ORACLE'S COOPERATIVE DEVELOPMENT ENVIRONMENT

ORACLE'S COOPERATIVE DEVELOPMENT ENVIRONMENT

A Reference and User's Guide

Kevin E. Kline

Butterworth-Heinemann

Boston Oxford Melbourne Singapore Toronto Munich New Delhi Tokyo

Library of Congress Cataloging-in-Publication Data

Kline, Kevin E., 1966–
  Oracle's cooperative development environment: a reference and user's guide/by Kevin E. Kline
      p. cm. — (Datamation® Book series)
      Includes index.
      ISBN 0-7506-9500-5
      1. Computer software—Development. 2. Oracle (Computer file)
  I. Title. II. Series.
  QA76.76.D47K564 1994
  005.75′65—dc20   94-48197
                                                              CIP

British Library Cataloguing-in-Publication Data

A catalogue record for this book is available from the British Library.

The publisher offers discounts on bulk orders of this book. For information, please write:

Manager of Special Sales
Butterworth-Heinemann
313 Washington Street
Newton, MA 02158-1626

10 9 8 7 6 5 4 3 2 1

Printed in the United States of America

To Dan and Shirley,
you've made this success possible.

To Kelly,
you've made the possibilities a success.

From my heart, thank you.

CONTENTS

4 INTRODUCTION TO ORACLE FORMS, VERSION 4.0   91

5 INTRODUCTION TO ORACLE REPORTS, VERSION 2.0   197

PREFACE

INTENDED AUDIENCE

This book is intended primarily for those who are knowledgeable about information systems in general, but not about Oracle7 or the Cooperative Design Environment (CDE) in particular. It is designed to cultivate readers' applications-development skills in Oracle and its many tools. Although this book does discuss the development and administration of Oracle databases, its main emphasis is the development of applications built around previously designed databases. Consequently, the coverage of database design is cursory, while the discussion of the application-development tools goes into much greater detail. However, novices and accomplished computer specialists alike can make good use of this book. As an introductory tutorial, novices can use this book as their first step in learning to use and work with the entire spectrum of Oracle application-development tools. Computer professionals who are proficient application developers, but unacquainted with the Oracle CDE specifically, will find this book to be an excellent tutorial in all of the Oracle basics, while Oracle professionals will discover many useful tricks and traps. In this capacity, the book is an excellent tool for computer professionals wishing to retrain, catch up on the latest RDBMS technology, or enhance their resumes for an upcoming job search.

ASSUMPTIONS

This book assumes that you are up to speed on the general use and meaning of relational database terminology and are somewhat familiar with relational database design theory. If you are completely new to relational databases, you might want to acquire one of the many fine books discussing relational database design. These books will provide greater insight into important database design concepts such as normalization, data modeling, and the logical and physical design of a database.

Although this book contains useful information that is, in many cases, applicable to earlier versions of the Oracle RDBMS and its development tools, it assumes that your primary interest is Oracle7 and the CDE. This book also assumes that you will not be required to install or administer the Oracle database, since the initial database installation and set up is beyond the scope of this book. Database installation and administration are very complex issues in their own right and could easily fill several large volumes.

CONVENTIONS

As with any hands-on guide to using a programming or computer language, you should understand the conventions used here in depicting examples of code and code fragments. This book contains the following conventions:

- In certain tables, commands are printed KEY[WORD], where KEY is an abbreviation acceptable to the programming language, although the entire command KEYWORD could also be used.
- Developer-defined keywords are also shown as uppercase clauses.
- SQL-, SQL*Plus-, and PL/SQL-required clauses are shown in lowercase.
- Parentheses surround options in a clause where one option is required. Phrases in a command that are entirely optional are shown in brackets. Each option is separated by a slash, as in the following:

```
(grant/revoke) system_privilege/role/publish... [with grant option]
```

- Triple dots (. . .) are used to show a block of code that was omitted for the sake of brevity or, in some cases, that a list of options may be used.
- All punctuation shown in examples is required.

USING THIS BOOK

This text is devoted to presenting not only the introductory concepts and basic skills that are required to use the CDE but also insightful case studies, examples, and professional-level hints and pointers along the way. Each chapter covers a specific tool of the Oracle CDE, or set of related tools. Oracle's capabilities are highlighted with a full complement of step-by-step examples that show exactly how to build a fully functional program that is portable and operable across dissimilar computer platforms, network environments, and terminal types.

Chapter 1 introduces the reader to the scope and approach of the book. It also discusses the fundamental concepts of application development, namely, the database, those who use and customize the database and its applications, and the suite of tools used to interface with the database.

Chapter 2 presents the basic concepts of designing and creating a well-crafted database using Oracle. This chapter gives readers a taste of the complexities of database management and provides them with the tools to design, create, and manipulate a basic database and its supporting applications.

Chapter 3 discusses the foundation tools of Oracle: SQL, SQL*Plus, and PL/SQL. As a foundation skill, a thorough knowledge of these three tools is essential before true skill can be gained in many of Oracle's other development tools. Hence, this chapter provides significant information for using SQL and its extensions to control and manipulate data inside of Oracle.

Chapter 4 shines a spotlight on Oracle's extremely powerful application development tool, Oracle Forms. This chapter introduces the reader to the basic construction of data entry and retrieval forms and menus. It reviews the basic interface and underlying concepts of Oracle Forms, making extensive use of examples throughout the text.

Chapter 5 focuses on the development of hard-copy reports using Oracle Reports. The CDE interface is discussed in specific detail, as are default and standardized report formats, building reports and data models, the Layout Painter, and printing.

Chapter 6 details the powerful multimedia capabilities of Oracle Graphics. This chapter discusses Oracle Graphics's charting and drawing capabilities, multimedia features, data access and file support, as well as programmatic and procedural controls.

Chapter 7 details Oracle's new documentation software, Oracle Book. It describes Oracle Book's capability to create and view sophisticated on-line hypertext and multimedia documents.

Chapter 8 presents several powerful Oracle tools designed to assist in the development, maintenance, or functionality of an application. Topics include loading non-Oracle data with SQL*Loader and keyboard remapping through Oracle*Terminal. It also provides an in-depth review of SQL*Net, Oracle's network connectivity tool.

The book also contains reference appendixes, which provide additional information about Oracle support networks and the inner workings of the Oracle RDBMS, SQL, and the CDE.

ACKNOWLEDGMENTS

Having done a great deal of technical writing in the past, I felt that writing a technical reference manual about the Oracle CDE, a software product I practically lived with, would be a fairly easy task. Far from it. In fact, this book owes much to the enthusiastic help of my friends and colleagues. If I forget to name you for your help specifically, please forgive me (and remember that I'm probably writing this very late at night).

First of all I'd like to thank Pat Burns, Liz Kennedy, and all of my colleagues at Nichols Research Corporation for all of their encouragement and support in my pursuit of Oracle expertise in general and this project in particular. Thanks to Bev Meeler, Shirley Reed, Neil Hamilton, and all those at the U.S. Army Missile Command Research, Development, and Engineering Center for making the Directorate-level Administrative and Budget Information System such a fine and exciting project.

At Oracle Corporation, a special thanks to Dennis Moore of Oracle's CDE Marketing Group for making all the loose ends come together and to Scott Dennison of Oracle Federal for getting the ball rolling. Credit goes to Aliza Lamdan, at Butterworth-Heinemann, for getting the tome in on time. Her enthusiastic support kept me going and kept the project on course. I'd like to acknowledge Annette Miller and Doug Stalnaker for their contributions in proofing and copyediting. A special thanks to Mary Baschab for her many creative inputs and her phenomenal skill with graphics.

Finally, I'd like to thank my wife for her fine technical editing and thoughtful review of the entire work. Her many comments helped turn techno-jargon into readable literature. Thanks for staying so devoted to me when I was practically chained to the computer for months on end. To Dylan, your crayon marks on my manuscripts were the most meaningful criticism I think I've encountered. Thanks for helping me learn that important lesson. And to Emily, your bright smiles and gurgles always made the work easier.

1 INTRODUCTION TO ORACLE7 AND THE CDE

INTRODUCTION

Oracle™ application-development skills are one of the most marketable talents available to computer professionals in the Information Age. The Oracle relational database-management system (RDBMS) has proven itself time and time again to be the tool of choice for information-management projects of all types and sizes because of its powerful database, its comprehensive suite of development tools, the Cooperative Development Environment (CDE), and its flexibility across a variety of computer platforms and networks. A thorough understanding of these development tools enables computer novices and experts alike to craft powerful and useful information systems quickly and easily.

One of the most noticeable strengths of Oracle is its unique and unified interface. The new Cooperative Development Environment has taken that strength to a new height by utilizing new graphic-user-interface (GUI) operating systems and terminal emulators. The CDE presents a standard "look and feel," reducing a developer's learning curve between one tool and the next, while enabling developers to program for a variety of computer types, from bit-mapped windowing systems to old-line character and block-mode computers. Furthermore, the CDE enables developers to more easily share work between the various tools and each other through shared libraries, triggers, procedures, and functions.

Even in its early days, the Oracle RDBMS was known for its cutting-edge technology. Oracle first appeared almost two decades ago and quickly earned its reputation as one of the computer industry's best high-performance, SQL-based database systems on the market. Oracle's creation is rooted in the database-interface programming language called the structured-query language, or SQL. SQL was originally developed at IBM in the late 1970s but was brought to market first by Oracle Corporation. Soon, SQL was adopted by the American National Standards Institute (ANSI) and the International Standards Organization (ISO) as the standard means of accessing and interfacing relational database-management systems.

Today, many popular relational database-management systems, like Oracle™, Sybase™, Informix™, and SQL Server™, hail SQL as their primary means of data management and control. Oracle's adherence to the SQL standard provides developers with the added benefit of computer programs that work equally well, unaltered, on dissimilar computer platforms using these other RDBMSes. Oracle has also implemented potent extensions to SQL through its PL/SQL and SQL*Plus instruction sets, adding powerful procedural extensions and report-writing capabilities to the SQL interface. Oracle's suite of development tools also extends to a variety of design and development products that encompass every aspect of systems analysis, design, and implementation.

Tool for the Information-Systems Professional

Oracle is a comprehensive, multifaceted application-development environment and relational database-development system that encompasses all the tools needed to create a fully functional information system and data repository. In fact, Oracle's diverse capability enables many information-systems professionals to cultivate specialized skills in a single Oracle tool. Hence, many Oracle developers are quite proficient in Oracle Forms, or SQL*Plus, or Oracle Reports, but relatively few are expert in all Oracle development tools. In many corporate information-system departments, individual computer users and developers are segregated into specific roles with a relatively narrow definition of job duties. The new Cooperative Development Environment will reduce the boundaries between experts of specific development tools by leveraging the use and functionality of the CDE's common, unified interface. Today, expertise in Oracle pays off, no matter what role you intend to play in information systems.

Although this book assumes some knowledge of information technology and processes, this chapter will explain the essential concepts of application development using Oracle7 (the current version of Oracle software), the basics of a relational database-management system, the common roles of users and developers, the general usage of the CDE, and the products available when using Oracle. Other topics discussed in this chapter include common features shared by tools of the CDE, a description of the example database, and a general approach to application development using the CDE.

WHAT IS A RELATIONAL DATABASE-MANAGEMENT SYSTEM?

Academically, a database may be defined as a shared collection of data represented in tabular form and designed to meet the informational needs of many users. A RDBMS is a software system used to create, manage, and secure databases, typically in one or more two-dimensional tables. More important, a RDBMS serves as the nontechnical interface between the actual physical data and representation of the data. Thus the RDBMS not only controls the physical handling of the data but also provides the tools for managing and maintaining that data. Many tasks may be performed with an RDBMS, such as:

- designing, creating, and modifying a database;
- designing, creating, and modifying applications that allow access to the database;
- manipulating data (inserting, updating, deleting, and retrieving data) either directly or through an application;
- protecting data from retrieval and tampering by unauthorized users; and
- transmitting data to networked sites and to many file formats.

ROLES ASSOCIATED WITH AN RDBMS

All of these tasks provide important capabilities to the RDBMS user. The importance of these capabilities depends on what needs to be accomplished. As an application developer, you may be responsible for maintaining and optimizing a large preexisting database and its applications, creating a brand-new application from scratch, or analyzing and using an existing application so that you can train others or write user manuals. However, most application developers will invariably have to perform all of these duties at one time or another, so let's investigate each of the roles that may be played.

The Database Administrator

The first and most essential component of an information system is the RDBMS itself. Most relational databases are complex enough to warrant a full-time manager, the database administrator. Simply enough, the database administrator (DBA) is the person responsible for the use and control of the database. As such, the DBA has a potent set of privileges that provide complete control over the database and its users, though the DBA need not be a user or application developer. Typically, the DBA has a very specific set of responsibilities, including:

- creating and maintaining database tables;
- backing up and restoring database tables;
- monitoring and optimizing database performance;
- controlling and monitoring user access;
- controlling the physical aspects of the database;
- importing and exporting data; and
- enforcing and maintaining standards for application developers.

The Application Developer

The RDBMS can serve as the nontechnical interface between physical data and representation of the data, but it will not perform as an efficient and user-friendly application without supporting programs to control data entry, manipulation, and retrieval. Depending on the organization, application developers may be responsible only for writing programs according to specifications provided to them by others. In other organizations, the developer not only is responsible for the creation and implementation of these programs but also provides additional input into the analysis and design process in a number of ways. In this extended role as a system analyst, a developer is lucky to devote half of his time to actual programming. The rest of the time the developer might be reviewing existing procedures (both formal and informal) that are to be automated, interviewing current and future users, or making design decisions about the system under development. Unlike the database administrator, the application developer may be required to perform a variety of duties. Most of these duties are a form of one of the following:

- analyzing and determining application requirements, both for informational and system capabilities;
- coding and documenting the software;
- testing the system and evaluating its performance (including many quality-assurance measures);

- implementing the system and training the users; and

- modifying and maintaining existing systems or components.

The End-User

Of course, an end-user is any person in the organization who uses the database application and, as such, may seem somewhat incidental to the development process. However, quite to the contrary, the user is one of the most important elements in the application development process. Users can provide feedback, and thus improve the application at every stage of development. Many developers utilize the application's end-user as a sounding board to help ensure successful installation and use of the final application. Involving end-users in the development process can add significantly to the satisfaction and value of the application. The success or failure of the application will be determined by its end-users. Users may be from any level or position of the organization, but they are the customer, and, as in other business situations, "the customer is always right."

THE ORACLE COOPERATIVE DEVELOPMENT ENVIRONMENT

Oracle offers the Cooperative Development Environment (CDE), an integrated set of application development tools used to produce forms, menus, and database designs. Taken together, the CDE tools provide application developers with all of the capabilities needed to design and create a fully functional information system while remaining well rooted in the ANSI standard SQL. The CDE further leverages systems development by allowing the components of the CDE to share code and text. The Oracle tools include SQL (and Oracle's SQL*Plus and PL/SQL extensions), Oracle Forms, Oracle Reports, Oracle Graphics, Oracle Book, and various utilities like SQL*Loader, Oracle*Terminal, Precompilers, and SQL*Net. Refer to Figure 1.1 for a graphical depiction of the CDE. Additional CDE tools that must be purchased separately include Oracle Data Browser, Oracle Glue, the Oracle Precompilers, Oracle ODBC, SQL*Net, and SQL*Connect. Each tool provides a unique and specific means of accessing and/or controlling data.

SQL*Plus

The SQL*Plus programming interface provides the most direct interface to Oracle data. Using SQL*Plus, developers can craft SQL programs and routines,

FIGURE 1.1 The Oracle CDE

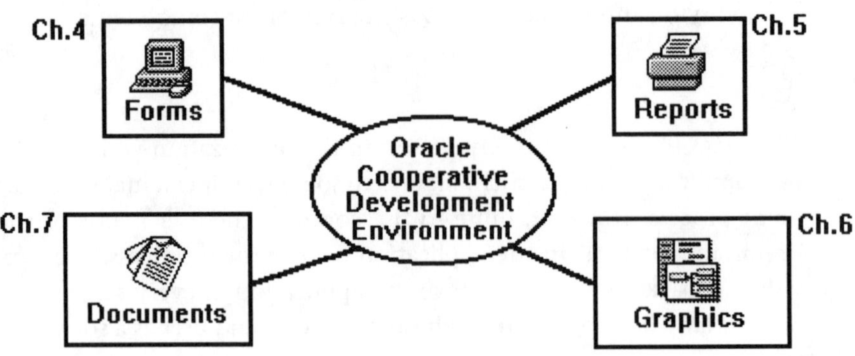

create and run reports, and query data directly from the Oracle RDBMS. SQL*Plus is compatible with the complete ANSI SQL command set but also includes extensions for line editing, help facilities, reporting, and control of system variables. SQL*Plus also allows use of Oracle's PL/SQL extension, enabling the developer to write procedures, uniquely define function keys, and write procedural SQL programs complete with conditionals, loops, and branches. Chapter 3 discusses SQL and its extensions.

Oracle Forms

For application users, Oracle Forms provides access to data stored in the Oracle RDBMS without the need to know any programming languages. For developers, Oracle Forms allows the creation of uniform form-based applications that provide efficient and secure access to data stored in Oracle. Oracle Forms provides other powerful capabilities to developers, such as applications that are easily portable to multiple computer platforms and uniform interfaces across different operating systems and architectures. Chapter 4 discusses the intricacies of Oracle Forms.

Oracle Reports

The Oracle Reports tool enables the developer to create polished reports and other forms of hard copy, with exact control over layout and presentation. Oracle Report's intuitive query builder and layout painter make report creation fast and easy. Chapter 5 details the use and capabilities of Oracle Reports.

Oracle Graphics

Oracle Graphics helps developers construct data-visualization and decision-support applications, such as charts, drawings, and multimedia programs. Since Oracle Graphics is a component of the CDE, developers can share code and PL/SQL text with Oracle Forms, Oracle Reports, and the Oracle RDBMS. Chapter 6 covers Oracle Graphics in detail.

Oracle Book

Oracle Book enables the creation of powerful on-line documents for use and inclusion within database applications. With Oracle Book, user manuals are electronically linked to the application itself, eliminating the need for constantly republishing and redistributing new manuals with each evolution of the application. Oracle Book's hypertext links allow users to click on the topic of interest, while word and phrase searches are also fully supported. Chapter 7 discusses the application development using Oracle Book.

SQL*Loader and Oracle*Terminal

The Oracle utility SQL*Loader provides a means of loading non-Oracle data, like ASCII flat files, directly into Oracle tables. The utility Oracle*Terminal allows the developer to remap function keys on different terminal types, so that users are required to perform the same keystrokes to invoke a given function regardless of computer type. The Import and Export utilities allow the developer to import and export Oracle tables to back up files. Chapter 8 discusses the Oracle utilities.

SQL*Net, Precompilers, and the Oracle Call Interface

SQL*Net is a connectivity tool that enables developers to design distributed applications and databases across geographically dispersed networks. The Oracle Call Interface (OCI) and Oracle Precompilers augment the power of applications developed in popular 3GLs (third-generation languages) and 4GLs (fourth-generation languages) by allowing direct calls to the Oracle RDBMS. OCI and the Precompilers allow the developer to merge Oracle SQL statements into a program's native code, whether it be COBOL, C, FORTRAN, PL/1, or Ada.

THE DATABASE EXAMPLE

In order to make the techniques and concepts clear, this book contains many examples showing the actual application and use of the Oracle tools. All of the examples in this book are based on the following sample database. In this case, the sample database is a collection of tables designed to help keep track of information useful in running an elementary school. The Lakeshore School database is composed of several tables, each one keeping track of a distinct set of information. The Lakeshore School tables are as follows:

STUDENTS	This table tracks information relevant to the student's present status. This table would have an entry to show each student's name, social security number, grade, home phone, etc.
TEACHERS	This table keeps track of information relevant to each teacher's current status. Records show the teacher's name, employee ID, room number, types of classes taught, etc.
STUDENT GRADES	This is a log of each student's grades from tests and projects while at Lakeshore School. One record represents one grade, and the students' class averages are calculated from the sums of their grades.
CLASS SCHEDULES	This is a list of classes offered at the school, and the time, location, and teacher of each class.
STUDENT SCHEDULE	This is a log of classes that each student is attending.
STUDENT ATTENDANCE	This simple table allows the teacher to mark each student as present, tardy, or absent for each class on each school day.

In addition to the primary tables tracked at the school, the school system keeps one table, Personnel, at the main downtown location. The Personnel table is accessible to the principal of Lakeshore School, and it tracks information relating to the pay and employment of the teachers and staff at the school and throughout the school system.

COMMON FEATURES OF CDE TOOLS

The CDE provides developers with a common interface among each of its distinct tools. By providing a unified interface, developers have reduced the learning curves necessary in mastering a new tool of the CDE. In addition, the CDE allows developers to share work between tools and among working groups of developers. Thus, a developer can create code once in Oracle Graphics to build powerful on-screen graphics, then import that same code into Oracle Reports to produce a hard-copy version of the graphic.

In addition to shared database features, like stored triggers and procedures, the basic operations that the developer must be familiar with are the same in all of the CDE tools: starting and quitting CDE tools, connecting to the database, working with modules, generating modules, running a module, and setting preferences within the given CDE tools.

Starting and Quitting the Oracle CDE

Each tool of the Oracle CDE may be invoked by launching its icon from the operating system. In addition, each CDE tool can be invoked using an operating system command line. For example, you could invoke Oracle Forms Designer from the command line by typing:

```
executable [module_name] [userid/password] [parameters]
```

The executable name could be the name for any of the CDE tools, such as F40DES for Oracle Forms Designer. Bracketed clauses are optional. If a module is not specified at startup, the CDE tool displays the File dialog allowing the developer to select a module. Alternately, you could create a new form, by cancelling the file dialog, then selecting the NEW command from the File menu option. For more details on the command line options for each CDE tool, refer to each tool's respective chapter.

Any of the CDE tools can be exited by selecting QUIT from the File menu. The CDE will prompt you to save or cancel any changes to all open modules prior to quitting.

Connecting to the Database

Many facilities of the CDE are unavailable unless connected to the database. Of course, any developer wishing to connect to the database must already have a user ID set up by the DBA. The CDE automatically connects to the database when a valid user ID is provided on the command line, as in the following:

```
f40des userid=kevin/triangle
```

Figure 1.2 Database Connect Window

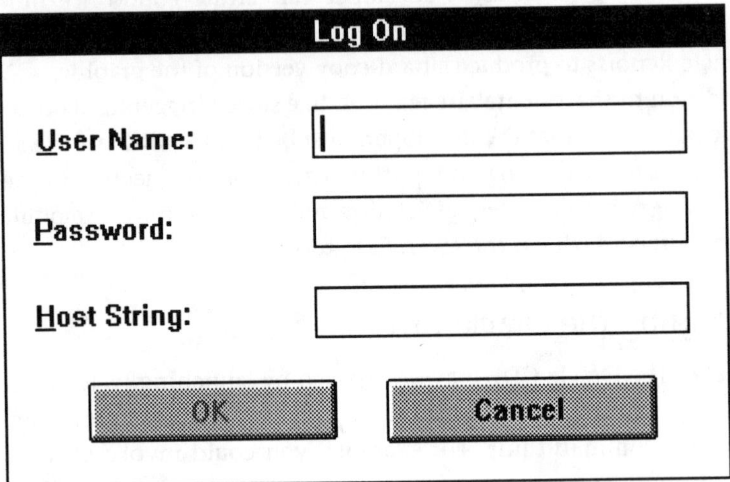

A developer can also connect to an Oracle database by selecting the CON-NECT command from the File menu. The developer must then type in a valid user name, password, and a database ID (if the database is at a remote loca-tion), as shown in Figure 1.2. The CDE then attempts to attach to the data-base when the Connect button is clicked.

Oracle Book works somewhat differently in that all documents created while connected are stored in the database, but all documents created while not connected are stored in a file.

Working with Modules

CDE applications are generally referred to as modules. Oracle Forms provides three primary modules: a forms module, a menu module, and a library mod-ule. Oracle Reports provides report modules and libary modules, while Oracle Graphics provides display modules and library modules, and Oracle Book provides document modules. The forms module contains objects and codes useful for the creation of forms, including windows, text fields, check boxes and alerts, lists of values, and PL/SQL triggers. The menu module contains a set of predefined menus and menu items, including a complete hierarchy of main menus and submenu objects with the commands needed to invoke other applications. The report module contains objects and codes useful for the creation of hard-copy reports, while display modules contain the structures needed to create on-line charts, and document modules contain structures needed to create on-line help documents. Library modules contain all the developer-created procedures, functions, and packages that are accessible from other locations in the application.

These modules can be combined and mingled to produce a complete and uniform application. Furthermore, applications developed in other Oracle CDE products may be called, opened, and manipulated using Oracle Forms. Thus, a chart from Oracle Graphics or a report from Oracle Reports can be retrieved into an Oracle Forms window and reviewed by the end-user. The benefits of such a modular design are obvious: enhanced flexibility, maintainability, and power.

Oracle products are renowned for their portability across computer platforms and operating systems. As a result, the CDE uses standardized naming conventions in the creation of the binary executable files and human-readable migration files. Additionally, CDE modules can be stored in the database. CDE files are stored with the following extensions:

Table 1.1   CDE File Extensions

Module	Binary	Text	Executable	Definition
Form	.FMB	.FMT	.FMX	Form definition file types
Menu	.MMB	.MMT	.MMX	Menu definition file types
Report	.RDF	.REX	.REP	Report definition file types
Display	.OGD	—	.OGR	Chart definition file types
Document	—	—	.ODB	Document definition file types
Library	.PLL	.PLS	.LIB	PL/SQL Library / PL/SQL Runtime Library

OPENING MODULES

You can open a new module by selecting NEW from the File menu. In Oracle Forms, you may then choose Form, Menu, or Library to open a new module of that type. The CDE behaves differently depending on the type of module opened. For an Oracle Forms form module, a default canvas is opened in the Layout editor. For an Oracle Forms menu module, the Menu editor is launched. For libraries modules, the CDE calls the Library Program Unit browser. Developers can open many modules at once within a single tool, although only one is active at a given time.

The method used to open an existing module depends on the method used to save the module. To open a module saved to a file, select the OPEN command from the File menu, then enter the name of the module to be opened and click the OK button. To open a module saved to the database, select the OPEN command from the File menu, then choose LIST to display all of the available modules stored in the database. Occasionally, a module may exist in the database but may not be available because you do not have access privileges. Enter the name of the desired module in the Open field and click the OK button to select the module.

SAVING MODULES

Modules can be saved to a file or directly to the database. To set the module preference for saving in Oracle Forms, select PREFERENCES from the Edit menu. Set the Object Access preference to FILE, DATABASE, or NONE. FILE saves modules to the file system. DATABASE saves modules to the Oracle database. NONE prompts the developer on a module-by-module basis. Then, select OK to accept the preference.

Setting the Object Access to NONE tells Oracle Forms to prompt for a specific location (file system or database) and module type each time a module is opened or saved. Developers may also use the Preference dialog to set the Display preference to either ALL FILES, FORMS, or MENUS. This display filters out the files/modules displayed in File dialogs used to save, open, rename, or delete a module.

SAVING AND REVERTING MODULES

Use the SAVE command on the File menu to save the module. If the form is new, specify the name. Specifying an existing name overwrites the previous version of the file. Use the SAVE AS command on the File menu to save the active form under a new name. Only the active form is saved when the SAVE or SAVE AS command is issued. If multiple modules are open, changes in each module must be saved separately. Also, only changes that have been applied and generated may be saved. The CDE will prompt the developer to apply changes if changes are pending when a SAVE command is issued.

Changes can be rolled back to the last save point by selecting the REVERT command from the File menu. Also, you can use the REVERT command on the Control menu to revert only those changes made within a specific editor or painter, such as the Layout editor in Oracle Forms.

It is important to remember that the CDE generally maintains changes and modifications at two levels: the object level and module level. Changes made by the CDE must first be applied to the object layer, a sort of intermediary buffer in system memory. Only after the changes have been applied can they be saved using the SAVE and SAVE AS commands. Changes are usually applied by clicking the OK or Accept button found on the object's property sheet, a pop-up dialog window that defines an object's behavior and appearance.

This methodology supports a multideveloper environment in which many developers might attempt to modify a single object at the same time. To avoid discrepancies between object definitions opened at different times or by different developers, the CDE uses the apply-save object-locking scheme. Each object is locked when it is opened and may not be reopened until the object is unlocked by applying or canceling any pending changes.

CLOSING, DELETING, RENAMING, AND CONVERTING

An active module can be closed without affecting other modules by selecting CLOSE from the File menu. The CDE will prompt the developer to commit unsaved changes to the module. If multiple modules are open, the CDE closes the active module and activates the next module.

You can delete a module stored in the database by selecting the DELETE command from the File menu. Next, select LIST to display all of the database modules available or enter the name of the module to be erased in the Delete field. Finally, click the OK button to delete the module.

Rename a module stored in the database by selecting RENAME from the File menu. Select LIST to display all of the database modules available or enter the name of the module to be renamed in the Old field. Enter a new name for the module in the New field (without an extension) and click the OK button to delete the module.

In Oracle Forms, to convert a form or menu from binary format (designated by the .FMB and .MMB extensions, respectively) to text format (designated by the .FMT and .MMT extensions, respectively) select the CONVERT command from the File menu. Text files are human-readable program code, similar to .INP files found in older versions of SQL*Forms.

GENERATING AND RUNNING MODULES

After creating and adding all of the appropriate objects and triggers, the developer can generate and run a module for testing and implementation. During generation, the CDE compiles all PL/SQL code in the module. If any errors are encountered, generation will fail and the CDE will display errors in the Generation Errors alert box. Generation and execution of a module are handled by other components within CDE, namely, the Generator and Run-time executables of the particular tool, both of which may be called from within CDE Designer tool. Thus, the developer may create the form within Oracle Forms Designer, generate the form, and execute it all in one session.

To generate the active module from Designer:

1. Select the GENERATE AS command from the File menu to call the Generate file dialog box, or select the GENERATE command from the File menu to generate changes and overwrite a preexisting module.

2. Supply a filename or accept the default filename in the Generate field. The CDE will assign an extension to the file based on the module type: .FMX for forms, .MMX for menus, etc. Alter the filename after each generation to create multiple versions of the runfile. Click ACCEPT to generate the runfile.

To execute a runtime module:

1. Select RUN from the File menu. The CDE Runtime tool will display the Runfile dialog box.

2. Enter the name of the executable module in the Run field. If a module is active, the Run field defaults to the name of the active module.

3. Enter any runtime parameters needed to execute the module.

4. Click OK to invoke the form.

Remember: Menus are not executed independently from forms. Similarly, libraries must be attached to a form, menu, display, or report module. Menus and libraries are attached to modules at design time and are loaded at run-time.

Setting Preferences

Design and runtime preferences can be altered by selecting the Preferences dialog from the Edit menu. Developers can use the Preference settings to customize the default behavior of the various CDE tools. Design and user preferences are numerous and vary widely from one tool to the next. Once the Preferences dialog has been invoked from the Edit menu, you may set design and user preferences according to your tastes. The SAVE PREFERENCES command on the Preferences dialog actually saves the current settings and establishes the default settings for future design sessions.

Getting Help

You can get on-line help within the CDE by selecting the HELP command from the Help menu. On-line help is available for the triggers, built-in routines, system variables, object properties, menu commands, and preferences. Figure 1.3 shows the Oracle Forms Help menu. Context-sensitive help is also available within different tools by pressing the [Help] function key. You can get additional help through three other help facilities: the show keys window, table/column browser, and built-in browsers.

The Help System contains several command buttons to aid in getting help for a specific question. The Contents button shows the table of contents of the help system. You can select a specific topic to get detailed help. The Index button shows the complete index of the help system. The History button displays the History window, showing all help topics recently reviewed in the order they were opened. The Backtrack button shows the help screen previous to the current help screen. Backtrack may be used many times to step all the way back through a help session. The Bookmark button puts a placeholder in the current help topic, allowing you to quickly call up that session. The Previous and Next buttons move between the help topics alphabetically. The Print button sends the current Help topic to the printer. The Find button searches for a specified string. Finally, the Dismiss button returns you to the position you were at before you invoked help.

Manipulating Items and Boilerplate Objects in a CDE Painter

Several of the CDE tools use a Layout Painter to create and manipulate objects, including Oracle Forms, Oracle Reports, and Oracle Graphics. Objects and items within these painters are manipulated in essentially the same way.

Before any object can be manipulated in any way, it must be selected. Use the Select or Single Select tool to select an item by clicking on it. Several items can be selected by holding the [Shift] (also called the [Constrain]) key and clicking on each item in succession. All of the items in a region may be selected by clicking outside of the group of objects (but within the region) and dragging the selection box until it surrounds all of the objects to be selected. An object may be added to the selection by using Shift-click. All objects in the workspace can be selected using the SELECT ALL command from the Edit menu. Deselect an object by clicking outside its boundaries or in an "empty" part of the workspace.

Once an object or group of objects has been selected, it may be manipu-

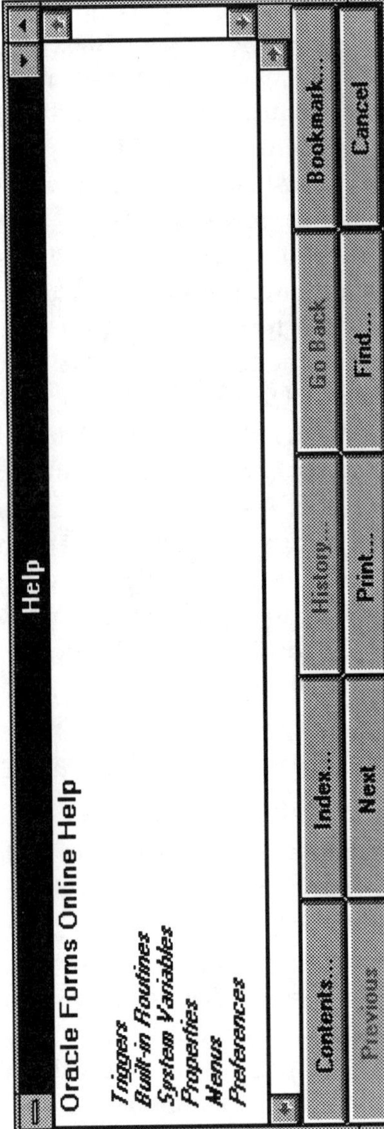

Figure 1.3   Oracle Forms On-Line Help

lated in various ways by doing one of the following: moving the object, resizing the object, cutting and/or copying the objects to the clipboard, pasting clipboard objects to the canvas, deleting the object, or duplicating the object.

Move objects by selecting them and dragging them to their new position. Move the object in small increments by selecting the object, then pressing the [Up], [Down], [Left], and [Right] keys. Incremental movement proceeds one pixel at a time with grid snap turned off, and proceeds one snap point (defined in the Ruler settings dialog) at a time with grid snap turned on. Use the [Shift]-drag feature to constrain the movement to vertical, diagonal, and horizontal directions. Resize the object by selecting it and dragging its selection handle to the desired size. Use the [Shift] key while resizing to constrain a rectangle to a square, and an ellipse to a circle.

Objects and groups may be cut or copied to the clipboard and, later, pasted back onto the canvas. Objects remain in the clipboard until displaced by another copied or cut object. To cut or copy an object to the clipboard, select the object or group of objects, then select the CUT or COPY command from the Edit menu. The objects are moved to the clipboard. The contents of the clipboard may then be pasted back onto a Layout editor canvas by selecting the PASTE command from the Edit menu. The object is pasted onto the canvas at the cursor position. Items and boilerplate material may be deleted by selecting the object or group of objects, then selecting the CLEAR command from the Edit menu (or by pressing the [Delete] key). Objects may be similarly duplicated by selecting the object or group of objects, then selecting the DUPLICATE command from the Edit menu. The duplicated item appears before the original. Items manipulated in this fashion receive new, default names, except for deleted items. Such items inherit all the properties of the original, including any triggers attached to the original.

SUMMARY

Oracle, as a tool for information-systems professionals, provides developers with a full-featured relational database-management system, designed to efficiently and effectively manage an organization's information. In the process of developing an information system, several primary support roles emerge: the database administrator, responsible for maintaining the database; the developer/analyst, who designs, codes, and implements information-system applications; and the end-user, who uses the information system only through the application.

The Cooperative Development Environment (CDE) is composed of several primary components. SQL*Plus is the CDE's direct, command-line programming interface. Oracle Forms allows the creation of screen-based applications. Oracle Reports enables the creation of intricate hard-copy reports and charts. Oracle Graphics helps developers construct visually informative charts, drawings, and multimedia applications. Oracle Book enables the creation of powerful on-line help documents for inclusion in other CDE applications. SQL*Loader provides a means of rapidly loading non-Oracle data into the database, while Oracle*Terminal allows the remapping of terminal-specific keys. In addition, several other Oracle tools enable the linking of CDE applications with popular 3GLs.

The database example used in this book has been briefly detailed by describing each of the database's specific tables. Finally, the common features of the CDE, namely, its basic operations, were discussed in some detail. Such basic operations include starting and quitting CDE tools, connecting to the database, working with CDE modules, setting CDE preferences, getting on-line help, and manipulating objects in a CDE Layout Painter.

2 CREATING THE DATABASE

INTRODUCTION

While a comprehensive discussion of database design and development could easily fill many volumes, chapter 2 will provide a basic introduction to the concepts vital to creating a database. It is important to remember that there is a big difference between creating a database and *designing* a database. Creating a database is the simple process of issuing the commands that bring it into existence. Designing a database involves much more complex processes such as normalization, performance tuning, and standardization. This chapter provides you with a crash course in basic database creation using Oracle. A thoughtfully devised database provides many benefits to its developers and users: minimal data redundancy; consistent, integrated data; enforced standards and security; easier application development and maintenance; data independent from database applications; and enhanced accessibility and responsiveness. The database must be an efficiently structured data repository, balancing the needs of speed, data integrity, and security. Furthermore, the database needs to accurately represent the information to be tracked and the relationships between different groups of information within.

This chapter will cover the basic concepts of a relational database, including creating and modifying the database through tables, views, and synonyms; controlling and monitoring user access to the database through roles; developer considerations like table constraints, enforced relational integrity, and stored procedures; and saving data and undoing mistakes.

Defining database tables and their relationship to each other is an important and difficult process. Many application developers, in hindsight, wished they had planned their table definitions just a little more carefully since their design affects every aspect of application development that follows.

CREATING TABLES

Creating database tables within Oracle is very easy and quick. The table is one of the most common forms used to store data today. Most aspects of modern life absolutely require the proper use and understanding of tables. Who could get through the workday without having a passing familiarity of how to read a checkbook register or use the yellow pages? In database terminology, a table consists of columns across the page or computer screen and rows down the page or computer screen. Veterans of the computer industry often call columns *attributes* and call rows of data *records*. So, a table describing a simple class schedule might look like the following:

TEACHER_ID	CLASS_ID	SUBJECT	PERIOD	ROOM
CK12	HIST05A	HISTORY	A	B315
PH04	MATH04D	MATH	D	A110
LM09	ENG06B	ENGLISH	B	A217

Within a relational database, each row of data in a table must possess a data element—a primary key that uniquely identifies the row. The key could be stored in one or several columns of the table. A single column value, or field, within a table serves as the primary key, but several fields combined together are called a *concatenated key*. The primary key field of one table might be stored in another table linking two related tables together. When a table's key is found in another table it is called a *foreign key*. For instance, the CLASS_ID field could be the foreign key linking the Class Schedule and Student Grade table.

Although the Class Schedule is an extremely simple example, it contains the three major data types common to Oracle: CHAR, DATE, and NUMBER. The SQL statement that would create this table is commensurately simple:

```
create table CLASS_SCHEDULE
(TEACHER_ID     VARCHAR2 (4) NOT NULL,
CLASS_ID       VARCHAR2 (9) NOT NULL,
SUBJECT        VARCHAR2 (20),
PERIOD         NUMBER (2),
ROOM           VARCHAR2 (3));
```

Actually, the spacing and style of entering the command is entirely up to you, although the syntax is not. The method shown here is somewhat clearer than writing one long command devoid of any breaks, since it more obviously displays fields, data types, and parentheses.

There are a few other simple rules to keep in mind when using CREATE TABLE:

- Columns must start with a letter of the alphabet and can include letters, numbers, or underscores, but not spaces or other special symbols.

- Each column must be separated by a comma, though the last column does not need a trailing comma.

- Columns must have a unique name within the table, from 1 to 30 characters in length, and the name may not be an Oracle reserved word (refer to appendix 1 on reserved words).

DOING IT RIGHT THE FIRST TIME

One of the hallmarks of a skilled and experienced application developer is the ability to build an application right (well, at least fairly close to right) on the very first attempt. Relational databases are very easy to build, but much harder to build well. You must facilitate the growth and evolution of the application through a clear and concise database structure. Fortunately, following a few rules can make the application significantly easier to create and maintain.

Naming Conventions

There is one very simple rule to follow whenever you construct a new database table: use regular English words to name tables and columns. A properly designed table should be entirely self-evident to developers and end-users alike. Many developers like to save space or typing time by using coded names or abbreviations for tables or columns. This practice makes long-term system maintenance and end-user interaction much more difficult. Take a look at the column heads from the CLASS_SCHEDULE table from earlier in the chapter:

```
TEACHER_ID
CLASS_ID
SUBJECT
PERIOD
ROOM
```

In general, all of the words are easily understood and recognizable to anyone who has ever seen a class schedule. Developers are no longer constrained to create tables and fields under eight characters in length, as limited by the old DOS-type computers, which makes using plain English words even easier. Other quick rules of thumb include:

- Always use consistent prefixes or suffixes in table and column names.

- Always use consistent underscoring between words in a table or column name.

- Abbreviations must be predefined and standardized because what might be an obvious abbreviation to one developer could be complete non-sense to another.

- Pluralization can be a problem when done inconsistently, so develop a rigid set of rules for pluralization in table and column names.

Poor naming habits can cause a world of trouble throughout the application's development and maturity. Consider a large development project, where several developers are creating tables that must interface with the tables of another developer. Unless a strict code of naming is adhered to, a team of developers could paint themselves into a tight corner by uncontrolled naming of tables and fields. Imagine the difficulties the maintenance staff will encounter if they cannot decipher the actual meaning of the abbreviated column and table names and the original developer is not available to explain them. Also, consider the problems caused by inconsistent naming. Who could immediately know that TEACHER_ID in one table is actually equivalent to TCHRID in another? The best way to correct this type of error is to avoid it altogether.

Building to Suit the Application

When constructing Oracle tables, application developers can build in several features that provide additional control over the data. In addition, developers can integrate numerous features into Oracle tables through data constraints and declared relational integrity. These data-checking features enable Oracle to automatically check data for correctness and validity. Use Oracle's integrity checks wherever possible, since Oracle will automatically execute the integrity checks any time an operation accesses the table.

Data Constraints

By specifying data constraints on one or more columns in a table, you instruct Oracle to enforce data integrity within the database that would otherwise require painstaking programming. Although data constraints do require a little more system overhead, they can significantly decrease your workload. Constraints can be placed on columns or on the entire table, though constraints that are composed of several columns must constrain the entire table. Constraints can enforce null status, key status, or validity conditions.

The STUDENTS table is used to track information about the student's present status. It also provides information about how to contact the child's parents in case of an emergency, as well as listing the student's homeroom teacher and classroom.

```
create table STUDENTS
STUDENT_NAME          VARCHAR2(30),
STUDENT_ID            VARCHAR2(4) UNIQUE,
GRADE                 VARCHAR2(2) NOT NULL,
ENROLL_DATE           DATE        DEFAULT SYSDATE,
HOMEROOM_CLASS        VARCHAR2(3) REFERENCES CLASS_SCHEDULE(ROOM),
SCHOOL_YEAR           VARCHAR2(5),
EMERGENCY_PHONE       NUMBER(10),
EMERGENCY_CONT        VARCHAR2(30),
EMERGENCY_ADDR        VARCHAR2(50),
ALT_EMERG_PHONE       NUMBER(10),
ALT_EMERG_CONT        VARCHAR2(30)
    PRIMARY KEY (STUDENT_ID, GRADE),
    CHECK (GRADE IN ('K', '0', '1', '2', '3', '4', '5')));
```

Each constraint used in this command instructs Oracle to perform a number of data-checking routines automatically. In the past, you would have to code these specific data-validation routines in each and every program that referenced this table and its fields. And even after you programmed in these data-validation routines, a user could still circumvent them by directly accessing tables through SQL. Now, you need only specify the data checking here. Oracle will do the rest.

Constraints may be placed on an individual row, like the UNIQUE constraint on the STUDENT_ID row, or they may be placed on the entire table, like the PRIMARY KEY constraint. The UNIQUE constraint placed on the STUDENT_ID column causes Oracle to check each and every student_id entered into that column. If a new student_id is identical to a preexisting one in the database, Oracle disallows the transaction. Like many other data constraints, the UNIQUE constraint helps prevent the most common types of data-entry problems. The UNIQUE characteristic could be applied to several fields, in which case it would appear at the end of the table description, written out like the PRIMARY KEY constraint. The PRIMARY KEY characteristic is similar to the UNIQUE constraint with the limitation that there may be many UNIQUE constraints but only one PRIMARY KEY. By specifying a primary key, you ensure that a unique combination of student_id and grade must be entered for those fields each time a record is created.

The NOT NULL status of the grade column indicates the column must have a not-null value. Anyone performing data entry on the record must provide a grade; it cannot be left blank. The default NULL status of a column allows the entry of null, or blank, values. The DEFAULT constraint found on the ENROLL_DATE column tells Oracle to automatically place the current date of when the transaction was processed, specified as SYSDATE, in that field. The user may overwrite the value that Oracle places there but could end up saving effort if the enrollment date of most students happens to be the date the record is keyed in.

The CREATE TABLE statement also contains two important clauses that instruct Oracle to maintain referential integrity checks on the table: the REFERENCES clause and the CHECK clause. The REFERENCES clause ensures that a specified foreign key (the primary key of another table) does exist when referenced in this table. The foreign key may be a single column or a concatenated key. In the STUDENTS table, the HOMEROOM_CLASS column references the CLASS_SCHEDULE table. Oracle would raise an alarm if the user were to try to type in a room that was not already recorded in the CLASS_SCHEDULE table. The referenced key need not be in another table; unique or primary keys within the current table may be referenced. You may also wish to apply a little foresight to the CREATE TABLE statement by attaching the ON DELETE CASCADE clause to the REFERENCES clause. The ON DELETE CASCADE clause tells Oracle to delete the dependent row when the independent row is deleted.

The CHECK clause provides an added level of data integrity to the STUDENTS table. In this case, the CHECK clause tells Oracle to make sure that the grade must be equal to the literals K or 0–12, since the students may be in kindergarten (K), preschool (0), or grades 1 through 12. CHECK can be used for any TRUE/FALSE comparison and can use SQL functions and literals.

Finally, it is very important to remember the issue of number precision when creating the table. Always be careful to specify the correct decimal precision for number fields in a table. And when guessing at the exact number precision, it is far better to be overgenerous in specifying number precision than to be frugal, because Oracle will either round off the number or entirely fail to record the data. Oracle will round numbers exceeding the decimal precision and will not insert records exceeding the total precision of the number field. For example, Oracle would not insert the value 12345678901.95 into the EMERGENCY_PHONE column because that value, counting the numbers preceding and following the decimal, exceeds ten digits in length, while Oracle would insert the value 195.9 into the database as 196, automatically rounding up to the decimal place.

In some circumstances, a developer may wish to create a table that is identical or similar to another preexisting table, possibly containing the same information. This can be easily accomplished by using the CREATE TABLE AS statement. For example:

```
CREATE TABLE student_homeroom
AS    select student_id, homeroom_class
      from students
      where school_year = '95/96';
```

The new table, STUDENT_HOMEROOM, has inherited a few columns from the STUDENTS table. Plus, the STUDENT_HOMEROOM table is instantly loaded with data showing each student and his or her homeroom class. The SELECT statement is very flexible and can contain columns derived from functions, calculations, or literal expressions. Derived columns of VARCHAR2 type will adjust their size as needed, while NUMBER columns will appear as simple number columns, without precision.

CREATING VIEWS

A *view* is a database construct that filters selected data from one or many database tables into a single virtual table. As a virtual table, a view is a specifically tailored subset of data providing the database developer with a means of strictly controlling data retrieval without constraining the underlying tables.

All views may be acted upon by using the SELECT statement, and single-table views also allow other database operations such as INSERT, UPDATE, and DELETE. Views are created using a SELECT statement, whether that is a simple query or complex multitable join that collates a single virtual table without actually storing any data. Views may also add special calculations to a given column or special security constraints. The view does not actually store any data of its own, rather it is automatically constructed by Oracle from database tables as it is needed. Consequently, a view always contains the most recently stored database values.

Views solve a number of security- and control-related problems encountered by the application developer. For example, a teacher and a principal require very different information to accomplish their jobs, but both require specific information about the students under their supervision. Furthermore, the principal needs summary information about the entire school, while the teacher requires much more information, but only about particular students. Views enable the application developer to create one cohesive table for all of the students and then add views that filter that data for the specific needs of its users.

Views can be constructed to filter out the rows or columns of certain tables. Using the students example, the teacher could view the entire row, that is, all of the columns that compose the students table, but only those rows that relate to her students. Rows containing data about any other student would be invisible. The principal can see every row in the table but does not have to see every column in the table, such as alternate emergency contact data. Plus, views can provide added simplicity to database queries by showing complex queries as simpler data sets or by placing more intuitive names on the columns of a table.

Views can contain subsets of rows, columns, or even special functions and calculations. The general command used to define a view is as follows:

```
CREATE VIEW view_name (column_name, column_name, ...)
AS    select_statement
WITH CHECK OPTION (CONSTRAINT constraint_statement);
```

View_name is the name given to the view. Column_name is the optional alias given to columns pulled by the view. If no column_name or alias is provided, the view uses the column_name as it appears in the SELECT statement. Select_statement must be a specific, valid SELECT statement whose WHERE statement is used to define the contents of the view. SELECT statements are detailed more fully in chapter 4. The command WITH CHECK OPTION tells Oracle to restrict inserts and updates through the view to data that the view can also select, based on the SELECT_STATEMENT WHERE clause.

Views can restrict the rows visible to a user. Using the students example discussed earlier, the teacher's view might be defined as:

```
CREATE VIEW teachers_view
AS    select *
      from students
      where homeroom_teacher = user
WITH CHECK OPTION;
```

When this CREATE VIEW statement is executed, the query is saved by Oracle and acted upon later, as the view is referenced. This view returns all columns in the table, but only those rows in the students table that meet the criteria of the WHERE clause. Note that this example uses the system variable *user*, which Oracle uses to track the user's system username.

Similarly, specific columns are visible in the principal's view:

```
CREATE VIEW principal
AS   select student_name, student_id, grade, enroll_date,
     homeroom_teacher, emergency_phone, emergency_contact,
     from students
WITH CHECK OPTION;
```

Since the WHERE clause is not used here, all rows are available to the principal; however, the columns have been limited.

The teachers_aid view restricts both columns and rows, and also adds in a simple function:

```
CREATE VIEW teachers_aid
AS   select class_id, student_id, test_grade
     round(avg(test_grade * 3),2) projected_grade
     from student_grades
     where teacher_id =
        select teacher_id from teachers where teacher_username = user)
WITH CHECK OPTION;
```

Under this view, Oracle checks the column teacher_id and makes it visible to the teacher aid by dynamically assigning the teacher_id based on a value stored in the TEACHERS table, allowing the aid to see the information on all of the assigned teacher's students. Once the query satisfies this requirement, the aid is provided with information about the student, including a simple grade projection for each student.

There are a few additional rules to remember when creating or using a view:

- The SELECT statement may not contain an ORDER BY clause, though it may contain a GROUP BY clause.

- Views that use `select *` will not work if a column has been added to the underlying table unless the view is dropped and then recreated.

- INSERT, DELETE, and UPDATE are allowed only on single-table views and only when all NOT NULL columns in the table appear in the view, when the view does not contain functions or calculations in the referenced INSERT or UPDATE statement, or when the view contains a GROUP BY, DISTINCT, or RowNum clause.

- Views are based on tables. If the underlying table is dropped, any references to the view will fail.

CREATING SYNONYMS

After creating a table or view, many developers like to create a shorter or more memorable means of referring to a table or view. This can be done quickly and easily by creating a synonym in this manner:

```
CREATE SYNONYM (PUBLIC) synonym_name
FOR object_name (@database_location)
```

This statement tells Oracle to treat all references to the synonym_name as if it were the actual object_name, including any user identifications. The PUBLIC keyword makes the synonym available to all users but can be used only by a role or user with DBA privileges; otherwise, the username must be included when referencing the synonym. The object_name may be the name of any valid table, view, or another synonym. @database_location refers to the location of a remote database accessible over the network configured for use with SQL*Net. For example:

```
CREATE SYNONYM jones
FOR personnel@downtown_link
```

Synonyms are equally easy to drop once created by using the DROP SYNONYM statement.

```
DROP (PUBLIC) SYNONYM synonym_name;
```

CREATING INDEXES

Indexes are constructs built on top of a table that speed the use and operation of SQL statements when the table is referenced. Indexes are especially useful for large tables where they can make a noticeable difference in performance, but probably should not be used for small tables (under about 500 rows in size). Indexes are invisible to the user and are used automatically when performing a SQL command on a table that has an index. To create an index, use the command:

```
create [unique] index INDEX_NAME on TABLE_NAME(column1, column2,...);
```

as in:

```
create unique index TEACHER_UX1 on TEACHERS(TEACHER_ID);
```

The index name must be a unique name, though many developers adopt a simple naming convention like using table_name_Ux or table_name_NUx, where _U indicates the index is a unique index, _Nux is a nonunique index built on TABLE_NAME, and x is the sequential number of the index (3 for the third index on that table). The columns shown in the command are the columns of the table that are indexed. Multiple columns can be indexed in a single table by issuing the CREATE INDEX command with multiple columns separated by commas.

Indexes can also be designed to shut out duplicate records created by INSERT or UPDATE statements. By adding the UNIQUE clause to the command, developers can ensure that no two records will possess the same values in their COLUMN clause. For example, a student database might have a unique index on social security number, since no two students should have the same one.

DROPPING OR ALTERING TABLES, VIEWS, AND INDEXES

Sometimes a database object, like a table, view, or index, needs to be completely discarded. Dropping database objects is a fairly simple process. To drop a table, simply use the DROP TABLE statement in this fashion:

```
DROP TABLE table_name (CASCADE CONSTRAINTS);
```

The table_name is the name of the specific object to be dropped. Dropping a table also drops its associated indexes and grants. The CASCADE CONSTRAINTS option erases the referential integrity constraints in other tables where they refer to the table to be dropped.

Views are even easier:

```
DROP VIEW view_name;
```

The DROP statement should be used only when the object is no longer needed, since errors will result in the application if a dropped object is referenced. Only a DBA may drop another user's table, view, or synonym.

Oracle tables, views, and synonyms may also be renamed using the SQL

RENAME statement. The new table name may not be a reserved word or the name of another table. The command is quite simple:

```
RENAME old_name TO new_name;
```

The new name may even be the same as another user's name or synonym, since Oracle interprets a table's uniqueness based on the user's name and the table name. So, TABLES JONES.PRODUCTS and SMITH.PRODUCTS could co-exist within the database. Even though the table names are the same, the user name differentiates them.

Oracle allows tables to be altered in two ways: by adding columns to an existing table or by altering the definition of a specific column. A few important rules apply to table modifications:

- Columns may be added at any time.
- Column width for VARCHAR2 and NUMBER fields may be increased at any time.
- Column number precision may be increased or decreased at any time for NUMBER columns.
- Column data types may be changed only when every row of the column is null.
- Column size may be decreased only when every row of the column is null.
- A NOT NULL column may only be added to tables with no rows.
- A column may be made NOT NULL only when all rows of the column possess a value.

Oracle allows table alterations through the standard SQL statement ALTER TABLE. Adding a column is quite straightforward:

```
ALTER TABLE table_name ADD(column_specification, column_specification);
```

as in:

```
alter table TEACHERS add(status_code varchar2(4) not null);
```

You should use the column_specification to declare the column's name, data type, and appropriate constraint. Remember that NOT NULL columns may be added only to tables with no rows. Modifying an existing column in a table is somewhat different:

```
ALTER TABLE table_name MODIFY(column_specification, column_specification);
```

as in:

```
alter table STUDENTS modify(student_name varchar2(35) not null,
    emergency_cont varchar2(35), alt_emergency_cont varchar2(35));
```

Here, the procedure used is the same as when adding a column, though the column must already exist in the table. The MODIFY clause can be used to change the data type, width, precision, or constraints.

USER SECURITY AND PRIVILEGES

Security is always a key concern to application developers. Information systems must provide the right users with the appropriate data at the right time. When an information system does not meet this requirement effectively, either by providing insufficient or unsecured data, then it fails to perform properly. Security within Oracle is maintained by an independent set of grants and privileges that must be set aside for each and every user. Oracle security is quite flexible and can be applied to specific tables and privileges, in addition to any security system implemented on the computer system where Oracle resides.

Overview of User-Role Creation

A user's ability to access and use Oracle is determined by that person's role. Users are granted a username and password, with an accompanying assortment of tables, views, and synonyms provided for that role (as well as any the user creates for personal use). Users may also provide grants and privileges on their own tables to other users. Privileges are typically divided into two sets: system privileges that affect the database tables in general, such as Connect, Resource, and DBA, and object privileges that allow the user to enact some sort of command (like INSERT or SELECT) on a table or other database object. To provide an overview example, let's step through the whole process of creating and assigning a role:

1. Create the desired role:

```
create role NEWUSER not identified;
```

2. Grant the role the appropriate system privileges:

```
grant CREATE SESSION, ALTER SESSION, CREATE TABLE, DROP TABLE, ALTER
TABLE, CREATE VIEW, DROP VIEW, CREATE SYNONYM, DROP SYNONYM to
NEWUSER with admin option;
```

3. Grant the role table privileges:

```
grant select on TEACHERS to NEWUSER with grant option;
grant all on STUDENTS to NEWUSER with grant option;
```

4. Grant the role to previously created users:

```
grant NEWUSER to LARRY;
```

5. If needed, set the role for the current session:

```
set role NEWUSER identified by LARRY;
```

Creating a user role requires a high level of authority in the database. The DBA will usually create any new roles for users needing access to the database. In many circumstances, the developer and DBA must closely coordinate the creation of new users and roles. However, using the CREATE USER command is quite simple:

```
create user username identified (by PASSWORD99 | externally);
```

In the CREATE USER statement, SALLY123 can be any user's name and PASSWORD99 can be any valid password. Alternately, the user can be identified externally by telling Oracle to enroll the user with the system logon and password. The "external" username and password are especially convenient, because users do not have to remember two separate passwords: one for the computer system and one for Oracle. Altering an Oracle username and password is similarly simple:

```
alter user SALLY123 identified by SAFE99;
```

Now SALLY123 should use the SAFE99 password to get into Oracle. Creating a username and password does not provide the user with much capability. The user's ability to work in the database is defined by the user's *role*, which must be assigned to the individual.

Oracle7 has five primary system privileges available to users, as shown in Table 2.1. Object privileges include ALL, ALTER, DELETE, EXECUTE, INDEX, INSERT, SELECT, UPDATE, and REFERENCES on a number of database objects.

Table 2.1   Oracle System Privileges

Privilege	Description
CONNECT	The basic user role allowing basic database connection. Object privileges for select, update, insert, and delete must also be assigned. Connect does allow users to create their own tables, views, synonyms, links, sequences, and clusters.
RESOURCE	Provides connect privileges, plus the power to create procedures, packages, triggers, and indexes. Resource also has fewer storage constraints than connect.
DBA	Has complete fiat over system privileges and grants, including other objects and system resources created by other users.
Exp_full_database	Used by the DBA to complete a full database export.
Imp_full_database	Used by the DBA to complete a full database import.

Using GRANT and REVOKE

Using the GRANT command allows you to grant access to personally developed tables and other database objects. You can also authorize the grantee to make grants to other users. REVOKE functions about the same as GRANT. Note the following:

```
(grant | revoke) system_privilege|role|public, ...
to username/role, ...
[with admin option]
```

The "with admin option" is used only with GRANT and allows other users to make specific privilege grants (like grant) on the table after they receive their own set of privileges on the table. Also note that the system privilege can be granted to everyone using the system (i.e., "public") or a predefined role, rather than just a single username. (Here and throughout the book the absolute value sign indicates an optional clause in a command, while a slash indicates a choice between one format and the other.) Suppose you need to create a GRANT statement for the basic new system user:

```
grant CREATE SESSION, ALTER SESSION, CREATE TABLE, DROP TABLE, ALTER
   TABLE, CREATE VIEW, DROP VIEW, CREATE SYNONYM, DROP SYNONYM
to newuser
with admin option;
```

Note that newuser is a defined role, a shared collection of privileges created using the CREATE ROLE command.

Granting system privileges extends only to connect, resource, or DBA levels of user authority and does not affect the actual tables, views, and synonyms that a user is given access to. Object privileges include ALL, ALTER, DELETE, EXECUTE, INDEX, INSERT, SELECT, UPDATE, and REFERENCES. Tables, and other database objects like views, are made accessible with this form of the GRANT statement:

```
grant OBJECT_PRIVILEGE (COLUMN_NAME, ...)
on OBJECT_NAME
to username/role
with grant option;
```

Users may invoke this form of grant to allow specified types of access to other users, like insert, update, delete, or select. Users may also grant execute privileges on procedures, functions, and packages. As with granting system privileges, grants may be made to an entire class of users or a specific username.

Also, remember that revoking a user does not, in any way, alter the tables or other database objects that the user created or populated with data. Those tables continue to exist and are fully usable by anyone with the appropriate grants. To fully erase a user and all of the database objects created by him or her, use the DROP USER command:

```
drop user USERNAME [cascade];
```

The cascade option drops all objects owned by the user, including referential integrity constraints. Dropping a user without the cascade option, while the user's tables continue to exist, causes Oracle to disregard the DROP USER command.

Creating a Special Role

You may also create a specially predefined role using the CREATE ROLE statement. The role is first created using the CREATE ROLE statement, then granted specific privileges using the GRANT command. Then, a user may be assigned to the role using the SET ROLE command and can access objects or privileges allowed by the role. When a user is granted a role, he or she gets all the privileges defined for that role. The CREATE ROLE statement is rather easy:

```
create role ROLE_NAME [identified [by password | externally] | not identified];
```

WORKING IN DEVELOPER GROUPS

In many Oracle application development projects, a number of developers will work together to implement and maintain a working information system. SQL contains a number of statements that increase the productivity of a large team of developers by allowing them to connect to remote databases and to create shared triggers, functions, PL/SQL packaged procedures, and other similar objects that may be called and referenced in other Oracle products such as Oracle Forms and Oracle Reports.

Links

In many situations, developers and users need to reference data located on the locally available database; however, applications can often be enhanced by allowing the user to query and alter data stored at remote databases. In many such situations, an Oracle application might be designed to run on a local PC (called a client) that does not even possess a database and be set up to automatically connect to a remote database server. Remote databases can be accessed using SQL*Net (described in chapter 8) and the SQL command CREATE DATABASE LINK. To create a database link, use this command:

```
create [public] database link LINK_NAME [connect to USER_NAME]
[identified by PASSWORD] [using 'CONNECTSTRING'];
```

The PUBLIC option is available only to database administrators but is very useful. When creating a database link, be sure to use the PUBLIC option to make the link available to all users; otherwise, only the creator has access to the link. Once the link is created, tables at the remote site can be accessed by prefixing the table name with @LINK_NAME in the FROM clause of the SQL statement (e.g., select * from TEACHERS@DOWNTOWN_LINK). To make references to remote databases easier to use, use the CREATE SYNONYM clause to create a simple synonym for the whole link string.

Stored Functions and Procedures

Another distinct enhancement available to developers is the ability to create and store custom-designed blocks of PL/SQL code within the database. PL/SQL code, discussed in greater detail in chapter 3, can be segregated into several different object types according to its application: functions, packages, procedures, and triggers. Using special SQL commands, developers can create and store predefined PL/SQL programs and make them available to all developers on the team. Additionally, changes made in a stored procedure do not have to be recompiled in every application that references them. The changes are immediately available throughout the application.

Functions are blocks of PL/SQL code that return a specific value. Procedures differ from functions in that they perform actions on data but do not necessarily provide data back to the calling operation. For example, a PL/SQL function (not to be confused with SQL functions like NVL or DECODE) might be designed to return the number of students in a given teacher's class who have passing grades. For example:

```
create function STUDENTS_PASSING (TEACHER in VARCHAR2, CLASS_ID in
   VARCHAR2) return NUMBER is NUMB_PASSING NUMBER;
BEGIN
   select count(grades)
   from student_grades
   where teacher_name = TEACHER
   and class = CLASS_ID
   and  average_grade >= 70;
     RETURN NUMB_PASSING;
EXCEPTIONS
     when others then message('Invalid value. Try again.');
     RETURN(-1);
END;
```

while a procedure might look like:

```
create procedure STUDENT_UPDATE (std_id IN)
AS begin
   update students set average_grade = (select avg(grades)
   from student_grades where student_id = std_id)
   where student_id = std_id;
end;
```

The syntax needed to create a function looks like the following:

```
create [or replace] function [USER_NAME.]FUNCTION_NAME [
(parameter_name [IN] data_type, ...) ] return DATA_TYPE (IS / AS)
pl/sql block
```

while the syntax needed to create a procedure looks like this:

```
create [or replace] procedure [USER_NAME.]PROCEDURE_NAME [
(parameter_name [IN / OUT / IN OUT], ...) ] (IS / AS) pl/sql block
```

The OR REPLACE clause recreates the function/procedure if it already exists in the database. Remember that all functions must have at least one parameter, so parameter lists are optional. Use the IN clause to tell Oracle to require the user to specify a value for the parameter. The OUT clause tells Oracle to pass a value back out of a procedure to the calling operation, and IN OUT performs both operations. The PL/SQL BLOCK clause is the actual PL/SQL definition of the function or procedure. A function can be compiled using the ALTER FUNCTION command, as in the following:

```
ALTER FUNCTION [USER_NAME.]FUNCTION_NAME [compile]
```

Attach the optional COMPILE clause to compile the function before it is stored, thus allowing you to see and isolate any errors before the function goes into general use. Note that functions and procedures can be used only in PL/SQL code, not SQL.

Stored Packages

Packages are groups of public procedures, functions, variables, exceptions, and other PL/SQL constructs. Packages offer some advantages over solitary procedures and functions, primarily in the areas of general organization and system overhead. For example, packages load multiple objects into memory at one time and allow multiple objects to share a single set of globals or cursors, while individual procedures and functions would have to be loaded and initialized separately.

Developers may customize PL/SQL packages using the CREATE PACKAGE and CREATE PACKAGE BODY commands. CREATE PACKAGE is used to create a public object used in other, external blocks of PL/SQL code, while CREATE PACKAGE BODY only defines the PL/SQL programming of the package. When creating a package, you must issue the statements in that specific order: CREATE PACKAGE, then CREATE PACKAGE BODY. Packaging PL/SQL code allows you to create objects that share data used in variables, declared constants, and cursors. The basic syntax for CREATE PACKAGE is as follows:

```
create (or replace) package [USER_NAME.]PACKAGE_NAME (is | as)
((declared_variables | declared_cursors | declared_exceptions |
declared_procedures | declared_functions); ...;) END [PACKAGE_NAME];
```

The OR REPLACE clause allows you to recreate the package without having to reissue grants and privileges associated with the old package definition, unless you alter a fundamental package specification, which requires recompilation using the ALTER PROCEDURE command. Examples of CREATE PACKAGE and CREATE PACKAGE BODY follow:

```
create package TEACHER_PACK as
      function STUDENTS_PASSING(TEACHER varchar2,CLASS_ID varchar2)
           return NUMB_PASSING;
      procedure STUDENT_UPDATE (TEMP_STUDENT_ID  varchar2)
      NO_GRADES exception;
end TEACHER_PACK;

create package body TEACHER_PACK as
      TEMP_STUDENT_ID varchar2;
BEGIN
function STUDENTS_PASSING (TEACHER in VARCHAR2, CLASS_ID in VARCHAR2)
      return NUMBER is NUMB_PASSING NUMBER;
      IS
      BEGIN
           select count(grades) from student_grades
           where teacher_name = TEACHER
              and class = CLASS_ID
              and average_grade = 70;
      return (NUMB_PASSING);
      END;
procedure STUDENT_UPDATE (temp_student_id IN)
      IS
      BEGIN
           update students set average_grade =
                (select avg(grades) from student_grades
                where student_id = temp_student_id)
           where student_id = std_id;
      END;
END TEACHER_PACK;
```

Once the package is created, the types, objects, and subprograms that it defines may be referenced in your programs. To reference a packaged object, simply call the "package_name. object_name" in the PL/SQL code. For example:

```
IF average_grade < teacher_pack.minimum_requirement THEN
alert_teacher;
END IF;
```

Oracle contains several built-in packages that can greatly assist your development. The package STANDARD defines the PL/SQL development environment and the types, exceptions, and subprograms available to every PL/SQL program. The package DBMS_STANDARD adds language facilities to applications that interact with Oracle.

Stored Triggers

Creating a trigger to be stored in the database is somewhat complex. To create a trigger, you must already have CREATE TRIGGER or CREATE ANY TRIGGER grants and privileges. Database triggers are event-driven; that is, they are specifically designed to "fire" automatically either before or after specific database events take place. Such database events include DELETEs, UPDATEs, and INSERTs. Stored triggers do not have to be referenced in a PL/SQL program to take effect; they automatically fire whenever the event takes place, even if it is in the SQL*Plus environment or in an Oracle Forms application. The general syntax of CREATE TRIGGER follows:

```
create trigger [USER_NAME.]TRIGGER_NAME [before / after] [delete /
insert / update [of column1, column2, ...] or [delete / insert /
update [of column1, column2, ...] on [USER_NAME.]TABLE_NAME
[referencing (old [as] old / new (as) new)] [for each row] [when
condition_list] PL/SQL block
```

The BEFORE / AFTER indicates whether the trigger should fire before or after the SQL action (delete, insert, or update). Thus, if your CREATE TRIGGER statement is used before DELETE, the trigger would fire before any record was deleted from the specified table.

When updating, use the OF COLUMN clause to ensure that the trigger fires only when the specified column is updated, not when any column of the table is updated. Use the REFERENCE clause to identify the table before the OLD and after the NEW trigger fires. Use the FOR EACH ROW statement to ensure that the trigger fires once for each row inserted, deleted, or updated and the WHEN clause to restrict the processing of the trigger to fire only when the condition list is met. In the example below, every time a record is inserted into the LABOR_BILLING table, an audit trail transaction is written to the AUDIT_TRAIL table recording the employee whose labor is being billed, the date of the record's creation, the amount of the transaction, the name of the operator, and the type of transaction:

```
create trigger INSERT_AUDIT_TRAIL
      before insert on each row
      on LABOR_BILLING
      begin
            insert into audit_trail(employee_id, transaction_date, value,
                  user_name, transaction_type)
            values(:teacher_id, sysdate, :amount, user, 'NEW LBR')
      end;
```

Note that the PL/SQL block cannot process COMMITs, ROLLBACKs, or SAVEPOINTs. A database trigger may be deactivated with the ALTER TRIGGER and ALTER TABLE commands. Also, remember that a table may have only three triggers for each SQL action of DELETE, UPDATE, and INSERT. A table may not have more than one trigger that fires for a single command, though a database trigger may hold execute commands.

SUMMARY

Chapter 2 introduces the basic concepts used in the creation of a database. After reading this chapter, you should be able to create, alter, and drop basic tables and views, using sound naming conventions. You should also be able to create basic synonyms to ease writing long table name strings.

Indexes are also available to speed processing on large tables and to aid in enforcing uniqueness. You should have an understanding of the creation of roles and the establishment of privileges for users, as well as an idea of how to take advantage of stored database links, procedures, functions, packages, and triggers.

3 THE FOUNDATION—SQL, SQL*PLUS, AND PL/SQL

INTRODUCTION

Anyone wishing to learn about Oracle must start with SQL and the Oracle SQL extensions SQL*Plus and PL/SQL. Without a proper understanding of the capabilities and use of SQL, application development is simply impossible. SQL provides direct interaction with the Oracle RDBMS, including insertion, modification, deletion, and retrieval of data. This chapter provides an introduction to the commands and capabilities of SQL within Oracle.

USING SQL IN A GUI ENVIRONMENT

All of the tools in Oracle's new Cooperative Development Environment are based on graphic user interfaces (GUI) like Microsoft Windows™, Macintosh System 7™, Motif™, or X-Windows™. All of the examples shown in this text are based on the Microsoft Windows GUI, including SQL*Plus, which can be invoked from Microsoft Windows by double-clicking the SQL*Plus icon. SQL*Plus first responds by calling the Connect dialog box, as shown in Figure 1.2.

Enter the username and password assigned in the appropriate fields. Users may also supply a database specification string that tells SQL*Plus to connect to a remote database, for example, the following:

```
CONNECT KEVIN/TRIANGLE@DOWNTOWN_LINK;
```

Otherwise, the CONNECT command defaults to the locally defined database. Remote databases are accessible only if they have been set up using compatible versions of SQL*Net (discussed in chapter 8) and network drivers. Once the database connection has established, the user is presented with the SQL*Plus interface, as shown in Figure 3.1.

Note that it is also possible to connect to the database using the SQL CONNECT command. Using the CONNECT command automatically disconnects the current session and commits all changes. Once connected, the SQL prompt indicates that SQL*PLUS is ready to receive commands. When ready to exit SQL*PLUS, simply type QUIT, EXIT, or select the EXIT command from the File menu.

SQL ON-LINE HELP

SQL contains an on-line help system, available to coach users through difficult spots. To list all available SQL and SQL*PLUS commands (but not PL/SQL commands), type:

```
HELP
```

Users can also get help by selecting the HELP command from the Help menu, as shown in Figure 3.2.

Users can also get information about specific SQL or SQL*PLUS commands, complete with examples, by typing:

```
HELP command name
```

For instance, typing HELP SELECT will retrieve a fairly involved discussion of the SELECT statement. Users can also get a list of currently available SQL topics by typing:

```
HELP TOPICS
```

DATATYPES

Data stored in Oracle tables must conform to constraints, called datatypes. When creating a table, you may choose from a wide variety of datatypes. Each datatype stores specific catagories of data, allowing you a great deal of control over insertion, modification, and retrieval.

Oracle recommends the use of a few specific datatypes but supports a wide variety of datatypes for compatibility with older versions of Oracle and with other SQL databases. The complete list of Oracle datatypes is shown in Table 3.1.

Figure 3.1   The SQL*Plus Interface

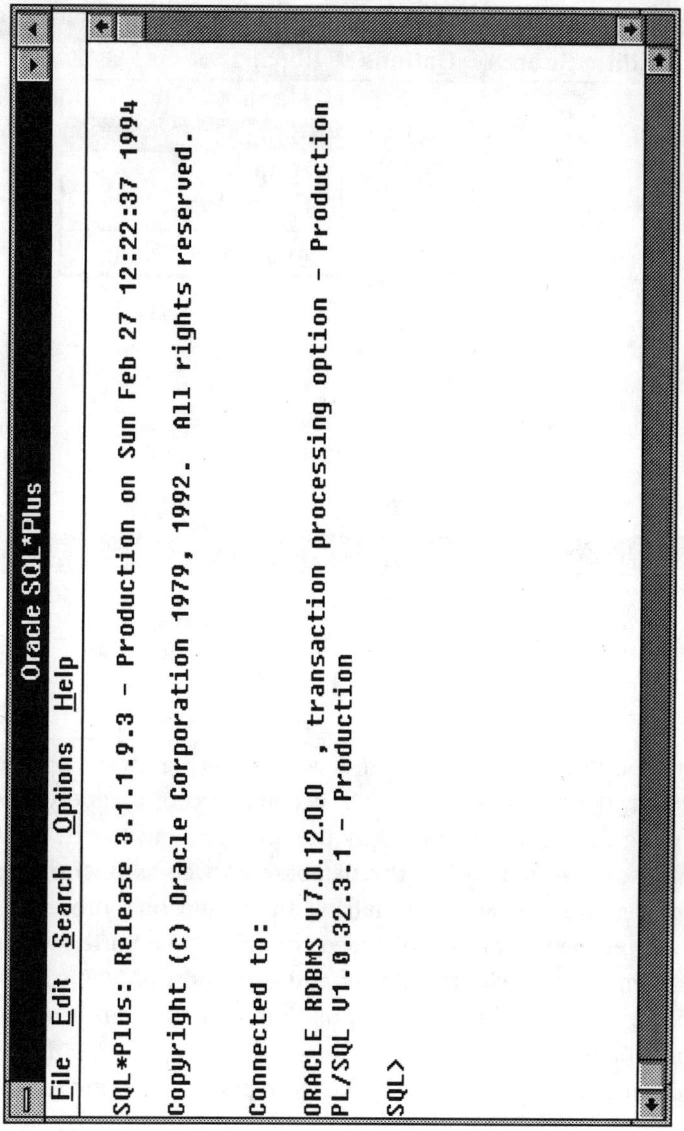

Figure 3.2   The Help Menu

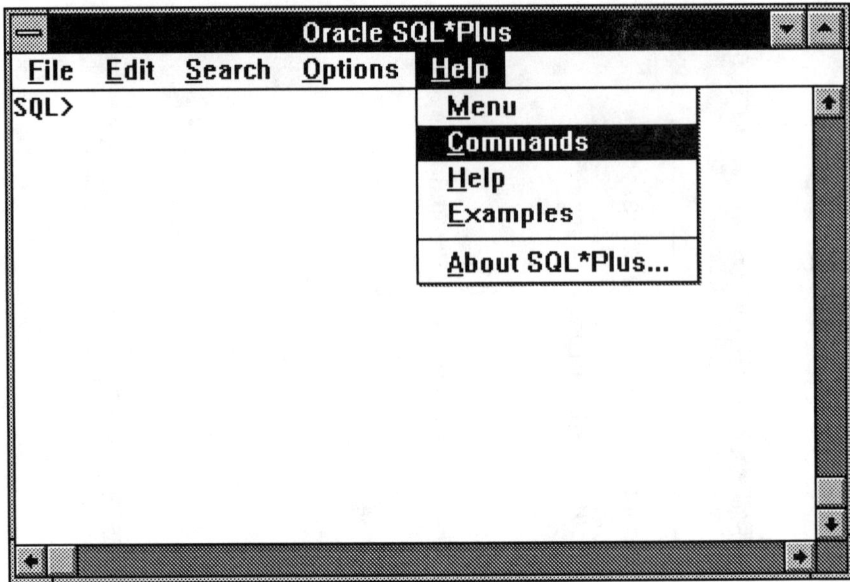

EDITING SQL STATEMENTS

SQL*Plus provides the application developer with a means of directly interacting with the Oracle RDBMS. SQL is composed of a variety of statements that can be dynamically defined by the user. You can insert, update, delete, and select data stored within the database, as well as perform a number of other procedures like report formatting and conditional processing.

SQL stores the most recently issued command in a buffer within the computer's memory to facilitate editing and execution of SQL commands. SQL provides a complete set of manipulation and line editor commands, as shown in Table 3.2.

For example, suppose you had just typed this command at the SQL prompt:

```
select student_id, student_name, homeroom_teacher
from STUDENTS
where grade > 4 and enroll_date between '01-SEP-95' and
'01-JAN-96';
```

Table 3.1 Oracle SQL Datatypes

Datatype	Description
CHAR(n)	Alphanumeric data between 1 and 255 characters, always of a fixed length, n characters long. Defaults to 1 character.
DATE	Oracle default format is DD-MON-YY.
LONG	Alphanumeric data up to 65,535 characters in length. Synonyms include LONG VARCHAR. Only one LONG field per table. LONG cannot be used in subqueries, functions, WHERE clauses, indexes, or clustered tables.
LONG RAW	RAW binary data with features of the LONG datatype.
NUMBER	Numeric floating-point data with no scale, capable of holding up to 40 digits in normal or scientific notation. Synonyms include DECIMAL, FLOAT, INTEGER, and SMALLINT.
NUMBER(n)	NUMBER of specified size n, up to 105 digits. Synonyms include INTEGER.
NUMBER(n,d)	NUMBER of specified size n with d digits of accuracy right of the decimal place.
RAW(n)	Raw binary data, not interpreted by Oracle, n bytes long, up to 255 bytes long.
VARCHAR(n)	Variable length alphanumeric string, n bytes long. Synonyms include VARCHAR2 in Oracle7.

You realize that some changes have to be made, so you review the entire command by typing L. You see that line 3 has an error, since you wanted to search for those equal to 4 rather than those greater than 4. You set the editor on line 3 by typing 3. Now, you need to change the greater than sign (>) to equal to (=). Changing data within the line editor is accomplished in this format:

```
C/OLD_TEXT/REPLACEMENT_TEXT
```

In this example, you would change the > to = by typing c/>/=. It is important to remember that the line editor searches the line from left to right for the first appearance of the OLD_TEXT string. When the editor finds the string, it replaces it with the REPLACEMENT_TEXT string. Be careful in those situations in which the OLD_TEXT string appears in the line more than once. In those cases, specify enough of an OLD_TEXT string to uniquely identify the entire phrase you want to modify. Alternately, you could have typed

Table 3.2   SQL Editor Commands

Command	Description
SAVE filename	Saves the contents of the SQL buffer to a disc file called filename. Operating system naming conventions apply. Use `SAVE filename REPLACE` to overwrite an existing file.
GET filename	Retrieves a stored SQL file into the buffer.
START filename	Executes a store SQL file. After execution, the file remains in the buffer. Synonyms include @.
RUN	Executes the current buffer command. Synonyms include /.
EDIT filename	Calls the operating system editor to edit a preexisting filename.
HOST command	Executes a specific operating system command. Operating system execution rules apply. For instance, to get a directory of files on a DOS microcomputer, type `HOST DIR *.*`.
@ filename	Runs the specified file.
@@ filename	Runs a nested command file.
a{ppend}	Adds specific text to the end of the current buffer line.
c{hange}	Changes text on the current buffer line using this format: c/old text/new text.
cl{ear}	Clears the entire buffer.
del	Deletes the current buffer line.
i{nput}	Adds one or more lines after the current buffer line.
l{ist}	Lists one or all buffer lines.
#	Places the editor on the specified line number.

`EDIT` at the SQL> prompt and used the system editor to interactively edit the buffer. Once done with the SQL query, you can save the query to a file using the SAVE filename command.

Besides learning the SQL buffer editor, application developers must become adept at the actual core of commands used by SQL. SQL commands fall into three groups: the Data Definition Language (DDL), the Data Manipulation Language (DML), and the Data Control Language (DCL). The DDL is composed of SQL commands that control the creation of database objects, including the CREATE, ALTER, and DROP commands. The DML—the command set most commonly used by developers—is used to create, alter, and retrieve data with commands like INSERT, DELETE, UPDATE, and SELECT. The DCL provides you with a command set capable of controlling user access and data storage through the GRANT, REVOKE, COMMIT, and ROLLBACK commands.

INSERTING DATA

Chapter 2 described the commands needed to actually create a database table. The SQL command INSERT allows data to be entered into a database
table. The INSERT command is not very practical for entering large quantities
of data on-line but is useful in many other circumstances. Used in conjunction with other Oracle tools, such as Oracle*Forms, INSERT is quite effective.
Basically, the INSERT command looks like this:

```
insert into TABLE_NAME(COLUMN_NAME, COLUMN_NAME)
[values([literal_value, function(literal_value)] [subquery];
```

As the example shows, you can use the VALUES clause to insert actual
literal strings into the database. Alternatively, you can add a subquery clause
to insert a list of values from another Oracle table. For example, suppose we
wanted to insert data into the CLASS_SCHEDULE table. We would type:

```
insert into CLASS_SCHEDULE
values('CK12', 'HIST05A', 'HISTORY', 'A', 'B315', '01-SEP-95',
   '01-JUN-96');
```

Character strings must be enclosed in single quotes, while date and numeric strings need not. Of course, the column must be of the same data type
as the data being entered, unless a conversion function like TO_CHAR or
TO_DATE is applied. In those cases where a null value needs to be inserted,
use the word *null* or empty single quotes (''). Furthermore, inserted values
must meet table and column constraints defined for the table. For example,
Oracle will disallow an INSERT command that does not insert a value into a
NOT NULL column. You may also insert into just a few specific columns, as
follows:

```
insert into CLASS_SCHEDULE (class_id, teacher_id, subject)
values('HIST05A', 'CK12', 'HISTORY');
```

You might opt to use a subquery to selectively move large quantities of
data from one table to another. When using a subquery, a valid SQL SELECT
statement may be used as long as you have access to the selected tables and
columns, and the data being selected is of the same data type required by the
insert statement. The subquery can contain literals, functions, and equations,
as well as directly selected values. For example:

```
insert into STUDENT_GRADES (student_id, class_id, test_grade)
   select student_id, class_id, '95'
   from STUDENT_SCHEDULE
   where teacher_id = 'CK12' and class_id = 'HIST05A';
```

The INSERT...SELECT statement is often used to quickly move large quantities of data from one table to another.

DELETING DATA

The primary means of erasing data from the database is the DELETE command. The DELETE statement allows you to remove one or more rows from a table based on the WHERE condition stipulated in the statement. For example:

```
delete from CLASS_SCHEDULE where subject like = '%BASKET WEAVING%'
```

In this example, you will delete every row in the CLASS_SCHEDULE table where the class has basket weaving (the class got canceled). The WHERE clause used here can contain the same level of detail available to SELECT and INSERT. Using a DELETE statement without a WHERE clause will cause Oracle to empty the entire table. Once you have deleted data, it can often, though not always, be recovered using the ROLLBACK statement discussed later in this chapter.

UPDATING DATA

The SQL command UPDATE provides you with a means of directly altering data within a table. Like INSERT and DELETE, UPDATE acts upon specified tables using criteria established in the WHERE clause:

```
update STUDENTS set enroll_date = enroll_date + 1 where grade = 3;
```

In this example, you simply wanted to increase the enrollment date of all third graders by one.

The UPDATE command may also contain SELECT subqueries to extract specific tabular or calculated values or to limit the effect of the UPDATE command on the table being altered. Using a SELECT subquery in the UPDATE statement's WHERE clause enables you to selectively update rows or columns within a table. You can also add any valid WHERE clause to the SELECT subquery, as shown in the example:

```
update STUDENTS set homeroom_class =
        (select room_number from class_schedule
         where class_id = 'HR112B')
    where student_id in
        (select student_id from student_attendance
         where attendance_date (between '01-JAN-96' and
         '31-JAN-96') and class_id = 'HB100C');
```

In this example, the class_id 'HR112B' represents a classroom that had water damage for a whole month; as a result, the class_id had to be altered for some records because students were relocated to a new classroom.

The critical point to remember when using INSERT, UPDATE, and DELETE statements is the need for careful application of the WHERE clause. Although the WHERE clause provides developers with the power to pinpoint the rows and columns to be affected, a sloppy WHERE clause could play havoc with rows or tables that were not meant to be altered. Since INSERT, UPDATE, and DELETE directly alter table data, always use extreme caution before making those changes permanent. In many cases, it is advisable to try out the command on a set of test data, then use SELECT statements to verify the effects of your DML command.

ROLLBACK AND COMMIT

Any work done by an INSERT, UPDATE, or DELETE statement can be undone or "rolled back" to its original, unaltered state. Conversely, data changes are made permanent when they are "committed," either explicitly or implicitly, to the database. Oracle uses the COMMIT statement to explicitly save data to the tables and uses the ROLLBACK statement to reverse changes to table data.

The COMMIT process can be invoked two ways: explicitly by issuing the COMMIT command (either by typing COMMIT at the SQL prompt or issuing the command in a trigger) or implicitly by performing certain other Oracle commands. Oracle commands that cause an implicit COMMIT include AL-TER, AUDIT, CONNECT, CREATE TABLE, CREATE VIEW, DISCONNECT, DROP TABLE, DROP VIEW, EXIT, GRANT, NOAUDIT, REVOKE, and QUIT. Issuing any of these commands causes Oracle to save all recent changes just as if the COMMIT command had been issued.

Some developers prefer to have Oracle automatically commit changes to the database. This can be accomplished by issuing the command SET AUTO-COMMIT ON. After issuing the SET command, Oracle will commit changes after every successful INSERT, UPDATE, and DELETE command.

The ROLLBACK command, invoked by typing ROLLBACK at the SQL prompt, enables you to undo any changes to database tables, *but only up to the point of the user's last commit*. Oracle actually buffers database changes, so that only the user working with the data will see changes immediately. All users who have authority to the table may continue to use it, but changes to the database won't be visible to other users until they are saved. Other users reviewing the data will continue to see older, unmodified data as long as the changes are not committed. Oracle will automatically rollback changes, even a long string of them, if the user is somehow disconnected from the database, usually through computer or network failure.

SELECTING DATA

You can extract information from the database through the SELECT command. SELECT and its permutations enable you to retrieve raw and calculated data from multiple tables and columns, with a wide array of search criteria, ordered and formatted to your specification. And since SELECT is based on relational database theory, all of the data is retrieved in a tabular format.

SELECT allows you to selectively retrieve columns and rows from the database. The most common and direct use of SELECT is to retrieve all of the information from one table. Single-table queries can extract all the data in the table using one of two methods, as shown below:

```
select *
from table_name;
```

or

```
select column1, column2, column3...
from table_name;
```

These two SELECT statements perform the same basic action. You can select all columns from the table using the asterisk (*), or wildcard, or can simply list every column in the table. Obviously, the asterisk is usually easier to type, especially in queries with many columns. Since these statements retrieve all of the data in a table, they are best used on smaller tables. When used on tables with many columns or rows, the selected data wraps around the screen (when it's greater than the screen width) and scrolls down the page (when longer than the screen height).

If you want to pull only a few specific columns, select the specific columns using a comma between them and the SELECT command, and add the FROM clause telling Oracle where to extract the data, as shown below:

```
select distinct student_id, student_name
from students;
```

This example also uses the DISTINCT clause. DISTINCT tells Oracle to filter out every duplicate record, only showing the selected information once. DISTINCT checks uniqueness in the combination of columns, not the first column listed. So, in this example each unique combination of student ID and student name will be displayed.

Aliases, or renamed column headings, may also be added to the query to quicken typing or make column headings more meaningful. You need not use double quotes to mark an alias, unless the alias contains spaces. For example:

```
select distinct student_names "NAME OF STUDENTS"
from STUDENTS;
```

Specific rows in a table can also be selected using a descriptive WHERE clause, just as in UPDATE, DELETE, and INSERT.

For example:

```
select teacher_name, teacher_id, primary_subject
from teachers where primary_subject = 'MATH';
```

This query will retrieve every row in the teacher table where the primary subject is MATH.

Functions and Operators

You have a number of comparison operators to choose from when writing the WHERE clause. The comparison operators shown in Table 3.3 provide you with a wide set of tools to establish search criteria in the SELECT statement.

Furthermore, you may also use the NOT operator to make any of the above operators test for negative conditions, like NOT BETWEEN VALUE1 AND VALUE2, NOT IN (VALUE1, VALUE2, ...), IS NOT NULL, etc.

Table 3.3   Comparison Operators

Operator	Description
=	equal to
!=, <>, ^=	not equal to
>	greater than
>=	greater than or equal to
<	less than
<=	less than or equal to
BETWEEN...AND...	between the two values
IN (VALUE1, VALUE2,...)	equal to any value in the list
IS NULL	has a null value
LIKE %VALUE%	has a value like the character string using the % or wildcard characters
NOT	reverses the functionality of an operator, like NOT BETWEEN..., NOT LIKE..., or NOT IN...
ALL	specifies that ALL values must exist to meet criteria; otherwise same as ANY, in this format: `[operator ALL list/subquery]`
ANY	acts as the LIKE operator, but in conjunction with =, !=, >, <, >=, <=, in this format: `[operator ANY list/subquery]`
EXISTS	used like ANY or ALL, but always used in conjunction with a WHERE clause, in this format: `[WHERE EXISTS subquery]`. EXISTS returns a true value when a subquery returns at least one row.

Comparison operators may also be used cumulatively with the AND and OR logical operators. When a SELECT's WHERE clause contains more than one condition, Oracle checks each condition individually. Oracle then combines the results and displays them in the order spelled out by the precedence of the logical operators. Comparison operators possess precedence in this order:

=, !=, >, >=, <, <=, IN, LIKE, IS NULL, BETWEEN

while logical operators possess precedence in this order:

NOT, AND, OR

Precedence may be altered through the use of parentheses. For example:

```
select student_name, student_id, enroll_date
from students
where grade >3 and emergency_phone is null or  emergency_contact is null;
```

This query will return all rows where the grade is greater than 3 and the emergency phone number is null, or any row where the emergency_contact is null, even in grades less than 3.

Adding parentheses to this query completely changes the results:

```
select student_name, student_id, enroll_date
from students
where grade >3 and (emergency_phone is null or emergency_contact is null);
```

This query will now retrieve any student in fourth grade or greater who has a blank emergency phone number or a blank emergency contact, since Oracle evaluates the conditions within the parentheses first.

Data retrieved by a query can also be sorted in ascending or descending order, according to your wishes. Oracle sorts data in ascending order by default. You may even sort across several different columns. For example:

```
select student_name, student_id, enroll_date
from students
where grade >3 and (emergency_phone is null or emergency_contact is null) order
by grade desc, student_id;
```

Here the query will retrieve the same data as in the previous example. This time the data will be sorted placing rows with higher grades first. Where rows have equal grades, the rows are then sorted numerically by the student_id.

SELECT statements can return not only the data stored in the database but also values calculated from the data stored in the database. In these circumstances, you can apply functions to certain elements of the SELECT statement. A long list of special functions, shown in Table 3.4, governs the behavior of CHARACTER strings, NUMBER strings, and DATE strings, as well as arithmetic and conversion functions.

SELECT statements can make use of any number of functions, both in the selected columns and in the WHERE clause. For example:

```
select upper(student_name) name, to_char (enroll_date,'MONTH DAY, YEAR')
"ENROLLED ON", grade, add_months((enroll_date - 10),2) CONTACT_DATE
from students
where enroll_date >('01-JAN-96') and (homeroom_class like '%HR%' or
homeroom_teacher like soundex('IS'));
```

Table 3.4 Conversion Functions and Set Operators

Function Type	Function	Description
Universal	nvl(value1,value2)	null value conversion; converts a null value to a specified non-null value
Numeric	+, –, *, /	add, subtract, multiply, divide
	()	altered precedence
	abs(value)	absolute value
	ceil(value)	smallest integer greater than or equal to value
	cos(value)	cosine of value
	cosh(value)	hyperbolic cosine of value
	exp(value)	exponent raised to the power of value
	floor(value)	largest integer smaller than or equal to value
	ln(value)	natural logarithm of value
	log(base,value)	base log of value
	mod(value,divisor)	modulus
	power(value,exp)	value raised to the exponent of expression
	round(value,place)	value rounded to the specified decimal place
	sign(value)	1 if value is positive, – if negative
	sin(value)	sine of value
	sinh(value)	hyperbolic sine of value
	sqrt(value)	square root of value
	tan(value)	tangent of value
	tanh(value)	hyperbolic tangent of value
	trunc(value,place)	value truncated to the specified decimal place
	vsize(value)	storage size of value
Character	(value1)||(value2)	concatenation, joins two strings together into one value
	ascii(value)	returns the ASCII value of the first character in the string
	chr(number)	returns the character equivalent of positive number
	initcap(value)	changes the first letter of the value to uppercase; NLS version is NLS_INITCAP
	instr(value,set, start_position,search_string)	returns the location of a set of characters in the specified value
	length(value)	returns the length of the value
	lower(value)	changes every letter in the value to lowercase; NLS version is NLS_LOWER
	lpad(value,spaces, characters)	pads a value to a certain length by padding the specified characters to the left side of the value
	ltrim(value,characters)	trims a value to a certain length by trimming specified characters on the left
	rpad(value,characters)	pads a value to a certain length by padding the specified characters to the right side of the value
	rtrim(value,characters)	trims a value to a certain length by trimming the specified characters on the right

---

Table 3.4 Conversion Functions and Set Operators *(continued)*

Function Type	*Function*	*Description*
	soundex(value)	returns values that sound like the specified value
	substr(value, start_position,count)	substring clips out a portion of a value starting at the start position and moving count characters to the right; NLS version is SUBSTRB
	translate(value,x,y)	converts characters within a value from x to y
	upper(value)	changes every letter in the value to uppercase; NLS version is NLS_UPPER
	userenv(value)	returns user environment information; values can be 'ENTRYID','SESSIONID', and 'TERMINAL'
	vsize(value)	returns the storage size of the value
Conversion	chartorowid(value)	changes a VARCHAR2 value to act like the pseudo-column ROWID
	convert(value,from,to)	converts a character value from a standard bit type to another bit type
	decode(value,if1,then1, if2,then2...else)	converts any char, date, or number string into any other char, date, or number string based on value
	hextoraw(hex_value)	converts a char string of hex numbers into binary or raw numbers
	rawtohex(value)	converts a binary string into hex numbers
	rowidtochar(rowid)	causes Oracle to treat the ROWID pseudo-column as a char string
	replace(value,x,y)	replaces x with y in value; synonym is translate
	to_char(value)	converts a number or date to a char
	to_date(value,'format')	converts a number or char to act like a date in the specified date format
	to_number(value)	converts a char string containing only numbers into a number string
Date	add_months(value,#)	adds # months to date value
	arithmetic	+ and – arithmetic functions can be performed on dates; number used in function is treated as number of days to be added or subtracted
	greatest(value)	finds greatest date in value or list of values
	last_day(value)	finds last day of the month of the value
	months_between(date1,date2)	returns date1 – date2 in months
	next_day(value,'day')	returns the date of the next day after date value
	new_time(value,'x','y')	returns the time in another time zone ('y') compared to this time zone ('x'); time zones are (xST/xDT, where ST is standard time and DT is daylight savings time, and x is chosen from this list): A (Atlantic), B (Bering), C (Central), E (Eastern), GMT (Greenwich mean time),

(continued)

Table 3.4 Conversion Functions and Set Operators (continued)

Function Type	Function	Description
		H (Hawaii-Alaska), M (Mountain), NST (Newfoundland), P (Pacific), Y (Yukon)
	round(value,'as')	rounds a date to 12 am if time is before noon or up to next day if after noon, using 'as' format
	to_char(date,'as')	converts a date to a char string using 'as' format
	trunc(date,'as')	truncates the date to 12 am, or according to the 'as' format
Group	avg(column)	returns the average value of column found in the table
	count(column/*)	returns the number of rows where column is not null or for the entire table (*)
	max(column)	returns the maximum not null value for that column
	min(column)	returns the minimum not null value for that column
	stddev(column)	returns the standard deviation based on not null values found in column
	sum(column)	returns the sum of all not null values found in column
	variance(column)	returns the variance of all values found in column
Set Operators	intersect	returns all distinct matching rows from two queries
	minus	returns all distinct rows in the first query that are not in the second
	union	returns all distinct rows from two queries
	union all	returns all rows from two queries

This statement pulls all of the recently enrolled students, showing their enroll_date and grade, contact_date, each student's enroll_date minus 10 days, but adds two months using the add_months function.

Special mention needs to be made of the DECODE statement, which provides powerful IF...THEN processing within a SELECT statement. Using the example just given, you could write a query that returns a different contact_date depending on the grade of the student. This lengthy query would retrieve somewhat more data than the previous query; another difference is that CONTACT_DATE is calculated according to the grade of the student:

enroll date plus ten days for fifth graders, enroll date plus twenty days for fourth graders, enroll date plus one month for third graders, enroll date plus one month and five days for second graders, and the enroll date plus two months for all other students.

Group functions are very useful for returning summary or higher-level information. For example:

```
select count(*), avg(test_grade), max(test_grade), min(test_grade)
from student_grades;
```

Group functions can also be forced to act only on distinct columns by including the DISTINCT keyword with the column name, as in `count(distinct student_id)`. Queries using group functions typically return a single value per function and group; however, queries using group functions can be broken into subgroups using the GROUP BY clause, as follows:

```
select grade, count(grade)
from students
group by grade;
```

The GROUP BY clause breaks the groupings out into subgroups; in this case, returning a list of grades and the number of students in each grade. The GROUP BY clause can also retrieve data conditionally using the HAVING clause:

```
select grade, count(grade)
from students
group by grade
having count(grade) >20;
```

This query returns the same information as the previous query, excluding those rows that have a count less than 20. GROUP BY and HAVING clauses can be used in the same SELECT statement as WHERE; however, placement of each clause must follow a particular syntax, as follows:

```
select...
from...
where...
group by...
having...
order by...
```

Figure 3.3 Set Operators

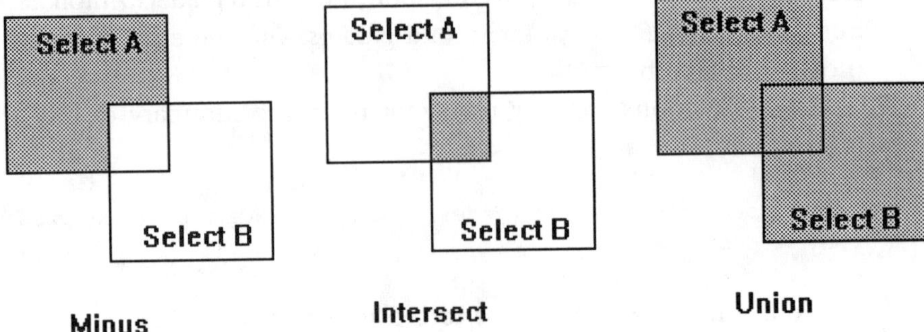

Set Operators

SELECT statements can also act upon entire sets of data using the set operators INTERSECT, MINUS, and UNION. Set operators all possess a similar syntax:

```
select1...
set operator...
select2...
```

However, since set operators act on the data retrieved by the respective queries, data between the two SELECT statements should possess a relationship. Each set operator retrieves different sets of data based on the interaction of the two queries, as shown in Figure 3.3.

The number of columns and the data types of each column must be identical between the two SELECT statements, although the columns do not have to have matching names. For example:

```
select student_name, student_id
from students minus
select students, student_id_code
from temp_student_attendance;
```

In this example, MINUS retrieves only those rows found in the first SELECT that are not found in the second. Note that the column names are different between the two queries, but the data types and sizes are not. The data retrieved by the second query must be identical to data found in the first query to be rejected. If the query had used INTERSECT instead of MINUS, the query would retrieve every distinct row that appears in both tables. If the query had used UNION, the query would retrieve all distinct rows in both tables, only excluding duplicates between the two tables. A variation of UNION, UNION ALL, retrieves all rows in both tables including every duplicate record of both tables.

JOINS

JOINS combines data found in two or more separate tables. The tables are listed in the FROM clause and the relationship between the two tables is defined in the WHERE clause, which may also be used to specify additional search criteria. JOIN commands may be quite simple, drawing data from multiple tables based on a simple equality condition in the WHERE clause, or can be quite complex, drawing data from multiple tables through nonequality relationships defined in the WHERE clause. The basic syntax for a simple JOIN command is shown below:

```
select table_name.column_name, table_name.column_name
from table_name1, table_name2
where table_name1.column_name = table_name2.column_name;
```

More complex joins may pull data from multiple tables based on a relationship not based on two or more equal column values. For example,

```
select st.student_name, st.student_id, avg(grd.test_grade)
from students st, student_attendance grd
where st.student_name = 'WINTER,DEAN';
```

An outer join, another type of complex join, combines data from multiple tables where there is no direct match in the other table. Oracle uses the plus symbol (+) to indicate an outer join condition. The syntax is essentially the same as a regular join, with the addition of the plus symbol on the table where data is not required to exist, as shown below:

```
select table_name.column_name, table_name.column_name
from table_name1, table_name2
where table_name1.column_name = table_name2.column_name(+);
```

or

```
select table_name.column_name, table_name.column_name
from table_name1, table_name2
where table_name1.column_name(+) = table_name2.column_name;
```

Subqueries

Subqueries retrieve data from a table based on the conditions established in another SELECT statement. Subqueries are allowed in INSERT, UPDATE, DELETE, and other SELECT statements. Of course, subqueries are also allowed within subqueries up to the practical limit of about 16. The typical single-row subquery must return only *one* result to complete the WHERE clause condition:

```
select student_name, grade
from students
where homeroom_class =
     (select classroom from teachers
      where teacher_name = upper('BLOOMFIELD'));
```

SELECT statements can contain several nested subqueries in separate components of the WHERE clause:

```
select student_name, grade
from students
where grade >= (select avg(grade) from students)
   and homeroom_class in
      (select distinct classroom from teachers
       where teacher_name = upper('BLOOMFIELD'));
```

A correlated subquery uses multiple queries but verifies, or correlates, their results within the information before it is retrieved. That is, a subquery may reference a column used in the main query. For example:

```
select student_name, grade
from students st
where homeroom_class in
     (select classroom
      from teachers
      where service >= (select avg(yrs_of_service)
          from personnel@downtown_link));
```

WRITING REPORTS AND PROGRAMS USING SQL*PLUS

SQL queries return data in a rather raw condition. Data is largely unformatted and the formatting that does exist is rather limited. SQL*Plus provides a command set that provides strong report-formatting features and is quite distinct

Table 3.5 SQL*Plus Commands

Command	Description
ACCEPT	accepts input from a user and stores it in a variable
BTITLE	defines title to appear at the bottom of every report page
BREAK	specifies the location at which a report should break
CLEAR	clears the definition of other SQL*Plus settings and commands
COLUMN	defines column formatting and printing
COMPUTE	used with BREAK to provide subtotal and summary information
COPY	copies data from one database to another
DEFINE	sets a user variable for the remainder of the session
EXECUTE	executes a single PL/SQL command
PAUSE	displays an empty line or text and waits for the user to press the [Enter] key
PRINT	displays the value of a variable
PROMPT	specifies a message or a blank line on the screen
REMARK	designates the trailing text as a remark; the symbols — and /* */ work similarly
RUNFORM	invokes Oracle Forms without a separate logon
SET	sets a large number of configuration parameters within the report; parameters are set for the duration of the session or until reset
SHOW	shows the settings of parameters defined by SET
SPOOL	extracts data to a file or printer
TTITLE	defines title to appear at the top of every report page
VARIABLE	declares a PL/SQL bind variable
WHENEVER OSERROR / SQLERROR	exits SQL*Plus if an operating system error or SQL error is encountered, respectively

from ANSI SQL. SQL*Plus commands are generally not portable to other SQL-based RDBMS products like Sybase or Informix. Another notable difference between SQL and SQL*Plus commands is that SQL*Plus commands do not require a semicolon. SQL*Plus commands are depicted in Table 3.5.

Formatting Reports

Oracle automatically formats the data retrieved from a query, many times in a format that is not very readable. For instance, a SQL*Plus query will retrieve money fields as straight numbers. However, you can control the appearance and behavior of data retrieved from queries using several useful commands, including BREAK, BTITLE and TTITLE, COLUMN, COMPUTE, and SET.

BREAK

This command prints a specified number of blank lines at a specified position, such as at the end of each page or after repeating values in a query. BREAK is often used with SKIP to print a certain number of blank lines and with COMPUTE (discussed later in this chapter) to print subtotals, totals, or other calculated values at important break groups. BREAK statements cannot be combined, since only one is active at a time. For example, to print a simple query that starts a new page with each new homeroom teacher and skips two spaces between each student, you would use the following:

```
break on homeroom_teacher skip page on student_id skip 2
select homeroom_teacher, student_id, student_name
from students
where grade = '3'
order by homeroom_teacher, student_id;
```

The general syntax for the BREAK command is:

```
BREAK ON [REPORT | column_name1, ... | ROW | PAGE]    [SKIP X | SKIP
PAGE] [NODUPLICATES | DUPLICATES].
```

BREAK ON REPORT causes Oracle to print computed totals or other computed information at the end of the report or query. ON REPORT is especially useful for printing grand totals. Oracle acts on the ON REPORT clause as the last BREAK. ON column_name suppresses the printing of duplicate values in a specified column. BREAK can specify several columns or column aliases to break on; however, the columns must be specified in the same order shown in the SELECT statement's ORDER BY clause. ON ROW tells Oracle to break on every row retrieved by the query. Oracle acts on the ON ROW statement before other BREAKs and should always be coupled with a COMPUTE statement or some other action statement, while ON PAGE tells Oracle to break at the end of every page, without regard to other breaks on COLUMN, ROW, or REPORT.

Oracle sets the breaks, nesting from the leftmost break to the right (for example, ON REGION ON SALES_REP ON PRODUCT_LINE). COMPUTE actions are then processed in reverse order, from rightmost (or least) break group toward the left (or largest break group). NODUPLICATES tells Oracle to print the first value of a break column, but to print blanks when the value is

Table 3.6 BTITLE/TTITLE Commands

Command	Description
COLUMNX	starts printing at column X of the current line
SKIPX	skips X lines; if X is null, then one line is skipped
TABX	moves X columns to the right (left if X is negative)
LEFT	left-justifies subsequent text
CENTER	centers subsequent text
RIGHT	right-justifies subsequent text
FORMAT	applies format same as the COLUMN command

a duplicate of a preceding row. Conversely, DUPLICATES ensures that each value is printed, even redundant rows. BREAK can be abbreviated as BRE.

BTITLE and TTITLE

BTTILE and TTITLE are essentially the same, in that they place and format a single or multilined title at the bottom or top of each report page, respectively. The titles may be formatted in a number of different ways using commands shown in Table 3.6.

Any number of text, variables, and options may appear in a TTITLE command. Each element is printed in the order it is placed in the TTITLE command. For example, to print TEACHER REPORT and the page number at the top of each page, you use the following:

```
ttitle left 'PERSONNEL REPORT' - right 'Page: ' format 99 SQL.PNO
```

To print a bottom title with PERSONAL IN NATURE in column 20, followed by ten spaces and LAKESHORE ELEMENTARY SCHOOL, enter:

```
btitle column 20 'PERSONAL IN NATURE' tab 10 'LAKESHORE ELEMENTARY SCHOOL'
```

BTITLE OFF suppresses and ON prints the bottom title, both without altering the bottom title text. Typing BTITLE alone prints all current BTITLE options, while only the most recent BTITLE command entered remains active. BTITLE can be abbreviated as BTI. Any number of text, variables, and options may appear in a BTITLE command. Each element is printed in the order in which it is placed in the BTITLE command.

COLUMN

This command tells SQL to retrieve a particular column in a user-defined format, with the header of your choice. Number columns must be formatted using 9s, while the width of alphanumeric columns can be specified by type A*x* (where *x* is the width of the column), as shown in the example below. Column statements may be combined.

```
column student_grade heading "Grade" format 99.99
column student_name heading "Name" format A25
select student_id, student_name, student_grade
from students
where student_grade = 90;
```

As with BTITLE, typing COLUMN alone will display all of the current settings for the COLUMN command; typing COLUMN column_name will display all of the current settings for that specific column. One or many COLUMN statements may exist at one time. Column attributes remain in effect until turned off or the session ends. In fact, several COLUMN statements may be applied cumulatively and are invoked in every query that calls that column. COLUMN may be abbreviated as COL. The syntax of the column command follows:

```
COL[UMN] [{column | column/alias} [option...] ];
```

The COLUMN command must reference the selected column or alias precisely as it appears in the SELECT statement. If the same column is selected from multiple tables, a single COLUMN statement will apply to both columns (since COLUMN ignores table name prefixes), unless they are given distinct aliases in the SELECT statement. COLUMN command options are described in Table 3.7.

Command options appear on the same line as the COLUMN command. Abbreviations from COLUMN options are that part of the option not held in brackets. For example, the OLD_VALUE command is abbreviated as OLD_V, WRAPPED as WRA, etc.

COMPUTE

COMPUTE works in tandem with the BREAK statement, printing summary lines and calculating certain functions on specifically selected rows. Used alone, it lists all COMPUTE definitions. The basic syntax for the command is as follows:

Table 3.7 COLUMN Command Options

Command Option	Description
ALI[AS] aliasname	Assigns a specified alias to a column, which can be used to refer to the column in BREAK, COMPUTE, and other COLUMN commands. Do not use this command to create distinct aliases; instead, use aliases in the SELECT statement.
CLE[AR]	Resets a column's display attributes.
FOLD_A[FTER] [n]	Inserts *n* carriage returns after the column heading and after each row in the column. The variable *n* is optional and does not affect the format of the column.
FOLD_B[EFORE] [n]	Inserts *n* carriage returns before the column heading and before each row of the column. The variable *n* is optional and does not affect the format of the column. Has the same effect as the NEWLINE command.
FOR[MAT] formatname	Sets the display format of the column. The format specification must be a literal, such as $9,999.99 or A10, but not a variable. Unless formatted otherwise, Oracle uses these defaults dependent on the column's datatype.
HEA[DING] heading_text	Alters the default column heading. Strings with blanks or punctuation marks must be enclosed in single or double quotes. Use the HEADSEP character (|) to make a multiline heading.
JUS[TIFY] value	L[EFT]/C[ENTER]/R[IGHT] values alter the justification of a column heading. NUMBERs default right and other data types default left.
LIKE {expr|alias}	Copies the display attributes of a column or expression previously defined with the COLUMN command to another column.
NEW_V[ALUE] variable	Sets up a variable containing the column value. Use NEW_VALUE to display column values, the date, or time in the top or bottom title. The column must be included in a BREAK command with the SKIP PAGE action. NEW_VALUE can also be used to create master/detail reports where there is a new master record for each page. This sort of master/detail reporting requires the column in the ORDER BY clause.
NOPRI[NT]|PRI[NT]	Allows a column to be printed or skipped. NOPRINT turns printing off; PRINT turns it on.
NUL[L] char	Displays the character used to represent a NULL value. The default for a NULL character is a blank space. Note: The SQL*Plus command SET NULL controls all NULLs in all columns, while COLUMN NULL is used to control a specific column.
OLD_V[ALUE] variable	Sets up a variable containing the column value. Otherwise, the same as new value.
ON|OFF	Turns on or off the display attributes for a column. OFF disables column attributes without affecting their definition, while ON reinstates them.
WRA[PPED]/ WOR[D_WRAPPED]/ TRU[NCATED]	Accommodates a CHAR string that is too wide for a column. WRAPPED moves the excess text to the next line. WORD_WRAP moves excess text to the next line, but does not split words. TRUNCATED merely cuts excess text off.

```
COMP[UTE] [function ...
   OF { quoted_select_expr / column / alias}...
   ON { quoted_select_expr / column / alias / REPORT| ROW}].
```

Allowable functions include AVG (average of non-null values), COU[NT] (count of non-null values), MAX[IMUM] (maximum value), MIN[IMUM] (minimum value), NUM[BER] (count of rows), STD (standard deviation of non-null values), SUM (sum of non-null values), and VAR[IANCE] (variance of non-null values). For example, the example query will print a teacher and his or her students, breaking and totaling on each teacher, with a grand total at the end of the report:

```
column student_grade heading "Grade" format 99.99
break on homeroom_teacher skip page on report skip 1
compute avg min max of student_grade on homeroom_teacher report
select homeroom_teacher, student_id, student_name, student_grade
from students where grade = '3'
order by homeroom_teacher, student_id;
```

Use spaces between multiple functions, columns, or aliases within the OF clause of the COMPUTE command, as shown in the example. Columns in the COMPUTE command must also appear in the SELECT statement. COMPUTE can be skipped by using the NOPRINT clause. Use the OF clause to pull the needed expressions or columns. Expression or function can be referenced in the OF clause by placing the expression or function in quotes marks, though columns and aliases do not need quotes. The ON clause tells Oracle to print the COMPUTE value at the break. COMPUTE prints its values and restarts the computation when the event occurs. Only the last COMPUTE command applies to columns with multiple COMPUTE statements. COMPUTE does have some restrictions, as follows:

- The expressions, columns, or aliases in the ON clause must be in the SELECT statement.

- The expressions, columns, or aliases in the ON clause must also be in the most recent BREAK command.

- If the ON clause uses ON ROW or ON REPORT, the most recent BREAK command must also use ROW or REPORT.

- At least one of the expressions, columns, or aliases in the OF clause must also be in the SELECT statement.

SET

Use the SET command to make a query appear more like a report. SET controls the entire environment settings for the current session. It controls everything from the display width for NUMBER and LONG data, to the enabling or disabling of column headers, to the number of lines and characters per page. The following example prints the previous query, plus provides page-formatting information:

```
whenever sqlerror exit;
whenever oserror exit;
set pagesize 60
set linesize 80
set header on
column student_grade heading "Grade" format 99.99
break on homeroom_teacher skip page on report skip 1
compute avg min max of student_grade on homeroom_teacher report
remark
remark  Written by C.K. Smith — 06/10/95
remark
   select homeroom_teacher, student_id, student_name, student_grade
   from students where grade = '3'
   order by homeroom_teacher, student_id;
clear columns
clear breaks
```

This program contains two other useful commands: CLEAR and REMARK. CLEAR resets all of the definitions assigned to other SQL*Plus statements, including BRE[AKS], BUFF[ER], COL[UMNS], COMP[UTES], and SCR[EEN]. REMARK indicates the presence of a comment in the program. CLEAR and REMARK may be abbreviated as CLE and REM, respectively. Also note that instead of typing the various SET commands, you can invoke the SET pick list, as shown in Figure 3.4, by issuing the SET OPTIONS command from the Options menu.

The SET command controls a vast array of system and environmental settings as shown in Table 3.8.

HANDLING ERRORS IN SQL*PLUS

The WHENEVER statement enables SQL*Plus programs to handle the occasional operating-system or SQL syntax error according to your specifications.

Figure 3.4 The Set Options Pick List

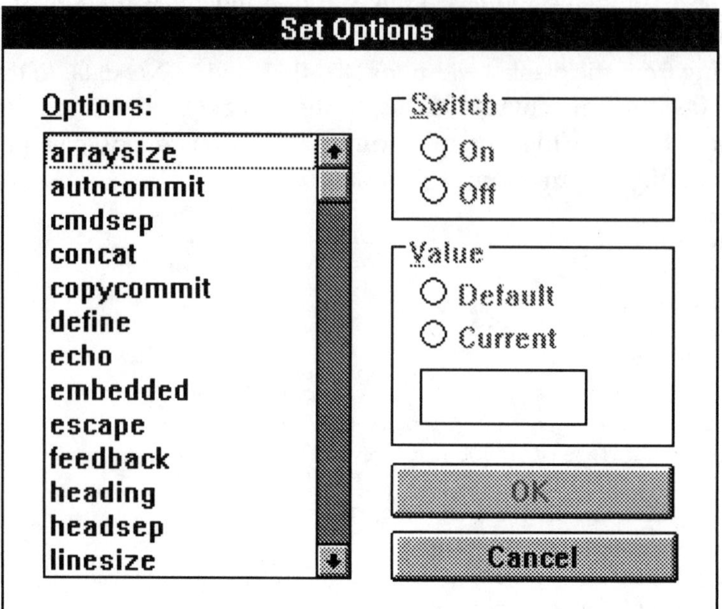

WHENEVER is available with two options, OSERROR and SQLERROR. Unless a WHENEVER clause is defined in your SQL*Plus programs, SQL*Plus will continue and take no action when an error occurs. If a WHENEVER clause is defined, the program will abort and exit SQL*Plus after it encounters the specified error. The general syntax is as follows:

```
whenever [oserror/sqlerror] exit [success / failure / (oscode error /
SQL error) ] [commit / rollback] continue [commit / rollback / none]
```

By specifying that the program should exit when an error is encountered, you give yourself several options in the construction of your error handler. If you choose to have the computer exit the program, you can request a SUCCESS code, FAILURE code, an OSCODE error number (for the OSERROR command), and a SQL error code (for the SQLERROR command). You can also specify whether the program should COMMIT or ROLLBACK any changes, or perform no action (NONE) before exiting or continuing.

Table 3.8 SET Variables

Variable and Syntax	Description
array[size] {20|n}	Specifies *n* number of rows retrieved from the database in one fetch.
auto[commit] {off|on}	Tells Oracle to automatically commit any pending changes to the database.
blo[ckterminator] {.|c}	Defines the nonalphanumeric character that ends a PL/SQL block to x.
buf[fer] buffer	Tells Oracle to use bufferx as the current buffer.
cmds[ep] {;|c|off|on}	Defines the nonalphanumeric character used to separate multiple SQL*Plus commands entered on one line to *x*.
con[cat] {.|c|off|on}	Defines the symbol used to delimit a variable from a character string that Oracle would otherwise see as a part of the variable's name.
copyc[ommit] {0|n}	Defines the number of batches processed before the COPY command commits changes to the database.
dcl[sep] {!|symbol}	Defines the symbol used to separate multiple operating-system commands entered on one line.
def[ine] {&|c|off|on}	Defines the prefix for a substitution variable.
echo {off|on}	Controls appearance of commands on the screen as they are executed.
embedded {off|on}	Allows new reports to start anywhere on a page, even on a page used by a previous report.
esc[ape] {\\\|c|off|on}	Defines the escape character.
feed[back] {6|n|off|on}	When *n* or more records are selected by a query, Oracle displays the "record selected" message.
flu[sh] {off|on}	Controls when output goes to the display device.
hea[ding] {off|on}	Turns the printing of column headings on or off in a report or query.
heads[ep] {||c|off|on}	Defines the character or symbol used as the heading separator character.
lin[esize] {80|n}	Defines the total number of characters displayed on a line before starting a new line.
long {80|n}	Defines the maximum width for displaying and copying LONG values within a range of 1 to 32,767, but less than MAXDATA.
maxd[ata] n	Sets the maximum total row width that SQL*Plus can process.
newp[age] {1|n}	Defines the number of blank lines printed between the bottom of one page and the top title of the next.
null txt	Defines the text to be printed when a query retrieves a null value.
numf[ormat] format	Defines the default format for displaying numbers in a SQL session.
num[width] {10|n}	Defines the default width for displayed numbers.
pages[ize] {14|n}	Defines the number of lines on the page.
pau[se] {off|on|text}	Defines scrolling on the terminal when running reports.
recsep {wr[apped]|ea[ch]|off}	Sets where the record separation occurs.

(continued)

Table 3.8   SET Variables *(continued)*

Variable and Syntax	*Description*
recsepchar {_|c}scan {off|on}	Defines the displays of a record separator between each record retrieved by a query.
scan {on|off}	Enables scanning for variables and parameters.
show[mode] {off|on}	ON displays the old and new settings of SQL*Plus SET variables.
spa[ce] {1|n}	Defines the number of spaces between columns, with a maximum of 10.
sqlc[ase] {MIX[ED]|LO[WER]|UP[PER]}	Defines the case of SQL commands and PL/SQL blocks, including quoted literals and identifiers, just prior to execution.
sqlco[ntinue] { >| text}	Defines the character sequence displayed as a prompt after a hyphen (-) is used to continue a SQL*Plus command on a new line.
sqln[umber] {OFF|ON}	ON sets the prompt for the second and subsequent lines of a SQL command or PL/SQL block as the line number.
sqlpre[fix] {#|c}	Sets the SQL*Plus prefix character.
sqlp[rompt] {SQL>|text}	Defines the SQL*Plus command prompt.
sqlt[erminator] {;|c|OFF|ON}	Sets to *c* the character used to end and execute SQL command.
suf[fix] {SQL|text}	Defines the default file extension that SQL*Plus uses in files created by SAVE and GET, but not SPOOL.
tab {OFF|ON}	ON tells SQL*Plus to use tabs to format blank space on reports, while OFF uses spaces to add blank spaces in output.
term[out] {OFF|ON}	Enables the display of output generated by command files.
ti[me] {OFF|ON}	Enables the display of the current time.
timi[ng] {OFF|ON}	Enables the display of timing statistics.
trim[out] {OFF|ON}	Enables the trimming of trailing spaces at the end of each line.
und[erline] {-|c|ON|OFF}	Enables or disables the symbol x, used to underline column headings.
ver[ify] {OFF|ON}	Tells SQL*Plus to display the text of a command before and after variables values are entered.
wra[p] {OFF|ON}	Enables or disables the truncation of the display of data items longer than the current line width.

PROGRAMMING USER INPUT AND VARIABLES IN SQL*PLUS ROUTINES

System Variables

Variables may be used in many SQL*Plus commands, notably BTITLE and TTITLE. System-supported variables include SQL.LNO, the current line number; SQL.PNO, the current page number; SQL.RELEASE, the current Oracle version number; SQL.SQLCODE, the current error code; and SQL.USER, the user name.

Passed Parameters

Parameters are substitution variables used only in command files. A parameter is given a unique name and designated by an ampersand (&) followed by a number (e.g., "&1"). Single quotes must be used for a parameter passing VARCHAR2 or DATE values. For example, this program asks for two parameter values:

```
select student_name, student_ID, grade
from students
where student_name = '&1' and grade > &2;
```

Parameter values can be assigned as arguments with the START command or else SQL*Plus will prompt the user for the appropriate value. When running the command file, enter parameter values in the exact order specified as part of the START command. The first argument must appear after the filename and represents the first parameter (&1), the second represents the second parameter (&2), and so on. For example:

```
SQL start student_check 'SMITH, ELLEN' 3
```

processes as:

```
select student_name, student_ID, grade
from students
where student_name = 'SMITH, ELLEN' and grade > 3;
```

Substitution Variables

Substitution variables are user-defined variables preceded by one or two ampersands. Single-ampersand variables retain their definition on their first occurrence but must have the value resupplied on each successive occurrence of the SQL command. Double-ampersand variables retain their value throughout the SQL command and the entire session. When a user variable is in a command, SQL*Plus executes the command as though it contained the value of the substitution variable, rather than the reference to the variable.

User variables can be used anywhere in SQL and SQL*Plus commands, except as the first word entered at the prompt. Users will be prompted for undefined user variables. To append characters immediately after a substitution variable, use a period to separate the variable from the characters as follows:

```
SQL  select *
from teachers
where primary_subject = '&e.history';
   Enter value for e:  american
```

This is interpreted as:

```
SQL select *
from teachers
where primary_subject = '&american history';
```

Despite user variables' usefulness, there are some restrictions on substitution. User variables or parameters cannot be used in SQL*Plus editing commands like APPEND, CHANGE, DEL, and INPUT, or in very simple commands where substitution would be meaningless, like HELP, REMARK, and TIMING. APPEND, CHANGE, and INPUT treat variables like any other text string. Plus, a variable or parameter should not be named after a SQL or PL/SQL reserved word. Reserved words are discussed in appendix 1.

User Features

SQL*Plus will automatically prompt the user for a good deal of information, but the way in which SQL*Plus performs the prompting is, by default, somewhat inelegant. It is quite easy for you to program in a few user-oriented features to make your programs more user-friendly, through the SET command or a few other SQL*Plus commands: ACCEPT, DEFINE, PAUSE, PROMPT, and SPOOL. This example program prints information about the current grades of students based upon parameters entered by the user:

```
REM
REM Sets the basic behavior and appearance of the program as a batch-mode application.
REM
SET VERIFY OFF;
SET ECHO OFF:
SET FEEDBACK OFF;
SET NULL '-'
SET SPACE 4
```

```
SET PAGESIZE 56

REM
REM Save the value of the current date to the TODAY variable.
REM
COLUMN SYSDATE NEW_VALUE TODAY NOPRINT

REM
REM Set up the top and bottom title.
REM
TTITLE LEFT TODAY CENTER BOLD 'SCORE STATUS' - RIGHT 'Page:' FORMAT 9
SQL.PNO -
    SKIP 1
BTITLE COL 27 'SCORE STATUS' TAB 6 'LAKESHORE ELEMENTARY SCHOOL'

REM
REM Sets up the display appearance of several columns.
REM
COL STUDENT_NAME HEADING 'Student' FORMAT A30
COL STUDENT_ID HEADING 'ID' FORMAT A4
COL ENROLL_DATE HEADING 'ENROLLED' FORMAT MONTH DD, YY
COL GRADE HEADING 'Grade' FORMAT 99
COL CURRENT_AVERAGE HEADING 'SCORE' FORMAT 999.99

REM
REM Sets up the main break group and summary totals.
REM
BREAK ON GRADE SKIP 2 NODUP ON REPORT SKIP 2
COMPUTE AVG OF CURRENT_AVERAGE ON GRADE REPORT

REM
REM Prompts for information from the end-user.
REM
PROMPT
ACCEPT GRADE CHAR PROMPT 'Enter the specific grade or leave blank for all grades:'
PROMPT

REM
REM Sets the program to spool output to a file called INVENT.LIS.
REM
SPOOL SCORE.LIS
SELECT STUDENT_NAME, STUDENT_ID, ENROLL_DATE, GRADE, CURRENT_AVG
    FROM STUDENTS
    WHERE GRADE = NVL(&GRADE, GRADE)
    ORDER BY GRADE, STUDENT_NAME, ENROLL_DATE
```

```
REM
REM Turns all the settings OFF.
REM
SPOOL OFF
TTITLE OFF
BTITLE OFF
CLEAR COLUMNS
CLEAR BREAK
CLEAR COMPUTE
SET SPACE 1
SET FEEDBACK ON
SET ECHO ON
SET VERIFY ON
SET PAGESIZE 23


REM
REM Prints the spooled document when the user is ready.
REM
PAUSE Press return to print the report.
HOST PRINT SCORE.LIS
```

ACCEPT reads the user's input into a stored variable for use in the SQL*Plus program. ACCEPT works in tangent with the PROMPT command. The syntax for the ACCEPT command is:

```
ACC[EPT] variable_name [NUM[BER] [CHAR] [PROMPT 'text' / NOPR[OMPT]] [HIDE]
```

If the variable_name does not exist, SQL*Plus creates it and can restrict the datatype to a NUMBER or CHAR based on the corresponding clause. If the response to the prompt does not match the specified datatype, the program terminates with an error message. PROMPT displays the text on-screen before accepting the value of the variable_name, while NOPROMPT skips a line and waits for input without displaying a prompt, and HIDE suppresses the display of a response as it is entered (useful for things like passwords).

The ACCEPT clause assigns a value to a variable in much the same way that SQL*Plus assigns the variable to a &variable object. As an alternative, you could use the DEFINE clause, which is roughly analogous to a &&variable object. The syntax for the DEFINE command follows:

```
DEFINE, format DEF[ine] [variable / variable = text_string]
```

The PAUSE and PROMPT commands achieve similar results. PAUSE displays an empty line on the screen with the optional text, then suspends operation until the user presses the [Enter] key. If the user leaves the PAUSE command blank, the program displays two blank lines, then awaits the user. Similarly, PROMPT sends the specified text to the screen or shows a blank line if entered alone. The syntax for the command is PROMPT text_string. When using PROMPT with the ACCEPT command, quote marks are needed around the text_string; otherwise, quotes are not needed.

SPOOL stores query results in an operating system file or sends the output to a default printer like LPT1. SPOOL alone lists the current spooling status. The general syntax of SPOOL follows:

```
SPO[OL] [file_name[.ext ] | OFF | OUT]
```

SPOOL file_name spools output to the named file, using a default extension if none is specified. OFF turns spooling off. OUT stops spooling and sends the file to the host computer's default printer. Use SET TERMOUT to spool output generated by command files without displaying the output on the screen.

USING PL/SQL

PL/SQL is Oracle's procedural language extension to SQL. PL/SQL provides condition handling, iteration, and nested processing in a block-structured language. PL/SQL's block structure allows for logical separation of variable declarations and program processes. In fact, PL/SQL variables are usable only in the block they are declared in (except for global or system variables). The standard syntax for a PL/SQL program contains a section for declarations, executables, and exception handling, as follows:

```
[DECLARE
   --temporary variable declarations]
BEGIN
   --PL/SQL and SQL statements

   BEGIN <<optional nested BLOCK_NAME>>
     --PL/SQL and SQL statements
   END;

[EXCEPTION
     --handlers]
END;
```

Declarations, which are optional, must be declared before the execution of the program. After declarations, the PL/SQL executables can contain any number of blocks (delimited by the BEGIN and END clauses), one after the other, as well as many blocks nested within each other.

Anonymous blocks, those blocks that do not have a name set off by angle brackets ("<<BLOCK_NAME>>"), cannot be referenced and are executed in sequential order. Named blocks are executed when they are referenced, using functions like GOTO. Exceptions and errors that are encountered can then be conditionally processed by the optional exception handlers. Exception handlers may even contain nested blocks of PL/SQL.

The Declare Block

PL/SQL initializes variables in the DECLARE block. The variables must be given a unique name within the context, along with a datatype and optional information like sizing information, a starting value, and NOT NULL constraint. Syntax for these types of variable assignments is shown in the following example:

```
DECLARE
     begin_date          DATE;
     end_date            DATE;
     student_count   NUMBER      := 0;
     teacher_name    VARCHAR2(20) NOT NULL := 'CHEU, KAREN';
```

Note that any NOT NULL variables must have a value assigned in the declaration block; otherwise, an error will result. Only one variable value may be declared per line. So, a declaration like `course_start, course_end` `DATE` would fail. In declaring a variable assignment, the word DEFAULT may be substituted for `:=`. DECLARE blocks can also create constants and elaborate variable assignments based on the value of expressions defined earlier in the block. For example:

```
DECLARE
     sales_tax        CONSTANT REAL := 0.07159;
     commission       REAL := 0.03;
     total_fee        REAL := (sales_tax + commission);
     service_fee      REAL DEFAULT 0.0015;
     mgt_fee          service_fee%TYPE;
```

To declare a constant value, prefix the datatype specifier with the word CONSTANT. Constants must be initialized as they are declared; otherwise, an error will result. The calculations shown in the TOTAL_FEE variable are acceptable; however, calculated variable assignments must appear after any variable used in calculating its value. So, if TOTAL_FEE had appeared in the DECLARE block before COMMISSION, the statement would fail. The %TYPE keyword can be used to duplicate the definition of a previously defined variable.

PL/SQL objects of all types (constants, variables, cursors, exceptions, procedures, functions, and packages) can have simple or complex names. A simple name merely refers to the object, whereas a complex name might qualify the table the object comes from and possibly a remote database link. For example:

```
employee_salary  --simple
personnel.employee_salary --qualified
employee_salary@downtown_link --remote
personnel.employee_salary@downtown_link --qualified & remote
```

PERSONNEL.EMPLOYEE_SALARY@DOWNTOWN_LINK is a very long object name representing a table at a remote database. In this case, you are well advised to create a simple synonym for the object, as with any long table, sequence, view, package, or stand-alone program. Synonyms are not available for constants, variables, cursors, exceptions, and packages procedures.

Declarations are limited in scope, or "context." That is, a declaration is usable only in the block it was declared in and in any sub-blocks under that calling block. If a declaration in a sub-block has the same name as a declaration in the main block, the value declared in the main block takes precedence. Declarations with the same name may be declared in blocks at the same level of context. Also note that declarations are initialized to NULL whenever a block or subprogram is entered.

The Processing Blocks

Once declarations are made, the PL/SQL program blocks can assign values to the declarations using a direct assignment via ":=" or by assigning the value in the declaration. For example:

```
BEGIN
   temp_date := '01-JUN-95';
   SELECT teacher_name, salary INTO employee, wage_rate
     FROM personnel WHERE employee_number = employee_id;
END;
```

Table 3.9 Operator Precedence

Operator	Usage
**, NOT	exponents and logical negatives
+, −	positive/negative values (not add or subtract)
*, /	multiply and divide
+, −, ||	add, subtract, and concatenate
=	equal to
!=	not equal to
<	less than
>	greater than
<=	less than or equal to
>=	greater than or equal to
IS NULL, LIKE, BETWEEN, IN	nonspecific comparison operators
AND	conjunctive
OR	comparative inclusive

In the PL/SQL statement, there must be a matching value for each variable selected using SELECT INTO. The value must also conform to the object's datatype. Boolean values may receive only a value of TRUE, FALSE, or NULL, as follows:

```
DECLARE
   trip BOOLEAN;
   . . .
BEGIN
   trip := FALSE;
   WHILE NOT trip LOOP
   . . .
   trip := (fetches >500);
   END LOOP;
END;
```

The sequence of assigning values to an expression depends on the operation being performed. Operations are done in particular order, depending on their precedence (priority). Precedence can be superseded by using a parenthetical reference. The operations within an expression are done in a particular order depending on their precedence. Table 3.9 shows the default order of operations from first to last. Items at the top of the chart have highest priority.

Be careful about operators when a NULL value might be involved. Since NULL indicates that no value is present, some unexpected results might arise. So, remember that comparisons involving a null yield NULL even when applying the NOT operator. Also be careful in a conditional control statement; since NULL produces an indeterminant value, no conditional processing will take place.

Within the processing blocks, PL/SQL provides access to all the functions available to SQL*PLus (except DECODE). There are more than seventy functions that assist in manipulating data. The group functions specifically designed for SQL (AVG, MIN, MAX, COUNT, SUM, STDDEV, and VARIANCE) are not strictly prohibited, but are only allowed on SQL processes in a PL/SQL block.

Conditional Programming in a Processing Block

Within a block of PL/SQL code, execution always begins at the start of the PL/SQL block and processes down through the code, line by line. By adding conditional processing, such as an IF-THEN statement or a LOOP, PL/SQL can perform different activities depending on the criteria specified.

The simplest conditional structure in PL/SQL is the IF-THEN statement and its variations. IF-THEN allows you to specify alternative actions depending on the circumstances at the time of execution. IF-THEN has three basic forms: IF-THEN, IF-THEN-ELSE, and IF-THEN-ELSIF. All forms of the IF-THEN statement must be closed with an END IF clause. IF-THEN statements are activated whenever the condition evaluates to TRUE. For example:

```
IF test_grade >= 90 THEN
   notify_teacher(teacher_name);
   UPDATE student_grades SET avg_grade = (select avg(grade)
         from student_test_scores);
END IF;
```

The IF-THEN-ELSE statement is slightly more elaborate and contains code that executes when the condition evaluates to FALSE or NULL. Using ELSE ensures that some sort of code is executed by the program. For example:

```
IF test_grade >= 90 THEN
   notify_teacher(teacher_name);
   UPDATE student_grades SET avg_grade = (select avg(grade)
         from student_test_scores);
```

```
   IF test_grade >= 98 THEN
      notify_dean;
   END IF;
ELSE
   UPDATE student_grades SET avg_grade = (select avg(grade)
      from student_test_scores);
END IF;
```

In this example, the teacher is notified (through the notify_teacher procedure) if the student's grade is an A, then the student's grades are averaged. If the student did not make an A on the test, then the student's average is calculated without notifying the teacher. Also note that an IF-THEN may be nested within a larger IF-THEN statement.

In other cases, the program must differentiate between many different options. In such a circumstance, the IF-THEN-ELSIF clause is most useful. For example:

```
BEGIN
   IF test_grade >= 90 THEN
      notify_teacher(teacher_name);
      IF test_grade >= 98 THEN
          notify_dean;
      END IF;
   ELSIF test_grade between 70 and 89 THEN
   ELSIF test_grade < 70 THEN
      alert_teacher(teacher_name);
   END IF;
   update_grades(student_name);
END;
```

In this example, the teacher is notified about good grades, and the dean is notified about truly exceptional grades. (Note that another IF_THEN_ELSIF clause could have been used instead of the nested IF-THEN.) The teacher is also alerted if a student is making poor grades. And since all three IF_THEN clauses update the student's grades, the multiple UPDATE statements are replaced with a single procedure call.

Additional conditional processing is available using one of the three forms of the LOOP statement: LOOP, WHILE-LOOP, and FOR-LOOP. Loops allow the execution of a set of statements many times over. You can easily control the number of times a loop is run. The most basic loop is the infinite loop:

```
LOOP
   counter := counter + 1
   IF counter = 50 THEN
     EXIT;
   END IF;
   /* And all other appropriate PL/SQL and SQL statements */
END LOOP;
```

This basic loop will infinitely execute the PL/SQL and SQL statements, processing down from the LOOP statement to the END LOOP statement, then returning to the top and starting again. An infinite loop like this can be broken by including an EXIT statement among the PL/SQL and SQL statements, perhaps in an IF-THEN statement. The EXIT statement is valid only within a loop and will cause the program immediately and unconditionally to exit from the loop.

The WHILE-LOOP statement builds a condition into the loop sequence. The condition is evaluated prior to the execution of each loop. If the condition is evaluated to TRUE, the loop is executed; if NULL or FALSE, the loop is bypassed in favor of the next statement. The general syntax of the WHILE-LOOP is as follows:

```
WHILE counter < 50 LOOP
   counter := counter + 1;
   /* And all other appropriate PL/SQL and SQL statements */
END LOOP;
```

The number of iterations through a WHILE loop is not specifically known, unless specified in the WHILE statement; however, FOR-LOOP enables you to specify the exact number of iterations to be performed by the loop using an upper and a lower boundary. The basic syntax is:

```
FOR counter IN 1..3 LOOP -- assigns values 1, 2, and 3 to counter
   reconcile_balances(acct_||counter);
   /* This will execute 3 times */
   /* All appropriate PL/SQL and SQL statements */
END LOOP;
```

The range is evaluated only when the FOR-LOOP is first entered. If the lower boundary and upper boundary are equal, the loop executes at once. If the lower boundary is greater in value than the upper boundary, the loop does not execute. The order of processing may be reversed by adding the REVERSE clause after the IN clause (FOR counter IN REVERSE 1..3 LOOP). The upper and lower boundaries may also be dynamically assigned using variables or even functions. For example:

```
SELECT COUNT(student_name) INTO students_enrolled
   FROM students;
FOR counter IN 1..students_enrolled LOOP
   FETCH var1 INTO...
   EXIT WHEN var1%NOTFOUND; -- exits when var1 is NOTFOUND
   ...
END LOOP;
CLOSE var1;
```

Note that the loop counter may be referenced only within the loop. The loop counter becomes undefined once the loop has been exited. Also note that the EXIT-WHEN statement allows the loop to be exited conditionally. If the EXIT-WHEN (or EXIT) evaluates TRUE, the loop is completed and processing is handed off to the next statement outside of the loop. For this reason, the next statement outside of the loop must be executable, even if it is a NULL statement. The loop may also be named by prefixing the loop with a developer-supplied name, enclosed in double angle brackets. For example:

```
<<CHECKER_LOOP>>
LOOP
   /* Any appropriate PL/SQL and SQL statements */
END LOOP checker_loop;
NULL;
```

Although it is contrary to good programming techniques, developers can enter and exit named blocks using the GOTO statement. The GOTO statement diverts processing to any normally labeled block, but not IF-THENs, LOOPs, and most exception blocks. But remember that GOTO statements are strongly discouraged in well-designed, structured code.

Another important command used in conditional programming is the NULL statement. The NULL command specifies inaction, merely passing control on to the next statement. Note that LOOPs must be followed by an executable command and IFs (and procedures) must contain at least one executable command. Make sure that at least a NULL follows the LOOP or is contained in the IF-THEN statement. NULLs can act as placeholders or add clarification to a program.

SQL Statements in a PL/SQL Processing Block

One of the advantages of PL/SQL is its seamless interconnection with SQL. PL/SQL can use all SQL data-manipulation commands, transaction-control statements, functions, group functions, pseudocolumns, and operators. PL/SQL also allows the use of comparisons, set operators and row operators as components of a SQL statement in a PL/SQL block. PL/SQL does not support the use of SQL*Plus commands and some SQL commands, like data definition statements (such as CREATE), session control statements (such as SET ROLE), and system control statements (such as ALTER SYSTEM). PL/SQL also does not support the EXPLAIN PLAN statement.

Cursors

Oracle processes SQL statements and stored information using "private SQL areas." A developer can custom-define a private work area using a *cursor*. Cursors are either implicit or explicit. Implicit cursors, usually built automatically for all SQL data-manipulation statements, retrieve and manipulate data in sets, even if the set retrieves only one row. Explicit cursors, usually custom-made, retrieve and act on data one row at a time. This allows PL/SQL programs to retrieve data, manipulate it, and process it one row at a time, much like COBOL or FORTRAN programs might.

Cursors are controlled using the OPEN, FETCH, and CLOSE commands. OPEN initializes the cursor and specifies the active set of data. FETCH retrieves data, one row at a time. With a conditional process like IF-THEN or LOOP, FETCH can retrieve many rows of data. Finally, CLOSE releases the cursor. Create a cursor by declaring it in the DECLARE block. For example:

```
DECLARE
   CURSOR get_scores IS
   SELECT student, student_id, grade
   FROM students
   WHERE average_grade > 79;
...
```

Cursors can also take parameters to influence the data returned. The parameter can be used only to replace a constant. For example:

```
   CURSOR get_scores1 (score_level IN NUMBER) IS
   SELECT student, student_id, grade
   FROM students
```

```
WHERE average_score > score_level;
```

Once the cursor has been defined, the OPEN statement executes the cursor's query. If the cursor issued a SELECT...FOR UPDATE statement, then OPEN also locks the database rows. Open a cursor by referencing it and be sure to include any parameters, if they are needed:

```
OPEN get_scores1(85);
```

Once the cursor is opened, the data may be retrieved only one row at a time using the FETCH statement. Each time the FETCH executes, the cursor steps to the next active row of data. For example:

```
FETCH get_scores1 INTO temp_student, temp_id, temp_grade;
```

The FETCH statement must contain an explicit INTO value for each column retrieved by the cursor. The value must the same datatype as the column. A typical fetch is used in an iterative LOOP of some kind:

```
OPEN get_scores1(65);
LOOP
    FETCH get_scores1 INTO temp_student, temp_id, temp_grade;
    EXIT WHEN get_scores1%NOTFOUND;
    -- PL/SQL code to process retrieved data
END LOOP;
CLOSE get_scores1;
```

When FETCH has run out of rows to return, it begins to return indeterminate values. The CLOSE statement should then be used to abort the cursor, as shown in the example. Once closed the cursor can be reopened, though any operations attempted on a closed cursor will return an INVALID_CURSOR exception.

All cursors have four attributes that may be utilized in PL/SQL programs: %NOTFOUND, %FOUND, %ROWCOUNT, and %ISOPEN. Appending each of these attributes to the cursor name can return valuable information and help control the cursor.

%NOTFOUND returns a TRUE value when the cursor is no longer able to FETCH rows and is useful for aborting LOOPs used by a cursor. The rest of the time (when the FETCH is returning records) %NOTFOUND is FALSE.

%FOUND is the exact opposite of %NOTFOUND. Use %NOTFOUND to see if the FETCH fails and %FOUND to see if it succeeds. For example:

```
LOOP
   FETCH tester INTO teacher_name, teacher_id;
   IF tester%FOUND THEN    -- fetch is successful
      INSERT INTO teacher_name VALUES (...);
   ELSIF tester%NOTFOUND   -- fetch failed
      EXIT;
   END IF;
END LOOP;
CLOSE tester;
```

%ROWCOUNT is used to return the number of rows fetched so far. When the cursor opens, %ROWCOUNT is zero; however, %ROWCOUNT moves ahead incrementally each time a fetch returns a row. Obviously, %ROW-COUNT could be used to influence the behavior of LOOP statements and other PL/SQL processes. %ISOPEN evaluates to TRUE as long as the current cursor is open. %ISOPEN is useful in IF-THEN conditionals to determine what sort of action the program should take.

Exception Handlers

PL/SQL processes predefined and custom-defined errors as "exceptions." So, when an error of some type arises, an exception is raised. When an exception is raised, normal processing stops and control passes to the exception handlers defined in the PL/SQL block or subprogram. To process these exceptions, developers write exception handlers.

A number of predefined errors can be raised by the system. For instance, any process that attempts to divide by zero raises the ZERO_DIVIDE exception, and any attempt to insert a value in a field that is inappropriate for its datatype (like an alphabetic character in a number field) raises the VALUE_ERROR exception. Table 3.10 shows a list of useful predefined exception handlers.

You can define custom exceptions in the DECLARE block, then check for them in the program. If the custom exception is encountered, the exception can be handled using the RAISE statement. For example, student attendance must be marked in the attendance book; it cannot be NULL. This example writes an exception to handle this problem:

```
PROCEDURE check_attendance IS
    attd_missing     EXCEPTION;
BEGIN
    SELECT student, student_id, attended INTO temp_std, temp_id, temp_attd
    FROM student_attendance
    WHERE teacher = teacher_id;
    IF attended IS NULL THEN RAISE attd_missing;
    ELSE calculate_attendance;
    END IF;
EXCEPTION
        WHEN attd_missing THEN notify_teacher;
        WHEN value_error THEN raise invalid_number;
        WHEN OTHERS THEN null;
END check_attendance;
```

Remember that an exception does not return a value; it indicates a certain condition. Consequently, the exception should be used to indicate what process should take place when that condition is encountered. However, exceptions can be cross-referenced similar to other PL/SQL objects. For example, if two or more exceptions need to process the same code, the code uses this statement:

```
WHEN value_error OR no_data_found THEN bell;
message('This is an invalid Student ID. Try again or press LIST.')
```

The OTHERS handler should be included in most PL/SQL programs, since it ensures that no exception will go unhandled. Remember that in nested programs, unhandled exceptions are passed to the enclosing program until the exception is finally handled or the exception fails and raises an error in the execution of the application (that is, the user sees an error message on the screen and the program may even be halted). Finally, very specific errors can be handled in an exception using the functions SQLCODE and SQLERRM to find out exactly which error occurred and to capture the error message, respectively.

Special PL/SQL Objects

%ROWTYPE sets up an object that represents a single row from a table or view. The row, or record, can then store all of the data retrieved from a cursor using the FETCH statement. The columns and datatypes in the record are the same as in the database. For example, two rows, one from a table and one from a cursor, can both be held in a %ROWTYPE object:

Table 3.10 Predefined Exception Handlers

Exception:	*Raised when process:*
CURSOR_ALREADY_OPEN	attempts to OPEN an already open cursor
DUP_VAL_ON_INDEX	attempts to INSERT or UPDATE a database column value that already exists within a UNIQUE index
INVALID_CURSOR	attempts an illegal cursor operation such as closing an unopened cursor
INVALID_NUMBER	attempts to use a character string where a number datatype was required
LOGIN_DENIED	attempts to log on with an invalid Oracle username/ password
NO_DATA_FOUND	attempts to SELECT INTO with no returned data
NOT_LOGGED_ON	attempts to issue a database call without being logged onto Oracle
PROGRAM_ERROR	encounters a PL/SQL internal problem, such as a function, that has no RETURN statement
STORAGE_ERROR	runs out of memory or encounters corrupted memory
TIMEOUT_ON_RESOURCE	encounters a timeout while Oracle is waiting for a resource like a table
TOO_MANY_ROWS	attempts to SELECT INTO one location but receives more than one row
TRANSACTION_BACKED_OUT	encounters a remote transaction that is rolled back because Oracle data might be erroneous at some nodes
VALUE_ERROR	attempts datatype conversion, but fails because of incompatible datatypes
ZERO_DIVIDE	attempts to divide a number by zero
OTHERS	[not actually an exception, OTHERS handles all exceptions not explicitly declared in the exception-handlers block]

```
DECLARE
      teacher_rec           teachers%ROWTYPE;
      CURSOR student_notes IS
      SELECT student_name, student_id,  homeroom_teacher
      FROM students
      WHERE ... ;
      student_rec    student_notes%ROWTYPE;
BEGIN
      SELECT * INTO teacher_rec
      FROM teachers
      WHERE ... ;
      ...
END;
```

Another useful PL/SQL object is a PL/SQL table, somewhat similar to a database table but with some differences. PL/SQL tables allow developers to create arraylike structures. These tables may be of any size and can have only one column and a primary key. The column can be any scalar type, but the primary key must be a BINARY_INTEGER. PL/SQL creates a table by first declaring and defining a TABLE type, then declaring the PL/SQL tables of that type. For example:

```
DECLARE
    TYPE employees IS TABLE OF CHAR(10) INDEX BY BINARY_INTEGER;
```

Once the table "employees" is declared, PL/SQL tables of that definition may be declared within the PL/SQL code:

```
employee_salary      employees;
```

The name "employee_salary" now represents an entire PL/SQL table. Rows of the table are referenced by table_name(seq_id). So, to call the third row of the PL/SQL table, use this command:

```
employee_salary(3) ...
```

Assign a value to the row using standard PL/SQL assignments:

```
employee_salary(3) := salary * 1.041;
```

Rows in a PL/SQL table do not exist until a value is assigned to them. Use a LOOP command with an INSERT or cursor to populate a PL/SQL table with values.

```
PROCEDURE fetch_teacher_data
        (rows             OUT  BINARY_INTEGER,
         teacher_tab      OUT  TeachernoTabTyp,
         name_tab         OUT  NameTabTyp)
IS
BEGIN
    rows := 0;
  FOR teacherrec IN (SELECT * FROM teacher)
  LOOP
    rows := rows + 1;
    teacher_tab(rows) := teacherrec.teacherno;
    name_tab(rows) := teacherrec.name;
  END LOOP;
END
```

Values in PL/SQL tables cannot be erased with the DELETE statement. Instead, use a LOOP to erase all values iteratively.

A PL/SQL object similar to a table or %ROWTYPE is a PL/SQL record. Records possess uniquely defined fields and datatypes. As with the other objects, RECORDS must be declared first in the declare block, then in the program. The basic syntax is:

```
DECLARE
   TYPE record_name IS RECORD
     (field_name1 {field_type | variable%TYPE | table.column%TYPE
         | table%ROWTYPE} [NOT NULL],
      field_name2 {field_type | variable%TYPE | table.column%TYPE
         | table%ROWTYPE} [NOT NULL], ...);
```

The field declarations are similar to variable declarations in that each field has a unique name and datatype. Plus, the fields may also be declared NOT NULL. Individual fields within a record may be referenced using a dot notation:

```
record_name.field_name ...
teachers.first_name ...
```

Values can be assigned to record fields through straight assignment using the := or by performing SELECT INTO statements.

LIMITATIONS OF PL/SQL

Although PL/SQL is a dramatic improvement over the EXEMACRO and trigger step method of programming in older versions of SQL*Forms, it still has a few limitations. First of all, PL/SQL has no means of handling input-output. There are no facilities within PL/SQL to print or store the data processed by your PL/SQL programs. This can usually be worked around by creating temporary tables, storing your information in those tables, and then using SQL*Plus commands to extract that data to a file or to a printer. Second, PL/SQL is not uniformly implemented across all products in Oracle's product line. So, you could have an early version of Oracle Forms, or some other CDE tool, that supports only PL/SQL, version 1, while the Oracle RDBMS supports PL/SQL, version 2.

A note on the positive side: PL/SQL is largely based on the programming language Ada. So, if you become quite proficient at PL/SQL, you are about halfway to proficiency in Ada.

CONCLUSION

SQL and its extensions SQL*Plus and PL/SQL serve as the basic foundation for most application-development activities using the Oracle CDE. This chapter presents the syntax and usage of standard SQL commands, like SELECT, INSERT, UPDATE, and DELETE. By the time you complete this chapter, you should be able to write complete SELECT, INSERT, UPDATE, and DELETE commands interactively or from a file. Programming and report writing using SQL*Plus are detailed, as well as methods of controlling the SQL*Plus environment using the SET command. Finally, this section details the techniques and style of the PL/SQL procedural extension to SQL.

4 INTRODUCTION TO ORACLE FORMS, VERSION 4.0

INTRODUCTION

Oracle Forms is your primary tool for creating screen-based applications for data entry, review, modification, and deletion. In simpler forms, you need not write actual programs, opting for application creation through simple menus, property sheets, and the Oracle Forms graphic Layout Editor. In more complex forms, you can add the power of PL/SQL programs and customized objects to provide enhanced conditional control.

You use three components of Oracle Forms to create and run applications: Oracle Forms Designer, Oracle Forms Generator, and Oracle Forms Runform. Oracle Forms Designer is used to build the application. Oracle Forms Generator is used to create an executable runfile. And Oracle Forms Runform is used by end-users to operate forms created by the developer—you.

Creating form modules with Oracle Forms is a straightforward process. Although Figure 4.1 shows the design process in a linear progression, the nonprocedural nature of Oracle Forms allows you to do much of the development in any order you prefer.

ORACLE FORMS DESIGNER INTERFACE

The Oracle Forms Designer Interface is a single window that displays the main menu, a message line, and a status line like the image shown in Figure 4.2. Work involving a form, menu, or library is launched from the main window and can be saved to a file or to the database. Once a form is opened, it can be constructed and modified using object property sheets, the Layout Editor, the PL/SQL Editor, and other design facilities appropriate for the application.

Figure 4.1 Overview of Form Creation

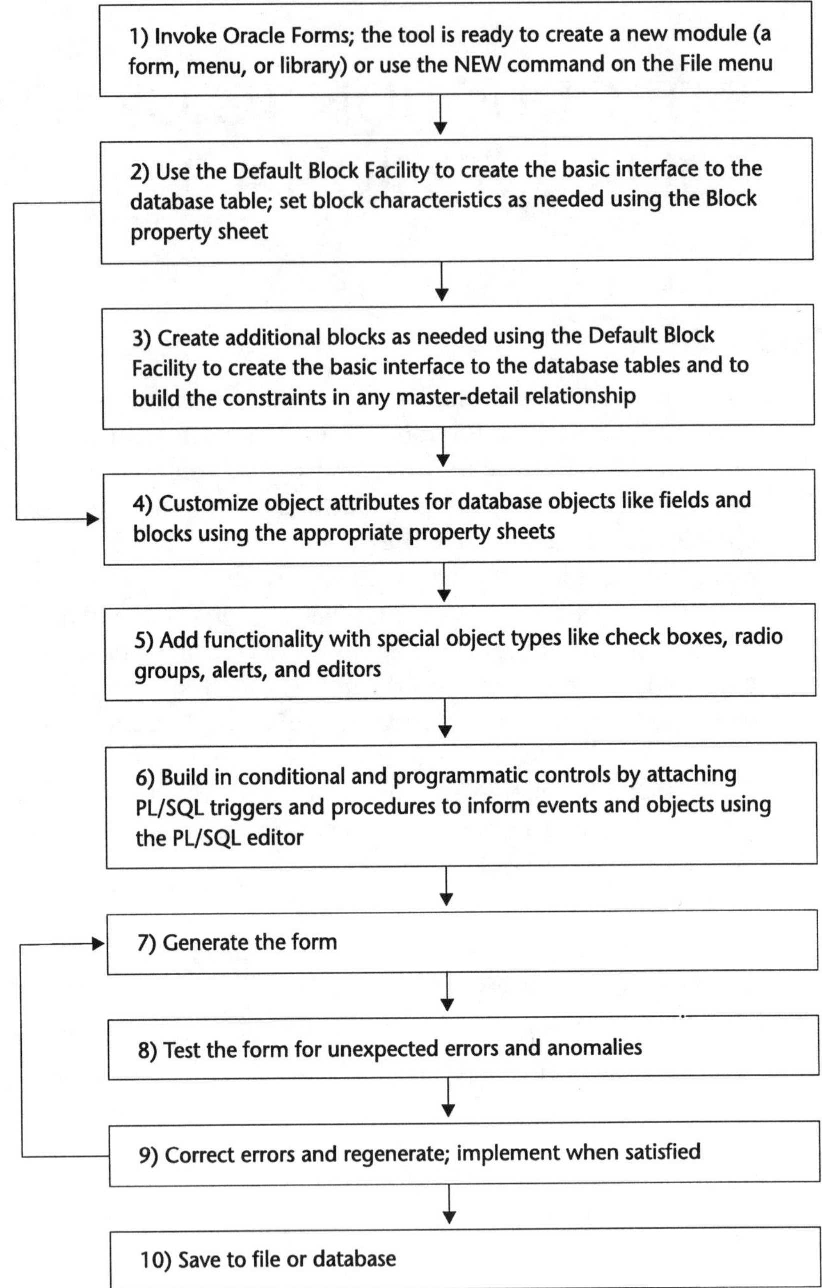

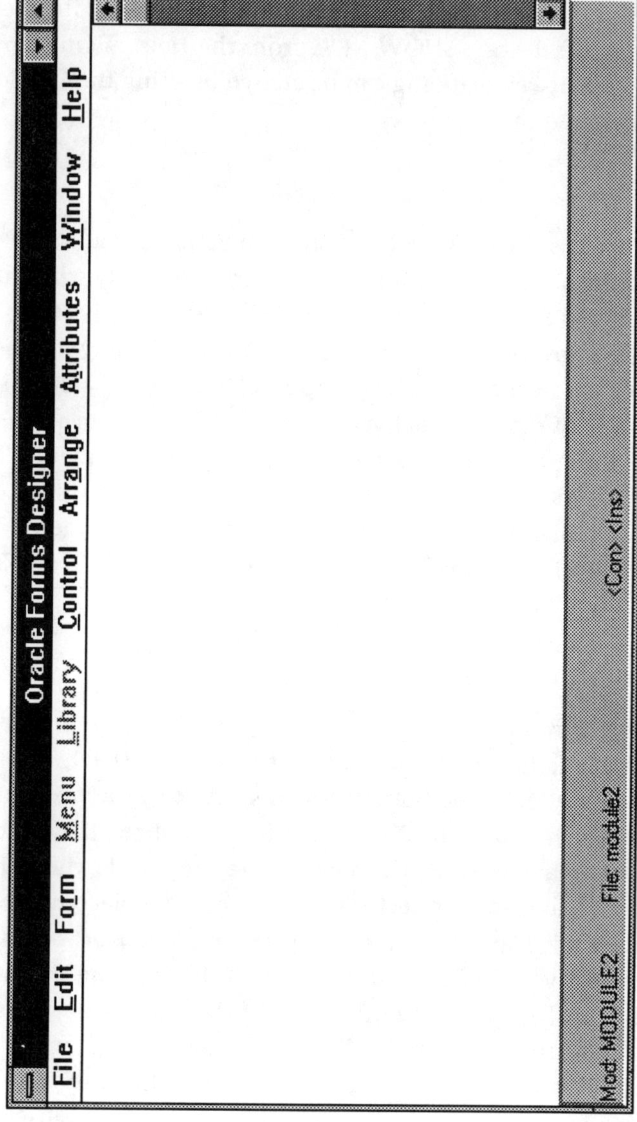

Figure 4.2 Main Designer Window

The Show Keys Function

To see the terminal-specific function keys for Oracle Forms, invoke the Show Keys window by selecting SHOW KEYS from the Help menu or by pressing Ctrl-K. The default-key mapping can be altered by using the Oracle Terminal program, described in chapter 8.

The Main Menu

The main menu is the primary location from which to launch many Oracle Forms operations. Some operations can be performed only when a module is active; others can be accessed at any time. The type of active form, menu, or library module governs when the Form, Menu, and Library menus are available, respectively. Commands on the respective menus are available only when that type of module is active.

None of the module menus are available when no modules are active. Also, many commands on the file menu are available only if a module is active. File commands that require an active module include CLOSE, SAVE, SAVE AS, REVERT, ATTACH/DETACH LIBRARY, GENERATE, GENERATE AS, and GET INFO.

The Message Line and Status Line

The second-to-last line of the main menu is the message line, used to display messages and help information related to the property sheets and tools being used by the developer. The bottom line displayed in the main menu is the status line, which is used to display information about the current session relating to the active module, the name of the current file, the status of referenced objects, database connect status, and insert/replace mode. The Mod status line item displays the name of the active module or is blank when no modules are active. The File status line item displays the filename for the current module. The <Ref> flag indicates if the current object is an object referenced from another module. The <Con> flag appears on the status line when Oracle Forms is connected to the database. The <Ins>/<Rep> flags appear depending on whether the text-editing mode is set to insert or replace typed text.

The Active Module

When a new module (form, menu, or library) is opened, it becomes the active module, with its name displayed on the status line. Many modules may be open at once, although only one is active at a time. Modules remain open until closed or until you quit Oracle Forms.

Many of the design tools, like the Layout Editor and property sheets, are invoked and displayed in separate windows. These windows can be nonmodal or modal. Nonmodal windows can be left opened whether or not you perform any action in the window, while modal windows disallow activity outside of the window and must be explicitly closed to leave the window, usually by clicking the OK or Cancel button or by some programming function. Nonmodal windows are also linked to specific modules and remain displayed until they are closed or their parent module is closed.

You can flip between active modules by clicking in the window of the module to be activated or by selecting the MODULE command from the Edit menu. When the MODULE command is invoked, a list of values appears allowing you to select a module to activate. After selecting a module from the list, click the OK button to open the module. Once a new module is activated, the name shown at the Mod item is updated to reflect that.

You can flip between different windows by clicking in the desired window or by selecting the name of the window from the Windows menu. The names of all open windows (except dialog boxes) are listed in the Windows menu, even inactive windows. The window names shown on the Window menu show the product name, the module name, and the window name (for example, FORMS: SCORES: Blocks).

Context and Navigation

Oracle Forms Designer is based on an object hierarchy, Form → Block → Item, where Form is the highest object in the hierarchy. In other words, each block must belong to a form, and each item must belong to a block. Designer keeps track of "where" the designer is working, from the top down. This is called *establishing context*.

You can quickly change context (the item, block, or form where work is being performed) within the object hierarchy by *zooming* to the specific location. Just use the [Zoom In] key to move down the hierarchy, from the form to a block, from a block to an item, or from an item to a property sheet. Use the [Zoom Out] key to move up the hierarchy. ZOOM is available in the Form module property sheet, the Block property sheet, the Item property sheet, and the Trigger property sheet. Note that the [Zoom In] and [Zoom Out] keys first accept changes to the object and then change the current context. If you zoom in to a level where no object exists, for example, from the block to the object level, then Designer will invoke the property sheet allowing you to create that object.

ZOOM moves you up and down the object hierarchy, but the NEXT and PREVIOUS commands move you laterally through objects on the same level. Thus, using the NEXT and PREVIOUS command would move you between blocks (if that were the current context) or between items within a specific block. Most windows contain Next and Previous icon buttons at the bottom of the box or accept the [Next Record] and [Previous Record] keys.

Oracle Forms validates the changes to the object before moving to the next. NEXT and PREVIOUS move the context to the next object or the previous object according to the sequence number of each object. For instance, if your current context is BLOCK2, clicking the Next button would move you to BLOCK3, while clicking the Previous button would move you to BLOCK1. NEXT and PREVIOUS are not available on objects invoked from the Layout Editor, since the Layout Editor establishes the current context as the single, invoked object.

Object-Naming Conventions

Developer-created objects must adhere to the Oracle naming conventions applied within Oracle Forms. When an object is created by clicking the New button in an object list, Designer creates a default object name in the format OBJECT_TYPEn, where OBJECT_TYPE is the type of object (block, field, etc.) and *n* is the next available sequence ID integer. The designer can then provide a new name for the object. The new name should not contain any special characters (except a dash "—" or an underscore "_") or spaces. All object names must be unique and should never be a reserved word or an Oracle keyword. Refer to appendix 1 for more information on keywords and reserved words.

Oracle Forms Designer Tools

Oracle Forms Designer contains many useful design tools: the Default Block Facility, the Layout Editor, the Menu Editor, the object lists, the various property sheets, the PL/SQL Editor, the Tables/Columns Browser, and the Built-Ins Browser.

THE DEFAULT BLOCK FACILITY

Oracle Forms Designer greatly aids the application development process by automating the creation of default blocks and their component items that

Figure 4.3 The Default Block Facility

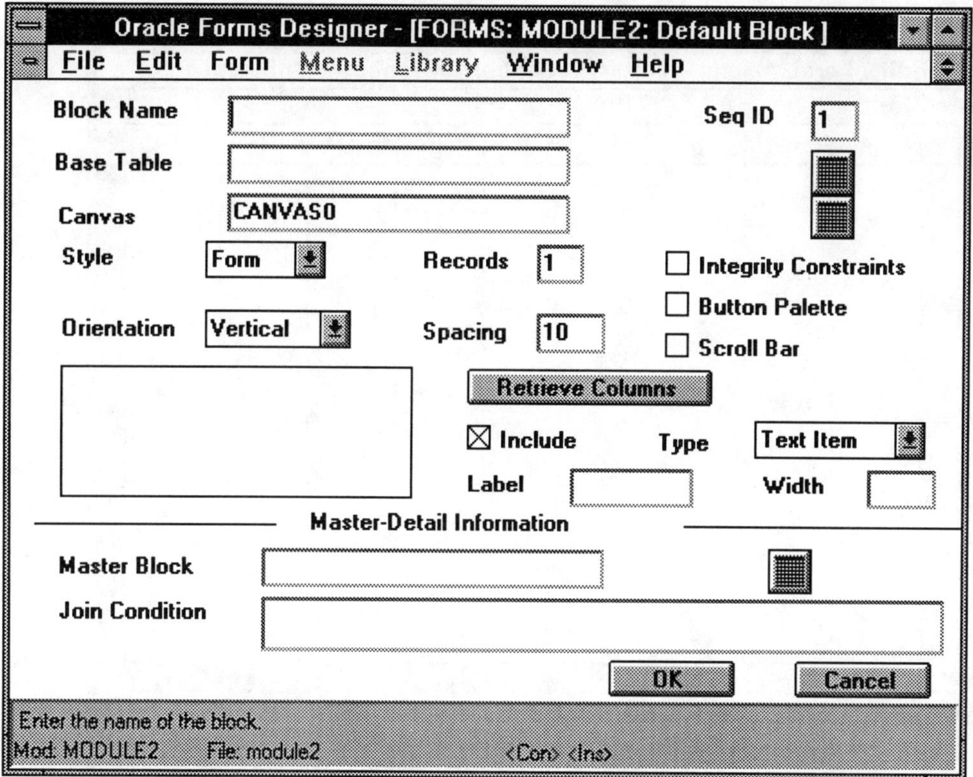

correspond to database table columns. By using the Default Block Facility,
developers specify the database table and columns that will serve as the data
elements of the block. Once they are specified, Designer automatically makes
the default canvas, blocks, and fields. Once created, the default block can
then be modified. The Default Block Facility, as shown in Figure 4.3, is available when a Form module is active by selecting DEFAULT BLOCK from the
Form module.

THE LAYOUT EDITOR

After the default blocks of the form have been defined, the Layout Editor,
seen in Figure 4.4, can put the finishing touches on the form. It enables you
to create and move objects, invoke item property sheets, and insert boilerplate text and graphics. To facilitate this process, it possesses rulers and grids,

Figure 4.4 The Layout Editor

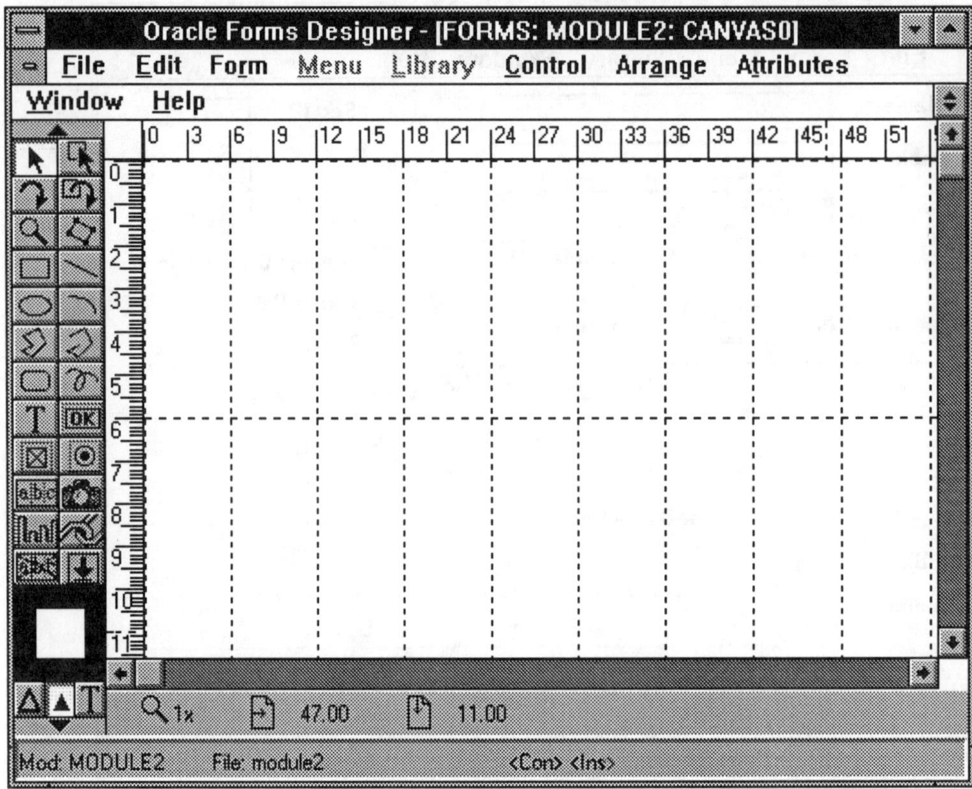

a full palette of drawing tools, support for many fonts and colors, and the ability to import and export text, images, and drawings to and from a canvas. Additionally, canvas objects can be hidden, or shown if already hidden, using the SHOW CANVAS command on the Arrange menu (somewhat similar to a page 0 field in SQL*Forms version 3).

More than one Layout Editor window can be open at a time, but only one can be active at a single time. When the Layout Editor is activated by pressing the [Layout Editor] key or by selecting the LAYOUT EDITOR command from the Form menu, you have access to commands on the Control, Arrange, and Attributes menus. Thus, you have access to commands that apply, cancel, and revert changes. A Form module must be active to invoke the Layout Editor.

THE MENU EDITOR

Customized menus that are used to invoke forms for runtime execution are built using the Menu Editor, seen in Figure 4.5. The Menu Editor is invoked by selecting the MENU command from the Editor menu. When a menu module is active, you can use the Menu Editor to create menus and submenus, append items to menus, and assign various commands to the menu.

OBJECT LISTS

The objects can be viewed and managed from object lists. Object lists display all the objects of a specific type from an active window. You call the object list by selecting the desired object type, like Window or Items, from the Form menu. Object lists enable you to invoke a property sheet for any existing object, delete an object, or create a new object through a default property sheet for that object type.

The type of object being manipulated is described in the Object Type list of values. Once an object type is selected from that list, all objects of that type from the currently active module are displayed in the object list in Figure 4.6. An object property sheet is invoked by double-clicking the object name on the object list. There are a number of commands also available from the Object List dialog box, including CLOSE, EDIT, NEW, OBJECT TYPE, and RE-MOVE. CLOSE quits the object list. EDIT calls the property sheet of the currently selected object. NEW calls the default property sheet (for the type of object shown in the object type) and creates a new object with the next available sequence ID (the sequential order of each object). REMOVE deletes the selected object from the object list.

PROPERTY SHEETS

By invoking the appropriate text item property sheet (see Figure 4.7), you are able to control the settings for the various objects of the current form or menu. A property sheet can be called from the Object List dialog box by selecting the appropriate object and selecting the Edit button or by simply double-clicking the object in the Layout sheet. Property sheets govern the standard behavior of a single object, like a field or a window, and are analogous to the Field Characteristics facility in SQL*Forms 3.0.

A number of commands control the behavior of a property sheet. The OK button, or the [Accept] key, accepts changes in the property sheet, then closes it. The Apply button executes a specific action, like executing a SELECT state-

Figure 4.5   The Menu Editor

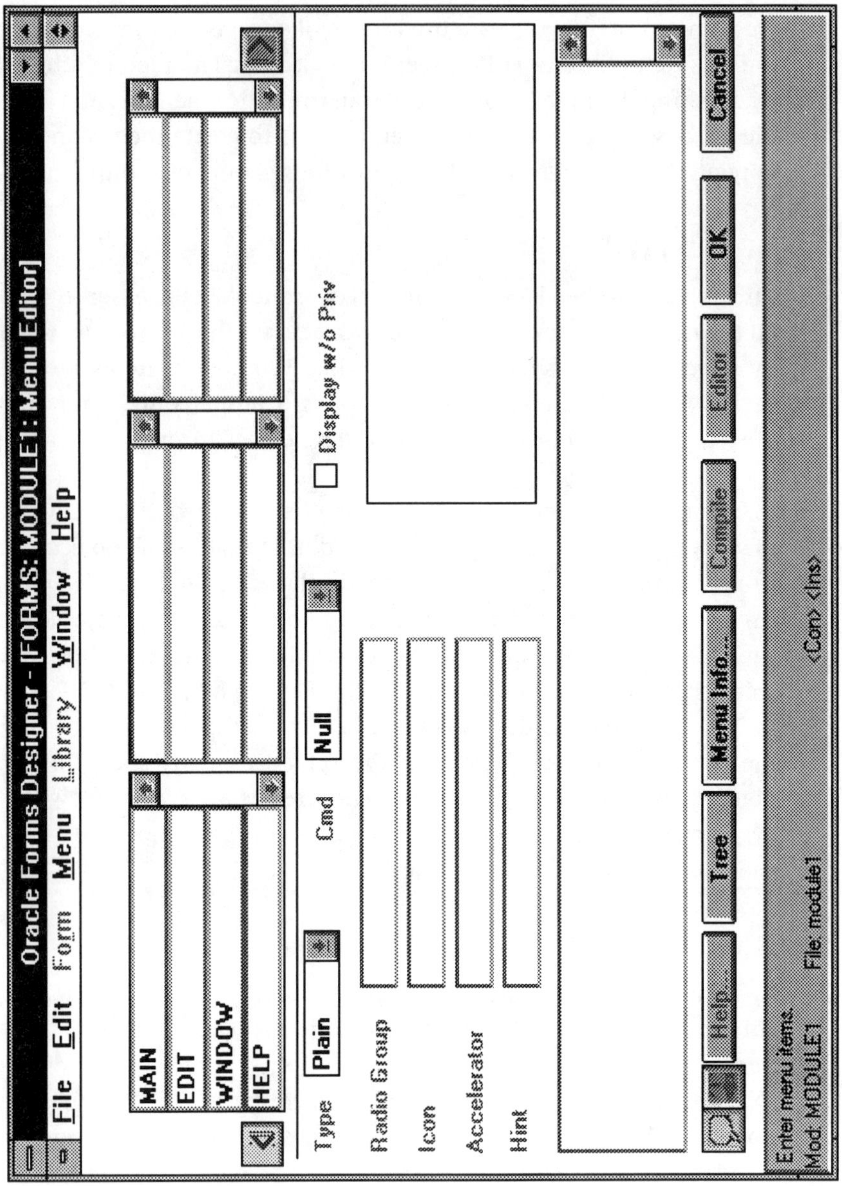

Figure 4.6   Object List Dialog Box

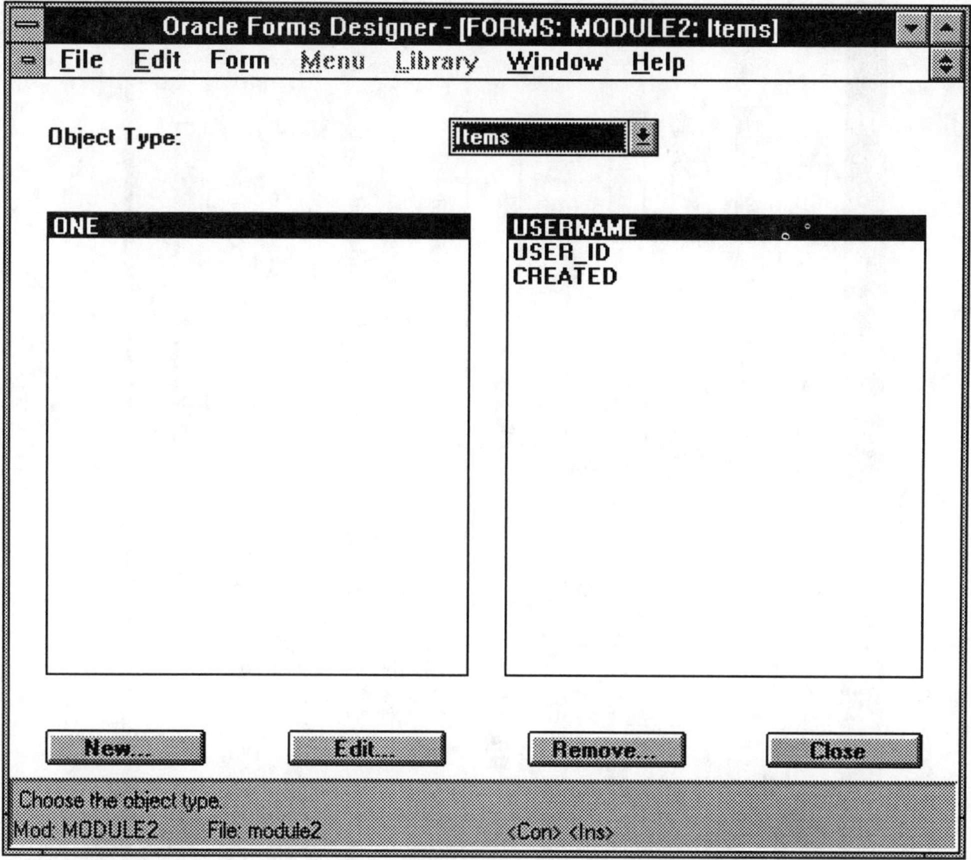

ment in the Query field of the List of Values property sheet. The Cancel button closes the property sheet without saving any changes. The Comments button invokes an editor, allowing you to attach notes to specific objects and modules as they are created. You can view the comments as part of the module code, by invoking the Comment editor or by printing Summary documentation for the module. The More button allows you to view additional pages of a multipage property sheet. The Next and Previous buttons, or the [Next Record] and [Previous Record] keys, allow you to move among more than one object of the same class. Finally, the Visual Attributes button calls the Visual Attributes dialog box, allowing you to set the font, color, and display attributes of the current object.

Figure 4.7 Text Item Property Sheet

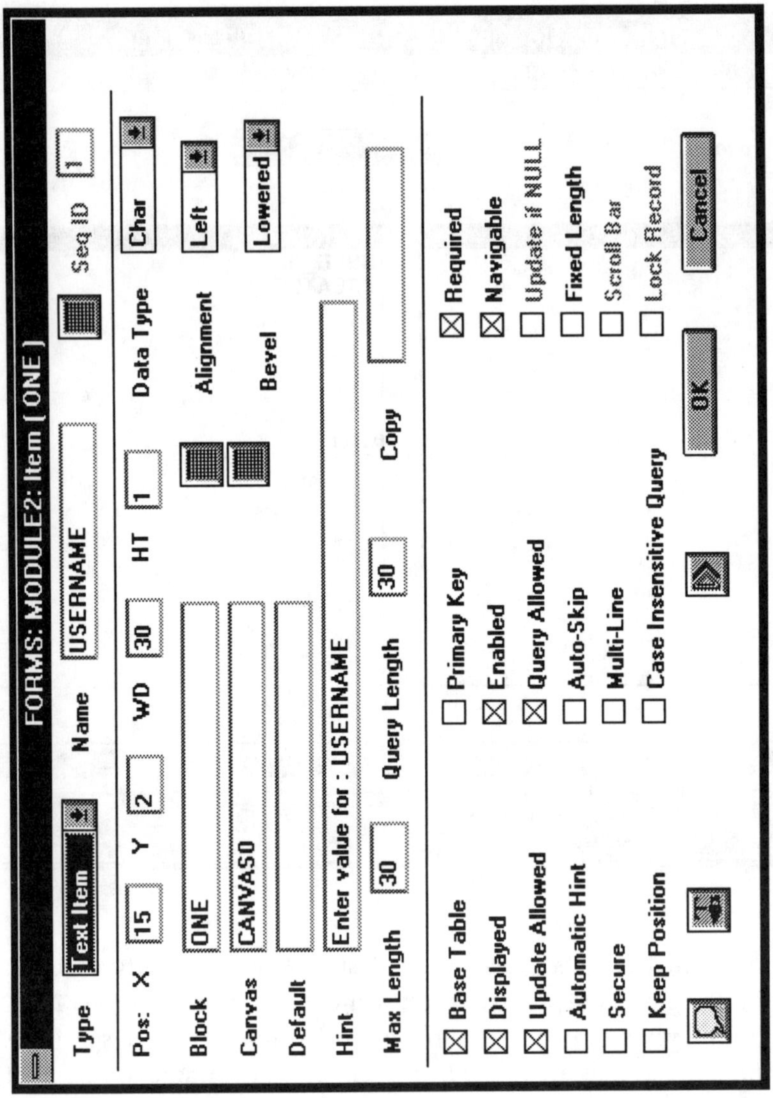

PL/SQL EDITOR

PL/SQL is an essential component of any Oracle Forms application. Designer uses the powerful PL/SQL Editor (see Figure 4.8) to edit and compile PL/SQL code for triggers and menu commands, or to create PL/SQL functions or procedures. Designer displays the PL/SQL Editor automatically if you attempt to compile a faulty trigger, menu item command, or user-named routine.

- To call the PL/SQL Editor in a form, select PL/SQL from the Form menu, then choose NEW or EDIT. When editing a Trigger property sheet, choose EDITOR.

- To call the PL/SQL Editor in a menu module, select PL/SQL from the Menu menu item to display the Program Units Browser, then choose NEW or EDIT.

- In a menu module when the current item is defined as a PL/SQL command, choose EDITOR in the Menu Editor.

- In a Menu Module property sheet, click the StartupCode button.

- When in a library module, call the PL/SQL Program Units Browser by selecting PL/SQL Program Units from the Library menu. Then click NEW or EDIT.

The PL/SQL Editor contains three primary components: the Source Text field, where the PL/SQL source code is written and edited; the Compilation Messages field, where compiling error messages are displayed; and the Status Line, which contains a <Not Modified>/<Modified> flag, indicating where changes have been applied, and also a <Not Compiled>/<Successfully Compiled> flag, indicating the code was successfully compiled.

PL/SQL Editor control buttons also provide added functionality to the editor. The Apply button applies the changes made to the trigger, although it does not save them to the module. Apply overwrites any previously existing trigger by the same name. The Cancel button undoes changes made since the last Apply or Revert and closes the editor. Compile examines the code for errors and generates the code. When successful, the status line shows the <Successfully Compiled> flag. The OK button applies changes to the code and closes the editor. The Revert button undoes changes made since the editor was opened or since the last Apply or Revert command.

Figure 4.8   The PL/SQL Editor

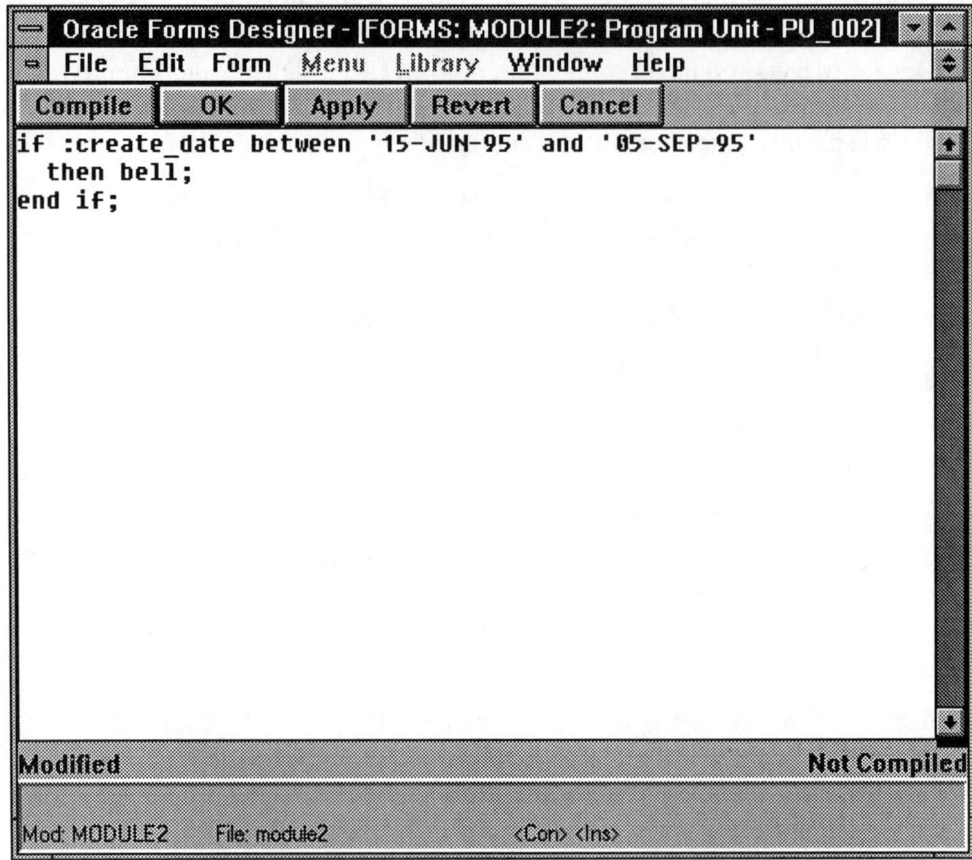

TABLES/COLUMNS BROWSER

The Tables/Columns Browser, seen in Figure 4.9, is used to select and paste tables, views, synonyms, and even complete SELECT statements into the current edit field. The Tables/Columns Browser is called by selecting the Tables/Columns command from the Edit menu. Select the desired table from the tables list, then click the OK button to see a list of all the columns contained in that table in the columns list.

Use the appropriate button at the bottom of the window to paste the selected table name, column names (all columns by default), or a complete SELECT statement (containing the selected table and column names) into the

Figure 4.9 The Tables/Columns Browser

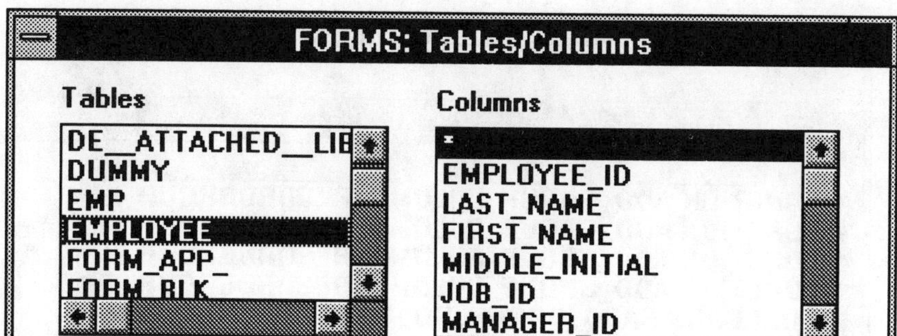

edit field, which is the field currently containing the cursor. Use the Close button to dismiss the Tables/Columns editor.

THE BUILT-INS BROWSER

You can call an alphabetical listing of all the built-in functions and procedures available for use in PL/SQL code and then paste the text for that packaged procedure directly into their edit field using the Built-Ins Browser (Figure 4.10). Invoke the Built-Ins Browser by selecting BUILT-INS from the Edit menu. The Browser displays both Oracle Forms built-ins and PL/SQL standard built-ins, though the Oracle Forms built-ins are displayed by default.

The Built-Ins Browser can remain open while work is being done in other windows. Built-ins are easily inserted into the current edit field (that is, the place where the cursor is currently located) by first selecting the desired built-in, then clicking either the Insert button or Insert w/ Args button. The Insert button pastes the name of the built-in and empty parentheses [( )] for any required parameters. The Insert w/ Args button pastes the complete text of the built-in, including any parameters.

Additionally, turn the Show Overloadings check box on to view the complete syntax of each valid built-in. In effect, an "overloaded" built-in can be written in one of several ways. Turning Show Overloadings on will display all valid configurations of the built-in. Turning Show Overloadings off will display only the default configuration of the built-in. For example, with Show

Figure 4.10   The Built-Ins Browser

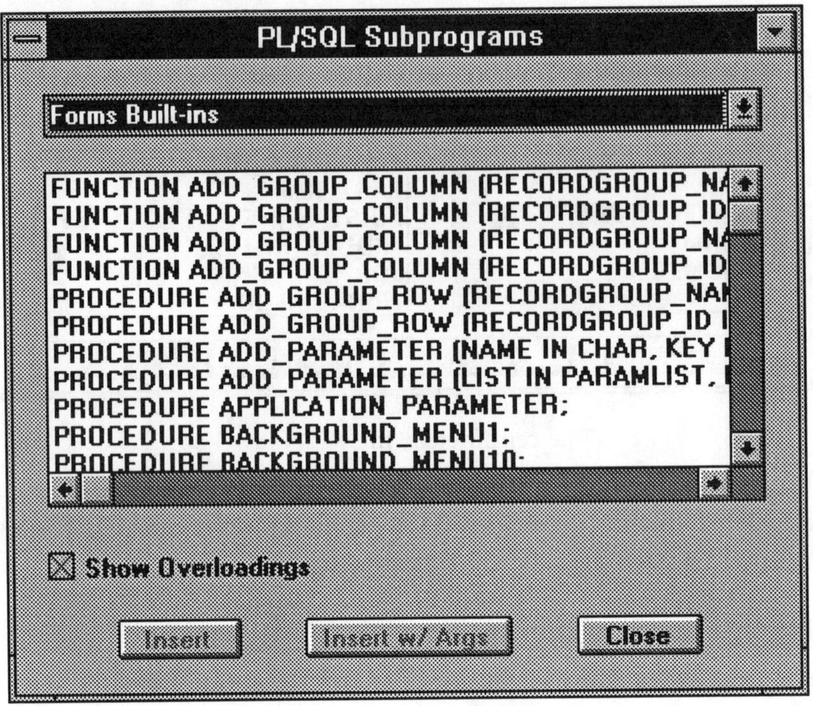

Overloadings on, the Built-Ins Browser displays the following for MOVE_WINDOW:

```
PROCEDURE MOVE_WINDOW(WINDOW_ID IN WINDOW, X IN NUMBER, Y IN NUMBER);
PROCEDURE MOVE_WINDOW(WINDOW_NAME IN CHAR, X IN NUMBER, Y IN NUMBER);
```

Two separate commands are displayed, since MOVE_WINDOW can be referenced by a window ID or by a window name. Note that the browser also indicates what datatype must be used for the various parameters; the window name must be in character format, and the distance X must be a number.

CUSTOMIZING THE PROPERTIES OF A FORM

Properties control the design-time and runtime behavior of a forms application. You can define these properties when in an active form by selecting the MODULE command from the Form menu. This calls the Form Module property sheet. You can then establish the design-time and runtime properties of the form and click OK to dismiss the property sheet.

Design-time Properties

Design-time properties affect design-time behavior and should usually be set before actual form development begins. Design-time properties include the form name and the form coordinate system.

The form name is an internally used title that appears on the status line during design. The form name is distinct from the filename used to save a generated form. Forms saved in the database use the form name defined in the form module Name property field. The form coordinate system defines the basic measurement units used to indicate size and position coordinates within Oracle Forms. Valid coordinate types include character cells (the default) or real units like centimeters, inches, pixels, or points. You need to be explicitly aware of the coordinate system you have designated, since Oracle Forms will interpret all coordinate positions by the method declared in this field.

Runtime Properties

Runtime properties affect the runtime behavior of a form and should usually be set before the form is generated. Important runtime properties include the validation unit, mouse navigation limit, cursor mode, savepoint mode, and the menu specification.

The Validation Unit field tells Oracle Forms at what object level validation events should occur. Validation is the process Oracle uses to confirm data stored in a form object, like a field or record, and occurs when the Leave-the-object event occurs. Validation units can be Default, Form, Block, Record, or Item. Of course, the default appears as Default and should be left as such unless the application has some unusual requirements.

The Mouse Navigation Limit field indicates how large the mouse navigation context is. Mouse Navigation Limit can be set to form (the default and most flexible setting), block, record, or item. A setting any lower than form restricts the user to the current object, like a block or record.

The Cursor Mode and Savepoint Mode fields are provided for developers creating applications that draw their data from non-Oracle databases. Accept the default settings for these fields when using an Oracle database; alter these fields only when connecting to non-Oracle databases.

The Menu Module field tells Designer which menu the form should use. Use the Default menu setting to provide standardized navigation, commit, query, and editing functions. Leave the field blank to detach the form from all menus. Specify a custom menu by setting the Menu Module, Menu Style, Use File, Starting Menu, and Menu Role properties. More information is provided on menus later in this chapter.

USING THE LAYOUT EDITOR

The Layout Editor (Figure 4.11) enables you to create and manipulate objects and invoke Item property sheets, as well as boilerplate text and graphics. To facilitate this process, Layout Editor possesses rulers and grids, a full palette of drawing tools, support for many fonts and colors, and the ability to import and export text, images, and drawings to and from a canvas. Additionally, canvas objects can be hidden, or shown if already hidden, using the SHOW CANVAS command on the Arrange menu (somewhat similar to a page 0 field in SQL*Forms version 3). Canvas objects are handled one at a time, in the Layout Editor, while the canvases themselves are displayed at runtime.

The Layout Editor can be invoked from any active form module either by selecting the Layout Editor from the Form menu or by pressing the [Layout Editor] key. When invoked, Layout Editor behavior is determined by the condition of the active canvas. If no canvas is active, Layout Editor creates one. If several canvases are active, Layout Editor displays a list of values allowing you to choose a specific canvas. If only one canvas is active, Layout Editor immediately displays that canvas. More than one Layout session can be active at a time, but only one session is allowed per canvas.

The Layout Editor is composed of these components: workspace, title bar, rulers, tool palette, visual attributes palette, and status line. The workspace is the area of the editor where objects are created and manipulated. The workspace size is independent of the window size, since you can scroll beyond the area actively displayed on the screen. The workspace size can be changed by altering the Layout Size after selecting the Layout Settings from the Arrange menu.

Title Bar and Status Line

The title bar shows the product (FORMS), the name of the active module, the name of the current canvas, and the name of the current block. The status line, shown at the bottom of the Layout Editor window, indicates the mouse

Figure 4.11 The Layout Editor

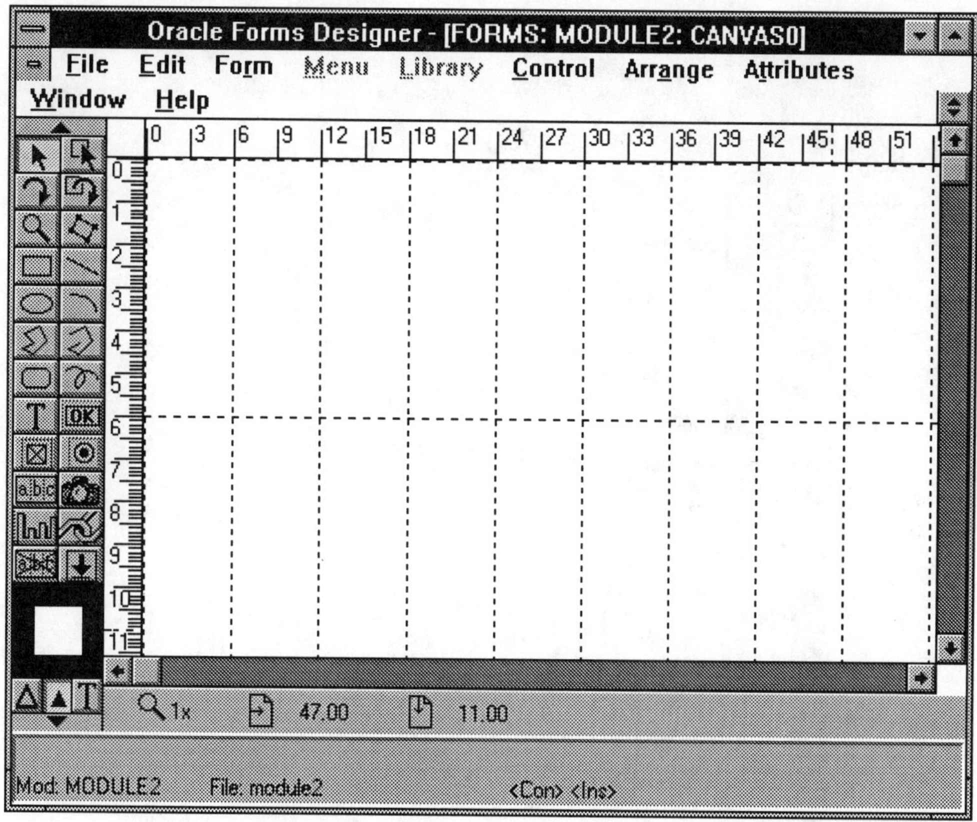

position, mouse drag distance (when creating or moving objects), rotation angle (when rotating an object), and the magnification level (when zooming in).

Rulers and Grids

Vertical and horizontal rulers provide sizing and arranging references. The rulers can be concealed by selecting the Rulers option in the Arrange menu. Ruler measurement units can be altered in the Ruler Settings dialog. Ruler guides, temporary markings used to line up objects, can be placed on the workspace by placing the pointer on the ruler, then clicking and dragging into the workspace. A ruler guide can be removed by dragging it out of the

Figure 4.12 The Tool Palette

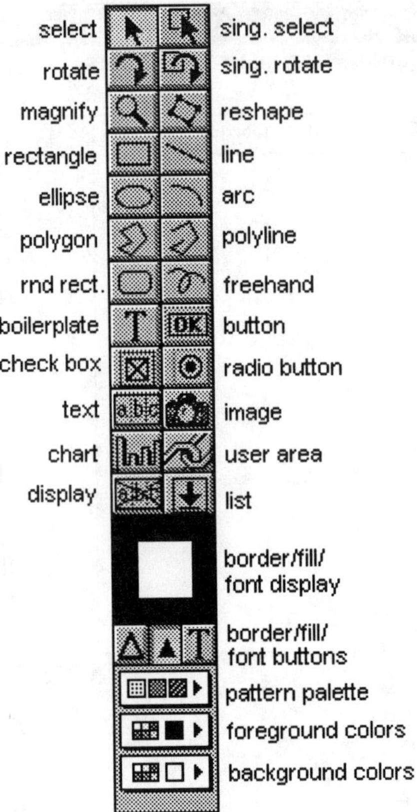

workspace. A grid is also displayed in the workspace to aid in positioning. Turn off the grid by selecting the Grid option from the Arrange menu.

Tool Palette

The Tool palette (Figure 4.12) is composed of a number of icons, each representing a different function for manipulation, boilerplate graphics, or item usage.

The Select tool starts as the default tool. A new tool can be selected as the active tool, usable for a single operation, by clicking its icon. The active tool is designated by a highlighted border. A new tool can be selected as the default tool, usable until a new icon is selected. A default tool is designated by a highlighted icon. Table 4.1 provides information for the creation of new items and boilerplate using the Layout Editor palette.

Visual Attributes Palette

The Visual Attributes palette is a section of the tool palette specifically devoted to the control of visual settings for the Layout Editor. The Visual Attributes palette contains the Attributes box, the Border/Fill/Font selector, the Pattern palette, the Foreground Color palette, and the Background Color palette.

The Attributes box shows the currently selected color and pattern settings. When no objects are selected, the box shows the default settings under which new objects will be created. When an object is selected, the box shows the object's border and fill pattern, as well as a "T" to show the color of any selected boilerplate fonts.

The Border/Fill/Font selector allows you to apply color and pattern choices to new and existing objects. Select the appropriate icon to apply a chosen color or pattern to the border of an object, its filling, or a font. Fonts do not have borders.

The Color and Pattern palettes work in tangent with the Border/Fill/Font selectors. Use the Color and Pattern palettes to choose the desired attribute and apply the attribute to a boilerplate object by selecting it with the border, fill, or font icon.

Creating and Saving Items

An existing item can be modified by double-clicking on the item to invoke its property sheet. Boilerplate items do not have property sheets. You create items in the Layout Editor, by doing the following:

1. Activate a block by selecting SET BLOCK from the Control menu. The item will be added to the active block.

2. From the Tool palette, select the tool icon that is appropriate for the type of item to be created.

3. Click once on the canvas to create an item with a default height and width, or create an item with a custom height and width by clicking on the canvas and dragging out the boundary of the new item.

4. Before the module can be saved using the SAVE or SAVE AS command on the File menu, the changes on the canvas must be applied. Apply the

Table 4.1 Tools Available in the Layout Editor Tool Palette

Manipulation Tools	*Usage*
Select	Used to select an object or a group of objects with a click, using [Shift]-click for each successive object.
Single Select	Used to select a single object that is part of a group.
Rotate	Used to rotate the currently selected boilerplate object or group (but not regular objects); rotate the object by dragging its handle; the status line shows the current angle of rotation.
Single Rotate	Used to rotate boilerplate objects that are part of a group.
Magnify	Used to enlarge or reduce the Layout Editor display by 2x; enlarge by clicking in the workspace; shrink by holding [Shift]-click; the click point becomes the center of the altered display.
Reshape	Used to reshape boilerplate graphic objects (but not regular objects) by clicking and dragging the selection handles.

Boilerplate Tools	*Usage*
Rectangle	Creates a rectangle at the click position—drag to its full size; use [Shift]-click to make a square.
Line	Creates a line at the click position—drag to its full length; use [Shift]-click to make a perfectly straight line.
Ellipse	Creates an ellipse at the click position—drag to its full size; use [Shift]-click to make a circle.
Arc	Creates an arc at the click position—drag to its full length; use [Shift]-click to make a circular arc.
Polygon	Marks each vertex; click to mark the vertex, then double-click at last line segment; use [Shift]-click to ensure perfectly straight lines.
Polyline	Same as polygon, except that the last vertex need not connect to the first.
Round Rectangle	Same as rectangle.
Freehand	Draws freehand graphic—click and drag to draw desired freehand graphic.
Text	Enters text at click position—quit by clicking outside the text box; edit existing text by clicking the text tool inside the text box; use the Scalable Bounding Box option in the Text Drawing option to allow multiline text with word-wrap features.

Item Tools	*Usage*
Button	Creates a Button item at the click position—drag to its full size.
Check Box	Creates a Check Box item at the click position—drag to its full size.

(continued)

Table 4.1 Tools Available in the Layout Editor Tool Palette *(continued)*

Item Tools	Usage
Radio Button	Creates a Radio Button item at the click position—drag to its full size; assign Radio Button to New or existing radio group.
Text	Creates a Text item (field) at click position—drag to its full size.
Image	Creates an Image item at the click position—drag to its full size (will display an "X" at the click position).
Chart	Creates a Chart item at the click position—drag to its full size (will display an "X" at the click position).
User Area	Creates an area on the screen under the control of a user-exit at the click position—drag to its full size.
Display	Creates a text item that cannot be edited at the click position —drag to its full size.
List	Creates a pop list or list box at the click position—drag to its full size; the default is a pop list.

new item to the object layer by selecting APPLY (or ACCEPT) from the Control menu. The item will not be available on object lists and property sheets until the APPLY or ACCEPT command is used.

The Control menu also contains other commands to apply or undo Layout Editor changes:

- ACCEPT: Applies changes made to the object layer and closes the Layout Editor.

- APPLY: Applies changes made to the object layer, allowing you to continue.

- CANCEL: Undoes changes made since the last APPLY command and closes the Layout Editor. If no changes have been applied using APPLY, then CANCEL undoes all changes.

- REVERT: Undoes changes made since the last APPLY command or since the Layout Editor was invoked. Use the UNDO command on the Edit menu to undo the most recent operation.

- SWITCH: Allows you to select and bring into the Layout Editor a different canvas from a list of values. When a new canvas is selected, Designer applies any changes to the current canvas then loads the new canvas.

Defining the Canvas View

The canvas is the foundation on which interface objects like alert boxes, text fields, and radio groups (and other boilerplate objects) interact with users. An object must be placed entirely on the canvas to be visible by users, and the canvas must be placed in a window to be displayed. Each canvas possesses a *viewport*, or definition of the canvas area that is displayed at runtime, which is called a *view*. Canvases can be displayed and hidden, resized, and possess visual attributes. Views can be displayed and hidden, moved, and resized (if the view is stacked). Views and canvases cannot be cleared, cut, copied, exported, or duplicated.

By default, both the canvas and view are hidden when Layout Editor is invoked. Show the canvas by selecting the SHOW CANVAS option from the Arrange menu. Show the view by selecting the SHOW VIEW option from the Arrange menu. Resizing a viewport or canvas is accomplished by clicking on the edge of the canvas to reveal the selection handle in the lower right corner. Resize the Layout Editor, if needed, to reveal the selection handle. Click and drag the selection handle to resize the canvas. Only a stacked view can be resized, though any canvas can be resized. Visual attributes for the canvas can be assigned using the Layout Editor border, fill, and font tools. Move the viewport by clicking it with the mouse and dragging it to the desired location.

Creating a Canvas View

Building a canvas view is the first step in building a forms application. The Default Block Facility automatically creates a canvas, as does the Layout Editor in a new form. However, you can manually create canvas views using the Canvas View property sheet by doing the following steps:

1. Select CANVAS VIEWS from the Form menu to display the Canvas View dialog and click NEW to call the Canvas View property sheet.

2. Enter a name and other properties as needed, including whether the canvas should be a content canvas (a full-screen canvas) or a stacked canvas (a pop-up window).

3. Click OK to apply the definition and close the dialog.

It is important to remember that stacked views, by their nature as pop-up windows, have a number of properties that do not apply to content canvases. Stacked-view properties include Bevel, Display Position (View in Window),

Table 4.2 Canvas View Properties

Property	*Description*
Bevel	A stack property that indicates if the stacked view should have a visible border; choose NONE to hide the border.
Display Position	A stack property that indicates the *x,y* coordinates of the stack's upper-left corner relative to the upper-left corner of the window.
Displayed	A stack property that tells if a stack is initially displayed (the default) or hidden when the window appears.
Name	The unique, internal name of the stack or content canvas object.
Position on Canvas	The position of the view's upper-left corner on the stack or content canvas; the default 0,0 shows the entire canvas.
Raise on Entry	Available to content and stack canvases; the Raise on Entry property raises a canvas to the forefront when entered (if turned on) or when entered and obscured (if turned off—the default).
Seq (Sequence)	Available to context and stacked views on the same window, Sequence numbers show the stacking and navigational order of views in the window.
Size (Wd/Ht)	Specifies the size of content and stack canvas or defaults to 80×24 character cells, or equivalent real units specified in the coordinate system.
Stacked View	An ON/OFF property that indicates if the canvas view is a stacked view or a content view (OFF is the default value) for its assigned window.
Vert/Horiz Scroll Bar	Tells if a stacked canvas view has a vertical and/or horizontal scroll bar.
View Size (Wd/Ht)	Tells the size of the view for a stacked canvas, which must be less than or equal to the canvas size.
Window	This required property tells the window where the canvas view is displayed. Window can be set to either Root_Window (the default) or a secondary window.

Displayed, Vertical/Horizontal Scroll Bar, and Viewport Size. If necessary, delete a canvas view by invoking the Canvas object list and clicking REMOVE. Any boilerplate is deleted with the canvas, and items assigned to the canvas become NULL-canvas items.

Canvas views are complex objects and contain a number of properties that influence their behavior. Use Table 4.2 as a reference when setting the properties of a canvas using the Canvas property sheet.

Creating Secondary Windows

Every form application possesses a root window that contains the GUI special functions, such as scroll bars and arrows, the iconify and maximize buttons, and the control menu. Many menus contain secondary windows programmed as pop-up windows or dialog boxes.

Display properties for the root window by selecting Windows from the Form menu. When the Windows object list appears, select Root_Window, then click on the Edit button. The root cannot be deleted from the Windows list, and many root-window properties cannot be altered, including Bordered (On), Closeable (On), Fixed Size (Off), Iconifiable, Inherit Menu (On), Name, Modal (Off), Movable (On), Remove on Exit (Off), Vertical/Horizontal Scroll Bar (Off), and Zoomable.

A form can have many secondary windows, which function as self-contained, stand-alone windows (sometimes called modeless) or as modal windows requiring an ACCEPT or CANCEL command before the user can exit. Create and define a secondary window by performing the following steps:

1. Select the WINDOWS command from the Form menu to call the Window object list, then click NEW to invoke the Window property sheet.

2. Enter the Name and property definitions for the window. Assign one or more canvas views to the window by entering the window name in the Window properties of the Canvas View property sheet.

3. Click OK to apply the changes and dismiss the window.

Designate a primary-content canvas view for a window by setting the View property to the name of an existing content view. Many properties depend on the mode of the window. Name, Size, Position, Title, and Canvas are applicable to both modal and modeless windows. The Modal property governs the mode of a window and is modeless (off) by default. Modeless windows may or may not have a border depending on the setting of the Border property. Certain properties are invalid when the Border property is turned off, including Closeable, Fixed Size, Icon Name, Icon Title, Iconifiable, Inherit Menu, Movable, Vertical/Horizontal Scroll Bar, and Zoomable.

Built-in functions and procedures allow you to display, hide, resize, move, and scroll windows. Such procedures include window routines and canvas-view routines. Window routines include FIND_WINDOW, GET_WINDOW_PROPERTY, HIDE_WINDOW, MOVE_WINDOW, RESIZE_WINDOW, SET_WINDOW_PROPERTY, and SHOW_WINDOW. Canvas-view routines include FIND_CANVAS, GET_CANVAS_PROPERTY, GET_VIEW_PROPERTY, HIDE_VIEW, REPLACE_CONTENT_VIEW, SCROLL_VIEW, SET_CANVAS_PROPERTY, SET_VIEW_PROPERTY, and SHOW_VIEW. Window event triggers include When-Window-Activated, When-Window-Closed, When-Window-Deactivated, and When-Window-Resized.

Working with Items

The Layout Editor controls many aspects of blocks and items, including setting block context, invoking Item property sheets, setting the spacing for multirecord blocks, creating items, and controlling block scroll bars.

Each Layout Editor window maintains a block context that identifies the current block for operations on items. The name of the current block is displayed in parentheses on the title bar of the Layout Editor window.

Block context is essential to the Layout Editor. Any item created in the Layout Editor is assigned to the current block, unless reassigned using the SET BLOCK command. Items are assigned to a different block by selecting the item or items, then selecting the Set Block dialog from the Control menu. At the Set Block dialog, choose the block to assign the items to.

Item property sheets control the behavior and appearance of items. In the Layout Editor, they can be invoked by double-clicking the item. Property sheets called from the Layout Editor differ from property sheets called from the Item object list in three ways. First, the Layout Editor property sheets are item specific, that is, the [Next] and [Previous] keys will not navigate to other items. Second, Layout Editor property sheets must be dismissed with OK or CANCEL before other work can begin. Finally, Layout Editor property sheets show all changes, even those not applied. Property sheets from the Item object list show only applied changes.

Developers often use blocks that display several records on the screen at one time. Such multirecord blocks are defined by setting the Displayed block property to greater than 1. The actual space between multiple records can be adjusted by selecting the multirecord item or items, then dragging the spacing handles to the desired spacing. With Grid Snap turned on, the distance must be at least as much as the defined snap point or cell unit.

To create a uniform GUI look and feel, you can add scroll bars to a block. To add or remove scroll bars, simply select the block, then set the Scroll Bar:Canvas property in the Block property sheet to the canvas having the scroll bars. The scroll bar can be positioned, resized, or formatted on the canvas using the Layout Editor.

The Layout Editor can create many types of items and boilerplate. The item or boilerplate must remain entirely within the canvas or else it will not be displayed at runtime. The Tool palette shows a different tool for each type of item. Remember that the item or boilerplate must be applied, then separately saved and generated to create a finished copy. Create an item by doing the following:

1. Select the block the item will belong to.

2. Select the item type from the Tool palette.

3. Position the cursor. The item's upper-left corner will appear at the cursor position.

4. Use a single click to create the appropriate item with a default width and height, or click and drag to desired size.

5. Apply changes by selecting APPLY from the Control menu.

Oracle Forms assigns the created item to the current block, unless there are no blocks in the form, in which case the Layout Editor will create a default block. In a multirecord block, the item will be repeated as dictated by the block definition.

Radio groups (groups of mutually exclusive buttons) require special attention since each individual radio button can be treated as a separate object by the Layout Editor. Create a radio group by selecting the Radio Button tool, then click and drag to place a radio button on the canvas. The Layout Editor prompts you to select an active radio group to attach the button to.

Importing Drawings and Images as Boilerplates

Images and drawings can be placed on the canvas as boilerplates in the Layout Editor using the IMPORT command from the Edit menu. Oracle Forms accepts many image formats: CGM, BMP, TIFF, JFIF, Oracle Graphics Format, PICT, and PCX. Note that boilerplate images are distinct from Image items. Image items are database elements, fetched at runtime, while boilerplate items are static and constantly attached to the canvas.

In this application, boilerplate images are useful for displaying company logos or static graphics. Also note that other form objects, like radio buttons or text items, can be placed on top of boilerplate images. When the form is saved and generated, the boilerplate image becomes a background component of the .FMX and .FMB files.

Formatting Objects

The Layout Editor enables you to format object settings such as font, color, pattern, and line width. New items created using the Layout Editor take on the current default attributes. When no item is selected, the Attributes box shows the current default color and pattern settings, while options on the Attributes menu show the default settings for other definitions like font, size, weight, and line. when an object is selected, it takes on the attributes defined in the Attributes box.

Visual formatting attributes can be set to default, to a named attribute, or to a set of custom attributes. Items set to Default are displayed in the default pattern, color, and font specified in the runtime resource file. To apply the default settings to an item, call the Visual Attributes dialog from the item's property sheet, then choose Default. Each visual attribute is a distinct Oracle object, distinguished by its name, that defines a collection of color, pattern, and font information. To apply a named visual attribute to an item, call the Visual Attributes dialog from the item's property sheet, then choose Named. Custom visual attributes are the patterns, colors, and fonts individually selected by you for a specific item.

Additionally, visual attributes can be controlled at runtime using various triggers to control the appearance of items, canvas views, radio buttons, and windows. Triggers that affect item appearances include DISPLAY_ITEM (to alter a single item in a multirecord block) and SET_ITEM_PROPERTY (to alter all the item occurrences in a multirecord block). Alter canvases, radio buttons, and windows with SET_CANVAS_PROPERTY, SET_RADIO_BUT-TON_PROPERTY, and SET_WINDOW_PROPERTY, respectively. Individual attributes cannot be set using these triggers; rather, you must define a named visual attribute that contains a collection of definitions, and your triggers must then reference the attribute, not a specific definition.

Object Attributes

Some item attributes cannot be defined in the Layout Editor, but most attributes can be defined using the Visual Attributes tool palette. Attributes can be defined for Font Type, Font Size, Font Weight, Font Style, Font Justification, Fill Pattern, Fill Foreground Color, and Fill Background Color. Font and text attributes can be assigned to buttons, check boxes, displays, lists, radio groups, and text items. The border characteristics of items cannot be altered.

As with items, a boilerplate's many attributes can be defined in the Layout Editor. Boilerplate text attributes can be defined for Font Type, Font Size, Font Weight, Font Style, Font Justification, Font Spacing, Border Pattern, and Fill Pattern. Boilerplate color attributes can be defined for BordEr Foreground Color, Border Background Color, Fill Foreground Color, Fill Background Color, and Text Color. Boilerplate border and line attributes can be defined for Line Width, Dash Style, and Arrow Style.

Width, dash, and arrow styles for lines can be assigned for use with the Line, Polyline, or Freehand tools. Line width can be set by selecting the LINE command from the Attributes menu, then choosing the desired line width. Dash style can be set by selecting the DASH command from the Attributes menu, then choosing the desired dash style. Similarly, arrow style can be set by selecting the ARROW command from the Attributes menu, then choosing the desired arrow style.

Arranging Objects

You must often arrange and manipulate objects and the placement of items in the Layout Editor. Such manipulations might include grouping objects, overlapping objects, aligning objects, and same-sizing objects.

GROUPING OBJECTS

Multiple objects can be grouped into and manipulated as a single, cohesive object. Grouping enables objects to be assembled and moved as a single unit, thus retaining relative position for objects in the group. To create a group, select two or more objects, then use the GROUP OPERATIONS:GROUP FUNCTION command from the Arrange menu. To disintegrate the group, click on the group, then select the GROUP OPERATIONS:UNGROUP FUNC- TION command on the Arrange menu.

OVERLAPPING OBJECTS

Objects can be arranged so that their boundaries overlap, thus obscuring other objects. Items always appear on top of boilerplate items. Among similar objects (item with item, or boilerplate with boilerplate), the most recently created item appears on top. Rearrange the position of a boilerplate by select- ing one of the arrangement commands from the Arrange menu: BRING TO FRONT, SEND TO BACK, MOVE FORWARD (to raise the object one layer), and MOVE BACKWARD (to lower the object one layer).

ALIGNING OBJECTS

In many cases, the aesthetic appeal of a form is made or broken by the alignment of the different objects on the screen. If the objects do not line up neatly, the whole form has a slipshod appearance. The Layout Editor can automatically align objects horizontally and/or vertically. To align two or more objects, select the desired objects, then issue the ALIGNMENT SETTING command from the Arrange menu. Specify the desired alignment, then click OK to accept the settings.

SAME-SIZING OBJECTS

Same-sizing is the process of making multiple objects the same size, both in height and/or width. To same-size multiple objects, select the desired objects to be made the same size, then issue the SAME SIZE command from the Arrange menu.

Color Palettes

Every form has a color or gray-scale palette containing 256 colors. The individual colors of the palette can be edited and entire palettes can be imported and exported for later use. A specific palette can be loaded when invoking Designer by specifying a Color Palette preference in the Edit Preference dialog; otherwise, the default color palette is loaded. Color palettes can be edited by first setting the Color Mode option to Editable in the Preference dialog on the Edit menu, then, after restarting Designer, selecting the EDIT COLOR command from the Attribute menu. Edit the color as desired. The new colors will be available after you restart Designer. Color palettes can also be imported from and exported to the database or to a file by selecting the Color Palette option from the IMPORT/EXPORT command on the Edit menu.

SPECIAL OBJECTS IN ORACLE FORMS DESIGNER

Objects are the building blocks of any form application. There are a number of object types used in Designer, including blocks, items, windows, canvas views, alerts, editors, list of values, records, and forms.

Blocks and Block Relations

Blocks are an extremely important part of Oracle Forms, since they serve as the basic functional unit that controls the use of database records. Oracle

Forms items must be assigned to a block, which must be created before any items. A form can contain an unlimited number of blocks, which are usually either *base table blocks* or *control blocks*. Base-table blocks are built on top of a specific database table or view, allowing you to control queries, updates, inserts, and deletes from the table. A base-table block must contain at least one field that corresponds directly to the columns of a database table. A control block is not necessarily related to a database table or view and does not contain fields that correspond to any database entity, unless specifically programmed to do so. The basic nature of the block is not explicitly defined; rather, the settings and items of the block determine its specific nature.

Forms that contain more than one block are often *master-detail* forms. Master-detail relationships relate the data between two or more base-table blocks (and their base tables) through a primary key to foreign key relationship. Master-detail blocks are easy to build with Oracle Forms and provide several important capabilities like coordinating query results between the master and detail blocks and ensuring that detail records directly relate to the master record (more on this later in the chapter).

The items of a block, just like a block itself, can be related to a base-table column or to a nonbase-table control item. A base-table block can include both control and base-table items, but a control block contains only control items. For example, buttons are always control items since they cannot store values or relate to a database column. Base-table items are directly related to a column from a database table. Control items are not directly related to a column from a database table, although the control item can be populated with a database value. Control items are useful for the following:

- displaying calculated values (like totals and averages);

- holding variables as a NULL-canvas (Page 0) field;

- displaying a database value from a table other than the base table of the block; and

- accepting input from the operator that is not related to a base table.

Creating Blocks

Base-table blocks are typically created using the Default Block Facility (see Figure 4.13) and then configured using the Block property sheet. Control blocks are created using the Block property sheet. Both a default block and a control block can be deleted at any time by selecting the BLOCK command

Figure 4.13 The Default Block Facility

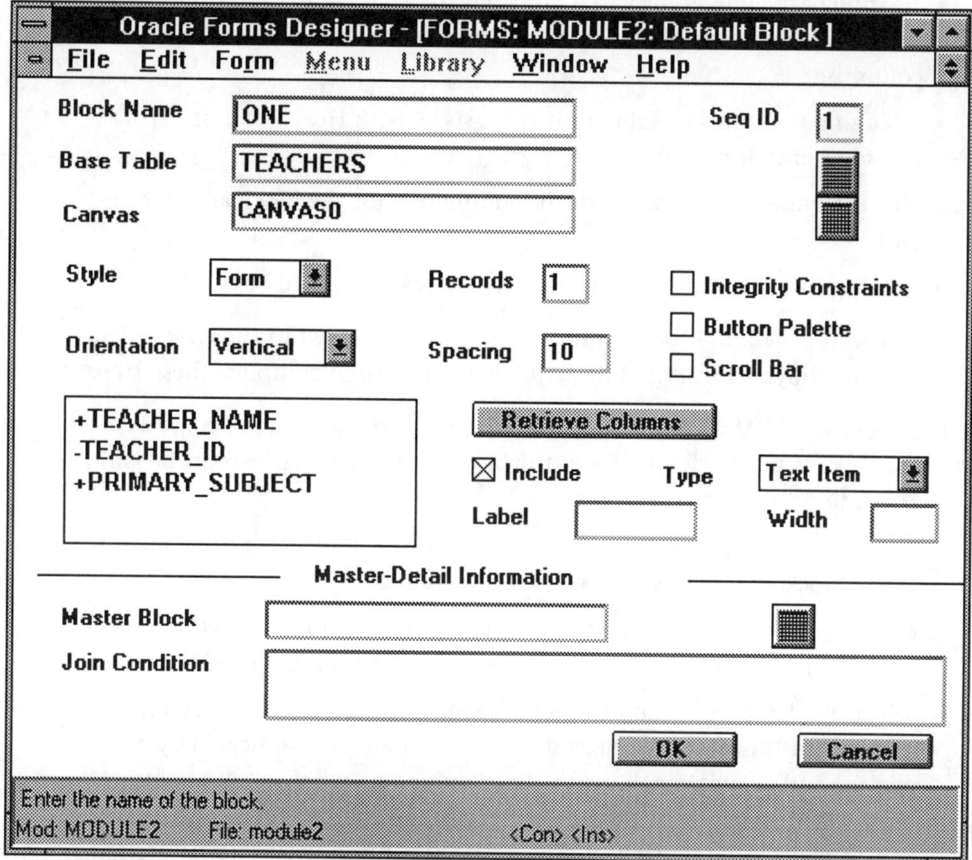

from the Form menu. When the Blocks object list appears, select the block to be deleted, then click Remove. The block and its items, triggers, and dependent relations are all erased.

THE DEFAULT BLOCK FACILITY

The Default Block facility eases the creation of base-table blocks and their corresponding base-table items. You need specify only the defining criteria about the block (like the database table, columns, and default layout) to use the block. Oracle Forms automatically completes the rest of the process by doing the following:

- creating a base-table block with default property values;

- creating base-table items and definitions for each database column specified, including setting the Required property to ON for NOT NULL columns;

- arranging the items in Tabular or Form style, with Horizontal or Vertical record orientation;

- creating boilerplate labels and a bounding box for the block and items; and

- creating a default canvas, when a canvas does not already exist.

Creating a default block requires you to be connected to the Oracle database and to have a form module active. You must then complete these steps:

1. Select the DEFAULT BLOCK command from the Form menu to display the Default Block Facility. Enter the block name. The name must be valid and unique among blocks.

2. Enter the name of the database table in the Base Table field that will serve as the block's base table, or use the list of values.

3. Enter the name of the canvas in the Canvas field. Designer creates the canvas if it does not exist and enlarges the current one, if need be.

4. Select the database columns that will appear in the block. By default, all columns in the table are selected to go into the block, indicated by a plus (+) and excluded columns with a minus (-). Double-click a column on the list to include or exclude it. Specify the column type, such as text item (the default), check box, etc. Set other column properties as desired.

   Two useful settings include Style and Button Palette. Style allows you to set the default form layout as Form, with columns in a two-column format and labels placed to the left, or as Tabular, which, depending on the Orientation setting, arranges columns in either a horizontal row with labels above or a vertical row with labels to the left. The Button Palette creates a button palette that allows navigation, querying, and committing in the current block.

5. If desired, turn on the Use Integrity Constraints option to enforce the constraints defined in the database (see chapter 2 for more information). The Use Integrity Constraints option provides control over primary key settings, default value constraints of columns, and can also create several

triggers to enforce integrity: When-Validate-Item, When-Validate-Record, and When-Remove-Record.

6. Click OK to create the block and close the window. Oracle Forms creates the block and arranges the items on the canvas as specified. Now use the Layout Editor to view and modify the block.

CREATING CONTROL BLOCKS

There are two ways to create a control block. First, to create a control block that utilizes database values, you can create the block as a default block. Then, after creating the block, clear the name from the table specified in the Base Table property. The second way creates a block without database values by selecting the BLOCKS command from the Form menu. Choose New to call the Block property sheet. Insert a Name and other desired properties, but leave the Base Table field blank. Click OK to create the control block and close the property sheet. Add new items to the control block using the Layout Editor or Item property sheets.

USING THE BLOCK PROPERTY SHEET

Block properties can be edited by invoking and editing the Block property sheet. Invoke the Block object list, listing all active blocks in the form by selecting the BLOCK command from the Form menu. Select the desired block, then click Edit. Edit the block properties, then click OK to apply the changes and close the property sheet. See Figure 4.14 for the Block property sheet.

A *displayed* value greater than 1 makes the block a multirecord block. The records in a multirecord block can be arranged vertically or horizontally based on the Horizontal Records check box. By default, the Horizontal Records value is off, causing records to appear vertically. The Scroll Bar button can be turned on to include a scroll bar for the specific canvas. The Scroll Bar displays horizontally or vertically depending upon the orientation of the block. The *Sequence ID* is the default order of the block used in navigation. Changing the Sequence ID reorders the block in relation to other blocks in the form. A block can also be listed in the Default Block menu by turning the In Menu check box to on. The block's name will appear in the Block menu, unless a new name is entered in the Block Menu field (the field directly below the In Menu check box).

Figure 4.14 Block Property Sheet

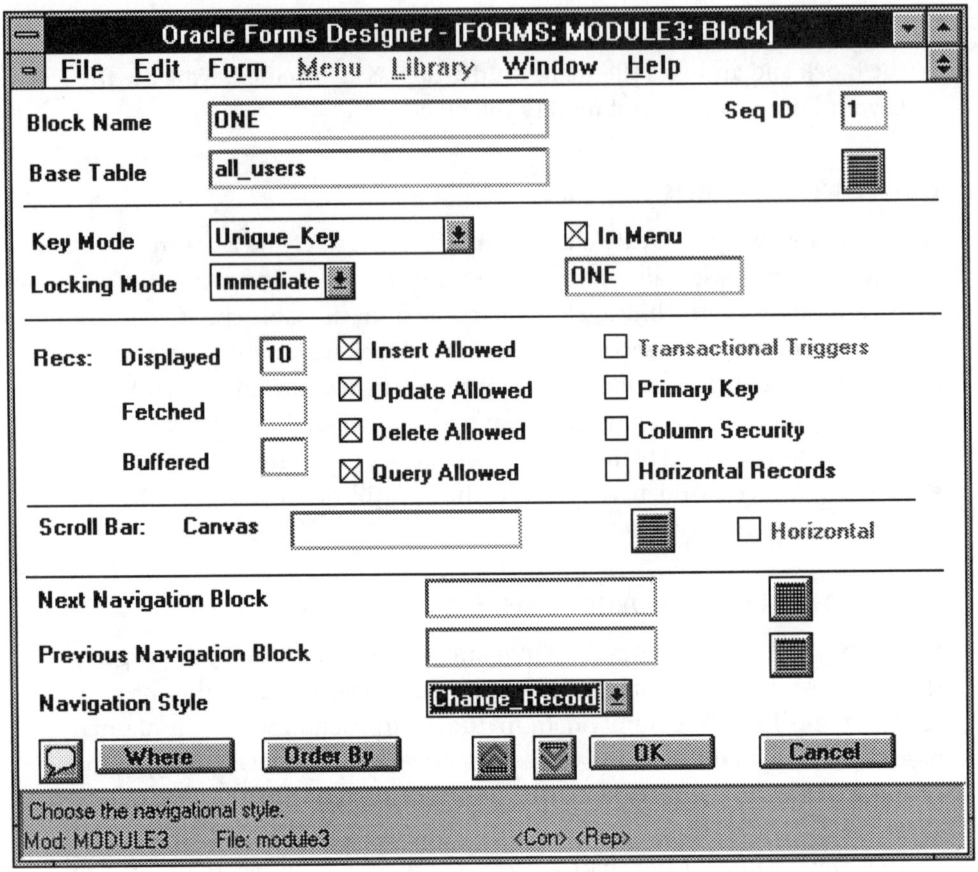

Certain values set in the Block property sheet apply only to base-table blocks. These options, shown in Table 4.3, are unavailable if the Base Table property is NULL.

Master-Detail Forms

As with other aspects of default block creation, Oracle Forms Designer incorporates a number of automatic procedures for the creation of *master-detail forms* (see Figure 4.15) that greatly ease your task. In order to take full advantage of Designer's capability of automatically writing triggers and procedures

Table 4.3 Block Property Descriptions

Property	Value Description
Base Table	Database table name used in this block.
Column Security	Enforces database column security. When on, operators must have update privileges on the columns to which the block's items correspond, enforced through dynamically setting the Update Allowed property on each column at form startup.
Fetched	Number of records fetched from the database at one time during a query. Cannot be less than Displayed.
Locking Mode	Tells when Oracle Forms should lock database records during form processing. Do not alter default unless using a non-Oracle data source.
Primary Key	Indicates whether Designer should enforce unique values for primary key items. The primary key items must have the item-level Primary Key property turned on.
Where/Order By	Optional conditions for restricting and ordering the rows by a query. All base-table blocks possess a default SELECT statement that acts as an unrestricted, unordered query unless lines are added here to perform that function. Use the built-in SET_BLOCK_PROPERTY to programmatically alter the default Where/Order By clause.
Navigation Style	Controls the method the block uses to move between records of the block. Valid settings are Same Record, Change Record, and Change Block. Same Record, the default, moves the cursor from the last item of the record to the first item of the same record. Change Record moves the cursor from the last item of the record to the first item of the next record. Change Block moves the cursor from the last item of the block to the first item of the next block.

that ensure the proper relationship between master and detail blocks, you should use the Default Block Facility to join the base tables.

A master-detail relationship is an association between two or more base-table blocks founded on the relationship of a primary key to foreign key between the base tables. For example, examine two tables in a database for use by elementary school teachers. The Teacher's table contains information about the teacher as an employee of the school system, while the Student table contains information about the students. A primary key to foreign key relationship exists between the Teacher table and the Student table in that

Figure 4.15 Master-Detail Form Example

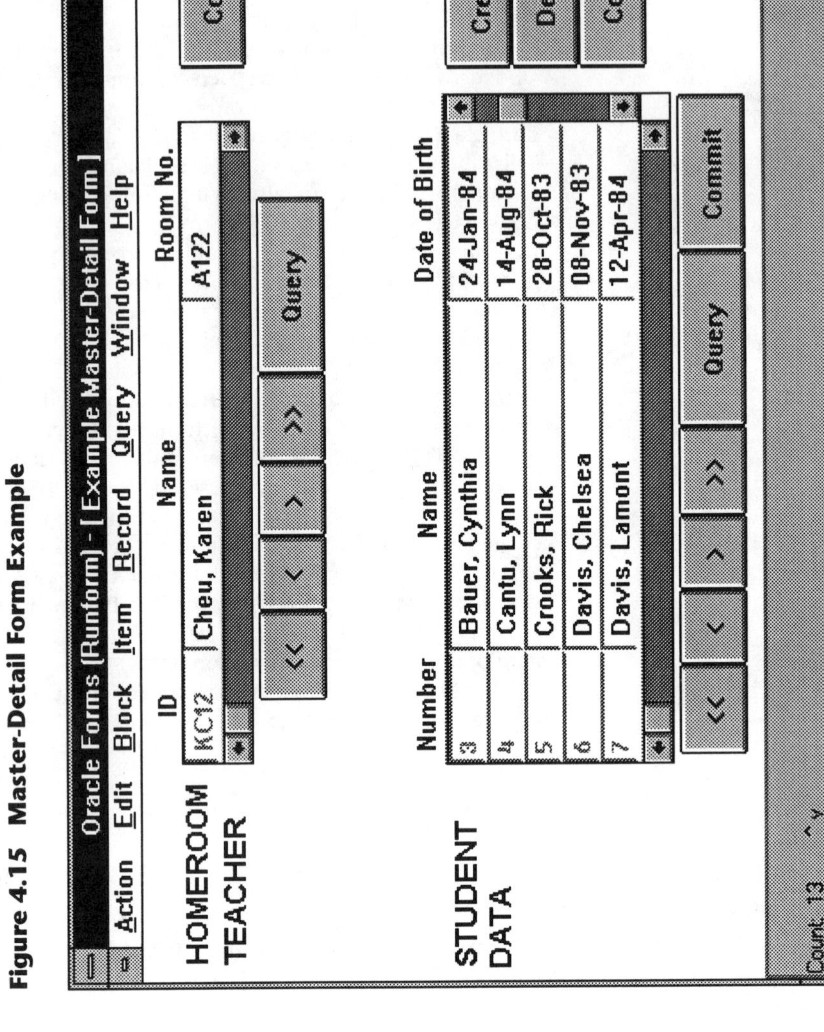

each student must have a teacher. The application includes a form based on this relationship where the Teacher block is the master and the Student block is the detail. More simply put, a teacher can have many students and each student must be assigned to one (and only one) teacher.

Designer's automatic master-detail procedure creates triggers and code that ensure that the detail block appears only for those master records to which the detail is linked. In addition, the triggers and code coordinate querying between the two blocks. For example, when the operator queries a different teacher record, Oracle Forms updates the detail block to show only students from her class. Similarly, when adding a student to the database, the operator must first select a teacher to assign the student to.

CREATING MASTER-DETAIL RELATIONSHIPS

Master-detail relationships can be created either in the Default Block Facility (at the same time a detail block is created) or in the Relation property sheet (see Figure 4.16). The master-detail relationship is based on the *join condition*. By defining the join condition, you link the primary key item(s) in the master block to the foreign key item(s) in the detail block.

The detail block serves as the point of creation for the master-detail relationship. The master block must already have been created.

1. Call the Default Block Facility and create the block as usual. Ensure that the foreign key columns have been included in the detail block.

2. Enter the name of the block that will serve as the master of the block being created, or use the list of values.

3. Enter the join condition that links the detail block with the master record in the Join Conditions field. The join condition for the example would be:

```
students.teacher_name = teachers.teacher_name
```

or, more generically,

```
detail_block.foreign_key_item = master_block.primary_key_item
```

4. Click OK to accept the Default Block definition and close the dialog. The relation is assigned the default name masterblock_detail block, which, in this example, is teachers_students.

To view or edit the properties of the relation, invoke the Relation property

Figure 4.16 The Relation Property Sheet

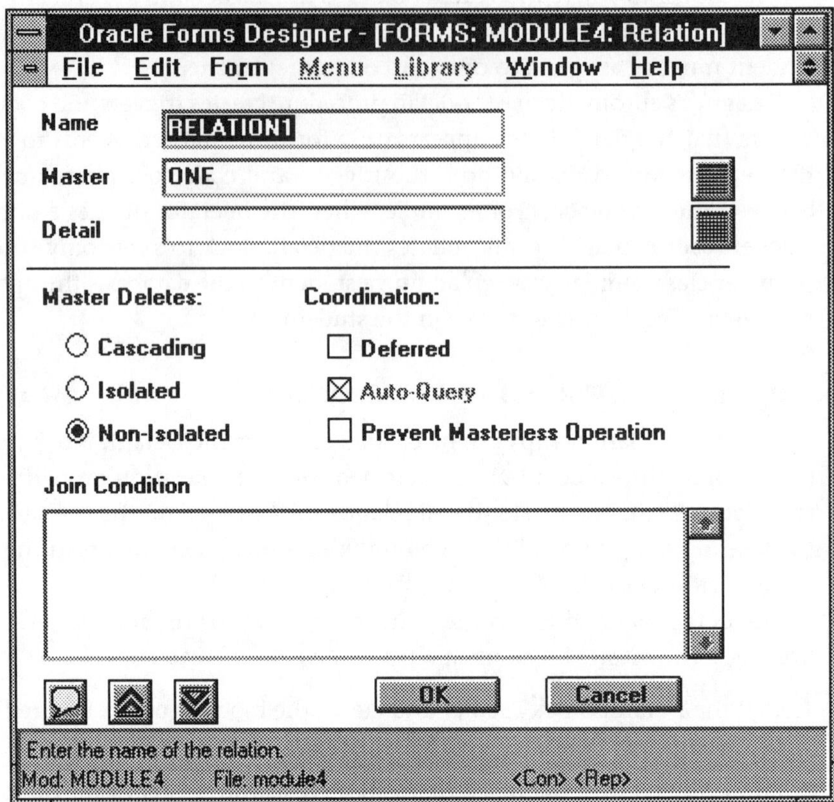

sheet. The Relation property sheet can also be invoked from the Form menu to create a new relation if the detail and master block already exist. Figure 4.17 shows the Relation object list.

The join condition must contain one of the following three elements:

- an item name that exists in both the master and detail block, such as teacher_name, since it exists in both blocks;

- an equating condition of two item names, where one exists in the master and the other exists in the detail block, such as students.home-room_teacher = teachers.teacher_name; or

- a combination of item names and equating conditions.

Figure 4.17 The Relation Object List

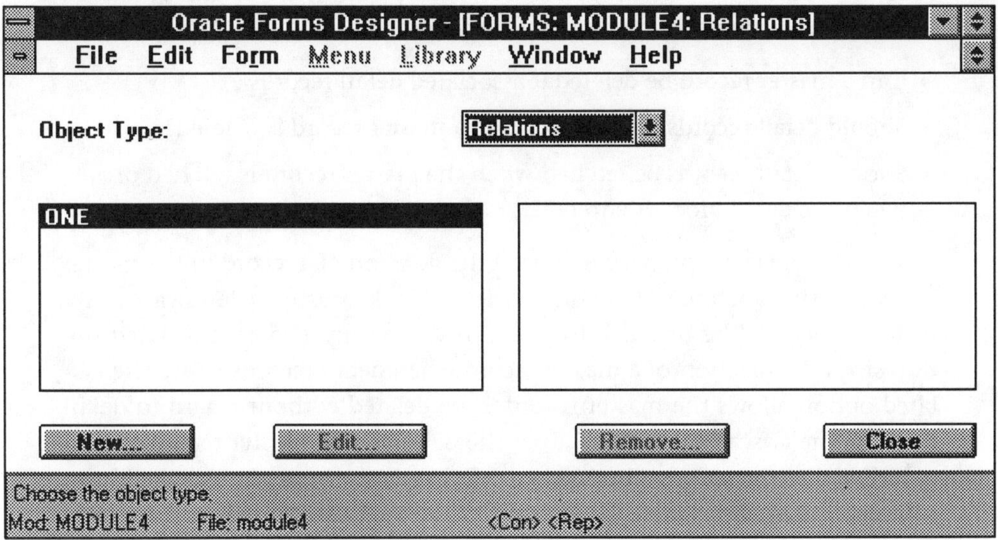

Once the relationship has been established using the join condition, Oracle Forms Designer creates the triggers that coordinate the behavior of the two blocks. Any event that calls a different record into the master block causes a coordinating event in the detail block. For example, if the operator uses the [Next Record] key to see the next record, Oracle Forms clears the detail block and retrieves all of the student records linked to that specific teacher.

The coordinating events of a master-detail form are based on the Copy property of the foreign key in the detail block. The Copy property is analogous to the Enforce Key found in SQL*Forms, version 3.0. Oracle Forms Designer performs a number of automatic functions to render the item invisible and make the operation seamless. Designer also sets the Canvas property to NULL as a NULL-canvas item and the following properties to OFF for foreign key items: Displayed, Enabled, Navigable, Query Allowed, and Update Allowed. Finally, Designer sets the Sequence ID of the items to the last in the block. Any boilerplate associated with the item is dropped.

When creating a relation, Oracle Forms generates the triggers and PL/SQL code needed to ensure proper coordination between the master and detail blocks. The default code generated depends on properties of the relation. In order to set the correct properties for the application, certain questions should be asked when creating a master-detail:

- Can a master record be deleted if associated detail records exist?

- Should detail records be deleted when a master record is deleted?

- Should detail records be fetched when the master record is fetched or when the detail block is entered?

The Master Delete properties control the deletion of a record in the master block and the deletion's effect on the detail block. Master Deletes can be set to Non-Isolated (the default), Isolated, or Cascading. The Non-Isolated option stops the deletion of a master record when detail records exist. The Isolated option allows the master record to be deleted without regard to detail records. The Cascading option causes the deletion of a master record and all of its detail records. Cascading deletes delete only the immediate detail block; subrelations are not deleted. Note: do not use Cascading deletes in Oracle Forms if Oracle7 Server is already using Cascading deletes.

The Coordination property controls the timing of data retrieval between a master and a detail block. Coordination properties include Immediate (the default), Deferred with Auto-query, or Deferred with No Auto-query. The Immediate option, best for forms where the detail block is visible with the master block, causes detail records to be fetched when the master record is fetched. The Deferred with Auto-Query option, best when the detail block is concealed, waits to fetch records until the detail block is entered. The Deferred with No Auto-Query option, best for detail blocks with many records or fields, mandates that the user explicitly execute a query in the detail block to retrieve detail records.

The Prevent Masterless Operation property controls the insertion and querying of records in the detail block. When turned on, a master record must be present for a detail or query details to be inserted. Most applications are better served with this option turned on. Note that this option does not prevent a user from navigating to the detail block and attempting a transaction; only the transaction itself is disabled.

EDITING MASTER-DETAIL RELATIONSHIPS

Relations can be edited at any time during the design and by programmatic methods at runtime. Edit relations by selecting the RELATIONS command from the Form menu and then editing the properties as desired. Use the SET_RELATION_PROPERTY built-in to alter relation properties at runtime and the GET_RELATION_PROPERTY to retrieve the current property information. For example:

```
    Set_Relation_Property ('teacher_kid', MASTER_DELETES,
DEFERRED_COORDINATION);
DECLARE
   master_block     VARCHAR2;
BEGIN
   master_block := Get_Relation_Property('teacher_kid', MASTER_BLOCK);
END;
```

TYPES OF MASTER-DETAIL RELATIONSHIPS

Many applications require simple master-detail relations with a single master block and a single detail block. Others require more complex, multiblock master-detail relationships. Oracle Forms Designer can handle an unlimited number of relations for a single form and can also allow a block to be the master and/or detail in many relations simultaneously. Such complex relations might include a detail block with two master blocks, a master block with many distinct detail blocks, or a master block with a detail block that is the master to another block. To create these kinds of relations, simply create each one individually as described in the section "Creating Master-Detail Relationships." Oracle Forms will create the triggers and code needed to support each relationship.

Items and Property Sheets in Oracle Forms

Items are the primary interface between an application's users and the database. Consequently, the ability to create items and to configure their properties is of great importance. Most items can be created and manipulated using the Layout Editor, but all items can also be created and altered using property sheets by following these steps:

1. Select ITEM from the Form menu to call the Items object list and select the source block for the item from the left-hand column.

2. Click NEW to call the default item property sheet. New items are automatically sequenced.

3. Change the Type selector to the item type desired to display the property sheet appropriate for that item type. Text is the default.

4. Establish properties for the item properties as needed. Properties are required on all items, including name, block name, sequence ID, and canvas ID. Leave canvas ID blank to create a NULL-canvas item (making it invisible during runtime). You can programmatically alter these settings using the SET_ITEM_PROPERTY built-in.

5. Click OK to apply the properties and close the dialog.

Items can be deleted by selecting the ITEM command from the Form menu, then selecting the item to be removed from the object list and clicking REMOVE. When an item is deleted, all triggers and code associated with it are also deleted.

Items can be converted to a different type without changing any other property. Both base-table and control items can be converted at any time during the design process, although base-table items must be compatible with the datatype of the corresponding database column. To convert an item type, simply invoke the item property sheet, change the Type selector, and click OK to apply the changes. Properties of the new type are automatically reformatted. Other properties, such as Name and Canvas, remain unchanged. So always change the Type first when altering an item, then change its properties. Other item properties are described in Table 4.4.

Oracle Forms provides special triggers for the manipulation of items. For example, button behavior can be controlled by the When-Button-Pressed trigger, check box behavior by the When-Checkbox-Changed trigger, list behavior by the When-List-Activated and When-List-Changed triggers, and radio group behavior by the When-Radio-Changed trigger. All items in a form can be affected by the When-New-Item-Instance trigger.

These triggers fire only when the operator changes the item's value with the mouse or keyboard, not when a program or another trigger alters the item. For example, clicking a radio button fires the When-Radio-Changed button. You can alter or retrieve item properties using these built-ins: DISPLAY_ITEM, GET_ITEM_PROPERTY, GET_RADIO_BUTTON_PROPERTY, SET_ITEM_PROPERTY, and SET_RADIO_BUTTON_PROPERTY.

Table 4.4 Item Properties

Property	*Description*
Position	X and Y coordinates mark the location of the upper-left corner of an item in relation to the upper-left corner of the canvas to which the item is assigned.
Size	WD and HT fields show the width and height of the item as specified in the Coordinate System units (character cells, pixels, etc.).
Displayed	The Displayed property—on by default—reveals or conceals an item at runtime. Some items are better hidden, such as global variables or foreign key items.
Datatype	The Datatype of the item is analogous to the datatype of database columns. Some item types cannot store information.

Item	*Storage*	*Database Datatypes*
Button	No	None
Chart	No	None
Check box	Yes	CHAR, DATE, NUMBER
Display	Yes	CHAR, DATE, NUMBER
Radio Group	Yes	CHAR, DATE, NUMBER
List	Yes	CHAR, DATE, NUMBER
Text	Yes	CHAR, DATE, NUMBER, LONG
User area	Yes	CHAR, DATE, NUMBER
Image	Yes	LONG RAW (must be long raw)

Property	*Description*
Default Value	Holds a value the item will always default to when a new record is created.
Max Length	The maximum number of characters the item can store; any excess is truncated.
Update	Update Allowed/Update if NULL: Only one of these properties can be active at a time. Items in a queried or committed record can be changed if Update Allowed is activated, while only NULL items in the record can be updated if Update if Null is activated.
Base Table	Must be active for a base-table item and is dependent on the Base Table block property.
Primary Key	Used to indicate the primary key items in the record, for base-table items.
Sequence ID	Indicates the navigation order of the item.
Navigable	Indicates that an item can be navigated to. This property is not usable with chart and display items.
Enabled	Indicates that the user can initialize an item that has the Navigable property set to on. Disabled items are usually ghosted and not navigable.
Mouse Navigate	Enables you to use a mouse. When turned on, users can activate text items, button items, check boxes, list items, and radio groups.
Query Allowed	Only allowed for check boxes, lists, radio groups, and text items. Oracle Forms skips over all other item types and items that have Query Allowed turned off while in Enter Query mode.

Items in Multirecord Blocks

The Displayed Block property tells Designer to create a block with many records or one record, thereby displaying many instances or one instance of the item in each occurrence of the record. By default, Designer allocates the minimum space required to display the items, though you can control the spacing manually.

Item Hints

In a user-friendly application, it is often appropriate to display context-sensitive help. Oracle Forms displays text for all navigable items except charts and user areas. Such help usually pertains to how the operator can enter valid data for the item, for example, "Enter the preparation date in this fashion DD-MON-YR." Display a hint for an item by doing the following:

1. Enter the hint text in the Hint field of the item's property sheet. No hint will appear if none is entered.

2. Turn the Automatic Hint on to display the text. Turning Automatic Hint off means the user must press the [Help] button to see the hint. The Default Block Facility creates default hints for each base-table item and sets the Automatic Hint property to ON.

Types of Items

Oracle Forms supports nine distinct types of interface items, similar to the datatypes found in SQL, around which an application interface is constructed. The Oracle Forms item types are button, chart, check box, display, image, list, radio group, text, and user area (see Table 4.5).

BUTTONS

Buttons are interface items that users select by mouse click to initiate an action. In a GUI, a button appears as a rectangular iconic box with a text label inside that describes the button's action. In character mode, a button appears as a text string within parentheses.

Buttons can be selected using the mouse or the keyboard, or as a part of the default navigation of a block. Default navigation to a button is dependent on the item's Sequence ID (some GUIs disallow keyboard navigation to a block).

Table 4.5   Oracle Forms Item Types

Item Type	Description
button	A rectangular area holding an icon or text label where users click to initiate actions.
chart	A variably sized, bordered rectangular display of an image created by Oracle Graphics. Users may view only a chart.
check box	A labeled ON/OFF box depicted as either checked or unchecked. Clicking in the box reverses its current condition.
display	A read-only text box whose value is programmatically assigned.
image	A variably sized, bordered rectangle used to display images.
list	A list of choices displayed as either a poplist (drop list) or a t-list (list box).
radio group	A group of two or more radio buttons, one of which is always selected using a mouse click.
text	A variably sized text field used to support a variety of data types, format masks, and editing capabilities.
user area	A variably sized, bordered rectangle calling a user exit, which is an external program written in a 3GL that is then linked to the form.

Create a button in the Layout Editor by following these steps:

1. Select the ITEMS command from the Form menu to call the Items object list. Change the item type to Button.

2. Set the properties of the button: set label, a text label that will fit within the button; set the Iconic property ON to display an icon named in the Icon Name field; and choose whether or not to make the default button the default choice in a group of buttons.

3. Click OK to apply the changes and close the property sheet.

4. Write and associate a When-Button-Pressed trigger with the button. The trigger does not store a value, but instead invokes some PL/SQL action, such as a calculation, navigational function, or display of a list of values.

CHECK BOXES

A check box is a binary indicator representing a value of ON or OFF, TRUE or FALSE. The check box appears on the screen as "checked" or "unchecked," its status being toggled by users with a mouse click. Check boxes can store and retrieve CHAR, NUMBER, and DATE values, as well as the ON and OFF type values. The check box can be set up to store a value like PASSED or FAILED in a teacher's grade book database. Use the Layout Editor to create a check box or define a check box by doing the following:

1. Select the ITEMS command from the Form menu to call the Items object list. Change the item type to Check Box.

2. Enter a text label in the Label property field. This text will appear to the right of the check box.

3. Set values for Checked Value and Unchecked Value that will be saved to the database. For example, enter PASSED in the Checked Value field if the check box should save that value to the database when checked. Blank indicates a NULL value. Be sure the Max Length setting will hold these values.

4. Set the other properties as desired, such as the Other Values property, which controls the form's behavior when a value other than the Checked or Unchecked value is entered. Valid settings are Checked in order to cause the box to default to checked status, Unchecked in order to cause the box to default to unchecked status, or Not Allowed in order to reject the invalid response. Enter an initial condition for the check box in the Default property field.

DISPLAY ITEMS

Display items are essential read-only text items. Users cannot navigate to display items, nor can they edit them. Note that multiline displays do not automatically word wrap; a newline character must be inserted to advance a line.

LIST ITEMS

A list item displays a list of predefined text entries as a pop list, as the default, or as a list box depending on the setting of the Style property. List items can display only a fixed number of entries, and each entry must be thirty characters in length or less. Of course, only one item may be selected on the list at one time, since selecting a new item deselects the previous item. Define a list item using the Layout Editor or follow these steps:

1. Select the ITEMS command from the Form menu to call the Items object list. Change the item type to List and set the display Style property to Poplist or List Box.

2. In the List column, type the exact entries to appear in the list item. Insert new elements in the list by pressing [Down] or [Insert Element]. Remove an element from the list by pressing [Remove Element].

3. Link a CHAR, NUMBER, or DATE value to each listed entry by typing the desired value in the Value field. The Value field is linked to the currently selected entry in the List column. A blank entry evaluates to NULL.

4. Specify a Default Value, if desired, and how to handle values other than values from the list using the Other Values property. Leave Other Values blank to indicate that other values are not allowed or enter a value from the list to cause that value to default.

RADIO GROUPS

Radio groups display a fixed number of mutually exclusive radio buttons; that is, only one radio item may be selected at a single time. Although radio buttons must be assigned to a single group, they can be sized, positioned, and formatted independently of each other. Each radio button has its own value, selected when the button is clicked. When you define a radio group, the property sheet shows the properties for both the radio group and the individual radio buttons.

Add a new radio button to a group by entering the button name in the Radio Button list of the Radio Group property sheet. Insert additional buttons in the list by pressing [Down] or [Insert Element]. Remove buttons from the list by pressing [Remove Element]. Note that button names are not displayed. Set the properties of a specific radio button by selecting it from the Radio Button list and doing the following:

1. Select the ITEMS command from the Form menu to call the Items object list. Change the item type to Radio Button and set the display label of the radio button in the Label property field.

2. Enter a CHAR, NUMBER, or DATE value for the radio button in the Value property field that is compatible with the Radio Group definition. The field should not exceed the items Max Length property. Leave the Value blank for a NULL value.

3. Assign display properties for Size, Position, Displayed, Enable, Visual Attributes, and an Other Values property. If there is no Other Values property and none of the items have a NULL value, assign a Default Value property.

TEXT ITEMS

Text items are the most common type of item found in a form and are defined on a two-page property sheet. They default to the CHAR datatype but can also be NUMBER, DATE, or LONG datatypes. They can be defined with the following datatypes for backward compatibility with older Oracle products: ALPHA, DATETIME, EDATE, INT, JDATE, MONEY, RINT, RMONEY, RNUMBER, and TIME. Text items, being one of the most flexible data types in Oracle Forms, possess numerous properties described in Table 4.6.

SPECIAL FEATURES IN ORACLE FORMS

Alert Items

Alert items are pop-up, built-in, and developer-created windows that display messages to notify users of application events or conditions. When an alert appears, the user must acknowledge and dismiss the alert. Alerts come in one of three varieties: Stop, Caution, and Note. Each respective alert indicates a higher level of message urgency, each with a unique icon. The appearance of an alert is governed by the GUI; you need only enter the message text for the alert. As many as three buttons can be displayed for a single alert, each with a different set of PL/SQL code. Once the message and buttons are defined, you must code a trigger to invoke the alert. To create an alert, do the following:

1. Select ALERTS from the Form menu, then click NEW to call the Alert property sheet. Enter a value in the Name property field.

2. Select the icon and message urgency: Stop, Caution, or Note. Then, enter the alert message of up to eighty characters in the Message field.

3. Define one or more buttons by entering a text label in the Button 1, Button 2, and Button 3 fields or accept the default labels: "OK" for Button 1 and "Cancel" for Button 2.

4. Choose the default button: 1, 2, or 3. This button is selected automatically by pressing the [Accept] key.

Table 4.6 Text Item Properties

Property	Description
Multiline Property	Makes a CHAR, ALPHA, or LONG text item display more than one line of text. The actual amount of text displayed depends on the size of the field and the type of font used. You must also set the Width, Height, Font Size, and Max Length properties to create the desired size text item. Multiline items may not Auto Skip, or possess Format Masks or Secure properties.
Wrap Style	Deactivates the carriage return as a NEXT_ITEM event for multiline text items. Values are Word Wrap (wraps to a new line between words), Character Wrap (wraps to a new line between characters), and None (prevents wrapping).
Scroll Bars	Provides a multiline item with scroll bars.
Max Length	Sets the maximum number of characters the item can store.
Required	Ensures an item must have a value before the record can be committed and before the user can use the [Next Item] key on that specific item.
Fixed Length	Makes the user enter a fixed number of characters in the item. The item must contain the Max Length of characters allowed (or be NULL).
Range-Low	Checks for a minimum specified range of valid entries.
Range-High	Checks for a maximum specified range of valid entries.
Case Restriction	Automatically ensures the case of text entered by a user. Valid entries are None (displays text exactly as entered), Upper (converts lowercase characters to uppercase), and Lower (converts uppercase characters to lowercase).
Alignment	Specifies the positioning (Left, Center, or Right) of text in the item.
Bevel	Enhances a text item's border for a three-dimensional look; set to Raised, Lowered, or None.
Secure	Hides the contents of an item, even as the user types a value.
Auto skip	Automatically advances the cursor to the next item when the user has entered a character in the last character of the field (designated by the Max Length).
Keep Position	Controls the position of the cursor within a text item. Oracle Forms ensures that the user's cursor appears in the exact position it held when the user last navigated to the field.
Format Mask	Holds a format mask to enhance the readability of numbers and dates. For example, entering the string "$999,990.00" into a text field would ensure that the number always appears with the dollar sign, place-holding commas (when needed), and leading zeros only at the dollars and cents level.
LOV (list of values)	Displays a precreated list of values for a specific text item. Once the list is created, the user could then press [List] to call the list for that specific item.

5. Click OK to apply the changes and dismiss the property sheet.

Once created, a form must display an alert using the SHOW_ALERT built-in from a trigger. This built-in returns a numeric constant: `Show_Alert(alert_name) Return NUMBER`. The number returned designates the button selected by the user: ALERT_BUTTON1, ALERT_BUTTON2, ALERT_BUTTON3. This value can be assigned to a variable to invoke other PL/SQL code in the When-Button-Pressed trigger.

An alert message can be changed during runtime using the CHANGE_ALERT_MESSAGE built-in procedure. This procedure allows you to reuse the same alert objects for many different objects. For example, a form can use many alerts that use the same OK and Cancel buttons, but the message can be changed depending on the circumstances.

Editors

Oracle Forms includes a default text editor in every form (see Figure 4.18), which can be invoked by pressing the [Edit] key or by selecting the EDIT command from the Edit menu. The default editor can be called up in a text item in a PL/SQL program through the EDIT_TEXTITEM built-in procedure. Developers, however, can create special-purpose editors with uniquely defined editor attributes. The editor can then be shown, independent of a text item, using the SHOW_EDITOR built-in.

When you are using a text editor, the application is in Edit mode, which prevents triggers from firing until the editor is dismissed by clicking OK or Cancel. You can perform search and replace, cut, copy, and paste within the editor (see Figure 4.19). When you are using the paste function and click OK, the contents of the editor are pasted into the text item.

The default editor is sized and positioned dynamically depending on the size and position of the text item. Settings for the editor can be defined by following these steps:

1. Call the property sheet of the text item and click the More button to call the second page of text item properties.

2. Use the Editor Pos: X/Y fields to enter the display position of the editor.

3. Leave the Editor Name field blank to use the default text editor or enter SYSTEM_EDITOR to use the operating system editor. Note the system editor is not available on platforms and is defined by the FORMS_EDITOR environment setting.

Figure 4.18 The Default Editor

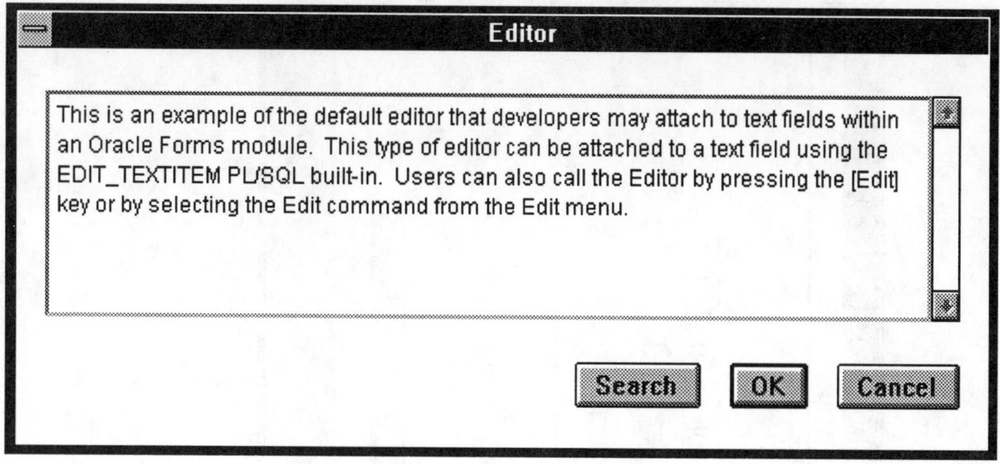

Create a customized version of the editor by following these steps:

1. Select EDITOR from the Form menu to call the Editors object list.

2. Click NEW to call the Editor property sheet.

3. Define the editor's properties for display size and position, wrap style, scroll bar, top and bottom titles, and visual attributes.

4. Click OK to apply the changes and close the editor property sheet.

5. Attach the editor to the appropriate text items or call the editor using the SHOW_EDITOR built-in procedure.

Image Items

Image items are vector or bit-mapped graphics created in the form at design time, but populated in the form at runtime. Like boilerplate images, image items can be in CGM, BMP, TIFF, JFIF, Oracle Graphics Format, PICT, and PCX image formats. Unlike boilerplate images, image items are not actually stored in the form definition file; rather, they are stored in the database and populated at runtime directly from database columns.

When creating an image item, you specify the canvas holding the image, the maximum size of the image (in bytes), and the height and width of the item. The image is then displayed by fetching it from a LONG RAW column

Figure 4.19 Editor Property Sheet

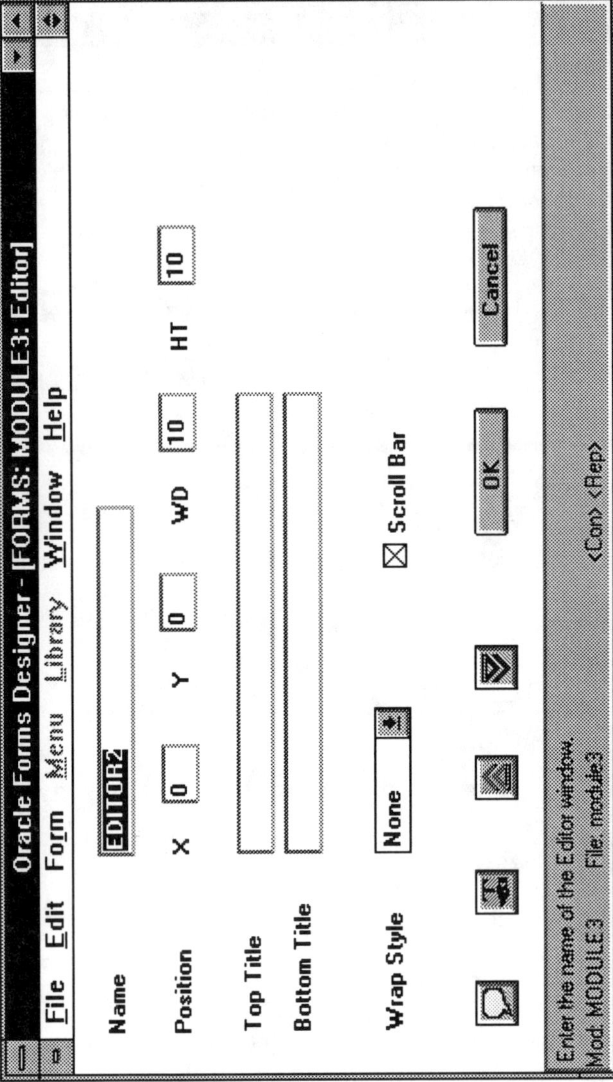

in the database, by a PL/SQL assignment, or by retrieving it from a file using the READ_IMAGE_FILE built-in. Note that image items must be built on LONG RAW database columns. So, even if an image is retrieved from a file using READ_IMAGE_FILE, it will still be stored in the database column.

Image items are created and defined just as other form objects are, either by using the Layout Editor or through the Default Block Facility. The Image Item property sheet allows modification of an existing image item. Image items can also be defined as base-table items or control items. When defining an image item, pay attention to the following:

- The datatype must always be set to LONG RAW.

- Turn on the Compression property to compress the image as it is loaded into the form. This creates smaller form executables.

- An image's Max Length property must be at least 1024 bytes. Images stored in a version 6 Oracle RDBMS cannot exceed 64 kilobytes compressed, while Oracle7 images cannot exceed 2 gigabytes compressed.

- Set the Sizing style property to control how images that are too large for their border are displayed. Select Crop to display the image at actual size, even though some of the image may be concealed. Select Adjust, the default, to scale the image to fit in the border. Scaled images are reduced in resolution.

- To conserve memory, set the Buffered block property to the minimal acceptable number, usually the number of records displayed plus two. Since Oracle Forms reserves memory for each item retrieved in a record (and image items are so memory intensive), a large amount of computer memory can be consumed.

Image items can be acted on by the When-Image-Activated trigger (for situations where the user has double-clicked the image) and the When-Image-Pressed trigger (for situations where the user has clicked the image). Several built-ins are available to process images as well: IMAGE_ADD, IMAGE_AND, IMAGE_SUBTRACT, IMAGE_XOR, and IMAGE_ZOOM.

Lists of Values

A list of values (LOV) is a modal single or multicolumn list displayed in a pop-up window and should not be confused with the list item object. LOVs (see Figure 4.20) are designed to be attached to one or more items in a form.

Figure 4.20   List of Values

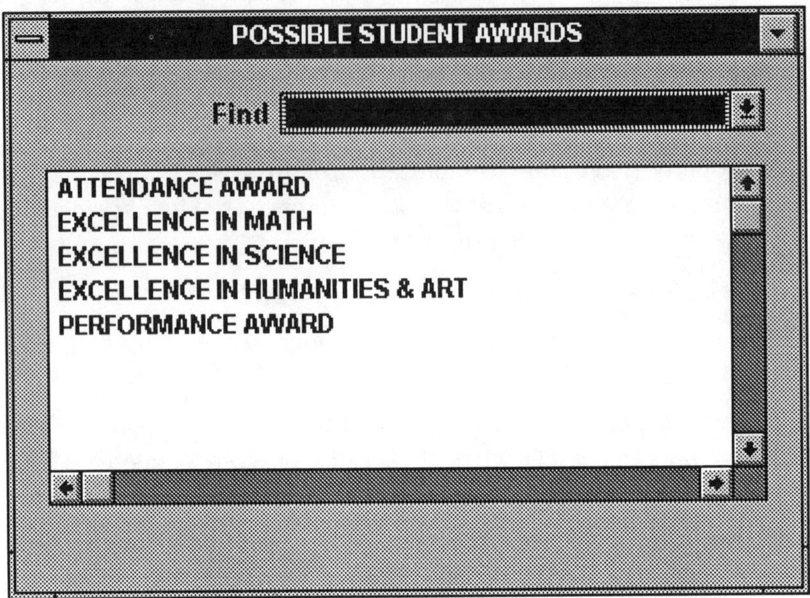

When the user enters an item with an LOV attached, the status line displays the <LOV> flag to alert the user that one is available. Operators can then call the list by pressing the [List of Values] key.

The list of values is a context-sensitive pick list allowing you to select a single value from a preset list of values. For instance, the LOV available in the Layout Editor allows you to specify the canvas to work in from a list of all available canvases. The LOV is a modal window, that is, it must be dismissed or an LOV item must be selected before any other work is performed. Figure 4.21 shows the LOV dialog box.

The LOV dialog contains powerful quick-search capabilities. If you wish to reduce a large list to a single value or set of values, merely type in the first letter of the string to be found. The LOV will then display all items that begin with that character, in alphabetical order. For example, if you want to find all the SET triggers in the Trigger property sheet LOV, just type the letter s to pull them in. Oracle Forms will display them in alphabetical order, segregating the trigger items alphabetically.

When you are quick-searching an LOV, the Find field displays the current search criteria. User-supplied criteria are shown in lowercase; characters com-

Figure 4.21 The List of Values Dialog Box

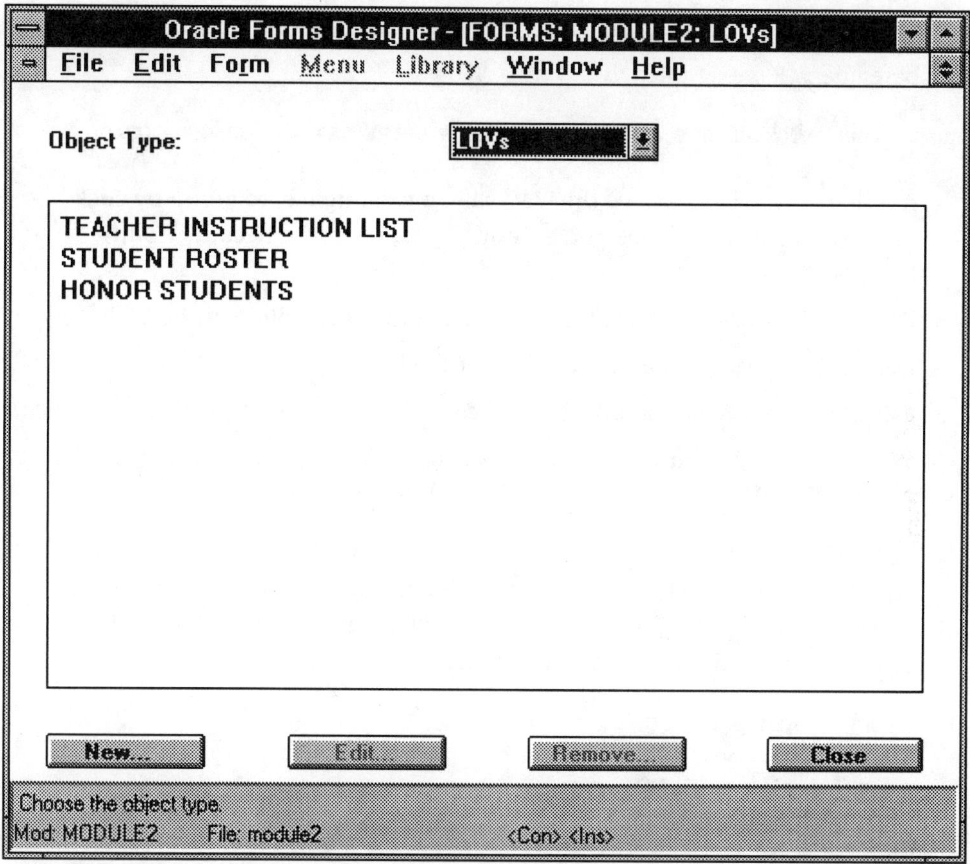

mon to all the line items are shown in uppercase. Pressing the [Delete Back] key undoes the last search character and expands the LOV.

LOV display data is stored in query record groups (basically, SELECT statements) or static record groups (a static array). You must designate the values displayed in the LOV, as well as an optional return value for the LOV. By selecting a return value, Oracle Forms pastes the assigned value into the item where the LOV was called from. Using this feature enables users to select an item from an LOV and insert it into the field. Follow the steps below to create an LOV:

1. Select LOV from the Form menu to invoke the LOV object list, then Click NEW to call the LOV property sheet. Enter the name of the LOV.

2. Enter the record group basis and return value of the LOV by creating a base query. For example:

```
SELECT TEACHER_NAME INTO :BLOCK1.NAME FROM TEACHERS WHERE GRADE = :BLOCK2.GRADE;
```

Alternatively, you can have the LOV call an existing record group by clicking the Record Group type and entering its name in the Record Group field.

3. Click APPLY to choose the record group columns to include in the LOV.

4. Define the appearance and properties of the LOV.

5. Click OK to apply the definitions and close the property sheet.

6. Write a trigger, like KEY-LISTVAL, to call the LOV (using the LIST_VALUES or SHOW_LOV built-ins) or attach the LOV to a text item.

Remember that an LOV can be reused within an application. This is useful in retrieving a return value into several different locations. A reusable LOV is built around the SHOW_LOV built-in and global variables that reassign the return value based on the user's current context. For example:

```
IF SHOW_LOV('LOV1') THEN
/* Assign the return value globals for LOV1 */
   :block1.one   := :GLOBAL.one;
   :block1.two   := :GLOBAL.two;
   :block1.three := :GLOBAL.three;
   :block1.four  := :GLOBAL.four;
END IF;
```

Use the GET_LOV_PROPERTY and SET_LOV_PROPERTY built-ins to control an LOV from within a PL/SQL program. SET_LOV_PROPERTY can alter the GROUP_NAME, LOV_SIZE, and POSITION properties.

Record Groups

Record groups are similar to database tables but are attached to a specific form module. Record groups are similar to a SQL view in construction and usage, except that they can have up to 255 columns of the CHAR, LONG, NUMBER, or DATE types. Like a SQL view, record groups can be based on a query but can also be static arrays or programmatically constructed groups. Query groups are essentially SQL views assigned to a specific form. Like views, the columns in a query record group receive their default names, data types, and widths from the defining SELECT statement. Static record groups are tables of data fixed at design time. Nonquery record groups are data structures defined at design time but populated with data programmatically at runtime.

Record groups are created and defined using the Record Group property sheet, as shown in Figure 4.22. Record groups provide the functionality of two-dimensional arrays wherever needed by the application. In fact, all LOV interface objects are record groups created using the LOV property sheet.

To create a query record group, perform the following steps:

1. Select the RECORD GROUPS command from the Form menu to call the Record Group object list, then click NEW to call the Record Group property sheet.

2. Enter a name for the record group in the Name field and set the Type selector to Query or Static. Query record groups are based upon a valid SELECT statement entered in the multiline edit box provided. Static record groups are based on your entries in a two-dimensional array in the Column Name and Column Value lists.

3. Click APPLY to validate the changes, then click OK to accept the definition.

You can create query record groups and nonquery record groups using PL/SQL code; static record groups cannot be created programmatically. Once a record group is created, it can be altered in these ways:

- by adding columns

- by populating the group with records

- by altering a query group's base query

- by adding and deleting rows

- by retrieving column values

- by flagging records as "selected"

Oracle Forms can manipulate record groups through a number of built-ins. Note that record groups are numbered internally (somewhat similar to the

Figure 4.22   Record Group Property Sheet

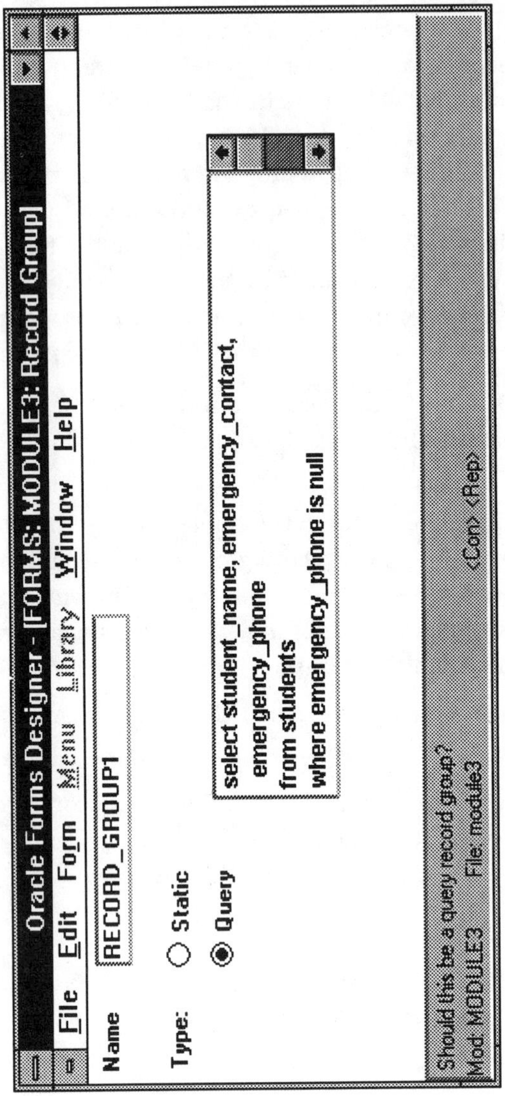

Table 4.7   Record Group Built-Ins

Function	Built-In	Type
Create/Delete Groups	CREATE_GROUP	Function
	CREATE_GROUP_FROM_QUERY	Function
	DELETE_GROUP	Procedure
Altering a Group	ADD_GROUP_COLUMN	Function
	ADD_GROUP_ROW	Procedure
	DELETE_GROUP_ROW	Procedure
Populating a Group	POPULATE_GROUP	Function
	POPULATE_GROUP_WITH_QUERY	Function
	SET_GROUP_CHAR_CELL	Procedure
	SET_GROUP_DATE_CELL	Procedure
	SET_GROUP_NUMBER_CELL	Procedure
Getting a Cell Value	GET_GROUP_CHAR_CELL	Function
	GET_GROUP_DATE_CELL	Function
	GET_GROUP_NUMBER_CELL	Function
Processing a Row	GET_GROUP_ROW_COUNT	Function
	GET_GROUP_SELECTION_COUNT	Function
	GET_GROUP_SELECTION	Function
	RESET_GROUP_SELECTION	Procedure
	SET_GROUP_SELECTION	Procedure
	UNSET_GROUP_SELECTION	Procedure
Row ID Functions	FIND_GROUP	Function
	FIND_COLUMN	Function

ROWID pseudo-column found in SQL). Any record group operations must act on columns and rows referenced by the row ID number. Table 4.7 shows the built-ins and their primary usage.

The type of record group and the method of record creation have a profound impact on the type of built-ins available to use on a specific record group. For instance, the ADD_GROUP_ROW built-in is invalid for adding a row to a static record group. Similarly, the ADD_GROUP_COLUMN built-in is invalid for a record group created at design time.

EVENT PROGRAMMING IN ORACLE FORMS

Programmatic functionality is added to an application through the use of PL/SQL triggers and procedures. Although PL/SQL is discussed in chapter 2, this section pays special attention to the use of PL/SQL within Oracle Forms.

Every trigger is fired by the occurrence of a specific event. A trigger is basically a uniquely named block of PL/SQL code written to add capabilities about and beyond the default capabilities of the form. Trigger names are normally an indication of the event that calls the trigger. For instance, the When-Button-Pressed trigger is directly linked to the Button Pressed event, where the user has clicked the mouse button. Triggers "fire" when Oracle Forms executes their code. See Figure 4.23 for a trigger property sheet.

Not only are triggers attached to a specific event, but they are also attached to specific objects within the form. The trigger can be attached to the form, a block, or an individual item, each with a narrower scope of execution. For example, a form might have several When-Button-Pressed triggers, one attached to the form and one attached to one of two buttons (an OK and Cancel button), each performing a separate action. When a Button Pressed event occurs, Oracle Forms processes the When-Button-Pressed trigger, either at the button item level (if the user clicked on one of the buttons) or at the form level (if the user did not click on one of the buttons). When more than one trigger responds to a specific event, the trigger with the lowest level of definition takes precedence. Of course, some triggers must be defined for a specific level, like the When-Record-Validated trigger.

Each predefined event has a specific built-in that controls the event's processing and can be referenced in a trigger. Choosing the event to build a trigger on top of is a very important step in forms development. The choice of the event affects the trigger name, when the event occurs, how it affects other events, and how it affects the form itself. Events, such as the Button Pressed event, can be externally invoked, while other events, such as Commit, are invoked by internal processes.

Triggers, like all Oracle Forms objects, are created using property sheets. (Some triggers are automatically created by Oracle Forms when you create master-detail relationships and other special functions.) When creating a trigger, remember that the trigger's name is determined by the event it is linked to, the form object (and, thus, scope) that the trigger is attached to, and the PL/SQL code of the trigger. Create a trigger in an active form by performing the following steps:

1. Select the TRIGGERS command from the Form menu to call the Triggers list window, then click NEW to call the Trigger property sheet. Trigger names appear on the list as "TRIGGER-NAME, BLOCK-NAME, ITEM-NAME," in alphabetical order based on scope.

Figure 4.23 Trigger Property Sheet

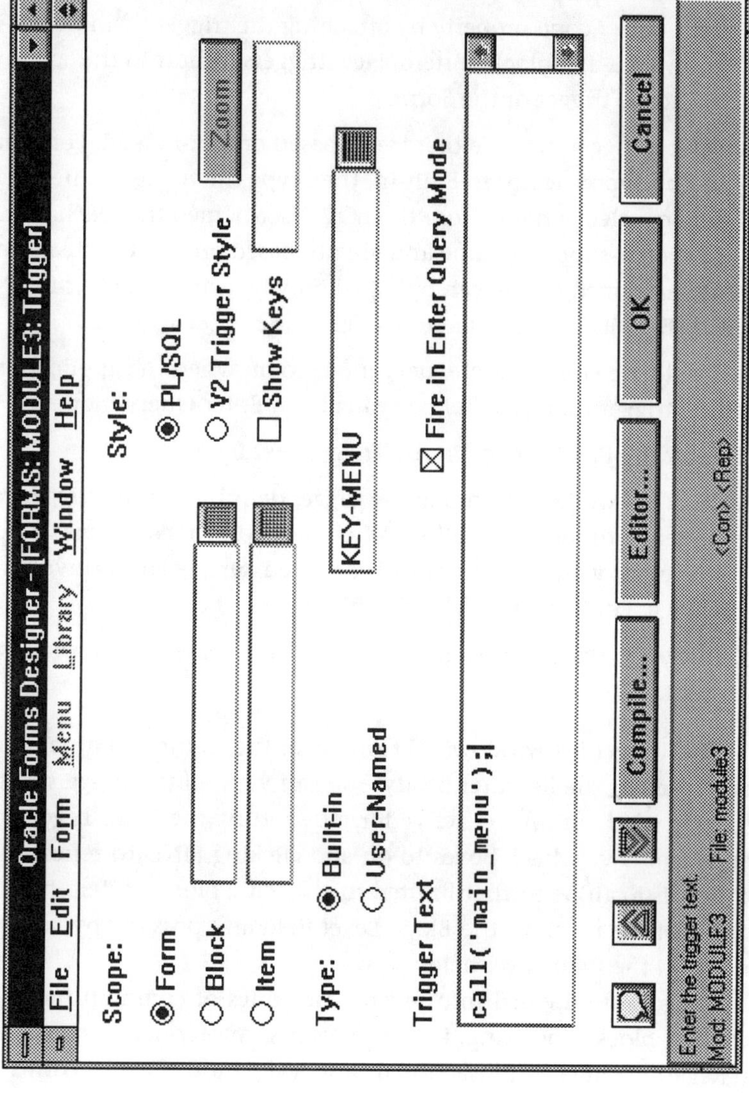

2. Set the trigger Style to PL/SQL. The V2 and Zoom trigger styles are included for compatibility with earlier versions of Oracle Forms.

3. Define the Scope property by attaching the trigger to an object in the form, such as a block or item. New triggers default to the scope of the last active trigger of the Form.

4. Enter a trigger name, either event-based or user-named. For event triggers, set the Type selector to Built-in, then type the trigger name in the Type field or select a name from the LOV. User-named triggers have a unique, developer-supplied name and are not based on any Oracle Forms event. A user-named trigger can be called only by using the built-in EXECUTE_TRIGGER (i.e., `Execute_Trigger ('trigger1');`).

5. Toggle the Fire in Enter Query mode to on when the application requires that trigger functionality be available in Enter Query mode.

6. Enter the PL/SQL code in the Trigger Text field.

7. Click COMPILE to compile the trigger definition. (The trigger can be accepted without compilation, when needed.) Oracle Forms will check the trigger for validity. If an error is detected, Oracle Forms invokes the PL/SQL Editor with a description of the errors.

8. Click OK to save the trigger definition and close the Trigger property sheet.

The Trigger list window offers many of the features of a standard list window, such as the list filter utility. You can view all the triggers in the list at a specific level within the active form by setting the Form Level, Block Level, and Item Level check boxes to on and clicking FIND to refresh the list. The trigger list can be further limited to a specific block or item by entering the name of the block in the Block Level field and possibly by adding the item name in the Item Level field.

Triggers are divided into several categories of common functionality, including block-processing, interface events, master-detail, message-handling, navigation, query, transactional, and validation. Oracle Forms contains a multitude of triggers. Table 4.8 contains a description of some of the most common.

Block-processing triggers initiate processes controlling record management in a block. Interface-event triggers, often called by an external event, initiate a process within the form interface. Master-detail triggers control the coordination between records in a detail block and the master record in the master block. Message-handling triggers fire in response to default and developer-defined messaging events.

Navigation triggers control navigational events, such as moving to the next block or the previous record. Navigational triggers are broken out into Pre-event, Post-event, and When-New-Instance triggers. Pre- and Post-event triggers fire as Oracle Forms navigates through the form through external or internal Oracle processes. When-New-Instance triggers do not fire on internal Oracle processes.

Query triggers fire just prior to and after a query is executed on a block. Transaction triggers fire at a wide variety of events that occur as a form interacts with its data. Validation triggers fire when Oracle Forms validates an item or record for accuracy of acceptable data values. Validation occurs at user inputs, programmed inputs, or default processing like the Commit process.

Writing PL/SQL Trigger Code

The executable section is the only section required in an Oracle Forms trigger. Triggers that do not have a DECLARE section do not need the BEGIN and END keywords. However, if a DECLARE section is a part of the trigger, the BEGIN and END keywords are required so that the compiler can recognize distinct components of the program. Proper use of the block syntax is essential in more complex triggers containing nested blocks of PL/SQL code.

SQL, procedural calls, value assignments, and built-in routines are used heavily in executable sections. Built-ins are packaged functions that are always available or "built in" to the PL/SQL command set. They are the basic PL/SQL commands that control the behavior of Oracle Forms. For example, the GO_Item built-in moves the context to a specific item on the form, while the NEXT_SET built-in advances the context to the next set of records. To call a built-in procedure within a block of PL/SQL code, simply type the procedure name and any required or optional parameters as a statement in the PL/SQL block, concluding with a semicolon. For example:

```
GO_ITEM('teacher_block.teacher_name');
```

Built-in functions are essentially the same as built-in procedures but with one noticeable difference. A built-in function returns a specific value (of a specific datatype), whereas a procedure causes an action. Hence, built-in functions are usually used to determine the current condition of the form for further activity by the trigger. For example:

Table 4.8 Common Oracle Forms Triggers

Category	Trigger Name	Description
Block	When-Create-Record	Performs the processs needed to create a new record in a block.
	When-Clear-Block	Performs the processs needed to remove all the records from the current block.
	When-Database-Record	Performs the processs needed to change a record status to Insert or Update, alerting Oracle Forms that the record should be processed by the next COMMIT_FORM operation.
	When-Remove-Record	Performs the processs needed to clear or delete a record.
Interface	When-Button-Pressed	Fires a process when a mouse or keyboard button is pressed.
	When-Checkbox-Changed	Fires a process when a check box is toggled with a mouse or keyboard action.
	When-Image-Activated	Fires a process when an image item is double-clicked.
	When-Image-Pressed	Fires a process when an image item is clicked.
	Key - * (all)	Replaces the default processing of an event key, like Key-EXIT or Key-HELP.
	When-Radio-Changed	Fires a process when a radio button is clicked in a radio group item.
	When-Timer-Expired	Fires a process when a programmatic timer expires.
	When-Window-Activated	Fires a process whenever a window is activated.
	When-Window-Closed	Fires a process whenever a window is closed with the CLOSE command.
	When-Window-Deactivated	Fires a process whenever a new window is activated and the old window is deactivated.
	When-Window-Resized	Fires a process whenever a window is resized.
Mas-Det	On-Check-Delete-Master	Fires when Oracle Forms attempts to delete a master record in a master-detail relation.
	On-Clear-Details	Fires when Oracle Forms clears detail records in a master-detail relation.
	On-Populate-Details	Fires when Oracle Forms fetches records into a detail block in a master-detail relation.
Messaging	On-Error	Replaces a default error message with a custom error message or process.
	On-Message	Replaces a default message with a custom message or process.
Navigation	Pre-Block	Performs a process before navigating to the block level.
	Pre-Form	Performs a process before navigating to the form level, like at form startup.
	Pre-Record	Performs a process before navigating to the record level.

(continued)

Table 4.8 Common Oracle Forms Triggers *(continued)*

Category	*Trigger Name*	*Description*
	Pre-Text-Item	Performs a process before navigating to a text item.
	Post-Block	Initiates a process on the current record after navigating from the block level to the form level.
	Post-Form	Performs a process immediately after leaving the form level.
	Post-Record	Initiates a process on the current record when navigating from the record level to the block level.
	Post-Text-Item	Initiates a process on an item when navigating from a text item to the record level.
	When-New-Instance	Triggers for Block, Form, Record, and Item instances. When-New-Instance triggers fire after the cursor has moved to the new instance. These triggers do not fire in response to internal navigational events caused by default processing.
Query-time	Pre-Query	Validates the current query criteria or provides additional query criteria.
	Post-Query	Performs a process after fetching each record, such as totaling values.
Transaction	On-Delete	Replaces the default record deletion processing.
	On-Insert	Replaces the default record insertion processing.
	On-Lock	Replaces the default record locking processing.
	On-Logon	Replaces the default database connect processing.
	On-Logout	Replaces the default logout processing.
	On-Update	Replaces the default update record processing.
	Post-Database-Commit	Supplements default database commit processing after the commit occurs.
	Post-Delete	Audits transactions after database record deletion occurs.
	Post-Forms-Commit	Supplements default database commit processing before the commit occurs.
	Post-Insert	Audits transactions before database record insertion occurs.
	Post-Update	Audits transactions after database updating occurs.
	Pre-Commit	Fires a process before the Post and Commit processes of the record commit action.
	Pre-Delete	Fires a process before the Post and Commit processes of the record deletion action.
	Pre-Insert	Fires a process before the Post and Commit processes of the record insertion action.
	Pre-Update	Fires a process before the Post and Commit processes of the record update action.
Validation	When-Validate-Item	Alters the default validation of an item.
	When-Validate-Record	Alters the default validation of a record.

```
DECLARE
      homeroom_teacher VARCHAR2 (5);
BEGIN
      homeroom_teacher :=
      Get_Item_Property('teacher_block.teacher_name',REQUIRED);
END;
```

You must be cognizant of the type of data returned by a built-in function. Many built-in functions return Boolean data, that is, either a TRUE or FALSE value. Also note that functions cannot be used in DML statements. Boolean results can be achieved by assigning the returned value of a function to a local variable, then referencing the variable in a DML statement.

However, some routines are illegal, or restricted, in certain triggers. A restricted routine is any built-in that moves the cursor from one item to another. Restricted routines cannot be used in any trigger that involves internal navigation. So, the GO_ITEM and NEXT_SET built-ins cannot be used in any triggers that fire in response to an internal navigation event (like any of the Pre- or Post-navigational triggers).

In addition to PL/SQL, triggers can use SQL. Triggers can use any DML SQL statement, but DML statements can desynchronize the state of the records in certain triggers.

Referencing Objects in Triggers

Oracle Forms objects can be referenced in a number of different ways: by name, by item value, by internal ID, and by indirect reference. To refer to an item or object by name in a PL/SQL trigger, such as in the GET_ITEM_PROPERTY example shown earlier, simply enclose the object name in single quotes: 'form_name', 'block_name', 'block_name.item_name', or even 'item_name'. As shown, an item can be referenced by its block and item name (which is the better method), or by just its item name (which is allowable only if the item name is unique in the form).

Item values can also be referenced, but only for items that store values. Items that store values include check boxes, display items, list items, radio groups, text items, and user-area items. To reference the value of an item, place a colon in front of the fully identified item name sans quotes. For example:

```
:block_name.item_name
:block_name.radio_group.radio_button
```

In this application, item values are similar to local or global variables. This syntax allows you to assign the value of an expression to a variable. For example, to apply a given percent scale to the student's grades, type:

```
:student.grade := avg(test_grade) * 1.05;
```

You can also assign the value of one item to another:

```
:student.teacher := :teacher.teacher_name;
```

Triggers can include SELECT statements that load an item value:

```
SELECT homeroom INTO :student.homeroom FROM teachers
WHERE id = :teacher.teacher_name;
```

Oracle Forms attaches a unique sequence ID to each item created in a form. The ID is an internal value somewhat similar to the SQL*Plus pseudo-column ROWID. You can find an object's specific ID by using the FIND_<object> built-in, where the <object> is any fully identified object class (i.e., window, LOV, alert, etc.). For example:

```
DECLARE
   object_id ALERT;
BEGIN
   object_id := Find_Alert('Alert1');
   ...
END;
```

In this example, once the object ID is assigned to a variable, it be can used to reference the object, rather than using the object's name. This provides two significant benefits in trigger writing: object IDs have improved performance over other reference methods, and using object IDs makes code more flexible and generic. For example, you may wish to write a trigger that displays a window and resizes it automatically. Rather than writing a new trigger for each window, the example built-in should suffice:

```
Resize_Window(object_id, 40, 40);
```

or, alternately,

```
Resize_Window((FIND_WINDOW('window1'), 40, 40);
```

Object names and IDs can be mixed in the same parameter list as long as the references point to a distinct form object. Each FIND_<object> built-in returns the specific datatype of the object. In the RESIZE_WINDOW example, the window ID is type WINDOW. If FIND_ALERT had been used instead, the returned value would have been of type ALERT, and so on. Objects that can be identified with FIND_<object> include Alerts, Canvases, Columns, Editors, Forms, Items, Lists of Values, Menu Items, Parameter Lists, Relations, Timers, Views, Record Groups, and Windows.

Objects can also be referenced indirectly in a trigger's text using the NAME_IN and COPY built-ins. As with the use of object IDs, indirect references to an item or variable provide some distinct benefits: since variables are used in the place of direct references, code can be much more generic, maintainable, and reusable, and indirect references are mandatory for referring to values in a form bind variable (item, parameter, or global) in a library or menu module. The NAME_IN built-in returns the value of the specified item or variable without referring to the item directly. NAME_IN always returns a CHAR string, so values that are DATE or NUMBER must be reformatted using the TO_DATE or TO_CHAR functions. For example:

```
:date_started := TO_DATE(Name_In('student.date_enrolled'));
grade_var     := TO_NUMBER(Name_In('student.test_grade'));
```

The COPY built-in copies the specified value into the specified variable or item without directly assigning a value to the item. For example:

```
:teacher.teacher_name := 'CHEU, KAREN';     -- direct reference
Copy('CHEU, KAREN','teacher.teacher_name'); -- indirect reference
```

The COPY and NAME_IN built-ins can even be used in conjunction in order to assign a value in a reference item:

```
/*  store the teacher's name in teacher_var reference item   */
Copy('CHEU, KAREN',Name_In('control.teacher_var'));
```

VARIABLES IN TRIGGERS

Triggers can include local variables that are usable only within the trigger in which they are defined, and global variables that are usable as long as the Runform session is in action (even across many different form modules). These variables can be declared in any trigger, menu-item command, user-named routine, or PL/SQL package. Additionally, NULL-canvas items can often be used as variables.

Local variables are assigned in the DECLARE block of PL/SQL routines and are available in the trigger or routine in which they are created. Local variables, also called declared variables, are described more fully in chapter 3 under the heading "The Declare Block." Global variables are accessible to any block of PL/SQL code accessed during the current Oracle session, even though many modules can be opened and closed. Unlike local variables, global variables are initialized rather that declared. For example:

```
:GLOBAL.department := :block1.employee_department;
```

Once initialized, global variables can store a character string of up to 255 characters. Once the global is given a value, it can be used in a trigger by calling its full name (in the example just given, ':GLOBAL.department'). Globals are not case-sensitive. The global can be assigned a new value at any time. The global's value can be cleared by using the ERASE built-in:

```
Erase('GLOBAL.department');
```

Global variables can also be created and initialized using the DEFAULT_VALUE built-in. DEFAULT_VALUE can be used on any variable whose value is NULL but does nothing to variables that are not NULL. If the variable to which the value is being assigned is an undefined global variable, Oracle Forms creates the variable, as follows:

```
Default_Value('GENERAL EDUCATION','GLOBAL.department');
```

Any item not attached to a specific canvas is an item whose Canvas property remains unspecified or NULL. NULL-canvas items are not displayed at runtime and cannot be seen or used by end-users. However, triggers and PL/SQL code can reference NULL-canvas items just like any other item in a form, using them to temporarily store values.

There are some constraints to remember when using global or NULL-canvas variables:

- NULL-canvas items can store CHAR, NUMBER, or DATE datatypes; global variables can store only character strings.

- NULL-canvas items can be sized just like other items using their Max Length property; global variables are always 255 characters.

- NULL-canvas items are available only in the form they were activated in; global variables are usable by any active form opened during the session.

- NULL-canvas items are erased, or set to NULL, by the appropriate CLEAR_<object> built-ins, like CLEAR_FORM and CLEAR_BLOCK; the value of global variables is affected only by ERASE.

- NULL-canvas items and global variables can be referenced in the default WHERE clauses of blocks, in record groups, LOVs, and other SQL statements.

EXCEPTION HANDLING IN TRIGGERS

When an error occurs in the PL/SQL code, an exception is raised. You can write exception handlers to react to specific types of errors in SQL statements, PL/SQL statements, and calls to user-named routines. When a statement raises an exception, control is transferred from the Executable block to the exception-handling section of the trigger.

In nested blocks, exceptions that occur in inner blocks drop out to the exception handlers of the enclosing block when no exception handling is present. The exception will continue to drop from inner blocks to enclosing blocks until the error encounters an appropriate exception handler or until the exception reaches the outer block, in which case the trigger fails and returns a runtime error. In fact, errors in called routines drop out to the calling routine, just as if they were nested PL/SQL blocks.

Exceptions are usually handled in one of three ways. First, you can write an exception handler for every possible exception raised. This is usually too arduous a task for a form with more than a couple triggers. Second, you can allow the Oracle Forms default postfailure trigger to handle the exception. Finally (and most commonly), you can write exception handlers for specific exceptions and let other exceptions be handled by the default processes. Error handling can be processed using certain built-in routines like ERROR_TYPE, ERROR_CODE, ERROR_TEXT, DBMS_ERROR_CODE, and DBMS_ERROR_TEXT.

ERROR TRAPPING

A built-in routine meets one of three fates: success, failure, or fatal error. When built-ins fail, a runtime error and error message occur, but no exception is raised within the trigger. Without an exception, the trigger does not actually fail and subsequent statements in the trigger are executed. However, you can trap the success or failure of a built-in to enable a more graceful failure or even to correct errors. A few built-in routines are particularly useful for this purpose, namely, FORM_SUCCESS, FORM_FAILURE, and FORM_FATAL. These built-ins deliver information about the outcome of the most recently executed built-in. Since built-ins do not raise an exception when they fail, you should write code to explicitly raise an exception in the appropriate circumstances using the RAISE keyword.

The FORM_TRIGGER_FAILURE exception is a commonly used, predefined PL/SQL exception available only in Oracle Forms. Since built-ins do not return an exception, here is a useful routine that tests the outcome of a built-in:

```
/*   In a Developer-Defined Routine   */
PROCEDURE Built_in_Validation IS
BEGIN
   IF NOT Form_Success THEN
      RAISE Form_Trigger_Failure;
   END IF;
END;
```

This procedure can be written to a library and then referenced in other triggers, as in this example:

```
/*   In a When-Button-Pressed Trigger   */
Go_Block('block1');
Built_in_Validation;
```

Developer-defined triggers can be created with error trapping in the same way that error trapping can be added to built-ins.

TRIGGERS IN ENTER QUERY MODE

Only a few triggers can fire in Enter Query mode. These triggers are as follows:

- Key-<Event>
- On-Error
- On-Message
- When-<Event> triggers, except:

    When-Database-Record
    When-Image-Activated
    When-New-Block-Instance
    When-New-Form-Instance

When-Create-Record
When-Remove-Record
When-Validate-Record
When-Validate-Item

When the trigger has the Entry Query mode set to ON, the trigger fires in both Enter Query mode and in Normal mode. However, you may want to add in trigger functionality that differentiates between Normal mode and Enter Query mode. Use the *SYSTEM.MODE* system variable to diagnose the form's current mode. For example, you could set a trigger to fire differently in Enter Query mode than in Normal mode:

```
/*   In a Key-<Next Item> Trigger   */
IF System.Mode = 'ENTER-QUERY' THEN
  go_next_item;
ELSIF System.Mode = 'NORMAL' THEN
  go_item('item3');
END IF;
```

Just as some built-ins are restricted in certain triggers, some built-in routines are restricted in Enter Query mode. These built-ins are the following:

```
ABORT_FETCH
BLOCK_MENU
CALL_INPUT
CLEAR_BLOCK
CLEAR_FORM
COMMIT_FORM
CREATE_QUERIED_RECORD
CREATE_RECORD
DELETE_RECORD
DOWN
DUPLICATE_RECORD
FETCH_RECORDS
FIRST_RECORD
GO_BLOCK
GO_ITEM (if it attempts to navigate out of the current block)
GO_RECORD
INSERT_RECORD
LAST_RECORD
LOCK_RECORD
LOGON
LOGON_SCREEN
LOGOUT
```

```
NEW_FORM
NEXT_BLOCK
NEXT_RECORD
NEXT_SET
POST
PREVIOUS_BLOCK
PREVIOUS_RECORD
SCROLL_DOWN
SCROLL_UP
SELECT_RECORDS
UP
UPDATE_RECORD
```

USING SYSTEM VARIABLES

In addition to built-in procedures and functions, Oracle Forms provides built-in system variables that supply information about the runtime condition of the form. These variables can be used by triggers, much like a built-in procedure, to diagnose and act on current conditions in the form. System variables are universally read-only, except for MESSAGE_LEVEL, DATE_THRESHOLD, EFFECTIVE_DATE, and SUPPRESS_WORKING. System variables include the following:

```
SYSTEM.BLOCK_STATUS
SYSTEM.COORDINATION_OPERATION
SYSTEM.CURRENT_BLOCK
SYSTEM.CURRENT_DATETIME
SYSTEM.CURRENT_FORM
SYSTEM.CURRENT_ITEM
SYSTEM.CURRENT_VALUE
SYSTEM.CURSOR_BLOCK
SYSTEM.CURSOR_ITEM
SYSTEM.CURSOR_RECORD
SYSTEM.CURSOR_VALUE
SYSTEM.DATE_THRESHOLD
SYSTEM.EFFECTIVE_DATE
SYSTEM.EVENT_WINDOW
SYSTEM.FORM_STATUS
SYSTEM.LAST_QUERY
SYSTEM.LAST_RECORD
SYSTEM.MESSAGE_LEVEL
SYSTEM.MODE
SYSTEM.RECORD_STATUS
SYSTEM.SUPPRESS_WORKING
```

```
SYSTEM.TRIGGER_BLOCK
SYSTEM.TRIGGER_ITEM
SYSTEM.TRIGGER_RECORD
```

SYSTEM VARIABLES DEFAULT VALUES

The current date and time can be inserted as a default value for certain types of items in the appropriate item property sheet:

```
$$DATE$$
$$DATETIME$$
$$DBDATE$$
$$DBDATETIME$$
$$DBTIME$$
$$TIME$$
```

Every call to a system variable like $$DATE$$ (the current date) requires overhead processing from the PL/SQL engine. These calls to the database can be avoided by writing the system variable to a local variable, then referencing the local variable as needed.

Writing PL/SQL Procedures, Functions, and Packages

You can create routines and procedures that can be called from other triggers or developer-created routines in form, menu, and library modules. Triggers are the primary means of adding functionality to a form; however, procedures are an excellent way to create modular and reusable blocks of code, eliminating the requirement to write the same code in several distinct triggers. Procedures are not event-driven, as are triggers. In fact, a procedure must be explicitly called to execute within an application. Create a PL/SQL procedure by performing the following steps:

1. Activate a module. The routine will be associated with the module.

2. Select the PL/SQL PROGRAM UNITS BROWSER command from the module (Form, Menu, or Library) menu. Note that the Xref button calls the Cross Referencing dialog for the currently selected PL/SQL program unit.

3. Click NEW to call the PL/SQL editor.

4. Enter, edit, and compile the procedure or function using the PL/SQL Editor. Note the sections on Procedure Syntax and Function Syntax in chapter 3.

5. Click OK to accept the procedure definition and close the PL/SQL Editor.

Both functions and procedures must have a unique, developer-assigned name that is constructed under the Oracle naming conventions. The main differences between stored functions and procedures discussed in chapter 3 and Oracle Forms functions and procedures are scope, since stored procedures and functions can be called from most any CDE tool, and the general syntax, since Oracle Forms procedures and functions do not need the CREATE command. For example, to define a procedure to calculate grades within an Oracle Forms module, type the following:

```
procedure CALC_GRADES (TEACHER in varchar2, STUDENT in varchar2) is
begin
   update STUDENT_GRADES set CLASS_AVERAGE =
      (select round(avg(test_scores),2) FROM student_grades
      where teacher_id = nvl(teacher, teacher_id)
         and student_id = nvl(student, student_id));
end;
```

There are a few other rules to remember when using a procedure or function. First, a routine can be called only from PL/SQL blocks in the same module. Second, a routine defined in a menu can be called only from a menu command or startup command. Finally, a routine defined in a library can be called only from a module where the library is attached.

PL/SQL LIBRARY MODULES

An Oracle Forms library module is a collection of PL/SQL code, such as functions, packages, procedures, and developer-defined program units. Once created, libraries are attached to any number of other Oracle Forms modules, such as a form, menu, or another library. Once attached, library programs can be called from triggers, menu commands, or routines. Libraries are loaded into memory at the same time as the calling module. In fact, libraries can reduce memory overhead by taking advantage of shared memory support. Libraries are fairly easy to create, as follows:

1. Select the Library option of the NEW command on the File menu. This command calls the Library object list. Click NEW to create a new library, EDIT to modify the currently selected library, or REMOVE to erase the currently selected library.

2. Create any procedures, functions, or packages according to the require-

Figure 4.24   Attached PL/SQL Libraries Browser

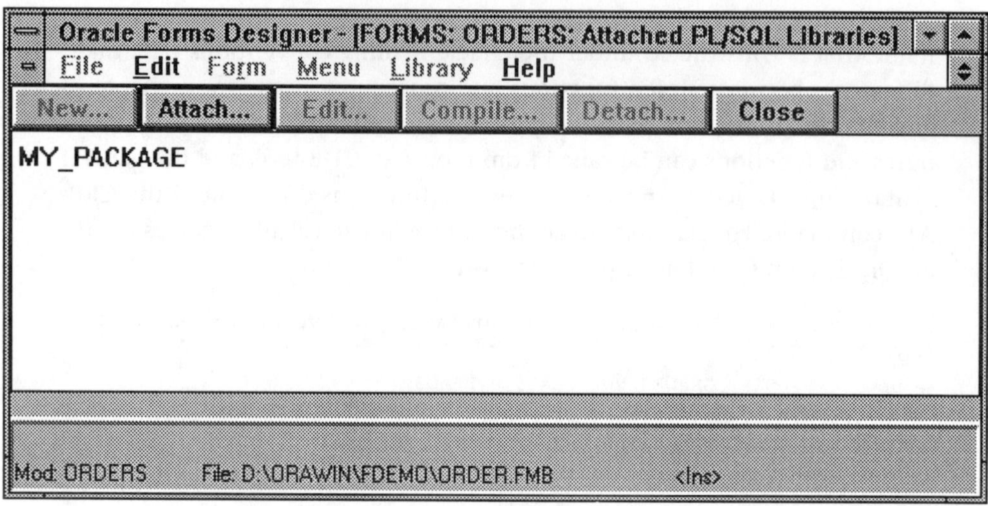

ments of the library. The program units are added to the library as they are created. When finished, save the library .PLL definitions to the database or to the file system. Since the library is compiled independently of any form or menu, refrain from using global or local variables (since this would raise an error). Instead, use the indirect referencing methods described earlier in the chapter.

3. Attach the library to an active module by selecting the ATTACH/DETACH command from the File menu, which will open the Attached PL/SQL Libraries Browser shown in Figure 4.24. Click the Detach button to detach a selected library from the active module. Also, double-click a library or select a library, then click EDIT to edit and modify an existing library (described later in this chapter).

   Select an active library or click Attach to call the Attach Library Dialog, shown in Figure 4.25. Specify the library name in the Library field, its source (file or database), its mode (read-only, read-write, or default), and the library's order (in reference to other libraries). Click the Attach button to return to the Attached PL/SQL Libraries Browser. Click CLOSE.

   Once attached, triggers and routines that contain reference library programs can be compiled. Now, you can reference library programs by

Figure 4.25 Attach Library Dialog

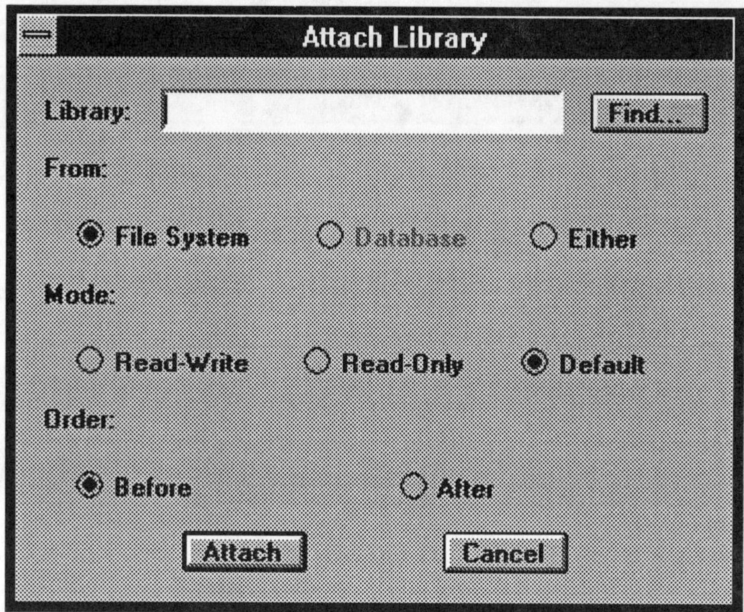

calling them in the form's PL/SQL code as if they were regularly coded procedures, functions, or packages.

4. Save the form to apply the changes.

5. Generate both the form and the library separately. Be certain to include the .LIB runfile with the .FMX form runfile or .MMX menu runfile at runtime.

Editing an Existing Library

When a developer double-clicks a library in the Attached PL/SQL Libraries Browser (or selects a library, then clicks EDIT), the Program Unit Dialog is invoked as shown in Figure 4.26. You can then import programming units from the active module into the library or remove programming units from the library. Note that the library must be defined as read-write.

The Edit Library Dialog is partitioned into two main work areas. The Library Contents box contains the programming units of the attached library,

Figure 4.26   Program Unit Dialog

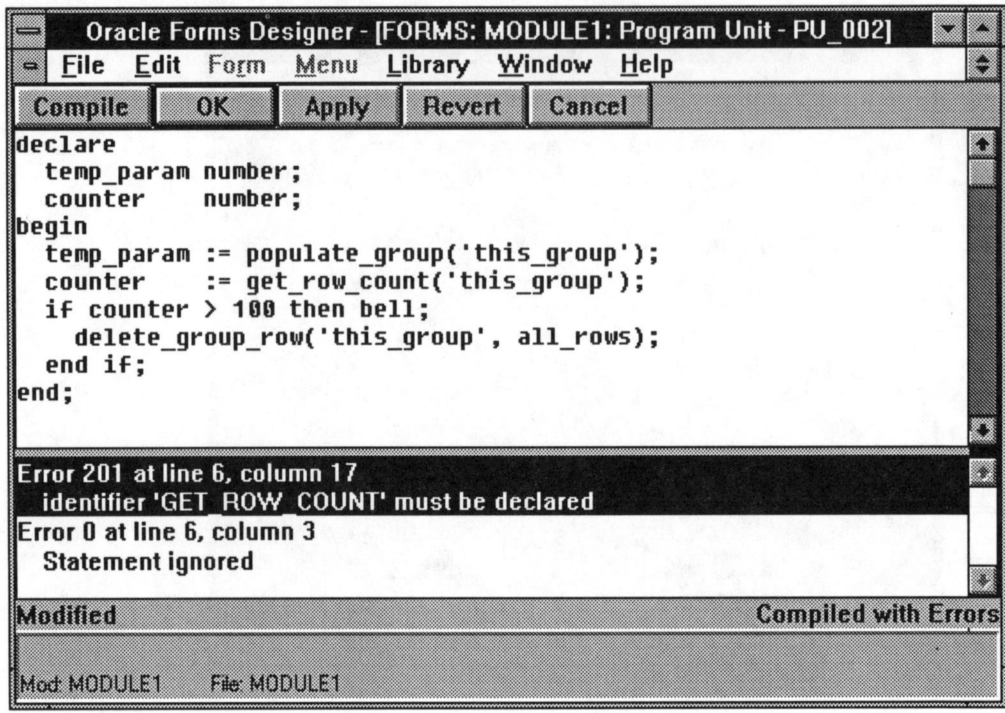

while the Loaded Program Units box contains a list of programming units in
the active form or menu.

You can copy a Loaded Program Unit into the Library Contents by selecting the program unit and clicking ADD. Conversely, a Library Contents Program Unit can be copied into the Loaded Program Units list, and thus into
the active module, by selecting the Library Content Program Unit and clicking LOAD. An individual program unit can be edited by selecting the item
and clicking EDIT. This function calls the PL/SQL editor for the selected item.
A library unit can be erased from the library by selecting the item, then clicking REMOVE. Note that none of the changes made will be permanent until
saved using the SAVE or SAVE AS commands.

The library can then be generated into a .LIB file, which must be present
with the runfile of any .FMX or .MMX that references it. Generate the library
by making the library module the currently active module, then select the

GENERATE (or GENERATE AS) command from the File menu. When needed, enter the filename of the library in the Generate field, although the library runfile must have the same name as the .PLL definition file.

COPYING AND REFERENCING OBJECTS

Oracle Forms allows you to effectively reuse existing objects through its Copy/Reference capability. Using Copy/Reference, objects can be created in one module then copied to another. In some situations, it is even more valuable to create an item in one module than to reference it in another module. Copying and referencing have distinct advantages and disadvantages when compared to one another. When an object is copied, its entire definition is recreated in the target module. If you discover that a change needs to be made in the object, it must be made in every form where the object was copied. When an object is referenced, a pointer to the original object is created in the target module. If you make a change in the original, it appears in all modules that reference it. It is for this reason that referencing is an especially effective development method in large, complex applications.

The COPY and REFERENCE commands can be used on most any form object or menu object. Copyable and referable form objects include alerts, blocks, canvas views, editors, form parameters, item, LOVs, PL/SQL code, record groups, triggers, visual attributes, and windows. Copyable and referable menu objects include menus, menu items, menu parameters, PL/SQL code, and visual attributes. Note that when an object is copied or referred, all objects owned by the original are also copied or referred, though visual attribute settings are not copied. So, copying a block also copies all of its items and triggers. To copy or reference an object, do the following:

1. In an active module, select the COPY/REFERENCE command from the Edit menu to call the Copy/Reference Dialog shown in Figure 4.27.

2. Set the Operation option to Copy (the default) or Reference as needed.

3. Enter the module of origination where the object will be copied or referred from in the Source field. The module must be saved in the database, and you must have full access to the object. Developers have full access to a module only if they are the owner of the module or have been granted access by the owner. To grant access to a module, select the GRANT MODULE command on the File menu. Then, enter the name of the module in the Module field and the complete name of the user (user ID) in the User field. Set the Operation to Grant, then click OK.

Figure 4.27   Copy/Reference Dialog

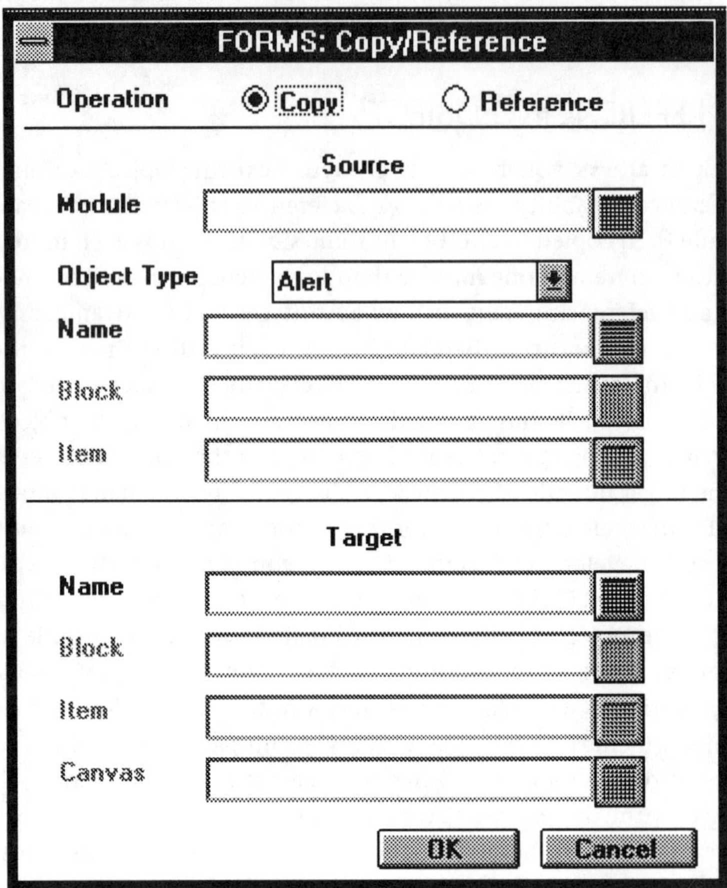

4. Identify the Object Type and name, including the block name for any items.

5. Enter the name of the copied/referenced object in the Target field, including the block name for any items. The Target name need not be the same as the Source name.

6. Click OK to accept the definition and dismiss the dialog.

Once an object is referenced, only a few aspects of it can be changed. (Of course, the original object can be changed, reflecting those changes in all its references.) Referenced blocks can be changed only in the values for block

Figure 4.28   Parameter Property Sheet

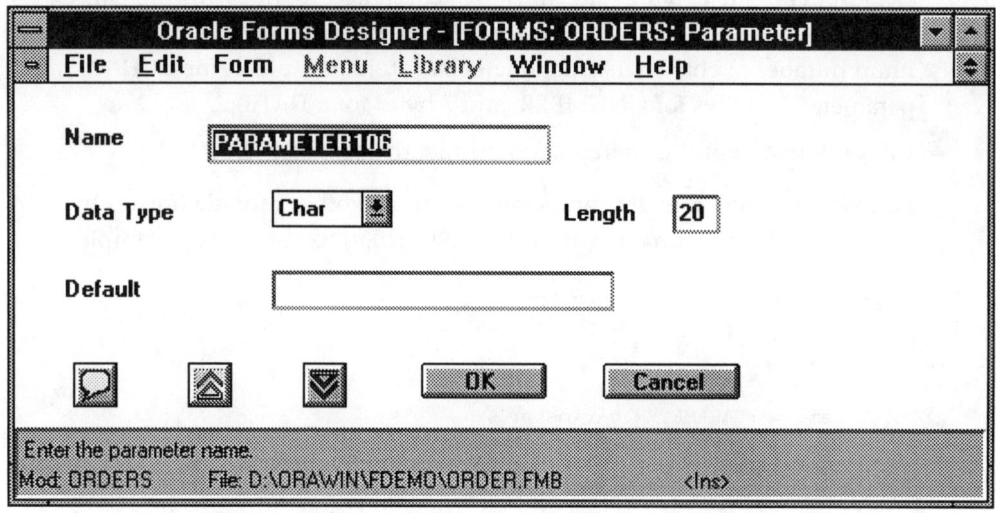

name, comment, or sequence ID. Referenced items can be changed only in
the values for comment, item name, position (X,Y), or sequence ID. Use care
when changing item names, since the name may have to be changed in any
PL/SQL program that references the item. Referenced triggers can have an
altered trigger name, trigger scope, or comment.

RUNTIME FORM PARAMETERS

Runtime form parameters are a method for passing a CHAR, NUMBER, or
DATE value to a form directly at startup. Parameters are passed to the module
by entering them on the command line that calls the module in the F40RUN
command or in the CALL_FORM, NEW_FORM, or RUN_PRODUCT built-ins.
Parameters must be predefined for a form, although a parameter can have a
default value assigned to it. Define parameters for a form by doing the following:

1. Call the Parameter object list by selecting the PARAMETERS command
   from the Form menu.

2. Click NEW to call the Parameter property sheet as shown in Figure 4.28.

3. Define the properties for the parameter as desired. Give the parameter a
   unique, internal name in the Name field. Data Type can be set to CHAR,

NUMBER, or DATE. Assign a default value to the parameter using the Default field. The default value must be kept in accordance with the parameter's data type and length. The Length number indicates the maximum number of characters a parameter can store (up to 64K for a CHAR parameter, 23 bytes for a NUMBER, and 7 bytes for a DATE).

4. Click OK to accept the changes and dismiss the property sheet.

Once created, a parameter can be referenced like other module objects by prefacing the parameter name with the string `:PARAMETER.`. For example:

```
:PARAMETER.parameter1 := 'CHEU, KARIN';
```

or

```
:block.item := :PARAMETER.parameter1;
```

Parameters can be referenced indirectly using NAME_IN or COPY, just as other objects can. Parameters can also be referenced in block properties, such as the default WHERE and ORDER BY clauses, in Default Value properties for items, and in Range properties for text items.

When using a built-in like CALL_FORM, NEW_FORM, or RUN_PRODUCT, parameters must be passed through a parameter list. Parameter lists are developer-constructed objects that contain a list of the parameter names, or keys, and their respective values. When calling a form from a block of PL/SQL code, you must have created the parameter list using the CREATE_PARAMETER_LIST built-in (items can be added using ADD_PARAMETER), then invoke the form using both the parameter list name and the appropriate built-in (CALL_FORM, NEW_FORM, or RUN_PRODUCT).

Parameters can be interpreted as text or data. Text parameters are used to pass a value for a parameter defined in a form called by CALL_FORM or NEW_FORM, or a complete command line for a product called by RUN_PRODUCT. Data parameters identify the name of a record group to the product called by RUN_PRODUCT. Although a DEFAULT parameter list is included with every form, parameter lists can be created and manipulated using several different built-ins, including ADD_PARAMETER, CREATE_PARAMETER_LIST, DELETE_PARAMETER, DESTROY_PARAMETER_LIST, GET_PARAMETER_ATTR, GET_PARAMETER_LIST, and SET_PARAMETER_ATTR.

INTEGRATING OTHER ORACLE PRODUCTS

As a part of the CDE, Oracle Forms allows you to call other CDE products, like Oracle Book and Oracle Graphics, and to call developer-created programs written in languages like C or COBOL. Parameters can be passed to these external products. In fact, the user can interact with external CDE products, passing data to and receiving data from the product.

The RUN_PRODUCT built-in is the primary means of accessing an external product. Standard RUN_PRODUCT syntax looks like the following:

```
RUN_PRODUCT(product, document, commode, execmode, location, list, display);
```

Each parameter is significant in the RUN_PRODUCT parameter list. *Product* indicates the specific Oracle tool to be called, whether it is FORMS, RE-PORTS, or GRAPHICS. *Document* indicates the name of the form, menu, report, or document to be used when the product starts up. *Commode* indicates the communication mode to be used by the product, either Synchronous (for products like Oracle Graphics, where control must pass to the called product until it is exited) or Asynchronous (when control returns to the calling form immediately). *Execmode* indicates whether the product should be executed in Batch or Runtime mode. Called forms should always be run in Runtime mode, but reports and graphics can be run in either mode. *Location* provides the path of the product, either as a file or database item. Finally, *List* identifies a parameter list to be attached to the called product.

Oracle Graphics can create a special item for use in a form called a Chart Item. Chart Items are special because they can be based on data contained in or queried from Oracle Graphics or Oracle Forms. Chart Items cannot be manipulated by users, so you must control them, and the information they display, programmatically. For example, a chart might be based on the data in a multirecord base-table block. To display a graph based on that block, you could write a Post-Query trigger that executes a RUN_PRODUCT call for each record in the block, thereby displaying a bar chart of the table's data.

Oracle Book must be called using the HOST built-in. You can retrieve context-sensitive help from an Oracle Book document by including the TARGET parameter in the host statement. Since Book documents include hypertext target items, you can programmatically zero in on the target appropriate to the application's needs.

DEBUG MODE

Debug mode greatly eases the process of finding and correcting errors and anomalies in an application through special debugging messages, break processing, and the Debugger facility. Run a form in Debug mode by setting Debug Mode to ON in the PREFERENCES command on the Edit menu (or by adding the parameter 'debug=YES' to the F40RUN command).

Debug messages display prior to the execution of a trigger to inform you exactly what the form is doing. Break processing allows you to interrupt the normal execution of a trigger to invoke the Debugger or perform some other check. Break processing is caused by including the BREAK built-in procedure in a block of PL/SQL code. Oracle Forms disallows break processing when the form is not running in debug mode.

The Debugger is a utility that informs you of the current state of the form by showing the current value of items and variables. The Debugger can be invoked by selecting the DEBUG command from the Help menu and is dismissed by clicking the OK button. The Debugger allows the display of system variables (the default), global variables, NULL-canvas items, all items, and parameter lists.

You can control other aspects of the DeBugger by setting the value for Automatic Update, Continue With Debug Messages, and Zoom options. Automatic Update immediately refreshes the value of an object, if its value has changed; otherwise, values are refreshed only when the Update button is pressed. The Continue With Debug Messages option allows you to turn off the display of messages at each trigger firing. Zoom displays the name and the entire value of a variable (very useful for some of the longer variables). Another important option is the Continue Modeless button, which allows you to view the Debugger while processing continues. The Continue Modeless button is available only when the Debugger is invoked programmatically.

ORACLE FORMS INFORMATIONAL REPORTS

If Oracle Reports is installed on the same computer as Oracle Forms and Designer is currently connected to the database, reports can be printed that provide detailed information about a specific form's triggers, procedures, and objects. This reporting feature contains a complete source code listing and object description.

The form document is made available by selecting the FORM DOC command from the File menu, then specifying the name of the module to be printed. You may also answer yes or no to four prompts: Summary Only, Show Triggers, Show Procedures, and Show Objects.

MULTIPLE-MODULE APPLICATIONS

Multiple forms and modules can be linked together to build complex, seamless applications that are modularly constructed and maintained. Oracle Forms enables you to connect a variety of forms and menus together, combined with other Oracle Forms products. Such a structure is excellent for client-server applications in which the client computer might execute the actual Oracle Forms application while the server computer maintains the Oracle RDBMS and data.

As described in the section "Runtime Form Parameters," a form should be invoked by the CALL_FORM or NEW_FORM built-in; RUN_PRODUCT is for nonform applications. The CALL_FORM built-in loads the specified form while keeping the calling form in memory. In fact, the called form can even remain on the screen. When the user exits the called form, control returns to the calling form. NEW_FORM, on the other hand, exits the current form and invokes the new form. Both CALL_FORM and NEW_FORM can pass parameters. CALL_FORM is unrestricted, while NEW_FORM is restricted to Normal mode only (it cannot be used in Enter Query mode).

Both CALL_FORM and NEW_FORM have only one required parameter, the form name. The following example uses CALL_FORM, though they both work the same:

```
Call_Form('form1');
```

In this example, Oracle Forms would apply the default parameters HIDE, NO_REPLACE, and NO_QUERY_ONLY to the CALL_FORM built-in. Conversely, you could specify:

```
Call_Form('form1',NO_HIDE,QUERY_ONLY,NO_REPLACE);
```

The HIDE parameter tells Oracle Forms whether or not the calling form should be hidden. A value of NO_HIDE indicates the calling form remains on the screen, overlaid by the currently active called form. This parameter is useful for the creation of forms with a pop-up window effect. Additionally, a form can be called in Data-Entry mode or Query-Only mode using the NO_QUERY_ONLY/QUERY_ONLY parameter. A form in Query-Only mode can query data from the database but cannot write new data or alter existing data. The NO_REPLACE parameter tells Oracle Forms not to replace the current menu module with one that might be attached to the called form.

A called form can be exited by using the EXIT_FORM procedure, the EXIT command on the default Action menu, or the [Exit/Cancel] key. To exit the called form and move to a new form, use the NEW_FORM procedure. It is often desirable to have users quit the entire application when they press the [Exit/Cancel] key or issue the EXIT command from the Action menu, as opposed to merely returning to the calling form. You should write a trigger to handle this function, such as the following:

```
/*    When-Button-Pressed Trigger    */
:GLOBAL.quit_check := 'quit';
Exit_Form;
```

Then, the calling form should use this code:

```
/*    In the trigger that called the other form    */
Call_Form('form2');
/*    Executes immediately upon return from form2    */
IF :GLOBAL.quit_check = 'quit' THEN
  Exit_Form;
END IF;
```

Integrate multiple forms with multiple menus using the DO_REPLACE and NO_REPLACE parameters for the CALL_FORM built-in. Using DO_REPLACE tells Oracle Forms to load the menu that is specifically attached to the called form. NO_REPLACE, the default, tells Oracle Forms to keep the current menu active. When using the NEW_FORM built-in, any menu attached to the new form is also loaded.

Posting Versus Committing in a Multiple-Form Application

In an application, calling and called forms can simultaneously issue DML commands to lock records, commit changes, and roll back posted changes. Application developers must understand and utilize the differences between posting and committing. Posting writes updates, deletions, and insertions to the database without committing them to the form. It can be initiated using the POST built-in. In contrast, committing writes updates, deletions, and insertions, then issues the COMMIT statement to commit the transactions to the database. In both actions, Oracle Forms performs validation and commit processing.

Forms are run in Post-Only mode when there are unposted changes in the calling form, providing some advantages to the multiform application. Posting writes transactions to the database, but the transactions can be programmatically rolled back because they have not been committed. This enables locks obtained in the calling form to be maintained until control is returned to it. Oracle Forms runs called forms in Post-Only mode when the calling form contains records that have been updated or deleted, but not committed. Oracle Forms locks the appropriate records (but not inserted records; they do not acquire locks) after changes are validated.

Savepoint and Rollback

By default all forms have the Savepoint Mode property turned on. Using this, you can "roll back" property changes in a form to the time when the last savepoint was issued. Whenever a form is loaded, a savepoint is issued on separate database transactions in distinct segments linked to a specific form module. Changes can then be posted and rolled back in the individual forms without affecting changes in other active forms. The NEW_FORM, EXIT_FORM, and CLEAR_FORM built-ins write or roll back changes in the current form before exiting occurs. The Rollback mode of a form is determined by the setting of the Rollback_mode parameter to TO_SAVEPOINT, NO_ROLLBACK, or FULL_ROLLBACK. Rollback_mode parameters are entered as optional parameters in a built-in procedure or in the command line F40RUN (i.e., `New_Form (ASK_COMMIT, TO_SAVEPOINT);`).

TO_SAVEPOINT is the default Rollback mode and rolls back uncommitted changes to the last savepoint. Posted changes, which are not committed, are also rolled back. Changes in a calling form are preserved, but changes and locks are lost in the current form when using this parameter setting. NO_ROLLBACK does not issue a rollback when exiting a called form, but locks obtained by the calling form remain in effect. Forms called with the FULL_ROLLBACK parameter automatically roll back all uncommitted changes pending in the current session. Remember that full rollbacks are illegal in a form running in Post-Only mode.

ROLLBACK and COMMIT are especially important in multiform applications because a single commit or rollback statement affects all open forms. This means that a rollback statement issued in Form1 affects Form2 and

Form3, since they were both active at the time the statement was issued. So, when building an application, proper use of posting and Rollback mode can control commit processing across several called forms. In many situations, it is a good idea to include the POST built-in in a block of PL/SQL code prior to calling the target form. It is also a good idea to check the form record status to ensure that at least one record is changed (using the string SYS-TEM.FORM_STATUS = 'CHANGED'), since attempting to post in a form without any changes raises an error.

When necessary you can find out the name of an active form in a multi-form application using the GET_APPLICATION_PROPERTY, as in the following built-in. Use the parameter CURRENT_FORM or CALLING_FORM with the built-in to find the name of the current form or calling form, respectively. Similarly, you can write an application that uses an end-user's username and password using the (USERNAME, PASSWORD) parameter.

```
DECLARE
    calling_form_name CHAR(20)  :=
    Get_Application_Property(CALLING_FORM);
BEGIN
    IF calling_form_name = 'form1' THEN Post;
        Exit_Form(NO_COMMIT,NO_ROLLBACK);
    ELSE
        Commit_Form;
        Exit_Form;
    END IF;
END;
```

BUILDING MENUS WITH ORACLE FORMS DESIGNER

Every form comes with a default menu to control navigation and transaction processing. However, you can create custom menus defined as separate modules, then attach forms to the menus. A menu is assigned to a form by putting the menu name in the Menu Module property of the Form Module property sheet. A NULL value indicates no menu is to be used for the form.

Menus created in Designer have a hierarchical design, much like a tree. Each menu contains a main menu with one or more submenus. At every level in the menu, menu items invoke commands or lower-level menus when selected by the end-user through the mouse or keyboard. Keyboard selections, or mnemonics, allow users to press a combination of keyboard characters, such as ALT-S, to activate the menu and select the command assigned to the ALT-S keystroke.

Table 4.9 Default Menu Functions

Action Menu Item	*Function Key*
Rollback	[Clear Form/Rollback]
Commit	[Commit]
Refresh	[Refresh]
Print	[Print]
Exit	[Exit/Cancel]

Edit Menu Item	*Function Key*
Cut	[Cut]
Copy	[Copy]
Paste	[Paste]
Edit	[Edit]

Block Menu Item	*Function Key*
Previous	[Previous Block]
Next	[Next Block]
Clear	[Clear Block]

Record Menu Item	*Function Key*
Previous	[Previous Record]
Next	[Next Record]
Scroll Up	[Scroll Up]
Scroll Down	[Scroll Down]
Clear	[Clear Record]
Remove	[Delete Record]
Insert	[Insert Record]
Duplicate	[Duplicate Record]
Lock	[Lock Record]

Item Menu Item	*Function Key*
Previous	[Previous Item]
Next	[Next Item]
Clear	[Clear Item]
Duplicate	[Duplicate Item]

Query Menu Item	*Function Key*
Enter	[Enter Query]
Execute	[Execute Query]
Last Criteria	[Enter Query]
Cancel	[Exit/Cancel]
Count Hits	[Count Query Hits]
Fetch Next Set	[Next Set of Records]

Help Menu Item	*Function Key*
Help	[Help]
Keys	[Show Keys]
List	[List]
Error	[Display Error]
Debug	[Debug]

Within an application, only one menu can be active at a time, be it the default menu or a custom one. You can take advantage of three PL/SQL built-ins to switch between multiple menus: HIDE_MENU to conceal the current menu, REPLACE_MENU to replace the current menu, and SHOW_MENU to display the current menu. The default menu built into every form is not a separate menu module but is a standard set of navigation, editing, and transaction commands that correspond to common Runform function keys (see Table 4.9). The default menu cannot be customized or edited in any way.

Custom menus can be formatted as pull-down, bar, or full-screen menus by specifying the desired style in the Form Module property sheet when the menu is attached to a form. Pull-down menus, the only style that allows tear-off menu features (menus that can be moved by the user to any position on the screen), are usually the best choice for most applications.

Just as forms are composed of blocks, canvases, items, and numerous other objects, menus are composed of various objects. Menu objects include the individual menus and submenus, menu items (plain text items, check boxes, radio buttons, and separators), and the associated menu item commands, menu substitution parameters, developer-named routines, and menu startup codes.

Just as in a form, the objects of a menu are defined through their property sheets. You can create a custom menu by following these steps:

1. Call the Oracle Forms Designer and open a new menu module by selecting the Menu option of the NEW command from the File menu. Open a predefined menu by selecting the OPEN command from the File menu.

2. Define the main menu, submenus, and individual items of the menu using the Menu Editor. When defining items of different levels, move to higher levels of the hierarchy with the Left-arrow button and to lower levels with the Right-arrow button.

3. Provide the commands to menu items.

4. Generate a menu module .MMX runfile.

5. Attach to the menu as many forms as desired by changing the properties in each form's Form Module property sheet.

The Menu Editor

Invoke the Menu Editor by selecting the EDITOR command from the Menu menu. The Menu Editor, shown in Figure 4.29, provides several useful capabilities. Use the Menu Editor to create menus and submenus, add menu items to menus, and assign commands to menu items. Menus and submenus are created by typing their names into the Main, Sub1, and Sub2 columns in the Menu Editor. The menus can be displayed either in List mode (the default mode) or Tree mode. In List mode, only the first column is active, with each item in the column representing the name of one of the main menu choices. In Tree mode, each pulldown menu is shown as a column listing its menu items, with the menu name at the top.

In both modes, menu items appear at runtime in the order they were created and listed in the column. In Tree mode, shown in Figure 4.30, you can

Figure 4.29 The Menu Editor (List Mode)

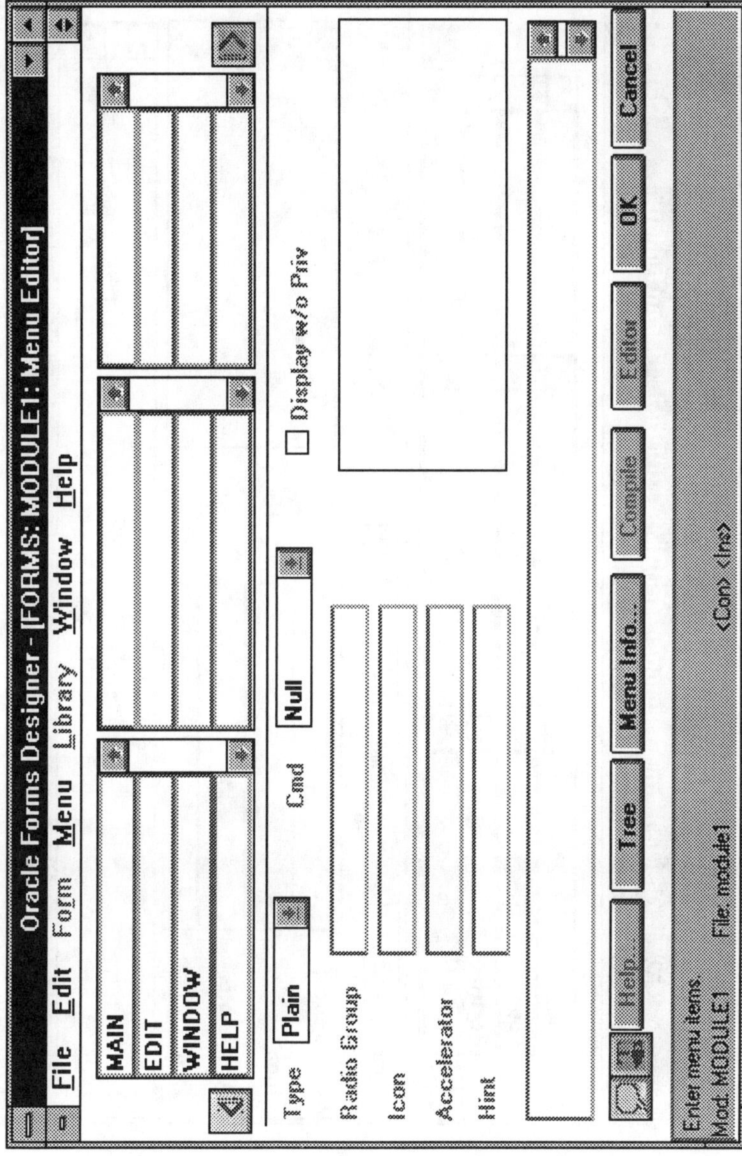

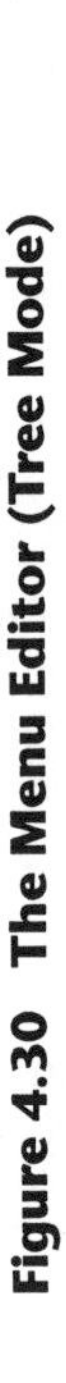

Figure 4.30   The Menu Editor (Tree Mode)

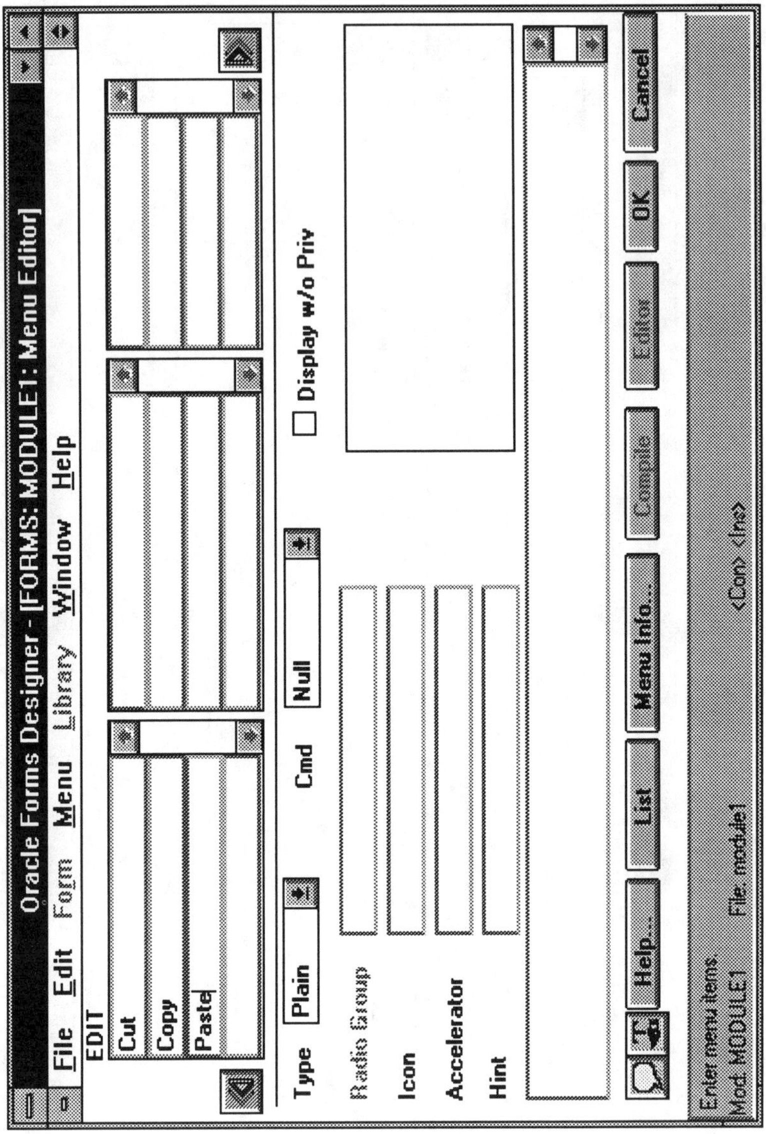

select a menu item by clicking it. When selected, submenus show their contents in the next column. You can toggle between the two display modes by clicking the List/Tree button. Use the Tree mode display style to add and manipulate menu items.

DEFINING MENUS, SUBMENUS, AND MENU ITEMS

The first step in creating a menu module is to create the main menu. Once it has been constructed, menu items that call submenus or execute commands can be added. To create a main menu and its elements follow these steps:

1. Call the Menu Editor in list mode.

2. Enter the unique name of the new main menu in the first column.

3. Select the main menu, then click the Tree button to switch to tree mode.

4. Enter the name of the new menu item on the first line of the menu column. Additional items can be added by pressing [Down] or [Insert Element], or can be erased by pressing [Delete Element]. Items appear in the order they were entered on the column.

To create a submenu in tree mode, do the following:

1. Select the menu item that calls the submenu.

2. Enter Menu as the item's Command (Cmd) property.

3. Enter the submenu name in the command field at the bottom of the Menu Editor.

4. Navigate out of the command field. The new submenu is created and its name appears over the next column. Create new items in the submenu by entering the name of items in its menu column.

To assign commands to menu items, follow these steps:

1. In tree mode, select an individual menu item from the desired menu.

2. Set the item's Cmd property.

3. Enter the text of the command in the command text field.

The PL/SQL command type provides complete Oracle Forms functionality to a menu item. PL/SQL menu items are structured as form triggers and can include blocks and built-ins. Compile and validate the PL/SQL menu items by clicking the Compile button.

Generating a Menu

A menu must be generated, placed into an .MMX menu runfile, and attached to a form before it can be run. Menu .MMX files are generated as forms or libraries but are always stored in the file system. Only the .MMB menu design file of a menu module can be stored in the database. A menu is attached to a form by opening the form and setting the Form Module property to call the runtime menu file. To generate a runtime file of the menu, do the following:

1. Enter the name of the main menu in the Menu Module property sheet. Call the Menu Module property sheet by selecting the MODULE command from the Menu menu. Enter the name of the main menu in the Main field.

2. Activate the menu module then select the GENERATE AS command from the File menu to call the Generate File dialog.

3. Enter a name for the .MMX file in the Generate field without the .MMX extension (which is added automatically).

4. Click OK to generate the file in the specified path and dismiss the dialog. Save the file using the SAVE AS command from the File menu.

To attach the menu to a form follow one of these steps:

1. Directly reference the .MMX file in an active form by entering its path and filename in the Module Name Form property sheet (called by selecting the MODULE command on the Form menu). Make sure the Use File property is turned on. This is the most preferable method of attaching a menu to a form.

or,

2. Attach the menu to a form through a database lookup. This method is available only when the menu design file is stored in the database and the form is connected to the database. To perform a database lookup, set the File and Directory properties of the Menu Module property sheet to specify the location of the .MMX file. Then, attach the menu to the form as in step 1, but turn the Use File property off.

Special Features in a Menu

Customized menus can include many special, user-friendly features like check boxes, radio buttons, separator menu items, mnemonic keys, accelerator keys, icons displayed on a menu item, menu titles, background menus, tear-off menus, substitution parameters, and hint text for menu items.

CHECK BOXES, RADIO BUTTONS, AND SEPARATOR MENU ITEMS

A menu item can be one of four types: plain (the default), check, radio, and separator. To create the desired item type, set the item's Type property in the Menu Editor to the desired type.

Check menu items are Boolean indicators, being either on or off, and are represented as plain items with or without a check mark to the right-hand side. Radio menu items, like form menu items, must be in a group of at least two or more and are displayed simultaneously. Radio menu items function in the same manner as radio form items and are assigned by selecting a menu item, then entering the name of the group in the Radio Group field of the Menu Editor.

Commands for check boxes execute when a user toggles the item. Commands for radio items execute when the item is selected. Check boxes are unchecked at menu startup, while only the first radio button of its respective group is toggled at menu startup. Use the GET_MENU_ITEM_PROPERTY built-in routine to find out the value of a menu item and the SET_MENU_ITEM_PROPERTY to change its startup value or current value. For example, set the value of a check box to checked:

```
Set_Menu_Item_Property('sub2_menu.checked1', CHECKED, PROPERTY_ON);
```

Separator menu items are simply visual tools for breaking distinct groups of menu items. Separator items cannot be selected but are created by setting the Cmd property to NULL. Although separator items can be used in a main menu or a bar-style menu, checks and radios cannot.

MNEMONIC KEYS

Mnemonic keys provide added efficiency through the use of quick keyboard commands, which can often be more expedient than mouse clicks. Mnemonic keys are special keystrokes that perform menu item commands without your having to use the mouse. For instance, the ALT-S keystroke often calls the Save operation. To add a mnemonic to any menu item, add an ampersand (&) in front of the character in the menu item name that will serve as the mnemonic. To create the ALT-S mnemonic, enter `&Save Changes` in the menu item name field. The first ampersand in a menu item name is treated as the mnemonic, with any additional ampersands treated as literals.

ACCELERATOR KEYS

Accelerator keys are five built-in functions, named [ACCELERATOR1] through [ACCELERATOR5], that perform the operations of one or many keystrokes on the menu. These keys are useful for reaching a navigational point deep in a menu or some other such function. To assign an accelerator, select the desired menu item, then enter the name of the accelerator key in the Accelerator property field. Then, using Oracle Terminal, assign an actual keystroke to the accelerator (something like Ctrl-T or ALT-U).

ICONS DISPLAYED ON A MENU ITEM

Icons can be assigned to menu items in a pull-down or bar menu in some GUIs. Add the icon by selecting the desired menu item in the Tree mode of the Menu Editor. Then, enter the filename of the icon source file in the Icon property field. If the operation fails because the file cannot be found, the icon reference is ignored and the item is displayed as regular text.

MENU ITEMS

In a pull-down or bar menu, the Title property of the Root Window defines the window title. If Title is NULL, the name of the main menu in the menu module serves as the title. In a full-screen menu, select the MENU INFORM command from the Menu property dialog to specify a Title of up to forty characters, a Subtitle of up to forty characters, and a Bottom Title of up to seventy-two characters.

BACKGROUND MENUS

A background menu is a single, special-purpose menu with the name BGM. Only one background menu can be defined for a module. Background menus provide two special capabilities. First, the background menu possesses ten special key functions. Second, authorized users can display the background menu items by pressing the [ShowBGM] key or by executing code containing the built-in routine SHOW_BACKGROUND_MENU. The background menu can be part of the regular menu hierarchy or a special-purpose menu.

Background menus are created and assigned menu items as regular menus, except that they are named BGMs. Menu items should be named BGM-1 through BGM-10. When adding a menu item, be sure to provide a descriptive comment in the Hint field since the hint is used as the item descriptor. Then, use Oracle Terminal to assign keystrokes to the menu items. The background keys can be programmatically executed using the BACKGROUND_MENU built-in procedure.

TEAR-OFF MENUS

Tear-off menus, available in some GUIs, are pull-down submenus that users can reposition on the screen. Make a menu tear-off by selecting the desired menu in the Menu Editor. Then click the Menu Info button and turn the Tear-Off property on.

SUBSTITUTION PARAMETERS

Substitution parameters are two-character variables whose value can be referenced in menu item command statements. You can define unique parameters or use the six built-in substitution parameters. Parameters are referenced in a menu command with an ampersand (&) and in PL/SQL code with a colon (:). The six built-in parameters are UN, PW, AD, SO, TT, and LN. UN is the current username. PW is the current password. AD is the directory of the runtime file. SO is the current menu item, or "selected option." TT is the terminal type used to log in. LN is the current language preference. The values can be used in triggers and routines, though the user is prompted for information only by calling the QUERY_PARAMETER built-in. Define a custom substitution parameter by doing the following:

1. Call the Parameter property sheet by selecting the PARAMETERS command from the Menu menu and clicking the New button.

2. Enter a two-character name for the substitution parameter.

3. Set the properties of the parameter as desired. Substitution parameters have a number of properties, shown in Table 4.10.

4. Click OK to accept the definition and dismiss the dialog.

HINT TEXT FOR MENU ITEMS

You can add on-line help for a particular menu item by adding up to seventy characters of text to the Hint field of the item in the Menu Editor. Hints are displayed in the message line of pull-down and bar menus and in the menu item descriptor of a full-screen menu. Additionally, help text can be added to the item by clicking the Help button to enter a help message in the Help Text editor. The help text can then be called by the user pressing [Menu Help] or by adding the MENU_HELP built-in procedure to a block of PL/SQL code.

Table 4.10   Parameter Properties

Property	*Description*
Case Restriction	Converts the user-supplied values to None, Upper, or Lower case.
Default	A default value for the parameter.
Fixed Length	Indicates the user must enter a value with the maximum number of characters (shown in the Size property).
Hint	Commentary displayed to the user at the prompt dialog.
Menu Parameters	In full-screen menus, the names of the menus associated with the parameters.
Name	The two-character parameter name.
Prompt	The text prompt displayed by the user on the Enter Parameter Values dialog.
Required	A value of ON indicates the user must enter a value for the parameter.
Secure	A value of ON indicates the parameter response is hidden as it is entered by the user.
Size	Indicates the maximum number of characters in the parameter value.

Menu Security

Security features, in addition to those available through grants, roles, and privileges established in SQL, are incorporated in Oracle Forms menu modules. These menu security functions enable you to control the availability of menu items for selected users through the creation and assignment of roles. As said before, these roles are distinct from those created and assigned in SQL, although Oracle Forms must be connected to the database for this function to work properly. In fact, menu items that are unavailable to specific users can be completely hidden or displayed as disabled, or ghosted, items. The basic steps in the creation and assignment of security roles follow:

1. Define the appropriate security roles by selecting the Role option of the GRANT command on the File menu. Click NEW in the Role Definition dialog.

2. Enter a security role name in the Role Name field.

3. Assign users to the role by listing their usernames in the User Name column.

4. Assign privileges for Debug, OS Command, and Background Menu by turning the appropriate value on or off. Click OK to accept the new role definition.

5. Enable the role for a specific menu by invoking that menu's Menu Module property sheet using the MODULE command from the Menu menu. Specify the role's access to the menu in the Security Roles field, then click OK to accept the role's assignment and dismiss the dialog.

6. Grant an enabled role access to specific menu items by invoking the Menu Editor in tree mode, then selecting the desired item. Enabled roles are displayed in the Security Roles list. You should grant access to the menu for a role by selecting the role from the role security list. Deselecting the role revokes access. Set Display w/o Priv to off to hide menu items that the user does not have access to or to on to display a ghosted (and disabled) menu item.

7. Open the Menu Module property sheet by selecting the MODULE command from the Menu menu. Set the Use Security property to on to enforce security roles or to off to ignore the security roles.

8. Click OK to accept the definition and dismiss the property sheet.

Only a developer with administration privileges may create or alter security roles. Developers with the SYSTEM privilege can grant and revoke menu security administration privileges for other designers by selecting the GRANT command from the File menu, then selecting ROLE ACCESS. They would then enter the name of the user wishing access in the User Name field, toggle the setting to Grant or Revoke, and then click OK to grant someone menu security administration privileges.

Programming Issues for Menus

Blocks of PL/SQL code can be written for menus, just as they are for forms using the PL/SQL editor. The code can then be applied within the menu according to your needs. Call the PL/SQL editor by selecting the PL/SQL PROGRAM UNITS command from the Menu menu, then click NEW.

A block of startup code can also be applied to a menu so that certain functions are automatically executed when the menu is opened. Startup code is useful to initialize parameters or variables (including globals) and to set the initial display value of special menu items (such as checks and radios). Write a block of startup code by selecting the MODULE command from the Menu

Table 4.11   Menu Built-Ins

Usage	*Built-In*
Set or retrieve menu item properties	GET_MENU_ITEM_PROPERTY
	SET_MENU_ITEM_PROPERTY
	FIND_MENU_ITEM
Show or hide the current menu	HIDE_MENU
	REPLACE_MENU
	SHOW_MENU
	MENU_REDISPLAY
Display or prompt for a substitution parameter value	APPLICATION_PARAMETER
	QUERY_PARAMETER
	MENU_PARAMETER
Execute background menu commands	BACKGROUND_MENU
	SHOW_BACKGROUND_MENU
Use full-screen menus	MAIN_MENU
	NEXT_MENU_ITEM
	PREVIOUS_MENU
	PREVIOUS_MENU_ITEM
	MENU_CLEAR_FIELD
	MENU_NEXT_FIELD
	MENU_PREVIOUS_FIELD
	TERMINATE
	WHERE_DISPLAY
Other useful built-ins	MENU_SHOW_KEYS
	DEBUG_MODE
	SET_INPUT_FOCUS

menu, then clicking Startup Code to call the PL/SQL Editor. Enter and compile the PL/SQL code as needed.

Remember that code in a menu can include anonymous blocks, built-ins, custom routines, and even linked libraries. Be careful not to directly reference any form objects; instead, use the NAME_IN or COPY built-ins. The built-ins shown in Table 4.11 are especially useful for menu applications.

Creating a Master Menu

In many multiform applications, a master menu is used to call submenus, form applications, SQL programs, and other routines. In Oracle Forms, this is best accomplished by creating a front-end form that exists only to display the main menu and execute the corresponding commands. Create the master menu by first creating a form without blocks or items, then attach the master menu to the form. Be sure to call the form holding the master menu using the NO_REPLACE parameter, otherwise its menu may be substituted improperly.

EXECUTABLES

Oracle Forms executables include the Designer, Runtime, and Generate components. The executables can be launched from their icons in the GUI or by a command-line prompt with any necessary arguments. Command-line executables can also include keywords to control the behavior of Oracle Forms, as shown in Table 4.12.

Designer

The Designer component is used to create and optimize the Oracle Forms applications. Designer is the portion used most often by developers. The command-line executable for Designer is F40DES. For example, to launch Oracle Forms Designer and to automatically load a module display to a non-default printer, you enter:

```
f40des module=student_list user=kevin/triangle
```

Runtime

The Runtime component invokes the Oracle Forms runtime environment, allowing end-users to run the module only. Runtime is the component of Oracle Forms most often used by end-users. The command-line executable for Runtime is F40RUN. For example, to invoke a module in Query-Only mode, you enter:

```
f40run module=student_list userid=( ) query_only=yes
```

Generate

The Generate component is used to call Oracle Forms Generate mode for compiling a form without any other intervention. The command-line executable form in Oracle Forms Generate is F40GEN. For example, to automatically log on and generate a module and then show statistics on the process, you enter:

```
f40gen module=student_list userid=kevin/triangle statistics=yes
```

Table 4.12   Oracle Forms Executable Keywords

Keyword*	Value**	Used By***	Usage
MODULE	=(filename and path)	D,R,G	Name of form to execute.
USERID	=(userid)	D,R,G	Database login, enter USERID=( ) to use the automatic OPS$ database login.
TERM	path and filename	D,R	Specifies a terminal definition file for key mapping; note that the preface "resfile:" must appear before the path and filename.
DEBUG	no/yes	R	Toggles the form in debug mode, showing message about the status of trigger execution.
KEYOUT	path and filename	R	Captures keystrokes for the current session to the specified file to be used as a macro for batch processing.
KEYIN	path and filename	R	Runs a macro file (created with KEYOUT) in batch mode.
OUTPUT_FILE	path and filename	R,G	Captures processing output to the specified file.
INTERACTIVE	yes/no	R	Shows the execution of forms running in batch mode and prints the output to file; for character-mode platforms only.
ARRAY	yes/no	R	Toggles array record processing.
BUFFER_RECORDS	yes/no	R	Toggles record buffering; speeds processing when turned on.
LOGON_SCREEN	no/yes	R,G	Displays the logon screen at startup; in the Generate executable, this keyword is LOGON.
BLOCK_MENU	no/yes	R	Displays the block menu upon entering the form.
OPTIMIZESQL	yes/no	R	Optimizes any SQL statements written in V2-style triggers.
OPTIMIZETP	yes/no	R	Optimizes transaction mode processing.
QUIET	no/yes	R	Turns off audible beeps found in the form.
STATISTICS	no/yes	R,G	When you leave the form, a message displays showing cursor usage.
QUERY_ONLY	no/yes	R	Invokes the executable in query-only mode, disabling the user's ability to create, delete, or alter data.
HELP	no/yes	D,R,G	Calls the Oracle Forms help screen.
OPTIONS_SCREEN	no/yes	R,G	Displays the options window for bit-mapped platforms only.
MODULE_TYPE	form	D,G	Indicates the current module type (form, menu, or library).
MODULE-ACCESS	file	D,G	Indicates whether to open and save to database or files.
VERBOSE	yes/no	G	Displays complete message while generating.

Table 4.12 Oracle Forms Executable Keywords *(continued)*

Keyword*	Value**	Used By***	Usage
SCRIPT	no/yes	G	Converts binary files to text files (e.g., FMB to FMT).
PARSE	no/yes	G	Converts text files to binary files (e.g., FMT to FMB).
GRANT_DESIGN	(user id)	G	Grants user privilege to menus.
REVOKE_USER	(user id)	G	Revokes user privilege to menus.
DELETE	no/yes	G	Deletes the form from the database.
INSERT	no/yes	G	Inserts the form directly into the database when generation is complete.
EXTRACT	no/yes	G	Moves the form from the database to a file of the same name.
UPGRADE	no/yes	G	Upgrades Forms 2.0, 2.3, 3.0, and Menu 5.0 files for Forms 4.0 files.
UPGRADE_ROLES	no/yes	G	Upgrades Menu 5.0 table privileges.
VERSION	3	G	The version to upgrade from: "version" for Forms 3.0, "version=23" for Forms 2.3, and "version=20" for Forms 2.0
GENERATE_ON_UPGRADE	yes/no	G	Generates a runform executable whenever a form is upgraded.
CRT_FILE	path and filename	G	Uses the specified CRT file when upgrading from Forms 2.0 or 2.3.
ADD_TRIGGERS	no/yes	G	Adds key-up/key-down triggers when converting Forms 2.0 and 2.3 triggers to Forms 4.0.
NOFAIL	no/yes	G	Adds the NOFAIL keyword to exemacros in Forms 2.0.
paramname	=(value)	D,R,G	Name(s) and value(s) of parameter(s) defined in the display. Values entered on the command line will overwrite any default value for the parameter.

*   Keywords are shown in the order they should appear in when writing an Oracle Graphics executable; that is, userid first, openfile second, and so on.

**   Default value appears first in the list. Values shown in parentheses may actually include a list of values, with each item separated by a comma. For example, when you open three files, the openfile keyword string might read `openfile=(myfile1, myfile2, myfile3)`.

*** D = the keyword is usable in Designer executables; R = the keyword is usable in Runtime executables; G = the keyword is usable in Generate executables.

CONCLUSION

The Oracle Forms application environment provides you with a powerful and comprehensive set of utilities for the creation and implementation of screen-based applications. These tools allow you to rapidly create forms and menus using Oracle Forms' default for block and trigger creation or to completely customize the form or menu to your requirements. Oracle Form's powerful default creation routines free you from having to code basic cursor movement, query behavior, security, and data commits. Instead, you can focus on the creation of event-driven processes using triggers and PL/SQL procedures.

After studying this chapter, you should understand the basic components of Oracle Forms, including the Layout Editor, Default Block Facility, and PL/SQL Program Units Browser. You should understand the functional concepts of context, navigation, and modality and how to create and manipulate objects such as buttons, check boxes, radio groups, and text items using both the Layout Editor and object property sheets.

You should have a good grasp of special features available in Oracle Forms, such as lists of values, alerts, editors, images, and record groups. The variations and intricacies of PL/SQL should be evident, and the use of procedures, functions, triggers, and libraries should be clear. You should have a basic grasp of the creation of menus and multiform applications using Oracle Forms, as well as of the integration of other CDE products into Oracle Forms modules. Finally, you should have a good idea how to launch effective Oracle Forms executable commands.

5 INTRODUCTION TO ORACLE REPORTS, VERSION 2.0

INTRODUCTION

Oracle Reports is a primary tool for creating, viewing, and printing high-quality reports. Using Oracle Reports, you can quickly and easily create reports of most any configuration and format, including master-detail reports, nested reports, form letters, matrix reports, and mailing labels. Oracle Reports includes powerful features that exploit the capabilities of the CDE, including the following:

- SQL for data retrieval;
- PL/SQL for conditional printing capabilities and packaged functions;
- support for a variety of colors, fonts, and graphic images;
- a data modeler for analysis of complex data relationships;
- a Layout Painter to format and structure the report; and
- a Previewer for quick testing and review of output.

Reports are constructed using three basic processes. First, you must open a new report definition by selecting the NEW REPORT command from the File menu, a somewhat similar process to making a forms module active in Oracle Forms. Next, you must define the data model, that is, the data elements, relationships, and values to populate the report. Finally, you should specify a report configuration, whether it be the Oracle Reports default or a customized layout.

Creating report modules with Oracle Forms is a straightforward process. Although Figure 5.1 shows the design process in a linear progression, developers can do much of the development, such as working in the Data Model Painter or Layout Painter, in any order they prefer.

Figure 5.1   Overview of Report Creation

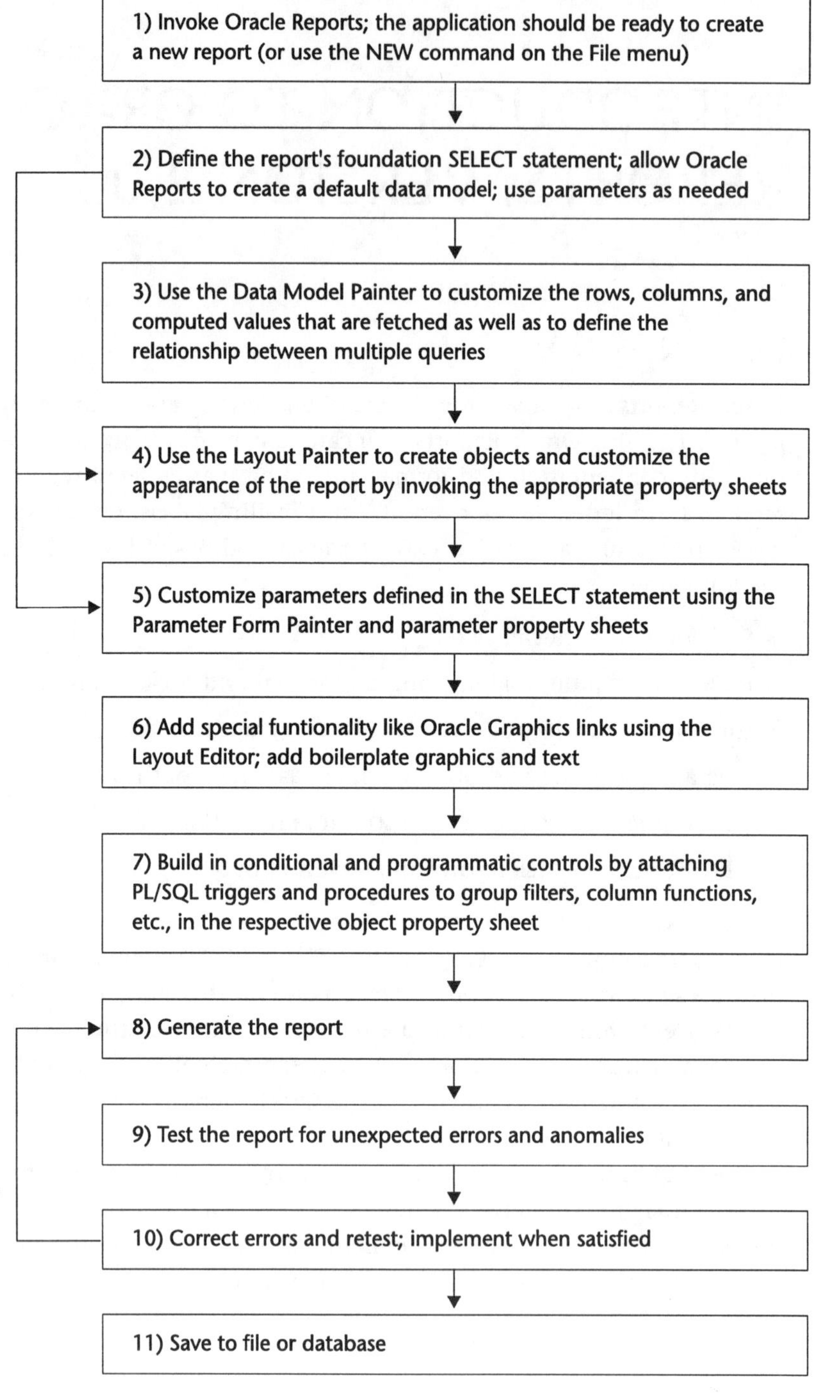

THE REPORT DATA MODEL

A report data model is the definition of the data elements that will compose the actual report. The report data model provides the definition for objects like queries, groups, columns, parameters, and links. Queries are simply the ANSI-standard SQL SELECT statements that fetch data from the database. A report can contain many queries, selecting data from many databases and from many machines.

Groups are a means used by Oracle Reports to break data up into logical sets, having an effect much like the SQL*Plus BREAK command. Oracle Reports automatically creates a default group for each query entered, but you can assign additional groups to a report. A column (the main building block of a group) represents the database columns pulled by the query's SELECT statement. Every column must be assigned to a group, either the default group assigned to the query or a custom group created by the developer. In addition, you can create additional columns that perform calculations or perform functions on other columns.

Parameters enable the developer to create flexible selection criteria and to alter the calculations or processing of a report at runtime. Parameters can be literal values in the query, like components of the WHERE clause, or can even replace entire expressions of the query, like the ORDER BY clause (thus allowing end-users to sort the report by the columns that they desire). Links create master-detail relationships between queries and groups through the use of matching columns. The developer can specify links as a standard join (column1 = column2) or as a specific SQL clause and arithmetic condition within the condition.

LAYING OUT THE REPORT COMPONENTS

Once the data model is defined, the developer can then tailor the appearance of the report using one of three methods. First, Oracle Reports provides six default layout styles for use by the developer: tabular, master-detail, form, form letter, mailing label, and matrix as shown in Figure 5.2. Second, the developer can use a default layout style, then modify it to specific needs. Third, the developer can create a completely customized report and modify any of its objects, including repeating frames, frames, fields, boilerplate, and anchors.

Figure 5.3 illustrates the components of a report. Repeating frames hold the records retrieved from the database and repeat as long as data is being

Figure 5.2 Default Report Layout Styles

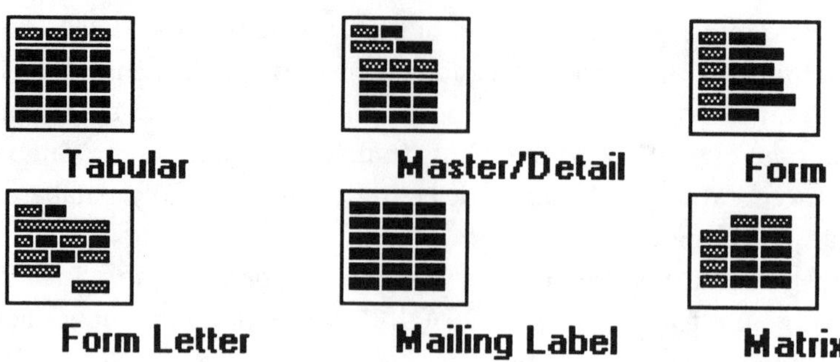

retrieved. Groups, assigned in the data model, appear in the layout as repeating frames. Frames are layout objects that enclose and control other layout objects. Thus, frames could be used to ensure that several objects always maintain their exact position relative to each other. Fields are essentially the data columns and their format definition. Fields are the common components of frames and repeating frames. Boilerplate, as in Oracle Forms, is the text and graphics that appear on the report whenever it is run without actually affecting the data retrieved by the report. Boilerplate includes field labels, drawn lines, or imported graphics (like a company logo). Anchors are used to attach objects of variable size to one another. Anchors ensure that an object always appears in its specified printing order and are especially useful for objects that might fluctuate in size.

OBJECT DEFINITIONS

Report objects, like Oracle Form objects, are defined and laid out using property sheets, painters, and tool palettes. Property sheets are dialogs that contain information detailing the behavior of specific objects. A different type of property sheet exists for each type of object used in Oracle Reports. Painters, such as the Data Model Painter, the Layout Painter (shown in Figure 5.4), or the Parameter Form Painter, are work areas that allow the developer to graphically manipulate the appearance of the report and its component objects.

Tool palettes, shown in Figure 5.5, contain the point-and-click painting tools that enable the creation and manipulation of report objects in a painter. Each type of tool appears as a distinct icon on the palette and is used to

Figure 5.3 Report Components

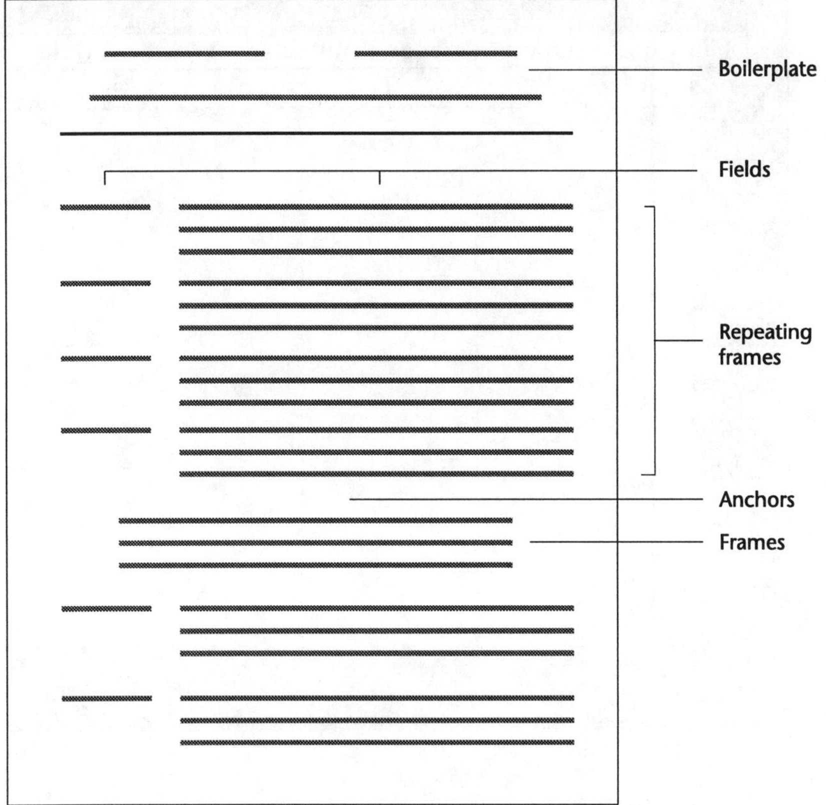

perform one specific function. To activate a tool for one function (until specifically deactivated), select the tool's icon and double-click.

REPORT FEATURES

Oracle Reports includes several features that make report writing as easy as possible, including intelligent defaulting procedures and an open architecture and development environment. Oracle Reports provides default capability creation, which is similar to Oracle Forms' automatic creation of triggers and procedures in master-detail relations. All the developer need specify is a SELECT statement and a default layout. Oracle Reports then creates the labels, columns, and report styling automatically. Oracle Reports' open archi-

Figure 5.4   The Layout Painter

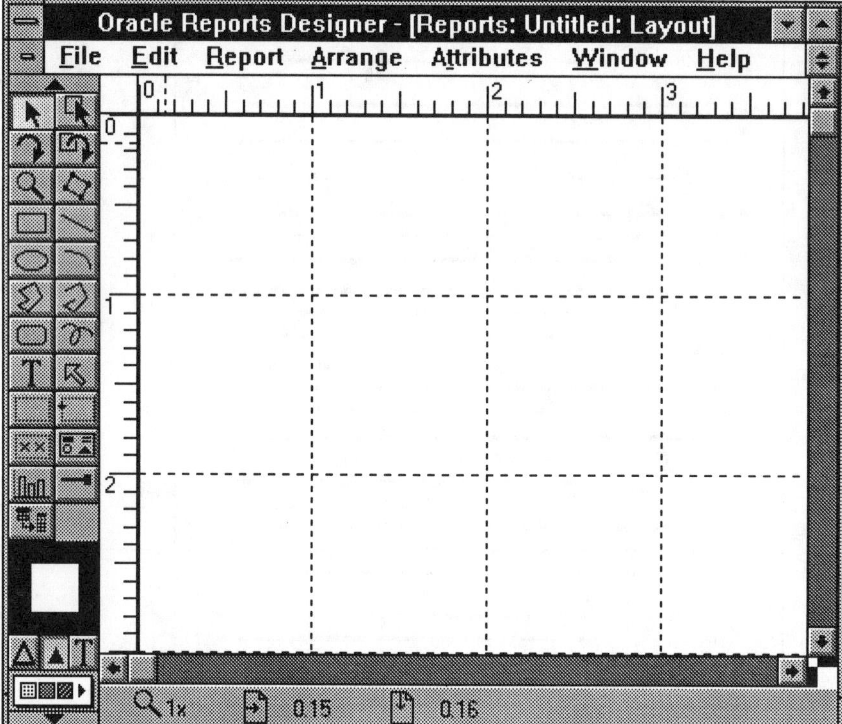

tecture allows the inclusion of PL/SQL code or even calls to 3GL programs (called user exits) without leaving Oracle Reports. In addition, Oracle Reports now provides a portable application-development environment so that reports created on one platform are portable across differing hardware, operating systems, and GUIs.

Oracle Reports is composed of two primary object categories: module objects and report-level objects. Within these object categories, each object type relates to a specific feature of a report; for instance, the query object represents the records and fields retrieved from the database in the report.

Module Objects

Oracle Reports module objects, different from Oracle Forms modules, are objects that can be used by one or many reports and even by other Oracle

Figure 5.5 The Tool Palettes

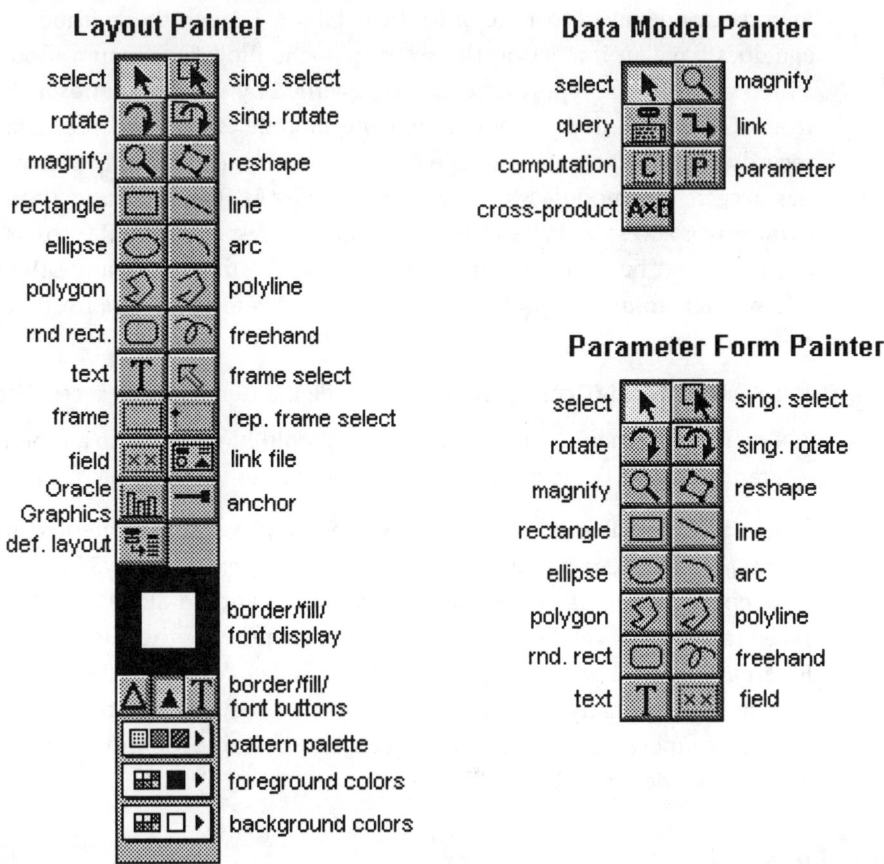

products. Oracle Reports modules could be reports, external queries, or PL/SQL external libraries (defined using Oracle Forms). Oracle Reports modules provide the same benefits as referenced objects in Oracle Forms, that is, quicker application development, because the capabilities built into a module can be written just once and used in many places, and ease of maintenance, because a change in the module is reflected in all the reports that reference it. Modules are initially created by using the NEW command on the File menu, then adding extra definition details such as the type and name of the module, etc. Modules can also be imported into a report without building a referential link using the IMPORT command from the Edit menu.

Saving and Generating Module Objects

Reports can be saved to a file or to the database, though the method of storage does have an impact on the security of the module. When a module is stored in a file, the report's security is governed by the commands and controls of the operating system. When the module is saved in the database, security rules of the database take precedence. Usually, the only person who has access to a module stored in the database is its owner and those the owner gives access to. When the owner grants access to a module, others may use the object but may not provide grants on the module to any others. To allow others to use a report, you add their names to the access list by doing the following:

1. Select the GRANT command from the File menu to call the access list.

2. Enter the usernames of the others who should have access to a module grant or delete those on the list whose privileges are to be revoked.

Just as Oracle Forms provides three module types (forms, menus, and libraries), so does Oracle Reports: external queries, external PL/SQL libraries, and reports. External queries are simply ANSI-standard SELECT statements saved to a file that can be used and reused in a report or other Oracle product. External PL/SQL libraries are also blocks of PL/SQL code saved in a file that can be used in many reports or other Oracle products. The report module type is composed of report-level objects and definitions, and references to external queries and PL/SQL libraries.

Report-Level Objects

Report-level objects are the individual building blocks of a report. They cannot be shared with other reports or by other Oracle products. Report-level objects might include a boilerplate object, such as a table, that appears in the report. They are created either by a default Oracle Reports process or specifically by the developer. They fall into one of three categories:

- data model objects: the rows, columns, and computed values fetched into the report;

- layout objects: the defining objects of the report's appearance; and

- parameter form objects: the defining objects of the Runtime Parameter Form's appearance, in which the user enters parameter values for the report.

The Report Object

There is only one object in a report definition that is not a report-level object: the report object itself. The report object defines the physical aspects of the report, such as its base unit of measure, its dimensions, and its major component sections.

UNITS OF MEASURE

A report's unit of measure is a scale that can be based on characters, picas/points, inches, or centimeters. All four units of measure are available in bit-mapped environments, though only the character scale is available in character-mode environments. However, unit of measure is device-independent, allowing the developer to create reports that run on any platform and printer that uses Oracle Reports version 2.0. Units of measure of a report can be changed by altering the Change Units setting in the Designer, using the R20CONV conversion utility, or even opening the report in an environment with a different default unit of measure, then saving the report.

DIMENSIONS

You can assign any length or width to a report, even if the report extends beyond the size of a single sheet of paper. Oracle Forms uses logical report definitions to establish the dimensions of a report. Thus, a report might be extra-wide, spreading across three physical pages (that is, pages printed out by the printer), though its logical definition shows only one very wide page. Keep in mind that margins must also surround each physical page of output.

COMPONENT SECTIONS

The major component sections of a report are the header, body/margin, and trailer. The report header is one or more physical pages at the beginning of the report showing important text, graphics, or data. The header is usually used as a declarative section, showing data such as the name of the report, who printed it, the date and time of printing, and perhaps a company logo. The body/margin section contains the meat of the report, displaying the primary informational text, graphics, data, and computations in positions relative to each other in the report's logical definition. Margins surround the body of the report on each physical page and can contain data of all sorts, such as headers and footers, dates, calculations, etc. Margins are definable only once in each report. The report trailer is printed at the end of the report

Figure 5.6 Physical and Logical Report Definition

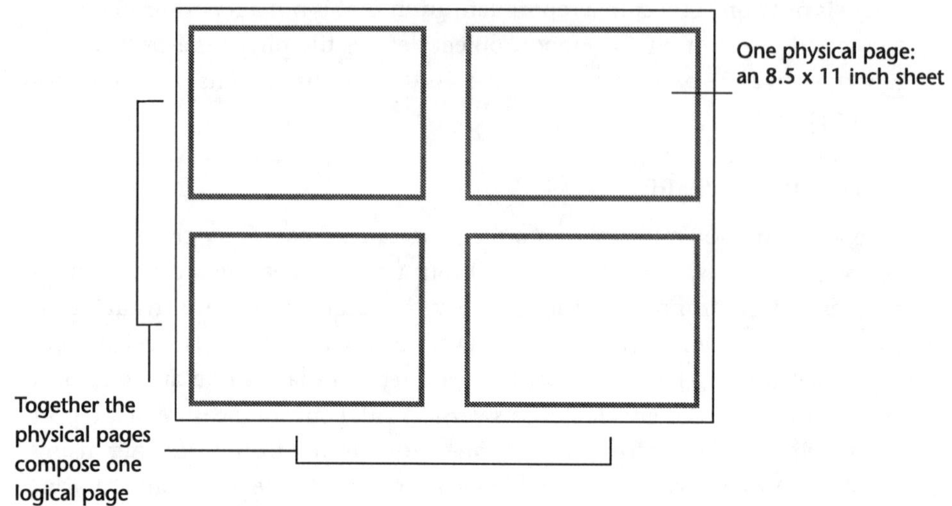

on one or more separate pages. As with the report header, the trailer can contain any information the developer desires. Figure 5.6 shows the physical and logical report definition.

DATA MODEL OBJECTS

Data models are used to graphically display the data and relationships used in a report. Oracle Reports includes a Data Model Painter to enable the developer to graphically construct report data models. The information shown in a data model might include the data retrieved from one or more local and remote databases and the data included by the developer. This information can be used in the report output, in calculations, or even to activate PL/SQL programs or user exits. Data model objects include queries, links, groups, columns, and parameters. For an example of a data model diagram, see Figure 5.7.

Queries

Queries are SQL SELECT statements that define the rows and columns to be retrieved into the report from one or more local or remote databases. They are available only in the report for which they were defined. For an example of a

Figure 5.7   Data Model Diagram

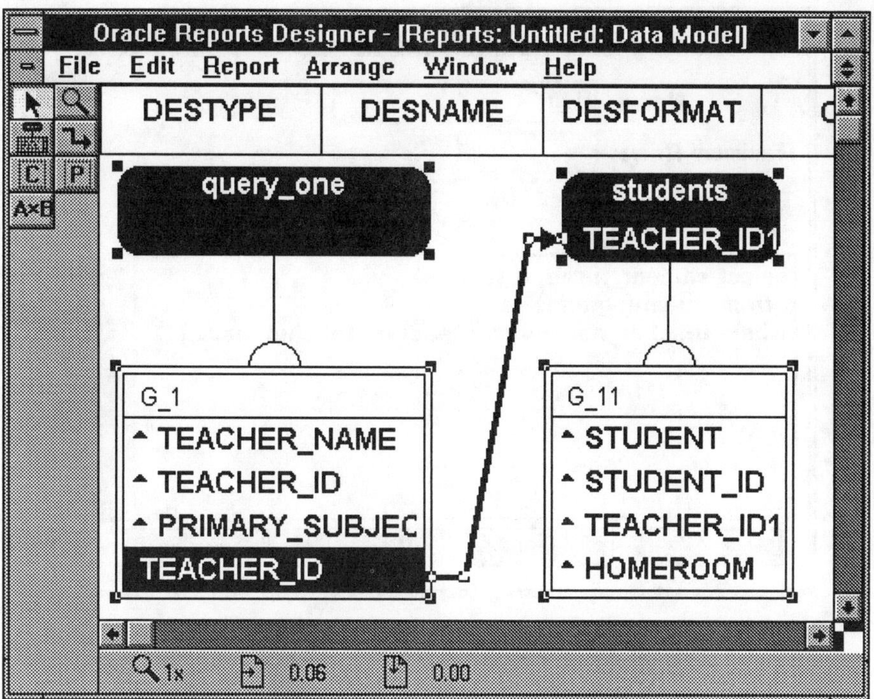

Query Property sheet, see Figure 5.8. Data model queries can use any SQL operation, including functions, set operators (like MINUS or UNION), and subqueries. Create a query in the Data Model Painter by doing the following:

1. Using the Query tool from the Tool palette, click in the painting region where the query object will be placed. The Query property sheet will appear. Modify an existing query object by double-clicking it.

2. Enter a SELECT statement in the multiline field on the Query property sheet, or enter the name of an external query to use. External queries can also be browsed using the List button. If an external query is used, it will appear in the multiline field as read-only.

3. Enter a unique name for the query in the Name field. Then, enter comments by clicking the Comment button or by embedding them in the query using the REM clause or comment delimiters (/* and */).

Figure 5.8   Query Property Sheet

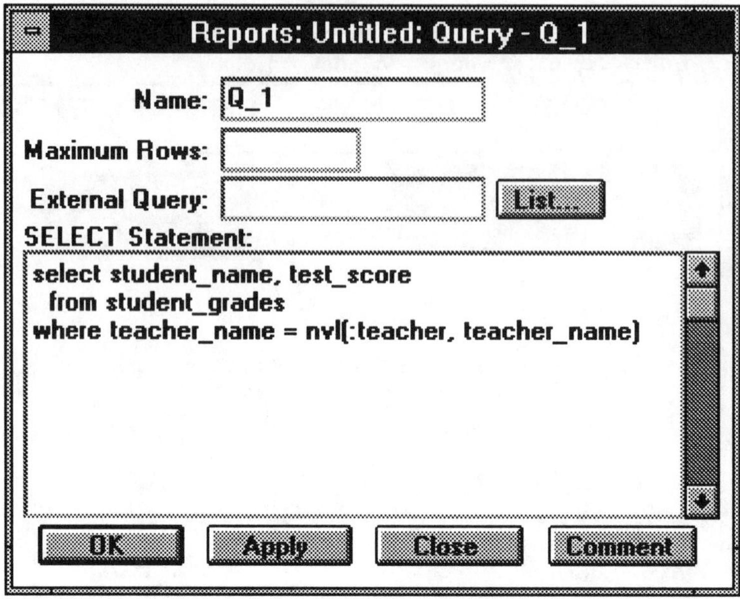

Queries are not necessary to create a report, but almost all reports have at least one query. When creating a report with a multitude of rows, you may find that the queries take a long time to execute and test. To speed testing, enter a small number (x) in the Maximum Rows field to restrict data retrieval to the first x rows retrieved.

A report with a single query is the easiest type of report to build and format. Single-query reports are usually formatted as tabular, mailing label, and form letter, as shown in Figure 5.2. However, reports can have any number of queries that may or may not be directly related to each other. Multiquery reports are useful for the following:

- multipart reports with unrelated bodies of data;

- multipart reports with related bodies of data;

- reports that have the same data sorted several different ways; and

- complex reports made simple by substituting a single, complex query with two or more simple queries linked together.

Multipart reports with unrelated bodies of data, or *master/master* reports,

Figure 5.9 Link Definition in the Data Model Painter

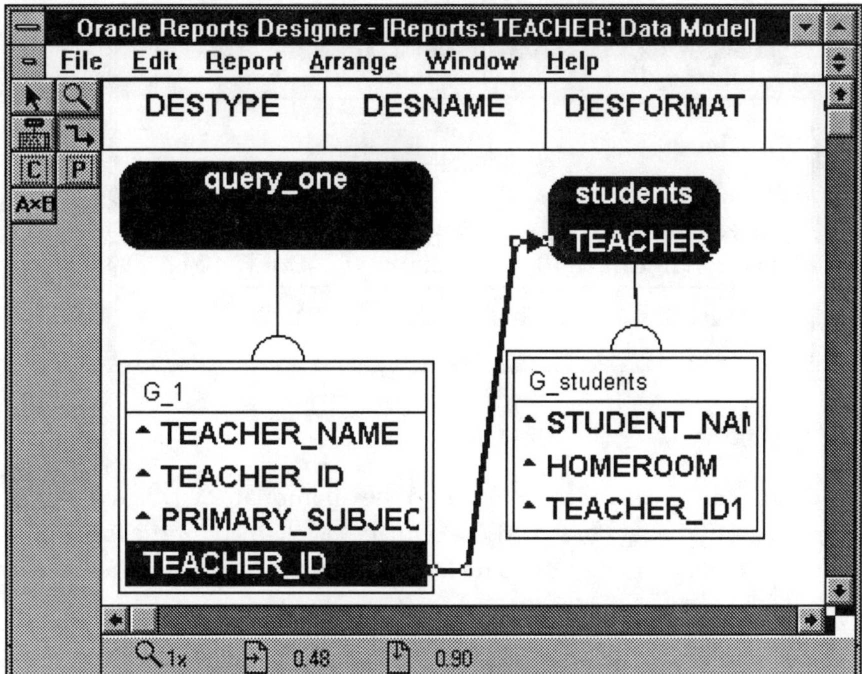

are used to display independent groups of data on the same report. For example, a report might select descriptions of teachers and of students, though the teachers and students are not linked to each other in any way.

Multipart reports with related bodies of data first fetch a *master*, or *parent*, record, then fetch the details that are dependent on the master. These *master/detail* (or sometime *parent/child*) reports are defined by creating two (or more) queries and one link between the queries. For example, a report showing a teacher and all of his or her students and their grades is a master/detail report with the teacher data acting as the master and the student data acting as the details.

Links

Links define the relationship of two or more SELECT statements, as is graphically displayed in Figure 5.9. A query can have many links, and queries can be linked to more than one other query. When you graphically create a link,

Figure 5.10 Link Property Sheet

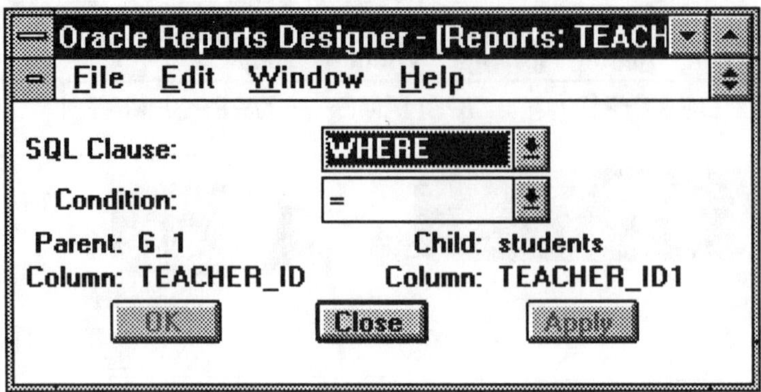

Oracle Forms converts the link into the appropriate SQL clauses to pull the correct child query based on the primary key defined for the link.

Links are created in the Data Model Painter by following these steps:

1. Using the Link tool on the Tool palette, click on the foreign or primary key in the master, then click on the foreign or primary key in a detail group. Or, quickly link the two groups without specifying the key by clicking the master, then the detail group. Double-click the link object to invoke its property sheet as shown in Figure 5.10.

2. Use the Link property sheet to enter the SQL conditions and operations, such as WHERE, HAVING, START WITH, etc.

Groups

Groups are useful objects that either filter the data displayed by a query or break the data into different sets. Filters may be one of two types: Oracle Reports packaged filters or custom filters. There are two packaged filters available, First and Last. The First package filter causes Reports to display only the first *x* number of records, while the Last package filter causes Reports to display only the last *x* records. Custom filters are blocks of PL/SQL code written by the developer to filter out data according to the needs of the report.

Break groups are useful for separating data into sets. Using Set Groups produces an effect similar to the BREAK command in SQL*Plus. For example, sets can be used to establish the position of calculated totals or to print the

Figure 5.11   Group Property Sheet

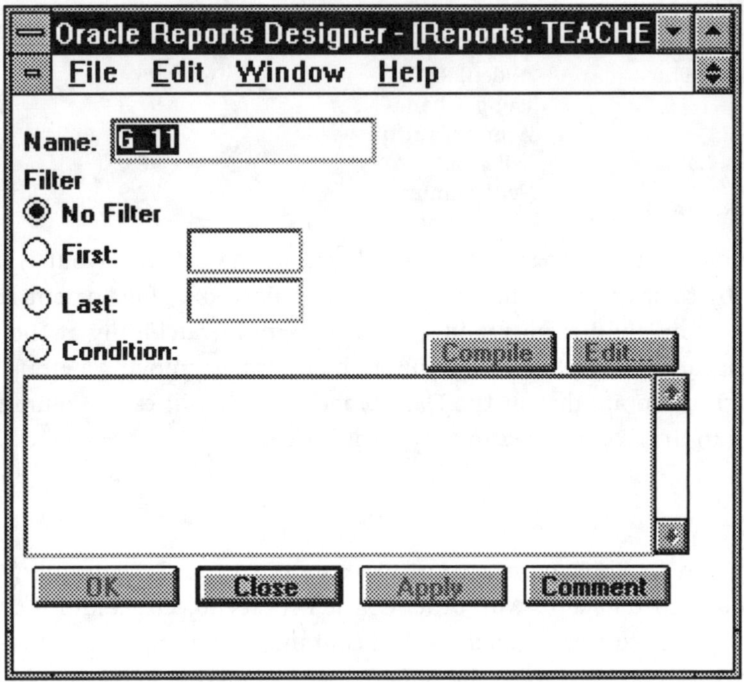

data into segregated groups. Set groups are divided into two types: default groups and custom groups. Default groups are generated by Oracle Reports as each query is created. Default groups automatically contain all the columns of a given query. Custom groups are used to produce breaks, to summarize data, or to create a matrix-style report. To create a custom group in the Data Model Painter, click on an existing column and drag it into a free region in the painter. The Group Property sheet, as shown in Figure 5.11, will appear.

Custom groups are usually subdivided into cross-product groups and break groups. Cross-product groups are used to create matrix-style reports and are covered more fully later in this chapter. Break groups, as stated before, segregate data into sets by an identical value that is printed one time as a header for the data's related records. For example, the honor roll shown in the following table is broken into break groups by assigning the Teacher_Name column to the break group, while leaving the other columns as part of the default group.

Teacher	*Student*	*Average*
Cheu, Karen	Brazelton, Terry	93.4
	Clanton, Nancy	91.7
	Schilb, Nick	94.0
Hernandez, Phil	Zaiden, Reid	96.4
	Tsung, Charles	97.8
	Wilson, Christy	95.0
Michaels, Lorna	Kelly, Pat	98.0
	Neuf, Gunter	92.9

The order in which groups are displayed in the default layout is determined by their order in the Default Layout dialog box. Thus, parent groups appear before child groups, and groups that are hierarchically at the same level appear from left to right, then top to bottom. So, moving a group from one position to another in the Data Model Painter will cause columns belonging to the group to be similarly displaced.

Columns

Columns in Oracle Reports act just like columns in a SQL*Plus query: they hold the fetched data. As with other Oracle Reports objects, columns may be default-type or custom-created. Default columns are automatically generated by Oracle Reports when a valid SELECT statement is entered. A column is assigned to each item selected by the query. Column datatypes and sizes default to the description stored in the database and are immediately assigned to the default group of the query where they originated.

One type of default column deserves special attention: the graphics column. Graphic columns retrieve graphics stored in the database, usually as a LONG or LONG RAW datatype. The Format settings of these graphics should be specified in the appropriate column's property sheet. Graphic columns can include pointers that specify graphic files stored in the operating system. In this case, the property sheet of the column should be set to Read From File in a specified format. In either case, Oracle Reports supports the BMP, CGM, JFIF, Oracle Graphics drawing, Oracle Graphics image, PCX, PICT, and TIFF image formats.

Custom-created columns are usually used to display computed values such as a column for sales tax. Custom columns can be created in the Data Model Painter by selecting the Computation tool from the Tool palette, then clicking on a group to attach the new column to a specific group or by clicking on an open area of the report to create a report-owned column. Double-click the

Figure 5.12 The Column Property Sheet

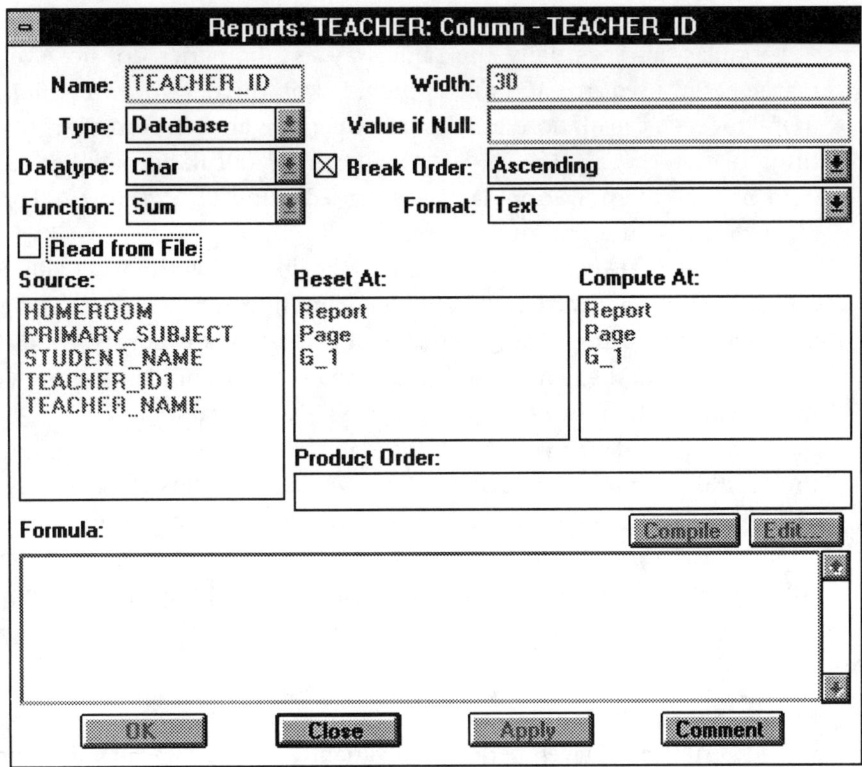

column to call its property sheet (as shown in Figure 5.12) and define its settings.

Custom columns fall into one of four categories: summaries, formulas, placeholders, and graphics columns (as described earlier). Oracle Reports provides summaries, defined in the Function field of the Column property sheet, to calculate values for a column, including the following:

Average	Standard Deviation
Minimum	Last
Count	Sum
% of Total	Maximum
First	Variance

In addition, summaries can further be broken down into running variations (like running totals or running percents) by setting the Reset at Field value to 0. Running variations are not available for First and Last summaries.

Formulas act essentially the same way as summaries do; however, the mathematics used in a formula is provided by the developer. Formulas are useful for such calculations as sales tax or perhaps an overhead charge (something like `:service_fee * 1.26`), where the calculation applies to each item in the column. Formulas are recorded using PL/SQL in the Formula block of the Column property sheet.

Placeholders are columns that merely take up space without actually fetching data from the database. Placeholder columns can be conditionally populated with data using PL/SQL. Thus, you can apply any sort of conditional operation you desire. For example, you can use a placeholder to show a commission only when the salesperson reaches his or her quota.

As with precedence within groups, column precedence is determined by the position of the column in the Data Model. Columns are generally read into the report from the top to bottom of the group. That is, the column that appears at the top within the group appears first on the report. Moving a column within its group reshuffles the order of all columns in the group.

Parameters

Parameters are system- and developer-defined variables whose values are assigned at runtime. Developer-defined variables, either *bind parameters* or *lexical parameters*, are especially useful in the selection of the Query object and in blocks of PL/SQL code. Both system parameters and custom parameters can be specified at the command line or by entering them in the Runtime Parameter Form when a report is called interactively. Additionally, both types of parameters can be assigned default values in the Parameter property sheet.

Oracle Reports provides several system parameters that affect the basic behavior of any report. The system parameters are described in Table 5.1.

Custom parameters are created in the Data Model Painter by first selecting the Parameter tool from the Tool palette. Click in an open area of the painter to create the parameter, then double-click the parameter to call its property sheet. Use the Parameter property sheet, as shown in Figure 5.13, to specify the exact details of the parameter's definition.

Note that bind and lexical parameters differ both in how they appear in Oracle Forms and in how they are used. Bind parameters, marked with a colon (:), are used to substitute a single column value or expression in a SELECT statement. For example,

Table 5.1   System Parameters

Parameter	Usage
destype	The type of report output, including file, printer, mail, or screen in PostScript format.
desname	Name of the destype output device, such as a printer's name or mail user ID.
desformat	The definition of the output (such as landscape or portrait) for character-mode environments.
copies	Number of copies to print.
currency	Currency symbol; the dollar sign ($) by default.
thousands	Thousands symbol; the comma (,) by default.
decimal	Decimal indicator; the period (.) by default.

```
select * from student_attendance where grade = :student_grade;
```

Whenever the report is run, the user can choose what grade level of students to check. Queries containing bind references are parsed for errors just once but are reevaluated each time the report is run. Lexical parameters, designated with an ampersand (&), are used to substitute entire clauses within a given SELECT statement. Unlike bind parameters, lexical parameters must be assigned a valid default value in the Parameter property sheet. They can then be referenced in queries. For example,

```
select * from student_attendance &WHERE_CLAUSE;
```

In this example, the user could run the report once and set the &WHERE_CLAUSE equal to the following:

```
where homeroom_teacher like 'HERNANDEZ%'
```

Then the user could run the same report later using the following:

```
where student_name like 'ANDERSON%'
```

CUSTOMIZING LAYOUT OBJECTS

Layout objects are used to control the appearance of a report. They determine the positioning and appearance of a report's data and boilerplate. In many cases, layout objects are used to design and control the appearance of the

Figure 5.13 Parameter Property Sheet

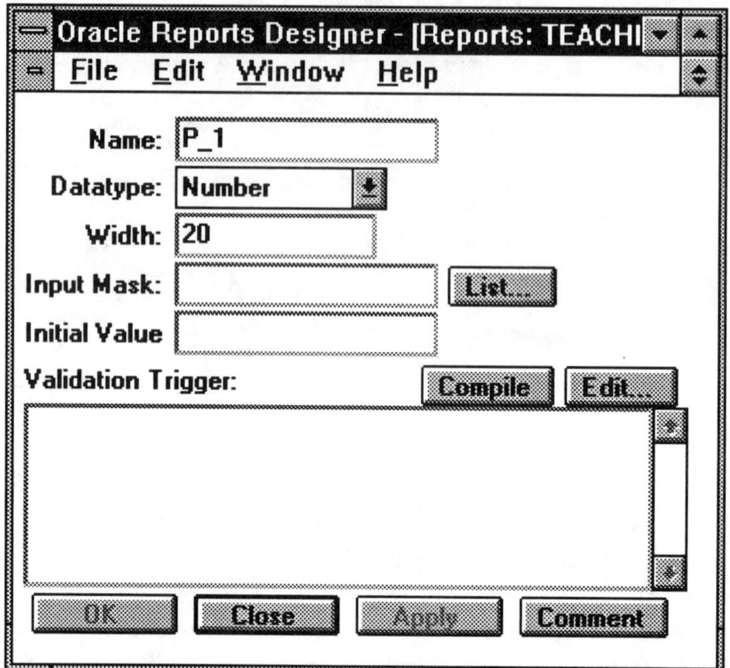

report but do not actually appear in the report themselves. There are six types of Layout objects: repeating frames, frames, fields, boilerplate, anchors, and matrix objects. Layout objects that do not actually appear in the report output include frames, repeating frames, and anchors.

Repeating Frames

Repeating frames act as placeholders for records, printing one time for each record in the group. Repeating frames define record-level information, like the print direction of the record (Down, Across, Down/Across, etc.) and the amount of space between records and columns. Repeating frames can even be nested one within another, usually to produce some sort of master/detail report. The display attributes of a repeating frame can also be altered using a PL/SQL format trigger and the PL/SQL packaged procedure SRW.SET_ATTR.

Repeating frames can be defined as expandable, contractible, variable, or

Figure 5.14 Repeating Frame Property Sheet

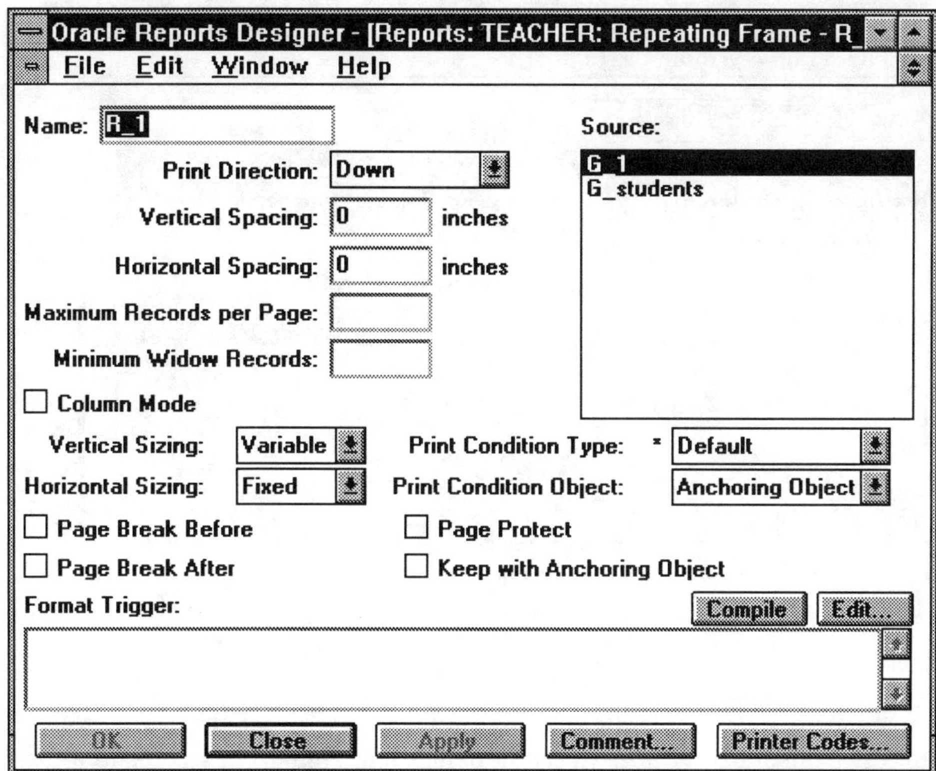

fixed horizontally or vertically. So, a repeating frame could expand vertically to print many records but, at the same time, retain a fixed horizontal length. Expandable repeating frames have a defined minimum size but can grow to show all the data held in the frame. Contractible repeating frames have a defined maximum size but can shrink if less data is held in the frame. Variable repeating frames can expand and contract freely, depending on the amount of data returned. Repeating frames of fixed size print data that exceeds the defined limits onto the following pages with the same x- and y-coordinates.

Repeating frame objects are created in the Layout Painter using the Repeating Frame tool. Double-click the repeating frame object to call its property sheet, as shown in Figure 5.14, and modify its definition as desired.

Figure 5.15   Frame Property Sheet

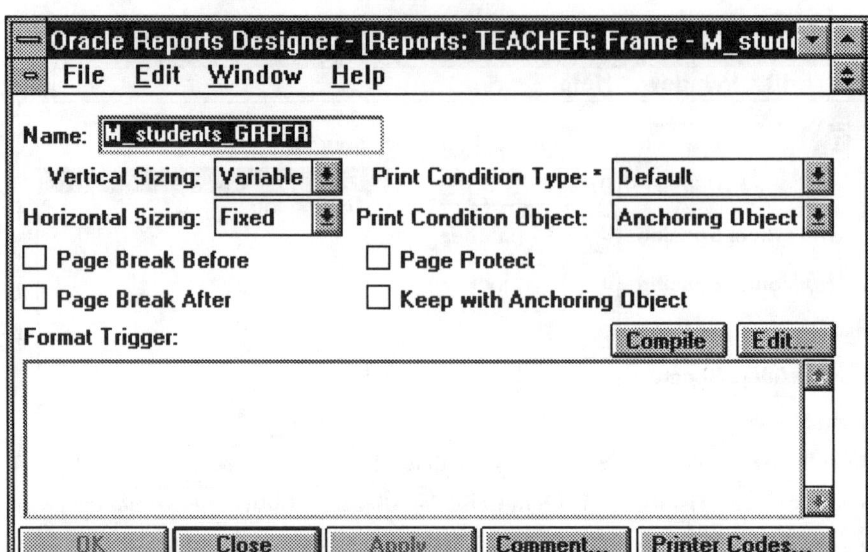

Frames

Frames share some similarity with repeating frames except that they are linked to individual records; repeating frames link a group of records to a page. Frames print as often as their enclosing or attached object, though the printing frequency can be modified on the frame property sheet. Frames are similar to repeating frames in definition and configuration. Oracle Reports automatically creates frames around objects, such as summary fields and boilerplate, when the default layout is being used. You can create frames to ensure that objects maintain their relative positions in a group during printing or to delineate sections in your report.

Use the Frame tool in the Layout Painter to create a frame object by clicking once in an open area of the painter. Modify its definition and invoke the frame property sheet, shown in Figure 5.15, by double-clicking on the frame.

Fields

Parameters and columns are stored in Oracle Reports fields. Field definitions control the display attributes and conditional logic for a field's contents. Col-

Figure 5.16 Field Property Sheet

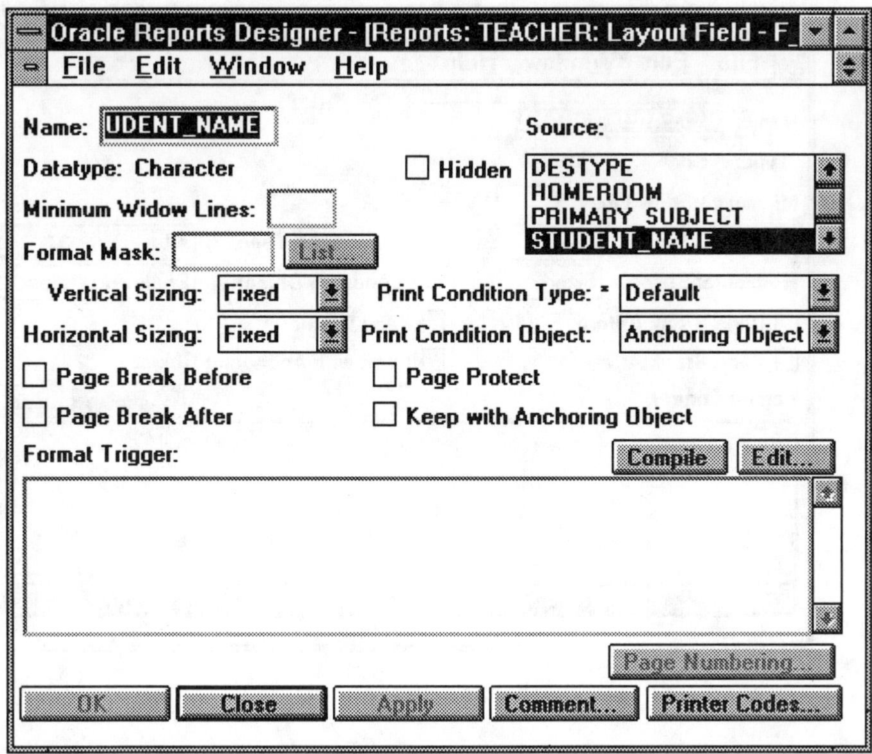

umns are parameters that do not have a field and are not printed with the report's output. By default, Oracle Reports creates one field for each column and puts the field in a repeating frame. The developer can control formatting attributes and field logic either through the repeating frame or through each field, as shown in the field property sheet represented by Figure 5.16.

Field-display attributes include justification (how the data should be placed), format mask (how numeric, date, and character data should look), and display attributes (coloring, fonts, style, and spacing). Data within a frame can be centered, left, right, flush-left (justified), flush-right (justified), or center-justified. Format masks control how numeric, date, and character data is displayed. For instance, a number format mask might show "$123,456.00," a date format mask might show "10/28/95" or "October the 25th, 1995," and a character format mask might show "ALL CAPS" or "lower-

Figure 5.17   Boilerplate Property Sheet

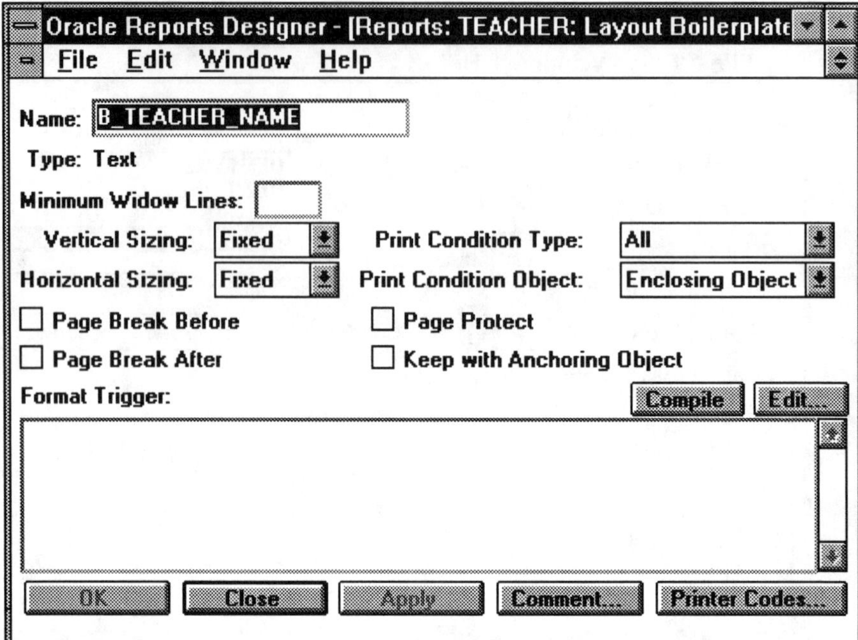

case." You can also attach format triggers to a specific field. Create a field using the Field tool to click in any open area of the Layout Painter. Call the specific field's property sheet by double-clicking on the field object.

Boilerplate

Boilerplate is the text, lines, and graphics that serve as labels and appear whether data is printed or not. Hence, boilerplate is often called *constant text* or even just a *label*. Oracle Reports creates default column labels from the name of the column pulled in the query's SELECT statement.

Boilerplate objects can be created in the Layout Painter in any open area. Tools available to create boilerplate objects include the Arc, the Polygon, the Ellipse, the Polyline, the Freehand, the Rectangle, the Line, the Rounded Rectangle, the Link File, and the Text tools. Existing boilerplate items can be modified by double-clicking the objects to display their property sheets, as shown in Figure 5.17, then altering their settings as needed.

Figure 5.18 Anchor Property Sheet

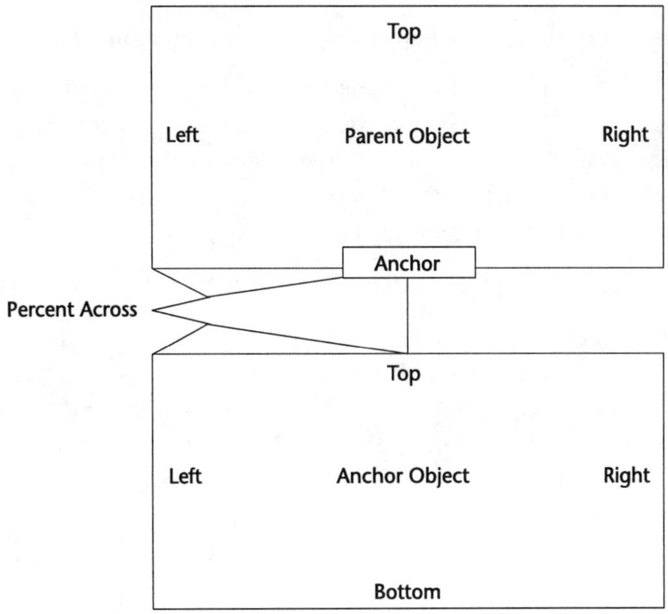

Anchors

Anchor objects maintain the relative positioning of all objects in a report's output. Anchors attach layout objects to each other, defining the order in which objects print and the vertical and horizontal space between objects. Because anchors establish relative distance, anchor settings are expressed as a percentage of the distance from the object's edge and from the object's parent. Anchors are divided into two types: *implicit anchors* created by Oracle Reports default utilities or *explicit anchors* created by the developer.

Implicit anchors, invisible in the Layout Painter, are automatically generated at runtime for each object. They prevent objects from overwriting each other. Explicit anchors, usually visible in the Layout Painter, must be attached by the child object to the parent object, in that specific order. Do not draw the anchor from the parent object to the child; draw from the child object to the parent.

Anchors are essential in establishing the relative positioning of groups on the report page. The x- and y-coordinate settings of the anchor, shown in Figure 5.18, are extremely important when anchoring a child object to a specific parent object. Consequently, there are several rules to remember when placing anchors. For objects whose parent object is above or below:

- The vertical distance between the two objects is fixed and constant.

- The horizontal positioning depends on the placement of the anchor, relative to the parent. For example, if a parent object's anchor is 50% from the edge (that is, at the center of the object) and the child object's anchor is 75% from its left edge, the child object will be 25% to the left of center on the parent object.

For objects whose parent object is to the right or left:

- Vertical distance between the parent and child object is relative. Since an object can have a variable length (that is, the report object might be based on a query that retrieves 10 or 100 rows depending on how it was executed), Oracle Reports first checks the actual length of the objects, then positions the objects at the anchor setting established for them in the Layout Painter.

- Horizontal distance between the two objects is fixed and constant.

For objects outside a repeating frame or regular frame:

- Create an anchor that is attached to an object inside the repeating frame or regular frame.

Avoid large areas of empty space in a report by creating *collapsing anchors*. Collapsing anchors cause child objects to move into the empty space that was allocated for a parent, while the child object maintains its position relative to the parent.

This is especially useful when a parent object might not be printed, when the parent and child appear on separate pages, or when a Print Condition is set between the two objects. Anchors can collapse horizontally, vertically, or both. Anchors are created in the Layout Painter by clicking the Anchor tool in an open area. An anchor setting can be established and modified by double-clicking the anchor object and calling its property sheet.

SPECIAL EFFECTS FOR REPORT LAYOUTS

There are a number of settings that can be applied to layout objects to produce special effects, including print condition, column mode, keep with anchoring object, page protection, format triggers, and layout definitions.

The setting Print Condition tells Oracle Reports when an object should print, relative to the printing of its parent, although other settings (such as Format Trigger) can override the Print Condition setting. Objects can be given one of several different settings to control printing:

- *All* prints an object, such as column headings, on all printed pages where the parent prints.

- *All But First* prints an object on all pages where the parent prints except the first logical page of the report, for example, page numbering that should appear only on the second and subsequent pages of a report.

- *All But Last* prints an object on all pages where the parent prints except the last logical page of the report, for example, an end-of-page summary replaced by an end-of-report summary on the last page.

- *Default* tells Oracle Reports to determine which condition to use.

- *First* prints an object on the first logical page where the parent object prints, for example, column labels that only appear once.

- *Last* prints an object on the last logical page where the parent object appears, as in a summary or group footer.

Column Mode is a setting that ensures the maintenance of space used by a repeating frame, even when it is empty. That is, when a column is empty, other groups will not move over and print in its space. For example, a report has three columns: ColumnA, ColumnB, and ColumnC. If ColumnB were to be empty, normally ColumnC would print in its space. However, with Column Mode turned on, ColumnC will print in its predefined position, even though ColumnB is empty.

The setting Keep with Anchoring Object ensures that a parent object always stays with its child object, even if it must bump down to a new page to do so. If the child object cannot appear on the current page, then the parent and child will both be printed on the next page. This setting works best when explicit anchors are defined between the objects, though implicit anchors are acceptable. When used with repeating frames, the objects are encapsulated for one record of the repeating frame. When used with a regular frame, all objects within the frame are encapsulated, including any subordinate repeating frames.

Page Protect sets all objects in a frame or repeating frame in order to keep them together on the same logical page wherever possible. If the objects cannot appear on the same page, Oracle Reports allows them to span multiple

Figure 5.19   Format Trigger

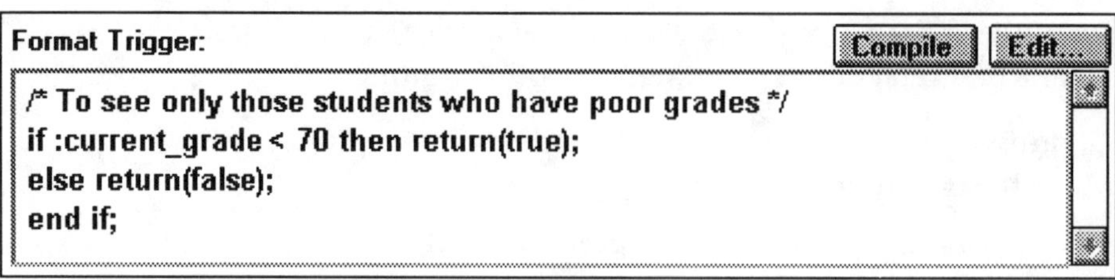

pages. This setting is useful for keeping groups of distinct data from appearing on the same page. For example, a break report showing teachers and their students could be split between pages, unless Page Protect was turned on. With Page Protect set on for teacher, the teacher and all related student records would always appear on the same page. When used with repeating frames, the objects are protected for one record of the repeating frame. When used with a regular frame, all objects within the frame are protected, including any subordinate repeating frames.

A format trigger, as shown in Figure 5.19, is a block of PL/SQL code that executes whenever the specified object is formatted. Format triggers are very useful for controlling conditional printing based on criteria supplied by the developer. For example, a format trigger could be used to display a field in boldface type whenever a student's grade drops dangerously low. Format triggers can alter a number of format attributes for a specific object, including the following:

- border pattern and color;
- interior pattern and color;
- font size, style, weight, spacing, and justification;
- format mask;
- character-mode attributes, such as highlighting; and
- access to a field's value.

The ability to link actions to a specific database value enables you to design extremely flexible reports, where one report can serve several different uses conditionally based on the values retrieved.

When designing the report, you need to remember the difference between the default report layout and an edited report layout. Default layouts can be used "as-is," or they can be customized, disregarded in favor of a custom design, or edited. Oracle Reports includes six default report styles: tabular, mailing label, form (across report), form letter, master/detail, and matrix. To create a default layout, follow these steps:

1. Select the DEFAULT LAYOUT command from the Report menu to call the Default Layout dialog box.

2. Select the preferred style and settings for the report.

3. Click OK to accept the definition and dismiss the dialog box.

After choosing a default report layout, Oracle Reports builds the necessary objects based on the report's data model and automatically places them based on the default layout. From there a developer can customize the report completely. Small touches can be added to the report, such as headings, added graphics, or text, or the developer can use the CUT, COPY, PASTE, MOVE, RESIZE, and EDIT commands to completely alter the default report layout. Alternately, the developer can go directly to the Layout Painter (without choosing a default style) and create all of the objects manually.

When using default report layouts, remember that previously defined layout objects are overwritten by default objects, unless the developer specifies that the new default objects should be created in a layout area different from the one used by the defined objects. Also note that one report can have many formats, such as a report with a tabular format on the first page and a matrix on the second.

Once a developer has established a data model and specified a report format, additional changes to the report's data model must be manually updated in the layout. For instance, if the developer adds a column to the report's query after the report layout was created, the new column will not appear on the report. The report layout must be edited to incorporate the new changes. If the changes are small, it is simpler to redefault the report, and thus re-create the report with changes intact. If the changes are numerous or extensive, add a new default style separate from the preexisting layout.

CUSTOMIZING PARAMETER FORM OBJECTS

When a report is run, a window called the Runtime Parameter Form will appear, which allows the user to enter optional information used by the report, such as a sort criterion for a query's SELECT statement, a specified

Figure 5.20   Sample Runtime Parameter Form

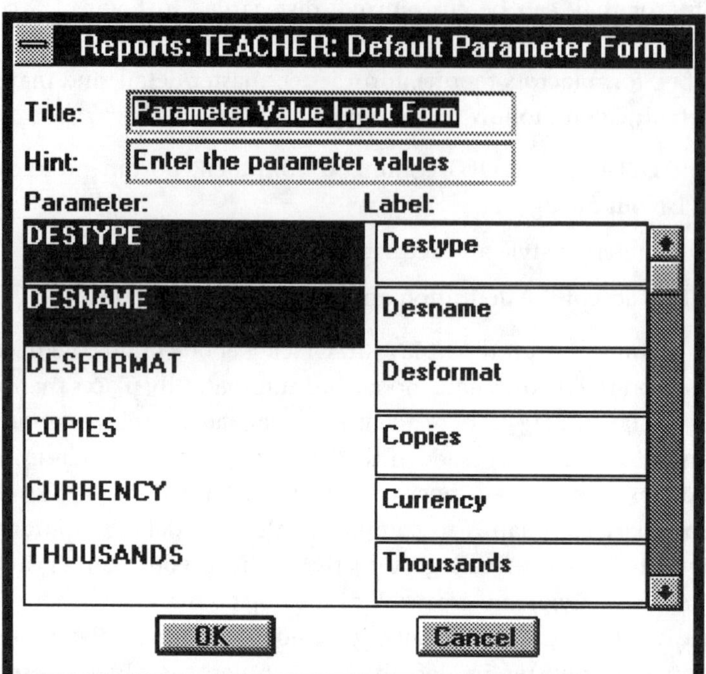

printer route or output device, or even a national language type. The Run-time Parameter Form can be custom-designed using fields and boilerplate, as shown in Figure 5.20, or it can be automatically created by Oracle Reports.

A field in the parameter form acts as an interactive prompt for data entry from the report user. A field represents a single specific report parameter and is created automatically by the Oracle Reports default Runtime Parameter Form build process. Runtime Parameter Form boilerplate procedure is the same as in the Layout Painter. It may be text or graphics provided by Oracle Reports' default procedure or custom-designed by the developer.

As with the layout of the report, you can choose the default parameter form style (there is only one style to choose), customize the default, or develop your own. Build a default parameter form by selecting the DEFAULT PARAMETER FORM command from the Report menu. Oracle Reports will create a default parameter form, based upon the definitions in the report's data model and incorporating any developer-defined variables, such as fields of the parameter form. Oracle Reports will also create a default parameter form at runtime, if the developer has not already done so.

USING PL/SQL WITH A REPORT

Oracle Reports is fully compatible with PL/SQL. Wherever conditional processing is needed in a report, PL/SQL code can accomplish the task. For example, PL/SQL code could modify report output whenever unexpected values were retrieved or could substitute a conditional parameter depending on the data to be fetched at the time. PL/SQL code can be included in a report in two ways:

- Via an external PL/SQL library, to which the report makes calls.

- Via internal report-level PL/SQL programs (such as format triggers or PL/SQL computations for specific columns).

External PL/SQL Libraries

External PL/SQL libraries are functions and procedures created and stored outside the report. As such, external libraries are specifically designed to be accessible and usable in many different Oracle products and applications. Typically, external PL/SQL libraries are sets of named functions and procedures that may or may not be logically related. Although libraries can be created in other products, you can create a library in Oracle Reports by performing the following steps:

1. Select the NEW command from the File menu, then select the EXTERNAL PL/SQL LIBRARIES command to display the Library Contents List. The Library Contents List shows all the procedures and functions stored in the current library, allowing the developer to modify or remove them as needed. The list is empty if none have been created.

2. Click NEW to call the PL/SQL Editor (as discussed in chapter 4). Enter the function or procedure, then click COMPILE. As the code is compiled, Oracle Reports checks for errors. The Compilation Messages portion of the Editor will display an error message as errors are encountered. Correct the errors, then click COMPILE again. Repeat until the code is free of bugs, then click OK to accept the routine. The Library Contents List will reappear, showing the name of the new function or procedure.

3. Select the SAVE or SAVE AS command from the File menu to name the

library and save it to the database or to a file, then select the CLOSE command from the File menu to dismiss the Library Contents List.

Now all the routines contained in the library are available to be referenced by any report objects accessible to the developer, as well as by several other Oracle products. To take advantage of a PL/SQL library, though, the library must be attached to the report. Attach a library to a report by doing the following:

1. In an active report, select the ATTACHED LIBRARIES command from the Report menu to call the Attached Libraries list. This list displays all the external PL/SQL libraries currently referenced in the report.

2. Click List to select the library to be attached. Click OK in the File dialog box to redisplay the Attached Libraries list, then click ADD to attach the library. When ready, click OK to accept the Attached Libraries list.

External PL/SQL Packages

External PL/SQL packages are groups of logically related PL/SQL types, objects, functions, and procedures. Packages are divided into package specifications and the package body. The main power of a package is its ability to create and pass global variables between different Oracle products. In Oracle Reports, packages are created as external PL/SQL libraries, except that the package specification, rather than library specifications, should be entered into the PL/SQL Editor. Then, save packages as regular entries in the library.

Oracle Reports is shipped with the SRW package, which contains the functions, procedures, and exceptions available to all reports, as shown in Table 5.2. SRW enables the alteration of field formats by running reports from within other reports, creating customized error messages, executing SQL statements, and other powerful functions. SRW does not have to be attached to be used, but SRW is available only within Oracle Reports.

Report-Level PL/SQL Routines

Report-level PL/SQL functions and procedures can be referenced from within a group, column, frame, repeating frame, field, boilerplate, parameter, or report trigger. Report-level PL/SQL code can be created using the appropriate property sheet or by selecting the PL/SQL command from the report menu (for creating a named function or procedure to be referenced in the appropriate property sheet).

Table 5.2 The SRW Package

Procedures/Function	*Usage*
srw.break	Suspends report temporarily but maintains display of all columns and parameters.
srw.do_sql	Executes a SQL DDL or DML statement within Oracle Reports.
srw.geterr_run	Fetches error messages encountered during the execution of srw.run_report.
srw.get_page_num	Fetches the current page number.
srw.message	Shows a message with the specified message number and text.
srw.reference	Appends the referenced object to the PL/SQL program's dependency list.
srw.run_report	Issues R20RUN command with any specified parameters.
srw.set_attr	Applies display attributes to the specified report object.
srw.set_field_<object>	Sets the value of a Char, Date, or Num field.
srw.set_maxrow	Sets a maximum limit on the number of rows returned by the query.
srw.user_exit	Invokes the specified user exit.

Exceptions	*Usage*
srw.context_failure	Raised when a package is called in the wrong context.
srw.do_sql_failure	Raised when srw.do_sql fails.
srw.integer_error	Raised when srw.message or srw.set_maxrow is called with a noninteger.
srw.maxrow_inerr	Raised when srw.set_maxrow encounters an internal error.
srw.maxrow_unset	Raised when srw.set_maxrow executes after the records have been retrieved.
srw.null_arguments	Raised when a block PL/SQL code is called with a null argument and an argument is required.
srw.program_abort	Aborts report execution when called by the PL/SQL program.
srw.run_report_batchno	Raised when srw.run_report contains string BATCH=NO.
srw.run_report_failure	Raised when srw.run_report fails.
srw.truncated_value	Raised when a user exits or the PL/SQL program assigns a value larger than is acceptable.
srw.unknown_query	Raised when srw.set_maxrow encounters an unknown or undefined query.
srw.unknown_user_exit	Raised when srw.user_exit cannot locate the specified user exit.
srw.user_exit_failure	Raised when the user exit failed.

GROUPS

Within a group, PL/SQL code is typically used to filter results. Oracle Reports provides the First and Last filters but allows developers to customize their own. Custom filters are created in the Group property sheet. Remember that filters do not reduce the amount of data returned by a query—that must be done through the query's WHERE clause—only the number of rows printed.

COLUMNS

Columns can contain PL/SQL formulas, which enable customized computations, and placeholders, which enable printing of fixed or predefined values. Column formulas and placeholders are defined in the Formula field found in the Column property sheet. Note that formulas and placeholders can be assigned only to custom-created columns, not default columns.

FRAMES, REPEATING FRAMES, FIELDS, AND BOILERPLATES

Oracle Reports objects can possess triggers that enable the developer to conditionally constrain (or even suppress) the appearance of data contained within these layout objects. Format triggers are created in the Format Trigger field of the appropriate layout object's property sheet.

VALIDATION TRIGGERS

Validation triggers test the parameter values entered in a Runtime Parameter Form. Oracle Reports stops processing according to the developer's specifications whenever an invalid entry is made. Validation triggers are created by entering the appropriate PL/SQL code in the Validation Trigger field on the parameter's property sheet.

REPORT TRIGGERS

Report triggers check the status of an object or change the logic of the report. They are created by selecting the TRIGGERS command from the Report menu, then choosing the specific type of report trigger. As with Oracle Forms, Oracle Reports triggers are event-driven and respond to a specific event in the report. You can attach a PL/SQL procedure, function, or package to these report events by issuing the appropriate Trigger command on the Report menu: BEFORE REPORT, AFTER REPORT, BETWEEN PAGE, BEFORE FORM, and AFTER FORM. After choosing the trigger, enter the PL/SQL code in the

Source Text field of the report trigger's property sheet. For example, you might want a BETWEEN PAGE trigger that calls the SRW.MESSAGE built-in at the end of each page to alert the user that a student had an exceptionally high or low grade.

CUSTOMIZING OBJECTS USING THE ORACLE REPORTS PAINTERS

Oracle Reports painters are work areas very similar to the Layout Editor found in Oracle Forms. Oracle Reports contains the Data Model Painter, the Layout Painter, and the Parameter Form Painter. When Oracle Reports is first invoked, the Data Model Painter and the Layout Painter are activated. Each painter can be invoked individually by issuing the appropriate command from the Report menu.

In these work areas, the developer can create, modify, and delete objects by manipulating their icons and/or adjusting settings in their property sheets. In general, an object is created in a painter by selecting the appropriate object tool and clicking in an open region of the painter. The object can then be modified through its property sheet. Note that clicking the object tool activates that tool for the next operation only. To make a tool active until replaced by another tool, double-click the appropriate tool icon. Additionally, objects can be deleted, cut, copied, and pasted using the appropriate command on the Edit menu. Objects can be resized by clicking the edge of the object and dragging to the desired size.

The Data Model Painter

The Data Model Painter, as shown in Figure 5.21, is used to create or modify the report's data model. You can select data, define data relationships, and perform computations on database values from the Data Model Painter.

The data model serves as the basis for retrieving and relating data from the database in order to produce a workable report. In most cases, the Data Model Painter is used to create data model objects, but the property sheets of the objects are used to do alterations and modifications. Table 5.3 describes all of the Data Model Painter tools and their various functions.

The Layout Painter

The Layout Painter, shown in Figure 5.4, is used to create or modify the report's format appearance by adding or modifying layout objects using the

Figure 5.21   The Data Model Painter

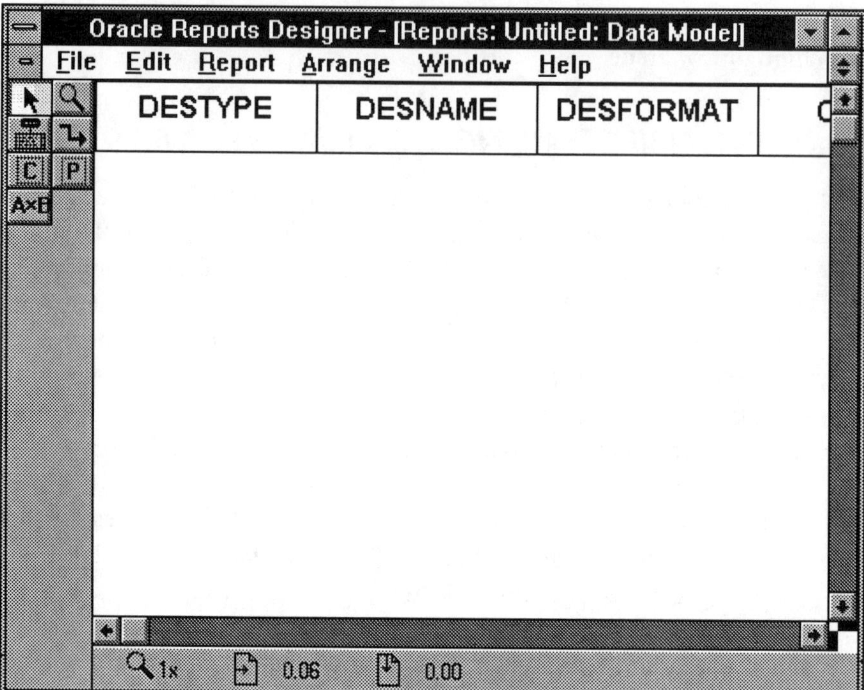

various tools found on the Tool palette. The layout is then used to generate the actual positioning of the report objects and the data that populates the report.

The Layout Painter creates a template, or a logical representation, of the report output. Objects are created and modified on the layout area, sometimes called the painting region, as icons, using the Tool palette, whose functions are described in Table 5.4. The object icons project the proportional size, relative position, pattern, color, and fonts that will be printed in the actual hard copy.

The Layout Painter divides reports into the header region, body region, and trailer region. The header is one or more pages that appear at the beginning of each report. The body, of course, is the main material of the report. And the trailer is one or more pages printed at the end of the report. All three regions can contain boilerplate of any type, as well as data and computations. You start in the body region but can navigate to other areas by selecting the

Table 5.3   Data Model Painter Tools

Tools	*Usage*
Select	Used to select an object with a click, or a group of objects using [Shift]-click for each successive object. With this tool, you can resize objects by clicking on the edge of the object and dragging.
Magnify	Used to enlarge or reduce the Layout Editor Display by 2×. Enlarge by clicking in the workspace; shrink by holding [Shift]-click. The click point becomes the center of the altered display.
Query	Creates a query when you click in an open area of the layout; once created the query can be further defined from its property sheet.
Link	Creates a link between a parent group and a child query by first clicking on the parent, then dragging to the child; once defined the link can be further defined from its property sheet.
Computation	Creates a new summary or formula column when you click in an open area of the data model layout; once defined the computation can be further defined from its property sheet.
Parameter	Creates a new parameter when you click in an open area of the Data Model Painter; once defined, the parameter can be further defined from its property sheet.
Cross Product	Creates a cross-product group (as a mathematical cross-product) around two or more other groups; once defined the cross-product group can be further defined from its property sheet.

PAINTER SETTINGS command from the Arrange menu, then selecting MAR-GIN, HEADER, or TRAILER in the Display Layout Using field and clicking the Apply button. Objects created in the margin will be overlapped by any object using the same territory in the body.

Parameter Form Painter

The Parameter Form Painter, shown in Figure 5.22, is used to define the Run-time Parameter Form's appearance by adding or altering the parameter form objects. Boilerplate and field objects can be specified in the Parameter Form Painter. Field objects created in the Parameter Form Painter might show default parameter values when the report is run, which the user can override by replacing them with literal values. The Runtime Parameter Form can even be several pages in length to meet the needs of the developer.

The Parameter Form Painter is automatically opened with the Data Model Painter and Layout Painter when the NEW command or OPEN command is issued from the File menu. The Parameter Form Painter can also be opened

Table 5.4 Layout Painter Tools

Tools	*Usage*
Select	Selects an object with a click, or a group of objects using [Shift]-click for each successive object.
Single Select	Selects a single object that is part of a group.
Rotate	Rotates the currently selected boilerplate object or group (but not regular objects). Rotate the object by dragging its handle; the status line shows the current angle of rotation.
Single Rotate	Rotates boilerplate objects that are part of a group.
Magnify	Enlarges or reduces the Layout Editor display by 2×. Enlarge by clicking in the workspace; shrink by holding [Shift]-click. The click point becomes the center of the altered display.
Reshape	Reshapes boilerplate graphic objects (but not regular objects) when you click and drag the selection handles.
Rectangle	Creates a rectangle at the click position; then you can drag it to its full size and use [Shift]-click to make a perfect square.
Line	Creates a line at the click position; then you can drag it to its full length and use [Shift]-click to make a perfectly straight line.
Ellipse	Creates an ellipse at the click position; then you can drag it to its full size and use [Shift]-click to make a circle.
Arc	Creates an arc at the click position; then you can drag it to its full length and use [Shift]-click to make a circular arc.
Polygon	Creates a polygon. Click to mark each vertex; then double-click at last line segment; use [Shift]-click to ensure perfectly straight lines.
Polyline	Same as polygon, except that the last vertex need not connect to the first.
Round Rectangle	Same as rectangle.
Freehand	Click and drag to draw the desired freehand graphic.
Boilerplate Text	Enter text at click position; quit by clicking outside the text box; edit existing text by clicking the text tool inside the text box; use the Scalable Bounding Box option in the Text Drawing option to allow multiline text with word-wrap features.
Frame Select	Selects frames or repeating frames and all objects contained therein.
Frame Tool	Creates a frame the same way a rectangle is drawn; alter the frame through its property sheet.
Repeating Frame Tool	Creates a repeating frame the same way a rectangle is drawn; alter the repeating frame through its property sheet.
Field Tool	Creates a field the same way a rectangle is drawn; alter the field through its property sheet.
Link File Tool	Creates boilerplate text, drawing, or image imported from file; the contents are displayed in a rectangular box in the layout and are linked directly to the specified file.
Oracle Graphics Tool	Creates an Oracle Graphics object directly associated with an Oracle Graphics display, which is executed and incorporated at runtime; otherwise, the object is drawn the same way a rectangle is.

Table 5.4 Layout Painter Tools

Tools	*Usage*
Anchor Tool	Anchors two objects together when you click on the child object, then on intermediate positions in the painter (to anchor the object to a specific spot), then double-click the parent object. Hold the shift key while clicking to constrain the anchored object to the nearest 25% increment.
Default Layout Tool	Defines a default layout for the specified portion of the painter. Specify the area as if drawing a rectangle. After the default area has been defined, the Default Layout Dialog box appears, allowing the developer to set any desired options. Click OK to accept the dialog or Cancel to abort it.

using the NAVIGATE command on the Edit menu, by clicking the Edit Parameter Form check box on the Report menu, or by issuing the DEFAULT PARAMETER FORM command on the Report menu.

Once the Parameter Form Painter has been called, the developer can use the tools on the Tools palette, described in Table 5.5, to place objects and invoke object property sheets. To create an item, select its tool and click (and drag as needed) in an open area of the layout. To modify an object, double-click the item to call its property sheet and make the necessary changes there. In general, the Parameter Form is only one page long, so navigation is not usually an issue, although navigation is accomplished using the scroll buttons and scroll bars. You can set the size and number of pages in the Parameter Form by invoking the Global Properties dialog on the Report menu.

USING THE PREVIEWER

When a report is executed, it can be displayed in the Previewer Window on the computer screen by setting the system parameter DESTYPE=Screen or Preview. The Previewer, shown in Figure 5.23, provides viewing functionality, which enables the user or developer to quickly view parts of the report and navigate through the report on-screen. Users can scroll one page at a time forward or backward, skip to the first or last page, or even zoom in on a specific page. The Previewer even supports split screens, so that data can be compared between multiple reports or different versions of the same report. In a split-screen setting (where one portion of the screen displays one report, and another section of the screen displays a different report), the developer

Figure 5.22   The Parameter Form Painter

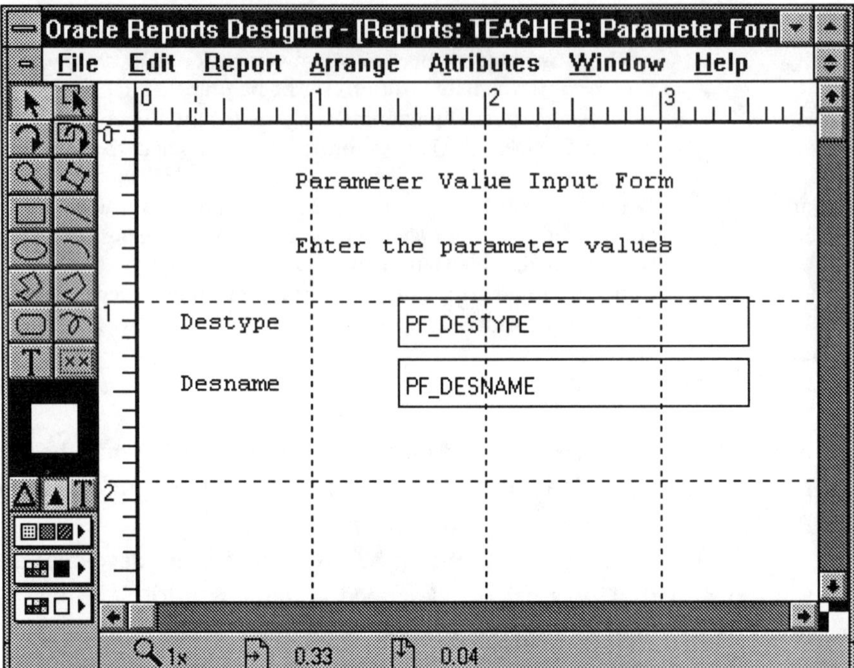

need only click in the split report window to activate it and navigate through it. The developer can alter the behavior of the Previewer by issuing the GLOBAL PROPERTIES command from the Report menu. For example, the developer could alter the global properties to support character-mode displays rather than bit-mapped displays.

The user can click the First and Last button to navigate to the first and last page of the report, respectively. The Previous and Next buttons move the user back to the previous page or forward to the next page. To the right of the Page button is a field that indicates the current page. To navigate to a specific page, overwrite the value in the page number field and click the Page button. The scroll bars can be used to view concealed sections of the report on the current page. The user can also use the Print, Close, and New buttons to print the report, close it, or open a new report.

Table 5.5 Parameter Form Painter Tools

Tools	*Usage*
Select	Used to select an object with a click, or a group of objects using [Shift]-click for each successive object.
Single Select	Used to select a single object that is part of a group.
Rotate	Used to rotate the currently selected boilerplate object or group (but not regular objects). Rotate the object by dragging its handle; the status line shows the current angle of rotation.
Single Rotate	Used to rotate boilerplate objects that are part of a group.
Magnify	Used to enlarge or reduce the Layout Editor display by 2x. Enlarge by clicking in the workspace; shrink by holding [Shift]-click. The click point becomes the center of the altered display.
Reshape	Used to reshape boilerplate graphic objects (but not regular objects) by clicking and dragging the selection handles.
Rectangle	Creates a rectangle at the click position. Drag to its full size; use [Shift]-drag to make a square.
Line	Creates a line at the click position. Drag to its full length; use [Shift]-drag to make a perfectly straight line (horizontal, vertical, or diagonal); change line attributes by selecting the object, then choosing the line type from the Attributes menu.
Ellipse	Create an ellipse at the click position. Drag to its full size; use [Shift]-drag to make a circle.
Arc	Create an arc at the click position. Drag to its full length; use [Shift]-drag to make a circular arc.
Polygon	Click to mark each vertex, then double-click at last line segment; use [Shift]-drag to ensure perfectly straight lines.
Polyline	Same as Polygon, except that the last vertex need not connect to the first.
Rounded Rectangle	Same as Rectangle.
Freehand	Click and drag to draw the desired freehand graphic.
Text Boilerplate	Enter text at click position with Returns for multiple lines; quit by clicking outside the text box; edit existing text by clicking the text tool inside the text box and altering the text as needed; alter the attributes for a text object by selecting the object, then providing definitions under the Attributes menu.
Text Field	Creates a Text item (field) at click position that allows end-users to enter text at runtime. Drag to its full size; use [Shift]-drag to create a square text field; enter default text for the field by selecting the field and typing the text within the field; click outside the field when done.

Figure 5.23   The Previewer

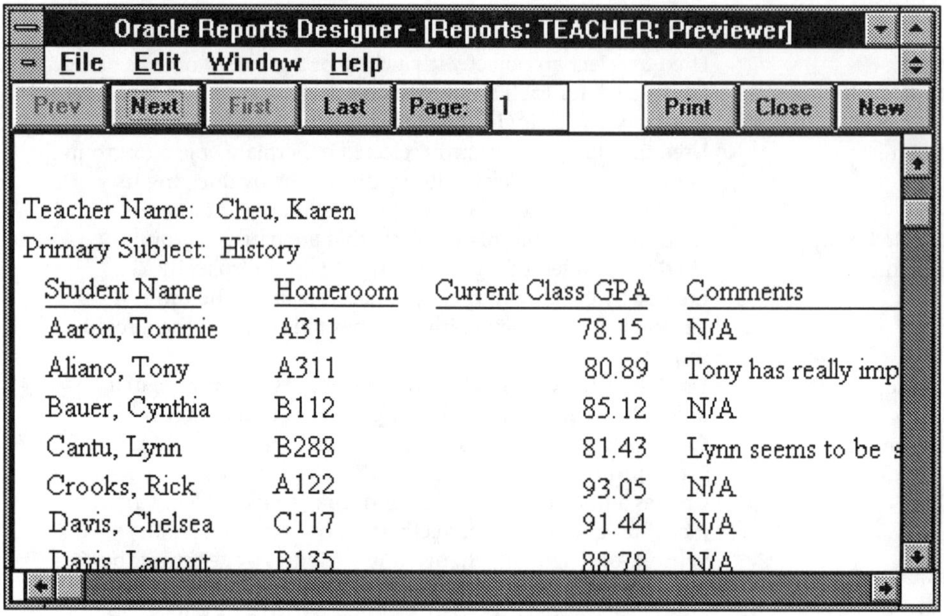

Oracle Reports Designer - [Reports: TEACHER: Previewer]

File   Edit   Window   Help

Prev   Next   First   Last   Page: 1   Print   Close   New

Teacher Name: Cheu, Karen
Primary Subject: History

Student Name   Homeroom   Current Class GPA   Comments
Aaron, Tommie   A311   78.15   N/A
Aliano, Tony   A311   80.89   Tony has really imp
Bauer, Cynthia   B112   85.12   N/A
Cantu, Lynn   B288   81.43   Lynn seems to be s
Crooks, Rick   A122   93.05   N/A
Davis, Chelsea   C117   91.44   N/A
Davis, Lamont   B135   88.78   N/A

EXECUTABLES

Oracle Reports contains five executables that perform certain important operations within Oracle Reports. Some executables exist to support upgrades from older versions of Oracle Reports; others provide new functionality. Oracle Reports executables include R20CONV, R20MPRT, R20MREP, R20RUN, and R20DES. They are issued using the syntax `R20xxx keyword=....` See Table 5.6 for a description of Oracle Report keywords.

R20CONV is used to convert one or more report definitions from one storage format to another. It replaces the DUMPREP, GENREP, and LOADREP executables found in SQL*ReportWriter, Version 1.1. For example, to convert a v1.1 .rex file to a v2 report stored in the database, enter the following:

```
r20conv userid=kevin/triangle stype=rexfile source=students.rex
dtype=database
```

R20MPRT is used to convert SQL*ReportWriter, Version 1.1 printer definition files, such as printdef.dat and pstscrpt.dat, to Oracle Reports printer driver definition files. This utility is especially useful for reports designed for very old and obsolete printer types.

R20MREP is used to migrate SQL*ReportWriter, Version 1.1 report definitions (those with a .rex extension) to the current version of Oracle Reports report definitions.

R20RUN is used to run previously designed reports. It can direct output via the Previewer to the screen, to a printer, to a specified file, a standard output (SYSOUT), or even attach the report to an Oracle*Mail electronic mail note. R20RUN is also the most commonly called executable from other Oracle products where the application need only run a report. For example, to run the status report after entering information in the report parameter screen from a VT-220 terminal, you enter the following:

```
r20run module=status_rpt paramform=yes term=vt220
```

R20DES is used to invoke the Oracle Reports Designer to design and run reports, as discussed in this chapter. Oracle Reports Designer stores report definitions either in the Oracle database or in a file according to the desires of the developer. For example, to open Oracle Forms Designer using a standard set of parameters stored in an ASCII file, you enter the following:

```
r20des userid=kevin/triangle cmdfile=myprefs.kev
```

CONCLUSION

Oracle Reports' powerful querying, formatting, and graphics capabilities make writing even complex master-detail or matrix reports easy. Oracle Reports' inclusion of several default formats makes creating informative reports a direct and speedy process. By including parameters and PL/SQL, you can build flexible and maintainable reports.

After studying this chapter, you should be able to create basic reports using the Default Report Layout facility. You should also be able to customize reports, as well as create and manipulate objects using the Layout Painter and Data Model Painter. You should understand how to use the Runtime Parameter Form to interactively prompt the end-user for more information, and you should know how to apply PL/SQL processing to various objects and events within the report. Finally, you should know how to write and execute Oracle Reports command-line executables.

Table 5.6 Oracle Reports Executable Keywords

Keyword*	Value**	Used By***	Usage
MODULE	(path and filename)	R,D	Name of report to be opened.
USERID	(userid)	C,R,D	Database login; enter USERID=( ) to use the automatic OPS$ database login.
STYPE	db/rdf/rex	C	Type of report source: database, rdffiles, or rexfiles.
SOURCE	(path and filename)	C	Source filename of report to be converted.
DTYPE	db/rdf/rep/rex	C	Type of report output: database rdffile, repfile, or rexfile.
DEST	(path and filename)	C	Target filename of the converted report.
DUNIT	cn/ch/i/p	C	Designated unit of measure: centimeters, characters, inches, or points.
PAGESIZE	n width $\times$ n height	C,R,D	Logical page size of converted report in DUNITS.
FORMSIZE	n width $\times$ n height	C	Size of Runtime Parameter form in DUNITS.
OVERWRITE	yes/no/prompt	C	Whether R20CONV should overwrite any existing object with the same name.
PARAMFORM	yes/no	R,D	Toggles the runtime parameter form.
CMDFILE	path and filename	R,D	A path and filename containing arguments for the executable.
TERM	path and filename	R,D	Name of a terminal definition to run.
ARRAYSIZE	n	R,D	The size in kilobytes for Oracle to use in array processing.
DESTYPE	sc/fl/prt/prv/so/mail	R,D	Type of destination device: screen, file, printer, previewer, or standard output mail.
DESNAME	path and filename	R,D	Name of the output device or filename.
DESFORMAT	format	R,D	The characteristics of the printer, such as wide, dflt (default), and so on.
COPIES	n	R,D	Number of copies to print.
CURRENCY	currency symbol	R,D	Currency character.
THOUSANDS	thousands symbol	R,D	Thousands character.
DECIMAL	decimal symbol	R,D	Decimal character.
READONLY	yes/no	R,D	Executes multiple queries simultaneously to enforce read consistency.

Table 5.6 Oracle Reports Executable Keywords *(continued)*

Keyword*	Value**	Used By***	Usage
LOGFILE	path and filename	R,D	Output file of PrintScreen actions.
BUFFERS	*n*	R,D	Size of virtual memory in kilobytes.
BATCH	yes/no	R	Runs reports in batch mode.
PROFILE	path and filename	R,D	File in which report performance data is stored.
RUNDEBUG	yes/no	R,D	Performs extra runtime checking for anomalous, but nonerror, conditions.
ONSUCCESS	ct/rb/no	R,D	Indicates if a commit, rollback, or noaction should occur when the report is completed successfully.
ONFAILURE	ct/rb/no	R,D	Indicates if a commit, rollback, or noaction should occur when the report fails.
KEYIN	path and filename	R,D	Name of keystroke macro file to read in at execution only; used in character-mode environments.
KEYOUT	path and filename	R,D	Name of keystroke macro file Oracle should read keystrokes into.
ERRFILE	path and filename	R	Name of file to store all error messages.
LONGCHUNK	*n*	R	Size of LONG columns in kilobytes.
PARAMNAME	(value)	R	Name(s) and value(s) of parameter(s) defined in the display. Values entered on the command line will overwrite any default value for the parameter.

*   Keywords are shown in the order in which they should appear when writing an Oracle Reports executable, that is, userid first, openfile second, and so on.

**   Values shown in parentheses may actually include a list of values, with each item separated by a comma. For example, to open three files, the destination keyword string might read `dest=(myfile1, myfile2, myfile3)`. Also note that values shown in the value column may be abbreviations of the required value. Check the Usage column for the full keyword value to specify.

*** C = the keyword is usable in the Conversion executable; R = the keyword is usable in the Runtime executable; D = the keyword is usable in the Designer executable.

6 INTRODUCTION TO ORACLE GRAPHICS, VERSION 2.0

INTRODUCTION

Oracle Graphics is a multimedia graphical display tool that enables dynamic links to Oracle (and non-Oracle) data sources. Displays created using Oracle Graphics reduce the reams of data found in many corporate reports to visually simple and concise graphics. It is this capability to quickly visualize complex or large data sets that serves as a decision-support tool for corporate decision makers. Oracle Graphics can act as a stand-alone application, or it can be integrated with other modules from other CDE tools, such as Oracle Forms, Oracle Reports, or Oracle Book, to create a comprehensive, full-featured application.

Oracle Graphics provides the developer with powerful graphical formatting capabilities, including the following:

- Image retrieval and display, including charts, line drawings, bit-mapped images, text, and sound from a variety of sources, including non-Oracle sources like Microsoft Excel (SYLK), Lotus 1-2-3 (WKS), and ASCII-delimited (PRN) files.

- Fifty-six predefined chart templates for quick customization.

- Artwork drawing tools for lines, polygons, and freehand shapes.

- Full procedural and conditional control using PL/SQL.

- Dynamic links to chart and drawing data sources, with automatic update capabilities.

- Interactive end-user facilities, such as buttons, and timers to ensure automatic program execution.

- Multiple, concurrent window sessions.

- Storage of graphics in files or the Oracle database.

- Import and export CGM drawings; BMP, JPEG, PCX, PICT, and TIFF images; and AIFF-C sound files.

While Oracle Forms and Oracle Reports applications are called modules, Oracle Graphics applications are called displays (even if they contain sounds). As with Forms and Reports, Oracle Graphics displays are built through the Oracle Graphics Designer, typically using the Layout Editor. The Layout Editor is the primary work area used to build displays. When Oracle Graphics is invoked, a new default display named DISP1 is opened. Along with the default window, the developer has access to the Tool palette on the left side of the screen and the Designer menus at the top of the screen.

Unlike form or report modules, displays rely almost entirely on their visual and graphic clarity. If the purpose and meaning of a display is not immediately evident, then it probably needs more work. The component of a display that end-users use and interact with is called the *visual framework*. The visual framework is composed of objects such as drawings, images, text, and charts. Objects, such as charts, can be dynamically linked to data from the database and can have added functionality provided by linked PL/SQL code. A display and its visual layout are composed of many objects placed on a single (or multiple) layer(s) in the Layout Editor.

Data used in a display requires a connection to the database. Any time an operation involves the database, an explicit connection to the database must be established. When data is retrieved, it is placed in the Data Table. Data used in Oracle Graphics can be derived from an Oracle database using a SQL SELECT statement or from a file, such as a spreadsheet.

The impact and power of an Oracle Graphics display depend on the presentation of the chart and the data it represents. A wide variety of charts can be defined using a chart template, and a wide variety of predefined templates is available for direct implementation or customization by the developer. The chart itself is drawn using the Chart tool (from the Tool palette) in the layout. After the chart is drawn, the query and chart template definitions are applied to the specified layout. Once the basic chart is defined, the data it represents (held in the Data Table) needs to be refreshed as the data values change. Whenever a chart is updated, both the chart template and data are rechecked and redisplayed.

OVERVIEW OF DISPLAY CREATION

Creating a display is, in many ways, a matter of personal preferences. Figure 6.1 shows a linear, straightforward method for creating an Oracle Graphics display; however, you can do different portions of the work at any point in the chart's creation, such as customizing the display with PL/SQL code.

As with other tools in the CDE, Oracle Graphics makes full use of parameters in both SQL SELECTs and in PL/SQL programs. Parameters are defined in the Parameter Table and serve as global variables in a display, while PL/SQL programs are written in the PL/SQL Editor. Oracle Graphics uses two types of PL/SQL programs: programs and packages. PL/SQL in Oracle Graphics behaves similarly to PL/SQL in Oracle Forms, using buttons and event-driven triggers.

Displays can be created for stand-alone use or can be called from other Oracle CDE tools, such as Oracle Forms or Oracle Reports. Similarly, displays can reference other Oracle products, for example, calling a form or report from a chart. Displays can also be created in a standard runtime version or an executable batch version and can be saved to the database or to files. When a display is saved to the database, a user must be specifically granted access to the display (using the GRANT command from the File menu) to access it. As with other products of the CDE, Oracle Graphics can be used to create PL/SQL libraries that can be referenced within a single display or multiple displays.

Components of a Display

The elements that compose a display provide a visual framework for data retrieval and presentation, dynamic data links, and the user interface. Display components include objects, color palettes, sounds, queries, chart templates, parameters, and blocks of PL/SQL code. Many of these components can be loaded from or exported to the file system (and outside of Oracle Graphics). Queries and parameters are the only components that cannot be exported. Of all the components, only objects and sounds are apparent to the end-user. All other components are used by the developer to create the display but are not seen by the end-user.

OBJECTS

Objects are the graphical elements of a display, such as drawings, images, text, and charts. Drawings are line-art graphics created and shown in the

Figure 6.1   Overview of Display Creation

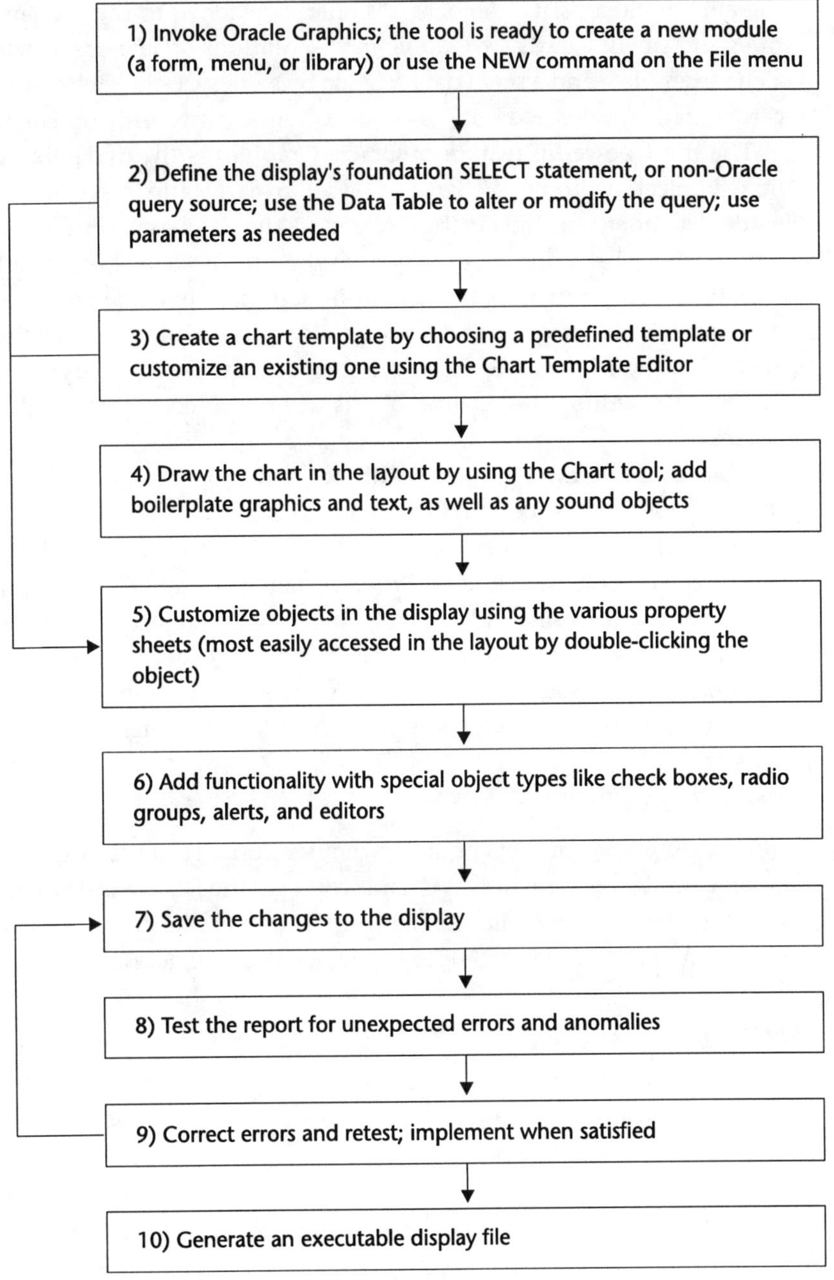

layout area. Images are bit-mapped graphics (created outside Oracle Graphics) imported into the display. Images might include scanned images or photographs. Text consists of blocks of boilerplate added to the display, such as titles and labels. Charts are graphic representations of data constructed using a chart template and a set of data fetched by a query. Data fetches into a chart can be static (performed only once) or dynamic (constantly updated).

The most powerful feature of Oracle Graphics is the dynamic, database-linked object. Although a chart can be set up as a static image, it can also be made dependent on information stored in the database. Thus, a chart's appearance and behavior could vary according to the data stored in the database based on programmatic calls to update the chart's appearance. Other objects, such as images or text, are created and manipulated in the layout area using the Tool palette. However, they can also be updated based on data or user interaction by attaching blocks of PL/SQL code to control their behavior.

Objects are defined by their attributes and properties. Attributes control the object's appearance, physical characteristics, and relationship to other objects. Attributes vary between object types but are usually defined by invoking the object's Attributes or Property dialog and specifying the appropriate options, or by using PL/SQL code to define the object's attributes. Attributes include such properties as the name of the object, any associated components (such as a query or block of PL/SQL code), any associated event (such as mouse-up or mouse-down), and display attributes.

COLOR PALETTES

Color Palettes are the sets of colors the developer establishes for use in the displays under construction. A default color palette is provided and is primarily dependent on the computer platform. However, the default palette can be edited and augmented according to the needs of the developer.

SOUNDS

Sounds, available only on systems that support this feature, can be recorded and played back according to the developer's specifications, for example, to alert or warn the end-user.

QUERIES

A query is the SELECT statement (or imported file) used to retrieve data into the display. A display can have one or more queries, although a display that

Figure 6.2 Oracle Graphics SQL Statement Editor

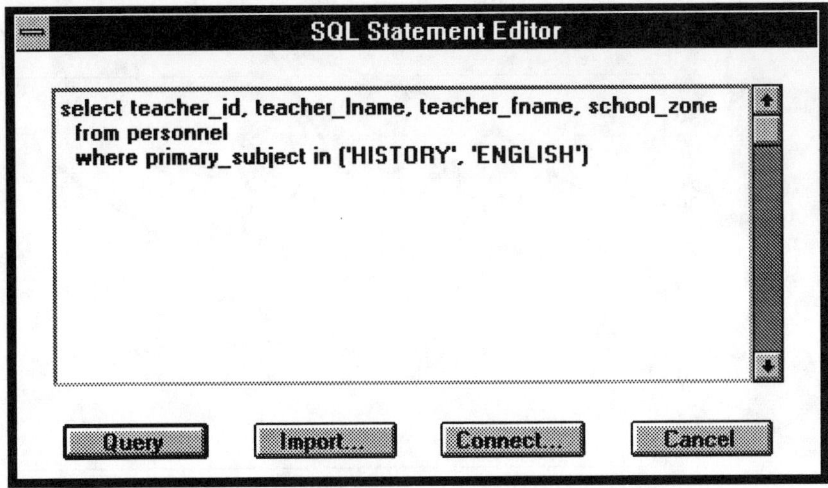

displays only static graphics need not have a query. Programmatic queries can also be used to pull data to create and modify other types of objects.

When creating a query, the developer must specify a filename and location if the query comes from something like a spreadsheet file. If the data needed for the display comes from the database, a standard SELECT statement is needed, as shown in Figure 6.2.

Data from the current query is fetched in columns and rows and placed into the Data Table. Once the chart is created, Oracle Graphics uses data held in the data chart, unless programmatically specified otherwise. The data retrieved by the query is evaluated as one of two types: category or value data. Category data is information that does not depend on any other data to have informational value. For example, a teacher's name has value completely independent of any other data. Value data is dependent on another piece of data. For example, the teacher's salary is not of much use unless you know which teacher gets that salary. In the chart, categoric data is plotted along the discrete axis and is not mathematically related, while value data is plotted along the continuous axis and is related mathematically, as shown in Figure 6.3.

CHART TEMPLATES

Chart templates are predefined chart configurations and properties stored in a file. Developers can select a chart template and quickly customize it to meet

Figure 6.3 Chart Components

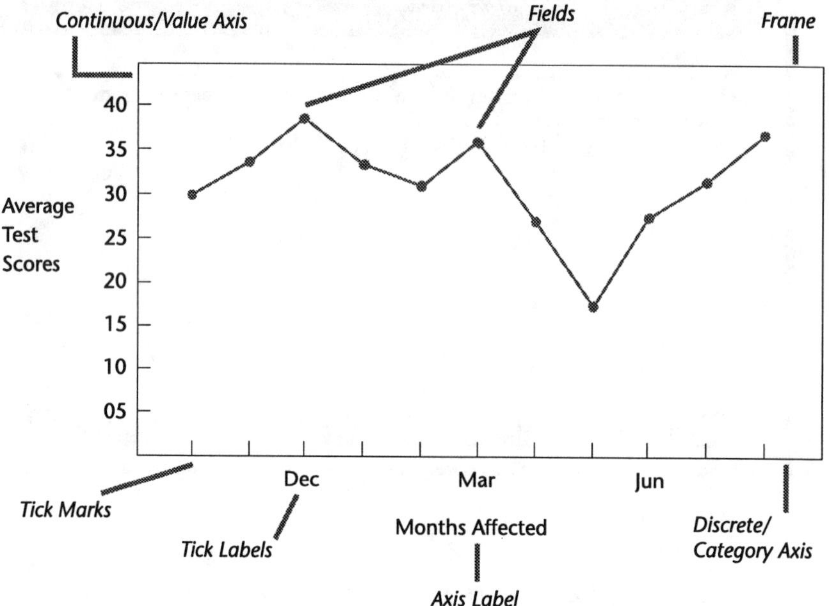

the needs of their display. Chart templates are used to define the basic format of a chart. They contain various definable components, which the developer can customize, and are useful for creating multiple charts with the same attributes but different queries. Chart templates are manipulated using the Chart Template Editor, shown in Figure 6.4. Oracle Graphics provides fifty-six predefined chart templates, divided into ten major categories: column, bar, line, mixed, pie, double-Y, high-low, Gantt, scatter, and table.

The major components of a chart template, the chart frame and field templates, can be easily adapted to the developer's needs. The chart frame encompasses the basic structure of the chart, such as the legend position and axis label fonts, but not the way data is plotted. The chart frame is the first item to appear in the Chart Template Editor, when a chart template is selected. Field templates determine the presentation of dependent data, such as lines or pie slices. Open a specific field template by selecting the SHOW FIELD command from the Control menu when the Chart Template Editor is active.

Figure 6.4 The Chart Template Editor

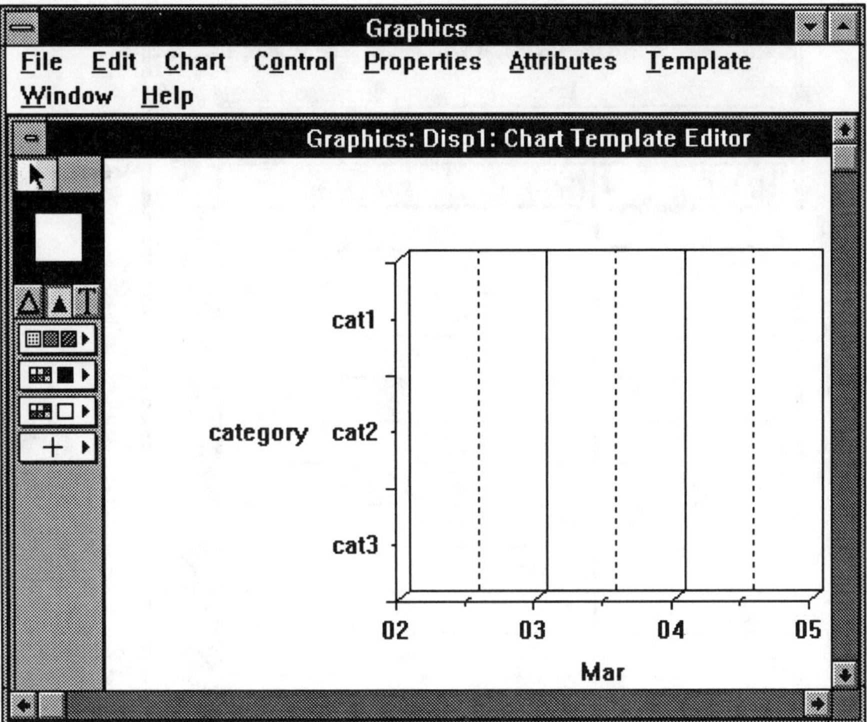

PARAMETERS

Parameters, like those in Oracle Reports or Oracle Forms, are global variables whose value is assigned at runtime. Parameters are added to the query's SELECT statement or to blocks of PL/SQL code to provide added flexibility in the routine. Each display possesses a single Parameter Table, shown in Figure 6.5, where each parameter is named; given a datatype of NUMBER, CHAR, or DATE; and assigned a default value (which can be overwritten at runtime).

Parameters are used in the SELECT statement of the query or in PL/SQL blocks as either bind or lexical references. Bind references substitute a single value, such as a character string, number, or date. Bind references are designated by a colon (:) added to the front of the parameter name. Lexical references substitute text embedded in the SELECT statement of the query with the value of the lexical parameter. Lexical parameters are designated by an

Figure 6.5   The Parameter Table

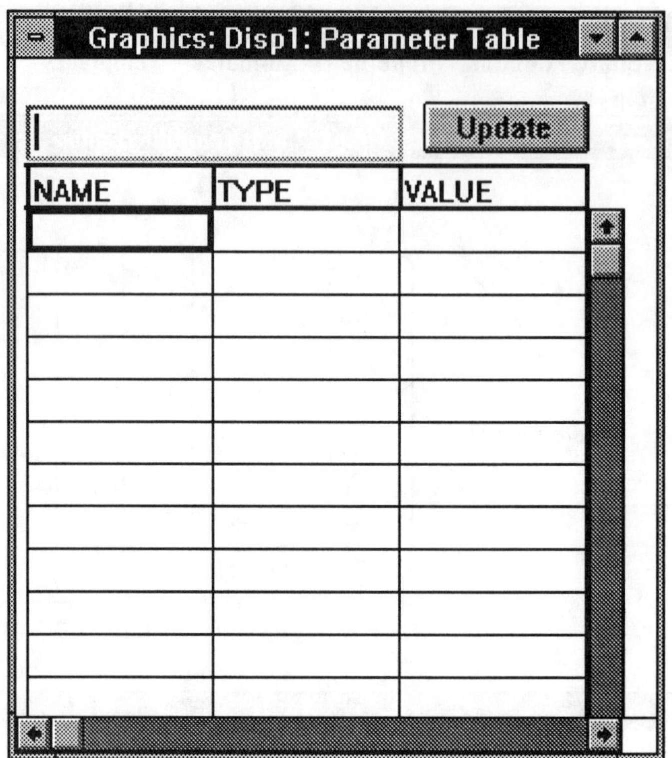

ampersand (&) added to the front of the parameter name. Refer to chapter 4 for more information on parameter usage.

Parameter values are assigned an initial value through the Parameter Table, by a PL/SQL program, or by arguments passed at runtime or through batch executables. At runtime, the parameters are substituted for their referenced value in the appropriate SELECT or PL/SQL program.

PL/SQL PROGRAM BLOCKS

PL/SQL program blocks are routines that allow the developer to programmatically create and modify objects, manipulate display operations, interface with the end-user, or control operations conditionally. PL/SQL blocks are created and accessed using the PL/SQL Program Units Browser, shown in Figure 6.6.

After a PL/SQL program unit has been opened using the browser, the code

Figure 6.6 PL/SQL Program Units Browser

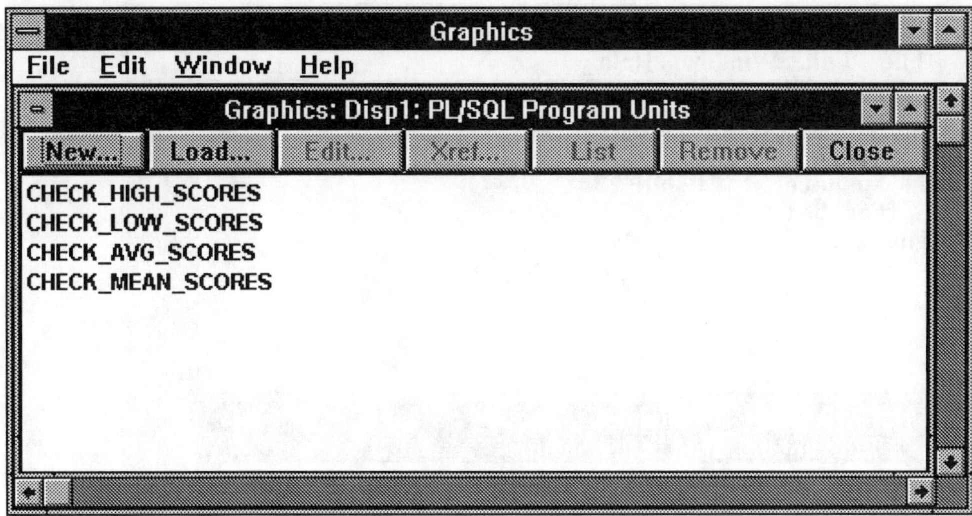

can be edited using the PL/SQL Editor. The PL/SQL Editor, shown in Figure 6.7, is used to write, edit, and debug PL/SQL code.

PL/SQL program units are broken into subprograms and packages. Subprograms are procedures and functions created by the developer, including two special types: the button procedure and the trigger procedure. The button procedure invokes a particular block of PL/SQL code when a mouse click or mouse click-and-drag occurs on a specified object or layer. The trigger procedure invokes a particular block of PL/SQL code under three sets of circumstances: when the display opens, closes, or a certain amount of time has passed. Packages are groups of related PL/SQL procedures, functions, datatypes, variables, and other PL/SQL objects available for use throughout the application. Packages can be referenced in blocks of PL/SQL code using the period (.) prefix along with the name of the package.

Built-Ins

Oracle Graphics contains a large collection of built-in extensions to the PL/SQL language unique to Oracle Graphics. Oracle Graphics built-ins provide functionality for datatypes, procedures, functions, and constants. Oracle Graphics also contains a number of built-in exceptions to aid in error handling.

Figure 6.7   Oracle Graphics PL/SQL Editor

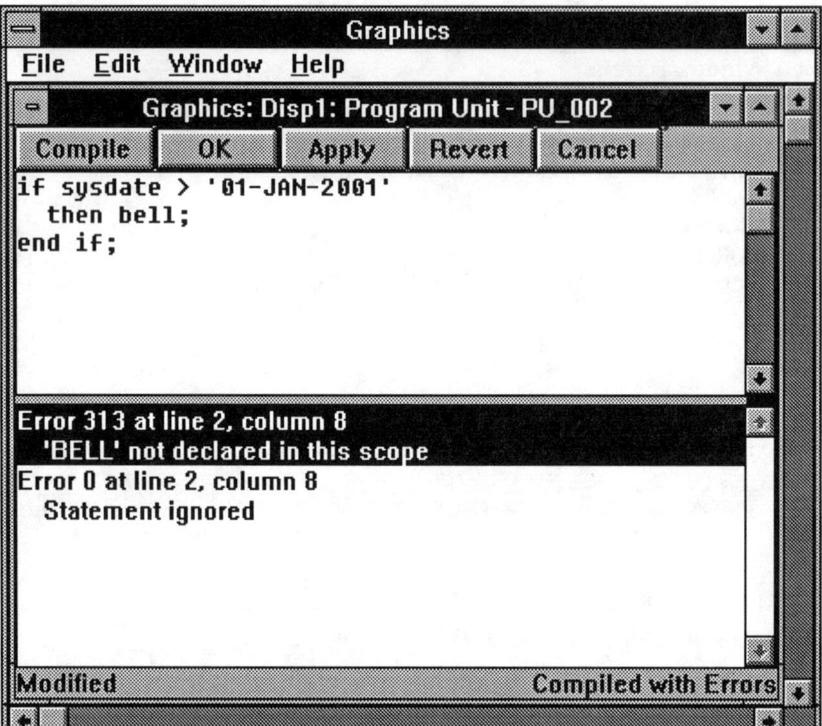

To make use of a built-in exception, the developer must write an exception handler. Exception handlers define and trap erroneous or anomalous conditions and include PL/SQL code to handle the condition. For more information on writing error handlers, refer to chapter 3.

In addition to PL/SQL code written internally within Oracle Graphics, developers can attach PL/SQL Libraries that are stored in the database or in a file. PL/SQL libraries are attached in Oracle Graphics using the Attached PL/SQL Libraries Browser.

USING THE DESIGNER WORK ENVIRONMENT

A number of elements in the Designer can be customized, including the default options, layout, layer settings, views, and windows. Default options, for example, control the basic use and appearance of the work environment.

Figure 6.8 The Preferences Dialog

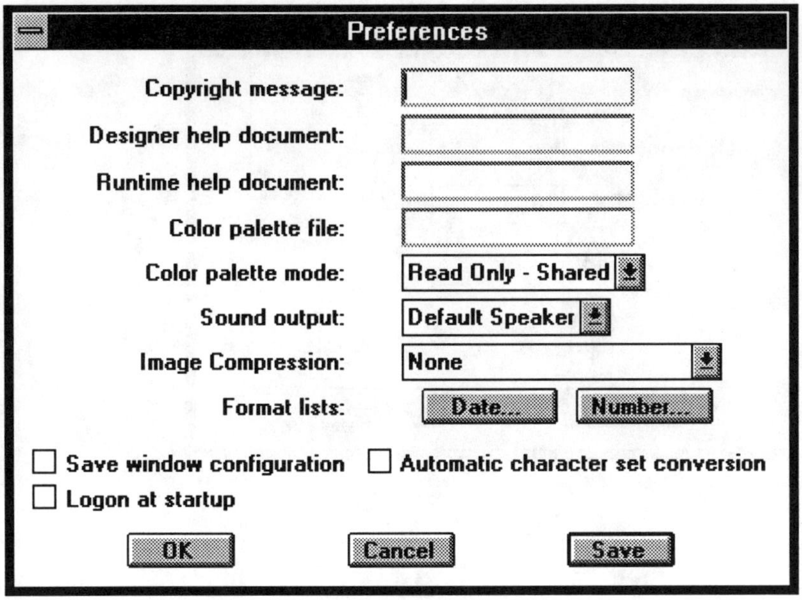

Defaults

Default options are available to control Designer Preferences, Layout Settings, and Ruler Settings and to access Grants and Page Setups. The Preferences Dialog, as shown in Figure 6.8, controls the settings for a copyright message, locations of Designer and Runtime help documents, color palette setting, a sound output device, date and number formats, automatic database connection, window configuration, and character set conversions.

The Layout Settings Dialog, shown in Figure 6.9, controls the dimensions of the layout area and how the layout will be divided into pages when printed, that is, left to right or top to bottom.

The Ruler Settings Dialog, shown in Figure 6.10, controls the default unit of measurement for rulers, grids, snap points per grid, and cell sizes.

Developers can control access to their objects by extending or revoking read, write, and execute privileges to other users through the Grant Dialog, shown in Figure 6.11.

Page Setup controls the default page size, orientation, and other printer output information. It is system-specific, and its dialog can vary from system to system.

Figure 6.9   The Layout Settings Dialog

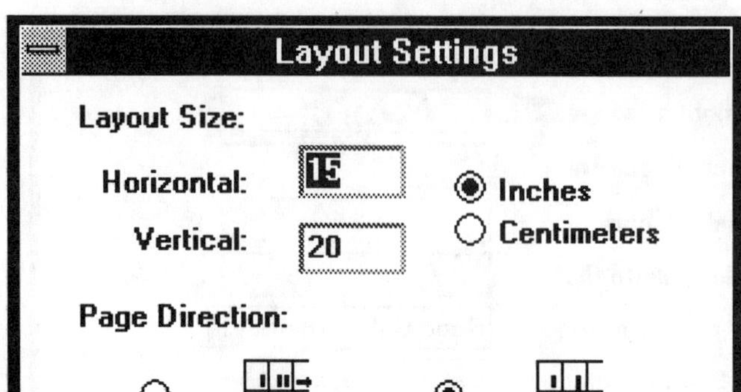

Display Layouts

Each display is created in a single layout area, as shown in Figure 6.12, where all elements of the display are created and manipulated using the Layout Editor and Tool palette. A status line provides the developer with task-related information about cursor position, mouse drag distance, angle rotations, and magnification level. Layout settings are illustrated in Figure 6.13.

Layers

Oracle Graphics objects can be placed in multiple layers in the layout areas. Layers enable the developer to overlap one object with another both during design and at runtime. Typically, objects on lower layers are concealed by objects on higher layers. The active layer is the area in which the developer is currently working and is always visible. However, layers can be shown and hidden throughout the display. By default, new displays possess only one layer, called *layer0*, which is automatically active. At runtime, the multiple layers of a display can be manipulated using PL/SQL code by making different layers active at different times or by changing the stacking order of layers to hide or reveal objects.

Figure 6.10   The Ruler Settings Dialog

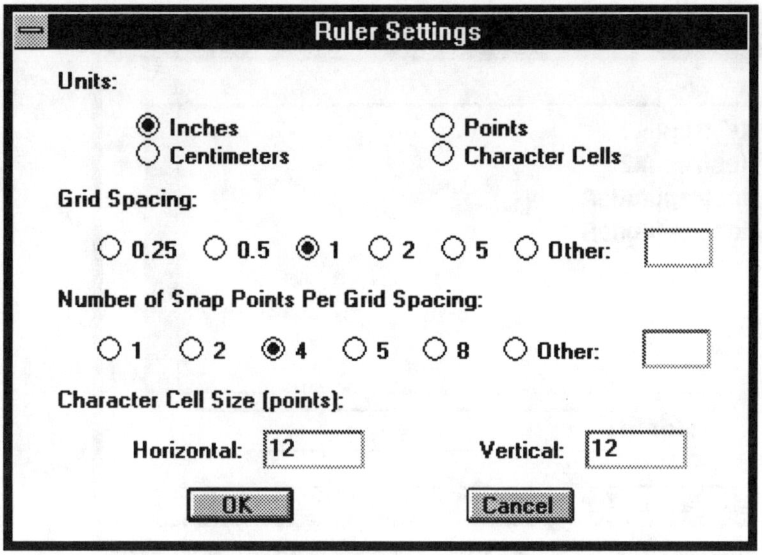

Ruler Settings

Units:
Inches   Points
Centimeters   Character Cells

Grid Spacing:
0.25   0.5   1   2   5   Other:

Number of Snap Points Per Grid Spacing:
1   2   4   5   8   Other:

Character Cell Size (points):
Horizontal: 12   Vertical: 12

OK   Cancel

Views

A display is created with one default view; however, developers can divide displays into as many as four views, each focusing on a different object or layer and each having its own default environment settings. Views are defined by moving the horizontal or vertical view handles scroll bar to a new position. They are available only to developers and cannot be used at runtime.

Windows

Windows can function as either work areas or display areas. Window work areas present the developer with various facilities, such as editors and browsers. Windows can also function as display areas, where objects are presented programmatically at runtime. Using PL/SQL, the developer can create, size, and position windows and the objects they display.

Figure 6.11   The Grant Dialog

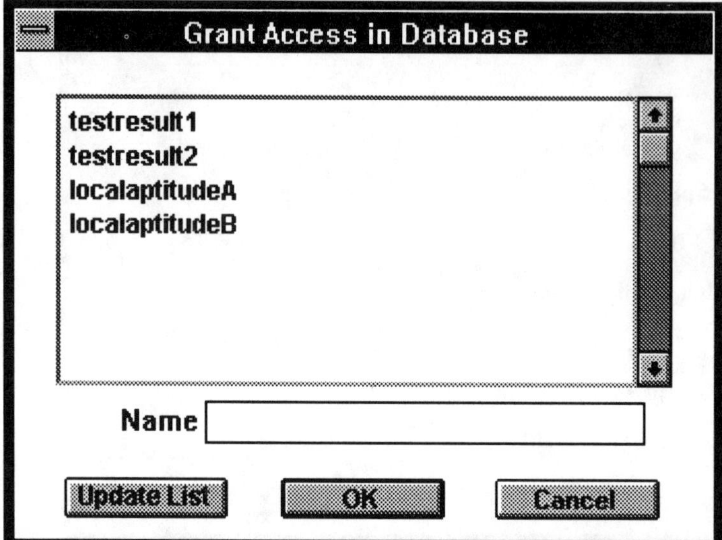

MORE ON CHARTS

Charts are the most important aspect of an Oracle Graphics presentation. Although a chart appears as a single item in the layout, there are three essential components used to construct it: queries, the chart template, and the chart region.

The query is the SELECT statement or file used to retrieve data for the chart. Only one query can be associated with a chart at any given moment, though the active query can be programmatically changed. The chart template defines the basic format of the chart and its attributes. As with a query, only one chart template can be active at a time. Chart templates can also govern subordinate field templates, such as bars, columns, pie slices, and lines. The chart region is the position the chart occupies. Charts can occupy only one region at a time, though they can be duplicated to appear multiple times in a single display.

Chart components help establish a number of the chart's properties; however, additional properties can be set by invoking the chart's Properties dialog or using PL/SQL programs. Additional properties include an associated button procedure and/or mouse event to call the chart, a mapping type for the chart's fields, and the static or dynamic nature of the chart.

Figure 6.12   The Oracle Graphics Layout Area

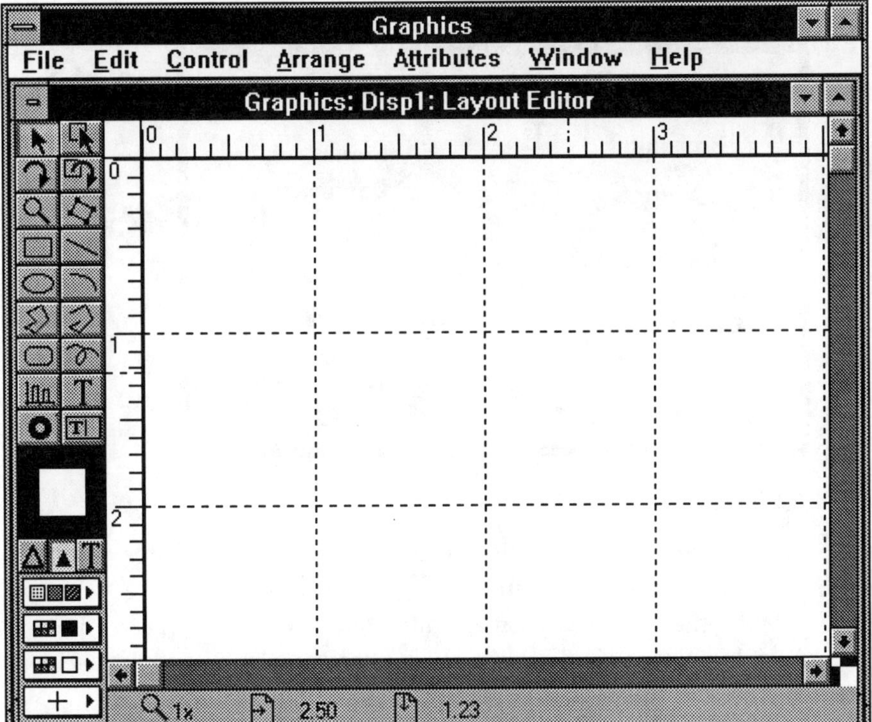

Field Mapping

Field mapping specifies which columns in the query will be included in the chart, the way they will be presented in the chart, the plotting order of the fields, and the association-dependent data fields with field templates. Oracle Graphics automatically does field mapping when a chart is created, based on the appearance of the columns in the Data Table and the current field template. These defaults can be altered by selecting the chart, then invoking its Properties dialog box, and setting the Field Mapping option.

Dynamic and Static Charts

A dynamic chart is linked to its data source and allows the developer to programmatically update its appearance whenever the chart's query is re-executed or its chart template changes. When a chart is updated, Oracle Graph-

Figure 6.13 Layout Settings

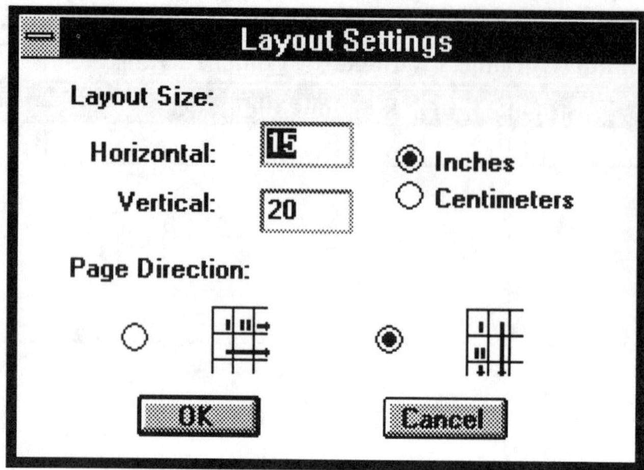

ics examines the Data Table and the Chart Template Editor and then redisplays the chart based on any new or modified information.

Static charts are based on an initial query but are then disconnected from their data source. Static charts cannot become distinct graphic elements that the user can edit without affecting their data sources.

Axis Charts

Most charts are axis charts, that is, charts whose data is plotted according to the edges, or axes, of the chart. An axis chart can contain two or three axes, which can be of the discrete, continuous, or date type. Discrete axes plot distinct values at fixed intervals, usually without any mathematical relation. Discrete axes are used to plot category, or independent, data. Continuous axes plot values by increments based on a continuous mathematical relationship. Continuous axes are used to plot value, or dependent, data. Date axes plot values starting with one date and changing until the chart reaches another date.

DISPLAY CONSTRUCTION USING ORACLE GRAPHICS

This section provides step-by-step details on how to perform tasks for creating and manipulating displays, objects, sounds, queries, charts, parameters, and PL/SQL code.

Display Generation

New displays are created by selecting the NEW command from the File menu. A new display is created by the default name of DispX, where X is the next available increment. Displays are saved by using the SAVE or SAVE AS command on the File menu.

The first time a display is saved, it must be directed to the file system or the database. If the display is to be saved to a file, select the File System option from the SAVE AS command on the File menu. After entering the filename, accept the dialog box to save the display. If the display is to be saved to the database, select the Database option from the SAVE AS command on the File menu. After entering the display name in the Name field, click the Save button. Save changes from then on using the SAVE command on the File menu.

To drop changes made since the last save action, select the REVERT command from the File menu. To close a display, but not the Designer, select the CLOSE command from the File menu. Oracle Graphics will prompt the developer to save any unsaved changes. The Designer can be exited entirely, by selecting the EXIT command from the File menu. Again, Oracle Graphics will prompt the developer to save any unsaved changes.

The developer can open an existing display by selecting the File System or Database option under the OPEN command on the File menu, depending on where the file is stored. Then, the developer can select the display from the File dialog box or Open From Database dialog box and click Open. The display can be printed as hard copy at any time by selecting the PRINT command from the File menu, though only the layers showing will be printed. Note: the printer may have to be set up using the PAGE SETUP command on the File menu.

Displays saved to the operating system can be deleted or renamed using operating system commands. Files stored in the database can be renamed by doing the following:

1. Select the Display option under the RENAME command on the File menu to call the Rename Module in the Database dialog box.

2. Enter the old name and the new name for the display.

3. Click Rename.

Similarly, displays saved in the database can be deleted by developers with the proper access grants by following these steps:

1. Select the Display option under the DELETE command on the File menu to call the Delete From Database dialog box.

2. Enter the name of the display.

3. Click Delete.

To run the most recently generated version of the display, select the File System or Database option under the RUN command on the File menu, depending on where the display is saved. Then, select the display from the File dialog box or the Open From Database dialog box and click Open. If the display needs to be generated into a runtime file usable by Oracle Graphics Runtime or Batch, select the display to be generated using the GENERATE command on the File menu. Developers can also grant access to one of their displays by following these steps:

1. Select the Display option under the GRANT command on the File menu to call the Grant Access option in the Database dialog box.

2. Enter the name of the display, and then click Grant to call the Grant dialog box.

3. Enter the username of the person to receive access, then click Add to add the username to the Access list. Revoke access to users by specifying their usernames, then clicking Remove to erase the usernames from the Access list.

4. Click OK.

Information about who created and last modified a display can be obtained by clicking the GET INFO command on the File menu. Click OK to dismiss the Get Info dialog.

Display Objects

Objects are the visual elements that make up the display. The Tool Palette is used to create and manipulate objects, as well as their characteristics, patterns, and colors. The Oracle Graphics Tool Palette, shown in Figure 6.14, is composed of a number of icons, each representing a different function for manipulating or creating a specific object type.

The Select tool starts as the default tool. A new tool can be selected as the active tool, usable for a single operation, by clicking its icon. The active tool is designated by a highlighted border. A new tool can be selected as the de-

Figure 6.14 The Oracle Graphics Tool Palette

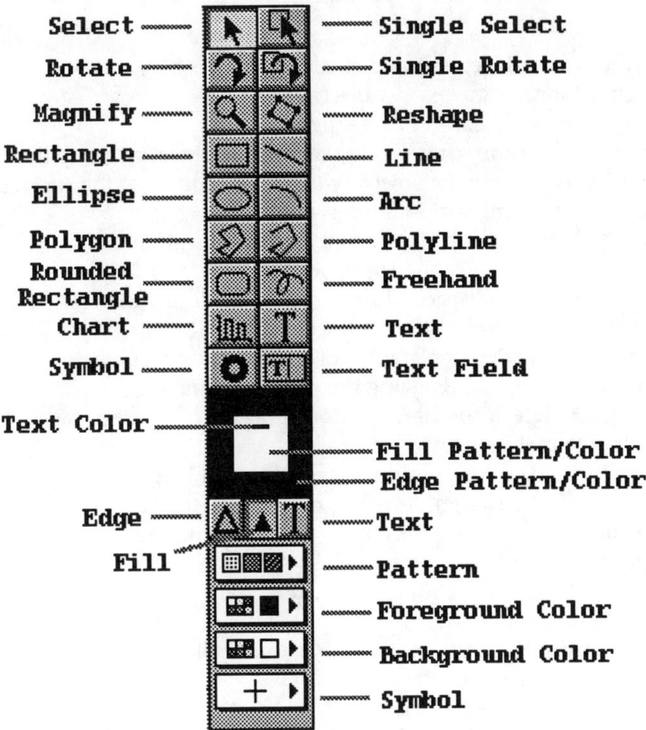

fault tool, usable until a new icon is selected. A default tool is designated by a highlighted icon. Table 6.1 describes each tool on the tool palette.

Before any object can be manipulated in any way, it must be selected. Use the Select or Single Select tool to select an item by clicking on it. Several items can be selected by holding the [Shift] (also called the [Constrain]) key and clicking on each item in succession. All of the items in a region can be selected by clicking outside of the group of objects (but within the region) and dragging the selection box until it surrounds all of the objects to be selected. An object can be added to the selection by using [Shift]-click. All objects in the workspace can be selected using the SELECT ALL command from the Edit menu. Deselect an object by clicking outside its boundaries or in an "empty" part of the workspace.

Multiple objects can be set up to behave as a single object by using the Group function. To create a single group object from multiple objects, select

Table 6.1 Oracle Graphics Tool Palette

Tools	*Usage*
Select	Used to select an object with a click or a group of objects using [Shift]-click for each successive object.
Single Select	Used to select a single object that is part of a group.
Rotate	Used to rotate the currently selected boilerplate object or group (but not regular objects). Rotate the object by dragging its handle; the status line shows the current angle of rotation.
Single Rotate	Used to rotate boilerplate objects that are part of a group.
Magnify	Used to enlarge or reduce the Layout Editor display by 2×. Enlarge by clicking in the workspace; shrink by holding [Shift]-click. The click point becomes the center of the altered display.
Reshape	Used to reshape boilerplate graphic objects (but not regular objects) by clicking and dragging the selection handles.
Rectangle	Creates a rectangle at the click position. Drag to its full size; use [Shift]-drag to make a square.
Line	Creates a line at the click position. Drag to its full length; use [Shift]-drag to make a perfectly straight line (horizontal, vertical, or diagonal); change line attributes by selecting the object, then choosing the line type from the Attributes menu.
Ellipse	Creates an ellipse at the click position. Drag to its full size; use [Shift]-drag to make a circle.
Arc	Creates an arc at the click position. Drag to its full length; use [Shift]-drag to make a circular arc.
Polygon	Creates a polygon. Click to mark each vertex, then double-click at last line segment; use [Shift]-drag to ensure perfectly straight lines.
Polyline	Same as Polygon, except that the last vertex need not connect to the first.
Rounded Rectangle	Same as Rectangle.
Freehand	Click and drag to draw the desired freehand graphic.
Text Boilerplate	Enter text at click position with Returns for multiple lines; quit by clicking outside the text box; edit existing text by clicking the text tool inside the text box and altering the text as needed; alter the attributes for a text object by selecting the object, then providing definitions under the Attributes menu.
Text Field	Creates a Text item (field) at click position, which allows end-users to enter text at runtime. Drag to its full size; use [Shift]-drag to create a square text field; enter default text for the field by selecting the field and typing the text within the field; click outside the field when done.
Chart	Creates a Chart item at the click position. Drag to its full size.
Symbol	Creates a symbol (as decorative artwork or a plot type for a chart template) when you click and hold the tool in order to open the symbol palette. Drag the cursor to the desired symbol then release; click with the Symbol tool to place the symbol on the layout; alter the symbol's attributes by selecting the symbol, then selecting the appropriate symbol definition from the Attributes menu.

the Group option from the GROUP OPERATIONS command under the Arrange menu. Ungroup the objects using the Ungroup option under the same command. Once an object or group of objects has been selected, it can be manipulated in various ways by doing one of the following: moving the object, resizing the object, cutting and/or copying the object to the clipboard, pasting clipboard objects to the canvas, deleting the object, or duplicating the object. Changes to objects can be reversed by selecting the UNDO command from the Edit menu.

Move objects by selecting them and dragging them to their new position. Move an object in small increments by selecting it, then pressing the Up, Down, Left, and Right keys. Incremental movement proceeds one pixel at a time with grid snap turned off and proceeds one snap point (defined in the Ruler settings dialog) at a time with grid snap turned on. Use the [Shift]-drag feature to constrain the movement to vertical, diagonal, and horizontal directions. Resize the object by selecting it and dragging its selection handle to the desired size. Use the [Shift] key while resizing to constrain a rectangle to a square and an ellipse to a circle.

Objects and groups can be cut or copied to the clipboard and, later, pasted back onto the canvas. Objects remain in the clipboard until displaced by another copied or cut object. To cut or copy an object to the clipboard, select the object or group of objects, then select the CUT or COPY command from the Edit menu. The objects are moved to the clipboard. The contents of the clipboard can then be pasted back onto a Layout Editor canvas by selecting the PASTE command from the Edit menu. The object is pasted onto the canvas at the cursor position.

A group of objects can be aligned along their top, side, or bottom edges (based on the Alignment Setting under the Arrange menu). To align a group of items, select the items, then select the ALIGN command from the Arrange menu. Items and boilerplate can be deleted by selecting the object or groups of objects, then selecting the CLEAR command from the Edit menu (or by pressing the [Delete] key). Objects can be similarly duplicated by selecting the object or group of objects, then selecting the DUPLICATE command from the Edit menu. The duplicated item appears before the original. Items manipulated in this fashion receive new, default names, except for deleted items. Such items inherit all the properties of the original, including any triggers attached to the original.

Imported and Exported Artwork

Artwork used in a display can be imported from or exported to the database or a file. Artwork can be simple, black-and-white line drawings or complex, colorful bit-mapped images. Images can be programmatically imported into the display using the og_import_image built-in or imported into the Layout Editor by selecting the IMPORT command from the Edit menu, then choosing the type of artwork to be imported. Indicate the settings as needed. Then, click OK to accept the settings and dismiss the dialog. The artwork is imported into the display.

To export a drawing using PL/SQL, use the og_export_image built-in. A developer can export an image from the Layout Editor by first selecting the image (or the entire layer for drawings), then choosing the EXPORT command from the Edit menu. When prompted, choose the type of artwork to be exported, then identify the desired settings as needed. Finally, click OK to accept the settings and dismiss the dialog. Artwork can be renamed, deleted, and secured through grants in the same way as displays.

Colors and Patterns in Objects

Colors and patterns can be defined for objects in the Layout Editor. Patterns can be applied to the border (edge) of the object or the interior (fill) of an object. They can be applied to the bounding box of a text object, but not the text itself. Patterns and colors can be applied to a chart using the chart template. To apply a pattern, follow these steps:

1. Select the object where the pattern will be applied, then click the Edge or Fill button on the Tool palette.

2. Open the Pattern palette by clicking and holding the palette icon.

3. Drag the cursor to the desired pattern and release. The palette is dismissed, and the pattern is applied to the object.

Colors differ from patterns in that an object can have color applied to the foreground (that portion shown dark) or the background (that part appearing light). Color can be applied to text from the Foreground Color or Background Color palette, when the Text radio button is selected. Color can be set programmatically using the og_set_attr built-in or can be set for systems that support color by following these steps:

1. Select where the foreground or background color will be applied on the object, then click the Edge, Fill, or Text button on the tool palette.

2. Open the Foreground Color palette or Background Color palette by clicking and holding the appropriate palette icon.

3. Drag the cursor to the desired color and release. The palette is dismissed, and the color is applied to the object.

The palette closes, and the color is applied to any selected objects and new objects you draw on the layout. The color also appears in the edge, fill, or text part of the Edge/Fill/Text display box, depending on which radio button you selected. The selection remains in effect for the current display until you change it.

On computers with color monitors, the color palette can be imported, exported, or manually edited for custom colors. Developers must set the Color Mode in the Preferences dialog to Editable before any color editing can be done. Color palettes are imported and exported in the same fashion as artwork. They are managed (renamed, deleted, and secured) in the same manner as displays. To edit a color palette in the Layout Editor, follow these steps:

1. Select the Edit Colors from the Attributes menu to call the Edit Colors dialog.

2. Choose a color and click the Edit button to call the operating-system color editor.

3. Edit the color according to operating system procedures, then accept the new color.

4. Rename the color as needed by entering a new name in the Current Color field and clicking the Rename button.

5. Click the OK button to accept the new color and dismiss the dialog.

Using Sounds

On systems that support sound, the developer can add audio recordings to displays for raising alerts or warnings at runtime. Sounds can be called using PL/SQL routines or can be defined in the Layout Editor by following these steps:

1. Select the SOUND command from the Control menu to call the Sound dialog box.

2. Record a new sound by clicking the New button. Oracle Graphics invokes the operating-system sound-recording facility, providing a default name for the sound file.

3. Record the sound according to the operating system procedures. Accept the dialog to return to the Sound dialog box.

4. Click the OK button to accept the new sound and dismiss the dialog.

PL/SQL can be used to record sounds. The following routine opens the Sound dialog box and allows the end-user to record a new sound:

```
procedure record_warning is
   new_sound     og_sound;
begin
   new_sound    :=    og_get_sound('new1');
   if not og_isnull(new1) then og_record_sound(new1);
   end if;
end;
```

Developers can also replay and edit audio objects. You gain programmatic control over playing sounds by using the og_play_sound built-in procedure in your Oracle Graphics triggers and procedures. Sounds can be renamed, deleted, or secured in the same fashion as displays and can be imported and exported just as if they were artwork. Play or edit a sound by following these steps:

1. Select the SOUND command from the Control menu to call the Sound dialog box.

2. Edit or play the sound by clicking the Edit or Play button, respectively. Oracle Graphics invokes the operating-system sound-recording facility, providing a default name for the sound file.

3. Edit or play the sound according to the operating system procedures. Accept the dialog to return to the Sound dialog box.

4. Click the OK button to accept the sound and dismiss the dialog.

Queries in Displays

Queries are the SELECT statements or data files that retrieve information for use in a display. Queries typically serve as the basis for charts but can also be executed using PL/SQL or can be used to create and alter objects. For queries to execute successfully, the user's session must be connected to the database (using the CONNECT command on the File menu). Alternatively, the query can draw data from a file, such as a spreadsheet, although the entire file must serve as the query. To specify a data file or SELECT statement as a query, follow these steps:

1. Select the SHOW DATA TABLE command from the Control menu to call the Data Table.

2. Select the NEW command on the File menu to call the New Query dialog box.

3. Enter a new name or accept the default. Enter the phrase SQL Statement in the Type field, then click the OK button to invoke the SQL Statement Editor dialog box. For more information on SQL SELECT statements, refer to chapter 3.

    To specify a data file, select a file type from the Type list, then click the OK button. Then, select the specific filename from the File dialog. Oracle Graphics populates the Data Table with data from the specified file.

4. Enter a valid SELECT statement in the SQL Statement Editor, then click the Query button. The query is executed and the data is fetched into the Data Table.

5. Dismiss the Data Table by selecting the CLOSE command from the File menu. The query remains active until replaced or edited by another.

The og_execute_query and og_update_chart PL/SQL built-in procedures can be used to programmatically control query execution and data retrieval in a PL/SQL program. Queries can be executed in the Layout Editor by selecting the Show Data Table from the Control menu, then clicking Query and selecting the desired query. Click the Execute button to run the query. Queries can be easily renamed or deleted by following these steps:

1. Select the SHOW DATA TABLE command from the Control window to call the Data Table.

2. Click the Query button and specify the query to be renamed or deleted.

3. Select the RENAME or DELETE command from the File menu, as required by the operation. A dialog box will prompt the developer to confirm deletion of the file. Click Yes to delete the query.

If the query is to be renamed, the Rename Query dialog box will appear, allowing the developer to enter a new name for the query.

4. Click the OK button to dismiss the dialog.

All references in the display to the renamed or deleted query must then be changed to the new name of the query or dropped altogether. Queries can be altered in a similar fashion, as follows:

1. Select the SHOW DATA TABLE command from the Control menu to call the Data Table.

2. Select the MODIFY command from the File menu. For SELECT statements, edit the query using the SQL Statement Editor and click the Query button. For file-based queries, select the filename from the file dialog box. When finished, the new data populates the Data Table.

3. Dismiss the Data Table by selecting the CLOSE command from the File menu. Note that the query remains in effect until replaced by another.

Building Charts

Charts are built by first defining a query, then creating a chart template, and finally drawing the chart in the Layout Editor. Once created, a chart can be modified and altered in a variety of ways, such as being converted to static artwork. Query creation is defined in the previous section.

USING CHART TEMPLATES

Creating a chart template begins with selecting a predefined chart template, which can be customized later by altering the chart frame and field templates. In fact, field templates can be added and deleted to vary the appearance of charts that may actually be very similar. Charts are renamed, deleted, and secured in the same manner as displays and can be imported and exported in the same fashion as artwork. To create a custom chart, the developer must select a chart template, customize the chart frame and field templates, then add or delete the appropriate field templates. A predefined or customized chart template is selected by following these steps:

1. Select the SHOW CHART TEMPLATE EDITOR command from the Control menu to call the Chart Template Editor.

2. Select the NEW command from the File menu to invoke the New Template dialog box.

To select a previously customized chart template, open the Template menu and specify the chart template. The specified chart template is pulled into the Chart Template Editor and remains active until replaced by another. Dismiss the Chart Template Editor by selecting the CLOSE command from the File menu.

3. Enter a new name or accept the default, then click the OK button. This action dismisses the dialog and opens the chart frame for a default chart template in the Chart Template Editor.

4. Specify a predefined template by selecting the Chart menu and choosing the desired chart type, such as Pie or Bar. Then, select the appropriate chart template as shown on the submenu for the chart type. The chart frame appears in the Chart Template Editor and remains active until replaced.

5. Dismiss the Chart Template Editor by selecting the CLOSE command from the File menu.

CUSTOMIZING CHARTS

The chart frame is used to define the basic structure and appearance of a chart without regard to the data plotted in the chart. When a frame is showing in the Chart Template Editor, select the SHOW FRAME command from the Control menu to begin customization.

Customizing the Axis Frame

Customizable properties of an axis chart include the baseline value, baseline mapping, and category width. These values can be customized by performing the following steps:

1. Double-click the chart component to be customized (or select the FRAME command from the Properties menu) to invoke the Axis Frame Properties dialog box.

2. Define the configuration for the Axis Frame.

3. Click the OK button to apply the definitions to the chart and dismiss the dialog.

Customizing Axis Properties

Axis charts use discrete, continuous, or date axis types, which can be specified by following these steps:

1. Double-click on the axis to be customized (or select the AXIS command from the Properties menu) to invoke the Properties dialog box for the specific axis type.

2. Define the configuration of the specific axis type, then click OK when done.

3. Click the More button to set additional options controlling tick label rotation, axis position, grids, and whether to hide or show objects in the More Axis Properties dialog box. Click OK to accept the settings and return to the Properties dialog box.

4. Click the OK button to apply the definitions to the axis and dismiss the dialog.

An axis can be altered from one type to another by selecting the axis, then choosing the AXIS TYPE command from the Properties menu and setting the axis type to the desired choice. The new axis type is applied immediately. Moving a legend is equally simple. To move a legend from one location to another, select and drag the legend frame to the new position.

Customizing Reference Lines

Reference lines are display lines that appear at certain specified locations on a chart. Add a reference line to a chart by selecting the ADD REFERENCE LINE command from the Control menu. When the Reference Line property sheet appears, enter the desired options, then click the OK button to apply the changes and dismiss the dialog. Edit an existing reference line by double-clicking the line (or by selecting the REFERENCE LINE command from the Properties menu), then setting the desired options in the property sheet. As usual, click the OK button to apply the changes and dismiss the dialog. Delete a reference line by selecting the reference line to be deleted, then selecting the DELETE REFERENCE LINE command from the Control menu.

Customizing Field Templates

Field templates control the form in which data is depicted in the chart, for example, as a pie slice or bar column. The field should be showing in the Chart Template Editor before it is altered or edited. Access a specific field template by issuing the SHOW FIELD command on the Control menu from within the Chart Template Editor, then selecting the desired field template from the list. Edit the properties of the field by following these steps:

1. Double-click the field template (or issue the FIELD command on the Property menu) to call the Field Properties dialog box.

2. Define the configuration for the Field Template. Note that colors and patterns are added to field templates in the same way they are added to objects.

3. Click the OK button to apply the definitions to the field and dismiss the dialog.

Field templates are not restricted to a single field. A field template can be assigned to one field, many fields, or remain unassigned. Hence, field templates can be created and deleted by the developer on an as-needed basis. A field template can be added to a chart template by following these steps:

1. Invoke the Add Field Template dialog by selecting the ADD FIELD TEMPLATE command from the Control menu.

2. Enter a new name for the field template. Click the OK button to dismiss the dialog and add the new field template to the chart template. It can then be customized as required. The field template will not appear in the chart unless it is associated with a chart field.

A field template can be deleted by calling the Delete Field Template dialog using the DELETE FIELD TEMPLATE command on the Control menu. After the dialog appears, select the field template to be deleted, then click the Delete button. Finally, click the OK button to accept the deletion and dismiss the dialog. Any chart field associated with the deleted template must be assigned a new field template.

Customizing Miscellaneous Values

Other miscellaneous values that can be customized include shadow, depth, and the default date or number format of an object. Charts can possess a shadow, whose size and direction can be altered using the SHADOW SIZE and SHADOW DIRECTION commands on the Properties menu, respectively. The depth of a chart can be altered by selecting the DEPTH SIZE command on the Properties menu. Note that shadow and depth changes may be evident in the chart frame or field template depending on the chart type. A chart object's date or number format can be customized by selecting the object, then setting its default format using the NUMBER ATTRIBUTE or the DATE ATTRIBUTE command from the Attributes menu.

Drawing the Chart

Creation of a chart requires the developer to specify a query (either a SQL SELECT statement or file) and then choose a customized or predefined chart template. The final step is to draw the chart on the layout. Once the chart is created, it can be populated with data using the UPDATE CHART command on the Control menu or using the og_execute_query and og_update_chart built-ins. A chart can be created programmatically using a PL/SQL program with a combination of the og_get_template, og_get_query, og_execute_query, og_make, and og_update_chart built-in routines.

The steps needed to draw a chart in the layout are as follows:

1. While in the layout, choose the Chart tool from the Tool palette.

2. Click and drag diagonally until the chart region reaches the desired size, then release. The Chart Properties dialog box will then appear. Hold the [Shift] key down while dragging to create a perfect square. Note that the chart region does not include labels or legends, which may be placed outside the region.

3. Specify settings as required or accept the defaults. By default, the current chart template and current query are used in the chart. If a different chart template or query is needed, select it from the Template or Query lists.

4. Click the OK button to draw the chart in the layout and dismiss the dialog. Dynamically updated charts will show a gearbox at their center. The chart can be converted to static artwork by issuing the command CONVERT CHART TO ARTWORK from the Control menu (the gearbox will disappear). The chart object, whether dynamic or static, can now be manipulated like any other object on the layout, including being moved, resized, or even deleted.

CUSTOMIZING THE CHART

Chart customization can include giving the chart a name so that it can be referenced in PL/SQL programs or linking the chart to a button procedure. Properties of a chart are modified by following these steps:

1. Double-click the chart in the layout to call the Chart Properties dialog.

2. Set the options as required.

3. Click the OK button to accept the changes and dismiss the dialog.

CUSTOMIZING FIELD MAPPING

By default, Oracle Graphics provides field mapping for the chart based on the query. However, the developer should update field mapping whenever certain chart properties are altered, including deleting or renaming field templates, adding a field template, deleting a column from the query, or changing a column name in the query by using an alias. The steps to modifying field mapping are as follows:

1. Double-click the chart in the layout to call the Chart Properties dialog.

2. Click the Field Mapping button to invoke the Chart Field Mapping dialog.

3. Changes to field mapping are not applied until they are explicitly accepted by clicking the OK button, even if Oracle Graphics has supplied the correct defaults. Developers can also alter field mapping, within these restrictions:
   - Use the Categories or Values lists to add a category or field value
   - Select a field, then set its plotting order, according to the requirements, as Top (first to be plotted), Bottom (last to be plotted), Up (moved up one in plotting order), or Down (moved down one in plotting order). Delete a field altogether by selecting the field then clicking Delete
   - Associate a field template to a value field by selecting the value field, then selecting from the Field Template list

4. Click OK to dismiss the dialog and return to the Chart Properties dialog box.

5. Click OK to apply the new field mapping and return to the layout.

USING PARAMETERS AND PL/SQL IN ORACLE GRAPHICS

Creating and Referencing Parameters

As in other tools, such as Oracle Forms, a parameter in Oracle Graphics is a global variable that is given its value at runtime by the end-user. Parameters can be used in a display's SQL SELECT query or in the PL/SQL routines used in the display. As a result, parameters can help the developer build a very flexible application. Parameters are defined by following these steps:

1. Select the SHOW PARAMETER TABLE command from the Control menu to call the Parameter Table.

2. Enter the name of the parameter, the data type, and the initial (default) value of the parameter in the entry field above the spread table. Click the Update button to explicitly apply the parameter definition, or click on the next cell to implicitly apply the existing parameter definition and start another. Edit a cell by selecting it, then changing the data in the entry field. Delete a cell by selecting it, then backspacing over the contents or issuing the CLEAR command from the Edit menu.

3. Issue the CLOSE command from the File menu to dismiss the Parameter Table.

Like other tools of the CDE, Oracle Graphics allows the developer to reference parameters as either bind variables or lexical variables after they are created in the Parameter Table. Bind references are used to represent a single literal value in a SQL SELECT statement or PL/SQL routine, such as the value of a date, character string, or number. Bind references are prefaced by a colon (:). Lexical references are used to represent entire strings in a SQL SELECT statement (but not in PL/SQL code), such as a complete WHERE clause (or portion of a WHERE clause) or ORDER BY clause. Lexical references are prefaced by an ampersand (&). A reference must first be named in the Parameter Table, then the reference can be used in a SELECT statement or PL/SQL routine. For more information on using references in SQL or PL/SQL statements, refer to chapter 3.

Values are assigned to a parameter in one of three ways: by using the initial, default value defined in the Parameter Table; by using a PL/SQL routine to define the value; or by specifying arguments in the Runtime or Batch executable. When the display is run, the parameters are substituted with their specified values in the SQL and PL/SQL routines.

Using PL/SQL in Oracle Graphics

PL/SQL provides the developer with programmatic control over most activities that can be accomplished in Oracle Graphics. Oracle Graphics developers can create PL/SQL programs and triggers, attach PL/SQL libraries, and compile PL/SQL code and check it for consistency.

Developers can use the PL/SQL Development Environment (or their own text editor and import the code) to write PL/SQL code in Oracle Graphics. Developers can create and customize PL/SQL code using the PL/SQL Program Units Browser, accessed by issuing the SHOW PL/SQL PROGRAM UNITS command on the Control menu. In the PL/SQL Program Units Browser, click the New button to begin a new PL/SQL program, click the Load button to load a program from a file, or click the Edit button (after selecting a PL/SQL program) to edit an existing program. Developers can also create a new PL/SQL button procedure or trigger procedure by selecting the New Button or NEW TIMER/TRIGGER command from the File menu.

Once the PL/SQL code has been created or edited to meet the developer's requirements, it can be compiled with all other PL/SQL codes in the display or individually. To compile the individual PL/SQL program, click the Compile button in the PL/SQL Unit Editor while editing the code. To compile all uncompiled PL/SQL code in a given display, first issue the SHOW PL/SQL BATCH COMPILER command on the Control menu, then select the Batch Compile from the File menu. When done, click the Close button to dismiss the Batch Compiler. The commands BATCH COMPILE (FORCE) or BATCH UNCOMPILE are also available from the File menu. BATCH COMPILE (FORCE) compiles all PL/SQL code whether or not it has already been compiled. BATCH UNCOMPILE discards compiled versions of the display (primarily so that the developer can migrate a "clean" version of the code to another platform for recompiling).

Built-Ins and Exception Handling in Oracle Graphics

Oracle Graphics contains a large collection of unique built-in extensions to the PL/SQL language. Oracle Graphics built-ins provide functionality for datatypes, procedures, functions, and constants that are not found in other CDE tools. Refer to Table 6.2 for a description of the more commonly used Oracle Graphics built-ins.

Oracle Graphics also contains a number of built-in exceptions to aid in exception handling and error trapping. To make use of a built-in exception, the developer must write an exception handler or use one of the many predefined exception handlers available in Oracle Graphics, shown in Table 6.3. Exception handlers define and trap erroneous or anomalous conditions and include PL/SQL code to handle the condition. For more information on writing error handlers, refer to chapter 4.

PL/SQL Libraries

In addition to using internal PL/SQL code, Oracle Graphics developers can attach PL/SQL Libraries that are stored in the database or in a file. PL/SQL libraries are attached in Oracle Graphics using the Attached PL/SQL Libraries

Table 6.2 Oracle Graphics Built-Ins

Built-In	Type	Description
og_activate_<object>	procedure	Activates the specified object, where <object> is a layer or timer.
og_append_dir	function	Returns a string specifying a local path for files.
og_append_file	function	Returns a string that specifies the path for a specific file.
og_center	procedure	Redraws the display using the specified coordinates as the center point.
og_clone	function	Creates a duplicate of a specified object.
og_close_display	procedure	Closes the display and executes the Close Display trigger for the specified display.
og_connect	function	Displays the Connect dialog and returns TRUE if the user clicks OK, FALSE if the user clicks Cancel.
og_data_changed	function	Compares new and old dates returned by og_execute_query and returns TRUE if any records are different, FALSE if none differ.
og_data_queried	function	Checks for the specified data category in the most recent og_execute_query.
og_deactivate_timer	procedure	Deactivates a specified timer.
og_delete_field	procedure	Deletes one or many fields from the specified chart object.
og_delete_point	procedure	Deletes one or many points from a polygon or polyline.
og_destroy	procedure	Destroys any specified object and any associated child objects.
og_draw	procedure	Draws the specified object in the layout.
og_execute_query	procedure	Executes the specified query and stores the results in the Data Table. This procedure maintains the "old" and "new" data, allowing the developer to code for situations with changing data.
og_export_<object>	procedure	Exports specified portions of the layout where <object> is a drawing, image, sound, or template.
og_generate_display	procedure	Generates the specified display.
og_get_attr	procedure	Gets the attributes of a specified object and assigns them to the record attribute.
og_get_<cell>	function	Returns a value for a specified query in the current row of the specified column, where <cell> is a date, character, or number cell.
og_get_<object>	function	Returns the handle of the specified object, where <object> is a button procedure, display, field, layer, object, point, query, schema, sound, template, timer, or window.
og_help	procedure	Invokes the specified runtime help document (set in the Preferences dialog).
og_hide_<object>	procedure	Hides the specified object, where <object> is a layer or window.

Table 6.2 Oracle Graphics Built-Ins *(continued)*

Built-In	Type	Description
og_host	procedure	Passes a command to the operating system.
og_import_<object>	function	Imports the specified object, where <object> is a drawing, image, sound, or chart template.
og_insert_<object>	procedure	Inserts the specified object into a specified position, where <object> is a field, polygon point, or complex/simple text.
og_isnull	function	Determines if the specified handle is a null handle.
og_logged_on	function	Returns TRUE if the user is connected to the database.
og_logoff	procedure	Closes the existing database connection.
og_logon	procedure	Connects to the specified database.
og_make	function	Creates a new object on the active layer.
og_move	procedure	Moves the specified object to another position on the layout.
og_next_row	procedure	Advances the implicit cursor associated with the specified query.
og_numcols	function	Returns the number of columns in the specified query.
og_numrows	function	Returns the number of rows in the specified query.
og_open_display	function	Opens the specified display and executes its Open Display trigger.
og_play_sound	procedure	Plays the specified sound.
og_point_in	function	Checks to see if the specified point falls in the fill region of an object.
og_point_near	function	Checks to see if the specified point falls along the edge of an object.
og_print	procedure	Prints the contents of the layout.
og_quit	procedure	Quits the current session.
og_record_sound	procedure	Invokes the dialog to record a sound.
og_rotate	procedure	Rotates an object clockwise the specified number of degrees.
og_same	function	Checks two objects for sameness.
og_save_display	procedure	Saves the current display.
og_scale	procedure	Resizes the specified object.
og_set_attr	procedure	Sets the attributes of the display or any specified object.
og_show_<object>	procedure	Shows the specified object, where <object> is a layer or window.
og_start_from	procedure	Sets the cursor to the specified row in the Data Table.
og_synchronize	procedure	Redraws all altered regions of the display.
og_update_bbox	procedure	Updates an object's bounding box.
og_update_chart	procedure	Updates the specified chart level settings, such as the axis data.
og_user_exit	procedure	Runs the specified user exit.

Table 6.3 Oracle Graphics Built-In Exception Handlers

Error Code	Exception Name	Error Code	Exception Name
102000	og_internal_og_error	102043	og_column_type_mismatch
102001	og_internal_tk_error	102044	og_invalid_column_name
102002	og_invalid_window_dimensions	102045	og_invalid_field_type
102003	og_invalid_object_handle	102046	og_main_window_destruction
102004	og_invalid_query_handle	102047	og_invalid_cursor_offset
102005	og_invalid_template_handle	102048	og_invalid_userexit_invocation
102006	og_invalid_buttonproc_handle	102049	og_userexit_failure_error
102007	og_invalid_sound_handle	102050	og_userexit_fatal_error
102008	og_invalid_window_handle	102051	og_userexit_unknown_error
102009	og_invalid_layer_handle	102052	og_invalid_chart_update_mask
102010	og_invalid_timer_handle	102053	og_invalid_row_number
102011	og_invalid_display_handle	102054	og_invalid_chart_creation_attr
102012	og_layer_not_child_of_root	102055	og_no_database_connection
102013	og_hide_active_layer	102056	og_invalid_external_location
102014	og_parent_not_group	102057	og_invalid_transfer_mode
102015	og_invalid_color_name	102058	og_invalid_event_mask
102016	og_invalid_pattern_name	102059	og_host_failure_error
102017	og_invalid_join_style	102060	og_invalid_bbox
102018	og_invalid_cap_style	102061	og_not_chart_object
102019	og_invalid_dash_style	102062	og_not_group_object
102020	og_invalid_object_type	102063	og_not_polygon_object
102021	og_root_object_destruction	102064	og_not_image_object
102022	og_invalid_arrowstyle	102065	og_not_text_object
102023	og_invalid_symbol_index	102066	og_invalid_arc_fill
102024	og_invalid_symbol_size	102067	og_invalid_field_template
102025	og_invalid_text_spacing	102068	og_missing_chart_field
102026	og_invalid_text_horalign	102069	og_invalid_field_datatype
102027	og_invalid_text_horjust	102070	og_invalid_data_value
102028	og_invalid_text_vertalign	102071	og_pctchart_zero
102029	og_invalid_text_vertjust	102072	og_no_dependent_fields
102030	og_open_display_failure	102073	og_piechart_sum_overflow
102031	og_invalid_child_index	102074	og_date_overflow
102032	og_invalid_child_del_total	102075	og_query_execution_error
102033	og_invalid_point_index	102076	og_sql_execution_error
102034	og_active_layer_del	102077	og_invalid_data_file
102035	og_invalid_point_del_total	102078	og_invalid_sylk_format
102036	og_invalid_cmptext_index	102079	og_invalid_prn_format
102037	og_invalid_cmptext_del_total	102080	og_invalid_wks_format
102038	og_invalid_smptext_index	102081	og_row_retrieval_failure
102039	og_invalid_smptext_del_total	102082	og_invalid_image_format
102040	og_invalid_field_index	102083	og_image_creation_failure
102041	og_invalid_field_del_total	102084	og_invalid_sound_format
102042	og_invalid_data_flag	102085	og_login_failure

Table 6.3 Oracle Graphics Built-In Exception Handlers *(continued)*

Error Code	Exception Name	Error Code	Exception Name
102086	og_logoff_failure	102105	og_generate_display_failure
102087	og_image_export_failure	102106	og_duplicate_display_name
102088	og_sound_export_failure	102107	og_invalid_query_source
102089	og_invalid_drawing_format	102108	og_invalid_date_format
102091	og_drawing_export_failure	102109	og_invalid_query_type
102092	og_template_export_failure	102110	og_null_module_name
102093	og_image_import_failure	102111	og_print_failure
102094	og_sound_import_failure	102112	og_invalid_timer_procedure
102095	og_drawing_import_failure	102113	og_invalid_timer_interval
102096	og_template_import_failure	102114	og_no_chart_data
102097	og_colors_not_writable	102115	og_display_closed
102098	og_font_not_found	102116	og_invalid_child_object
102099	og_invalid_column_index	102117	og_no_sound_output_device
102100	og_logon_disallowed	102118	og_no_sound_input_device
102101	og_logoff_disallowed	102119	og_too_many_data_rows
102102	og_env_var_error	102120	og_sound_conversion_failure
102103	og_env_var_notfound	102121	og_invalid_compression_type
102104	og_save_display_failure		

Browser. Access the PL/SQL Libraries Browser by issuing the SHOW AT-TACHED LIBRARIES command on the Control menu. Developers can click the New button to begin a new library or use the Edit button to modify an existing one (and the Compile button to save any changes). To attach a library to the current display, select the PL/SQL library from the list and click the Attach button. To detach a library from the current display, select the library from the list and click the Detach button.

Validity Checking

Developers can use the Oracle Graphics Consistency Checker utility to ensure that PL/SQL routines in the display are completely valid. An invalid PL/SQL routine might include code that contains a reference to a trigger that does not exist or a variable name that has no assigned value. Developers can invoke and use the Consistency Checker by selecting the SHOW CONSISTENCY CHECKER command on the Control menu. Then, select the CONSISTENCY CHECK command under the File menu to get a report of inconsistencies in the message display field. When done, select the CLOSE command on the File menu to dismiss the dialog.

Triggers

Oracle Graphics allows the use of three important triggers: Timer, Open Display, and Close Display triggers. Timer triggers execute a block of PL/SQL code at specified intervals, such as when updating a chart every minute or two. Timer triggers do not count execution time within their specified interval, so a trigger that is set to run every 90 seconds and takes 10 seconds to run itself will fire every 100 seconds. You can programmatically abort a timer using the og_deactivate_timer built-in. Figure 6.15 shows the Timer Trigger Dialog.

The TIMER TRIGGER DIALOG command can be found under the command menu. Clicking the New button will create a new timer for your display, which you can rename in the Rename field. Specify the PL/SQL procedure you want executed (which is created using the PL/SQl Editor) and the interval at which you wish it to execute in the appropriate fields. Then, click Apply to apply the timer to the display and OK to exit the dialog. Here is an example of a timer trigger procedure you might create using the PL/SQL Program Units Browser:

```
procedure update_chart is
   my_query      og_query;
   my_chart      og_object;
begin
   my_query := og_get_query('Student Grade Query');
   my_chart := og_get_object('Student Grade Chart');
   og_execute_query('my_query');
   og_update_chart(my_chart, OG_ALL_CHUPDA);
end;
exception when og_no_database_connection then message('Not connected
to database');
```

Note that the Timer Trigger always fires after any Open Display Trigger you have specified.

The Open/Close Display executes a block of PL/SQL code whenever you open or close the display. Good uses for this type of trigger include setting the initial behavior of the display and optionally printing the display. Assign Open Display and Close Display triggers by issuing the OPEN/CLOSE DISPLAY TRIGGER command under the Control menu in the Layout Editor. Once the dialog appears, assign your previously created PL/SQL procedures to the Open trigger and Close trigger as desired, then click OK to exit the dialog.

Note that with any of the three triggers, you can use only stand-alone, previously created blocks of PL/SQL code. You cannot execute PL/SQL proce-

Figure 6.15 Timer Trigger Dialog

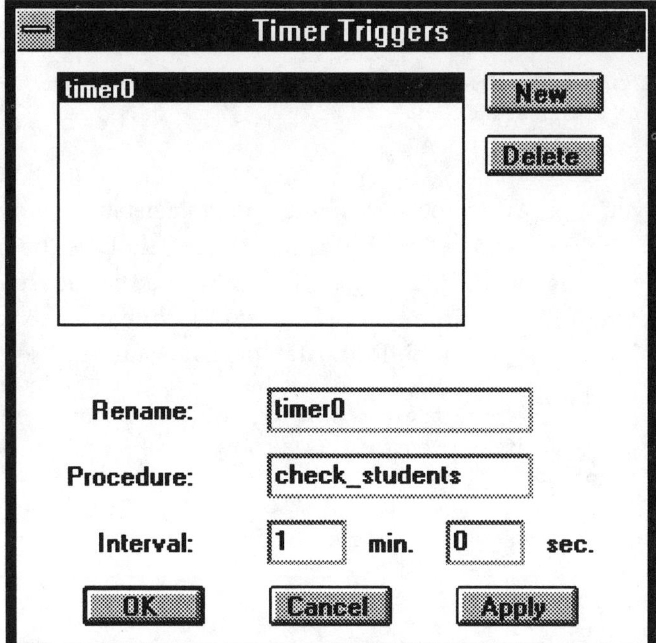

dures contained in a package unless you first create an Oracle Graphics procedure that specifically calls that package.

Button Procedures

You can program your display to perform certain activities, at the click of a mouse, on either an object (such as a button) or an entire layer. You can specify a PL/SQL procedure to fire on the following mouse events: mouse down, when the mouse button is depressed; mouse up, when the mouse button is released; mouse move down, when the mouse is moved with the button depressed; and, mouse move up, when the mouse is moved without the button being depressed. Mouse move up is applicable only to layers, not to objects.

To program a button procedure, you must associate a procedure with the object and set it up so that it will accept one or more mouse events, either in the object's Property dialog or using PL/SQL procedures. Button procedures have to have four specific arguments, as shown in the default procedure header built by the PL/SQL Program Units Browser when you select a new button procedure:

```
procedure PROCEDURE_NAME(buttonobj in og_object, hitobj in og_object, win in
    og_window, eventinfo in og_event) is
    ...<<<PL/SQL code>>>...
```

In this case, you supply the procedure name, though a default is provided. Buttonobj is the object associated with this procedure. Hitobj is the object that detects the mouse event. Win is the window where the mouse event should be detected. And, eventinfo is a specific set of information about the procedure, stored in the og_event built-in datatype. For example:

```
procedure move_n_spin_display(buttonobj in og_object, hitobj in
og_object, win in og_window, eventinfo in og_event) is
    move_offset og_point;
begin
    if eventinfo.event_type = OG_MOUSE_DOWN then
       move_offset.x := 1.5 * OG_INCH;
       move_offset.y := 1.5 * OG_INCH;
       og_move(buttonobj, move_offset);
    else eventinfo.event_type = OG_MOUSE_UP then
       og_rotate(buttonobj, eventinfo.mouse_position, 45);
    end if;
end;
```

CUSTOMIZING THE DESIGNER WORK ENVIRONMENT

A number of the work environment features can be customized, including preferences (described earlier in the chapter), layout, rulers and grids, layers, views (also discussed earlier in the chapter), and drawing options. When the Designer work environment is customized to the developer's tastes, the settings remain in effect for the current and subsequent sessions until reset.

Customizing the Layout

By customizing the layout, developers can create a personalized layout appearance. Layout settings, as discussed earlier, control layout size and page direction. The developer can display the entire layout on the screen by issuing the FIT TO WINDOW command on the Arrange menu or can use the

MAGNIFICATION command to increase or decrease the size of the layout view. Additionally, the developer can hide or show layout elements like palettes, the status line, rulers, ruler guides, grids, and page breaks. To hide or show a specific element, select the element type from the Arrange menu (which contains an entry for each element) and toggle the item as hidden or shown. Some elements, such as rulers and grids, can be further customized by selecting the RULER SETTINGS and GRID SNAP commands, respectively, from the Arrange menu, then altering their settings as desired.

Customizing Layers

Layers are a very powerful feature of Oracle Graphics; they allow the display to hide and show various objects at designated times. For example, a button on one layer can invoke a piece of artwork on another layer. To add a layer to the display, follow these steps:

1. Invoke the Layer Settings dialog by issuing the LAYER SETTINGS command on the Arrange menu.

2. Click the New button. A new layer with the default name of LayerX (where *x* is the next available increment) appears as the active layer. If multiple views exist, the layer is added to all views, though it is active only in the active view.

    The layer can be renamed by reinvoking the Layer Settings dialog. Select the layer to be renamed from the Existing Layers list and alter the name as required in the Rename field. Click the Rename button to replace the old name.

3. Click the OK button.

Layers must be activated for the developer to perform any work on the layer. To activate a single layer, open the Layer Settings dialog by selecting the LAYER SETTINGS command on the Arrange menu. Then, select the layer to activate from the Existing Layers list, and click the Activate button. The layer becomes active and visible, if it was hidden. Now, click the OK button to dismiss the dialog. Layers can be activated using PL/SQL code, as shown in the following example:

```
procedure activate_a_layer(layer_no in number, window_name in og_window)
is
      the_layer         varchar2(6);
      my_layer          og_layer;
```

```
begin
     the_layer         :='layer'||to_char(layer_no);
     my_layer          :=og_get_layer(the_layer);
     og_activate_layer(the_layer, window_name);
end;
```

Layers and the objects they contain can be hidden or shown at any time. In fact, many layers can be hidden or shown at one time. The active layer is always the topmost layer. You can make another layer the active layer simply by clicking on it. You can hide or show a layer in PL/SQL by using the og_hide_layer and og_show_layer built-ins or by following these steps:

1. Invoke the Layout Settings dialog box by issuing the LAYER SETTINGS command from the Arrange menu.

2. Select the layer to be hidden or shown from the list of Existing Layers.

3. Click the Hide/Show button. All layer names will appear in a pop-up list. Hidden layers that are now shown will display a plus sign (+) in front of the layer name, while previously shown layers that are now hidden will display a minus sign (-) by the layer name.

4. Click OK.

Layers lie one on top of another. The order in which layers are placed is called the stacking order. Developers can control the stacking order by calling the Layer Settings dialog (from the Arrange menu) and selecting a specific layer from the list of Existing Layers. After choosing the layer that will be moved in the stacking order, click the Up button (moves the layer up one), the Down button (moves the layer down one), the Top button (moves the layer to the top of the stack), or the Bottom button (moves the layer to the bottom of the stack). Then click OK. Use the Delete button to delete a selected layer and all of its objects from the stack.

Customizing Drawing Options

The general drawing options, as well as options for other important visual properties of the display, are controlled through the Attributes menu. Developers can specify defaults for these properties so that the developers' preferences are automatically applied as the default in the layout. The Attribute menu offers control over font; text spacing and justification; the appearance of lines, dashes, arrows and symbols; color editing; and freehand drawing options. Drawing options are available to govern the default General drawing settings, Arc drawing settings, Text drawing settings, and Rounded Rectangle drawing settings. To alter any of the desired settings, select the appropriate command from the Attributes menu and configure the settings as desired. The configuration remains in effect until changed.

EXECUTABLES

Oracle Graphics executables include the Designer, Runtime, and Batch components. The executables can be launched from their icons in the GUI or by a command-line prompt with any necessary arguments. Command-line executables can also include keywords to control the behavior of Oracle Graphics, shown in Table 6.4.

Designer

The Designer component is used to create and optimize the Oracle Graphics display applications. Designer is the portion used most often by developers. The command-line executable for Designer is OG20DES. For example, to launch Oracle Graphics Designer and to automatically load and print a display to a nondefault printer, enter:

```
og20des openfile=my_display print=yes printer=aux_printer
```

This example shows how developers can also provide their usernames and passwords, as well as specify the automatic generation of two files (and print only the first of two files), when Oracle Designer is loaded:

```
og20des userid=(kevin/triangle) openfile=(my_file1, my_file2)
   generatefile=(my_file1, my_file2) print=(yes, no)
```

Runtime

The Runtime component invokes the Oracle Graphics runtime environment, allowing end-users to run the display only. Runtime is the component of Oracle Graphics most often used by end-users. The command-line executable for Runtime is OG20RUN. For example, to run a display using the end-user's automatic OPS$ login and to automatically execute commands stored in the file MY_COMMANDS, enter the following:

```
og20run userid=( ) openfile=my_file cmdfile=my_commands
```

Table 6.4   Oracle Graphics Executable Keywords

Keyword*	Value**	Used By***	Usage
USERID	=(userid)	D,R,B	Database login; enter USERID=( ) to use the automatic OPS$ database login.
OPENFILE	=(filename and path)	D,R,B	Path and filename of display to be opened.
OPENDB	=(display_name)	D,R,B	Name of display in the database to be opened.
PRINT	=(yes/no)	D,R,B	Yes prints the display to the default printer.
COPIES	=(n)	D,R,B	Number of copies of the display to be printed.
PRINTER	=(printer_name)	D,R,B	Name of the printer used in the PRINT command.
PRINTFILE	=(filename and path)	D,R,B	Name of file to print in PostScript format.
EXPORTFILE	=(filename and path)	D,R,B	Name of file to export display using Oracle format; even hidden layers are exported.
EXPORTCGM	=(filename and path)	D,R,B	Name of file to export display using CGM format; even hidden layers are exported.
EXPORTBIT	=(16/32)	D,R,B	Specifies CGM file format as 16- or 32-bit.
EXPORTDB	=(db_name)	D,R,B	Name of database object to export display as drawing in Oracle format; even hidden layers are exported; users must also be logged in using USERID.
GENERATEFILE	=(filename and path)	D	Name of file where the display will be generated; PL/SQL will be compiled and errors will be shown in LOGFILE.
GENERATEDB	=(display_name)	D	Same as GENERATEFILE command, but contents will be stored in database; users must be logged in using USERID.
SAVEFILE	=(filename and path)	D	Name of file where display will be saved.
SAVEDB	=(display_name)	D	Name display will be saved under in database; users must be logged in using USERID.
CLOSE	=(yes/no)	D,R	Indicates the executable should be closed when processing is finished.
QUIT	=(yes/no)	D,R	Indicates the Oracle Graphics session should be terminated when processing for all open displays is finished.

Table 6.4 Oracle Graphics Executable Keywords *(continued)*

Keyword*	Value**	Used By***	Usage
CMDFILE	=(filename and path)	D,R,B	A text file that contains valid command-line arguments, allowing the developer to create standard sets of arguments; it may contain arguments for one single-line command only, with command keywords separated by a space or blank line.
LOGFILE	=(filename and path)	D,R,B	A text file in which any error messages will be written (if they cannot be shown in an alert box).
MODULE	=(filename and path)	D,R,B	Synonym for openfile.
PARAMNAME	=(value)	D,R,B	Name(s) and value(s) of parameter(s) defined in the display. Values entered on the command line will overwrite any default value for the parameter.

*   Keywords are shown in the order in which they should appear in an Oracle Graphics executable ,that is, userid first, openfile second, and so on.

**   Values shown in parentheses may actually include a list of values, with each item separated by a comma. For example, to open three files the openfile keyword string might read `openfile=(myfile1, myfile2, myfile3)`.

***   D = the keyword is usable in Designer executables; R = the keyword is usable in Runtime executables; B = the keyword is usable in Batch executables.

Batch

The Batch component is used to call Oracle Graphics Batch mode for directing the output of a display to a file, printer, or even the database. The Batch terminates automatically when all processing is completed. The command-line executable for Batch is OG20BAT. For example, the following batch command opens and prints multiple copies of a file, prints a CBM image of the display to file, and utilizes a date parameter:

```
og20bat openfile=c:\graphics\employee\my_file3 print=yes copies=3
    exportcgm=c:\images\file3.cgm dateparam='14-JUN-95'
```

CONCLUSION

Oracle Graphics provides the developer with a powerful multimedia graphic display tool, including direct dynamic links into an Oracle database. Developers can use Oracle Graphics, including its capability to link to non-Oracle data sources, to quickly simplify and condense data that is difficult to interpret (because of quantity or other factors). In addition, Oracle Graphics's sound capabilities provide the developer with a complete multimedia presentation tool.

After studying this chapter, you should understand the basic steps needed to create an Oracle Graphics display and the basic components of a display, from the objects, layers, and palettes to the queries, PL/SQL procedures, and templates that make up a chart. You should understand the placement and manipulation of display objects that you create or import using the tools of the Layout Editor and the display object property sheets.

Additionally, you should know how to use chart templates to take advantage of the numerous, predefined chart types that Oracle Graphics makes available, as well as how to modify a predefined chart template. You should be able to use PL/SQL to create procedures, triggers, and button events within your display. And finally, you should be able to customize your own working environment within Oracle Graphics, as well as write effective command-line executables to invoke displays created with Oracle Graphics in other CDE products, such as Oracle Forms or Oracle Reports.

7 INTRODUCTION TO ORACLE BOOK, VERSION 1.0

INTRODUCTION

Although the idea of on-line help is not new, the quality and frequency of on-line documentation have risen dramatically only since developers began to provide meaningful help in the Windows environment. For many years, the best users could hope for was an occasional hint on the status line and an afternoon spent browsing the user manual. Now, within a Windows or other GUI-based application, end-users practically demand a clearly and accurately written help system, complete with hypertext links to bind together related topics.

This chapter explains how to use Oracle Book to create and use on-line electronic documents as a form of on-line help within other Oracle applications. Provided is a step-by-step overview of the Oracle Book Tag Language, Oracle Book file creation and implementation, and the general usage of Oracle Book documents. By including Oracle Book documents in their CDE applications, developers can improve the usability and appearance of their information system (and make themselves look a little better in the eyes of the end-user too!).

ORACLE BOOK OVERVIEW

Oracle Book enables developers to create electronic user manuals that are available from anywhere within an Oracle CDE application. Oracle Book documents are very similar to more common paperbound software user manuals. They can contain pictures, graphs, and tables, as well as instructions and text. However, Oracle Book documents are much more powerful than regular text documents since they can be placed where the user can take greater advantage of their information: within the application. Oracle Book documents can also augment hard-copy user manuals by including audio effects and video animation.

Oracle Book provides a number of important benefits for the application developer, including improved communication of information and instructions through a seamless integration of text, sound, images, and video; greater control of distribution with reduced costs compared to paper-based document production; easy modification of documents with updates immediately visible to users; and powerful documents that can access other documents or invoke other programs through hypertext links.

Oracle Book contains three main programs: Oracle Book Runtime, Oracle Book Designer, and Oracle Sound. The Oracle Book Runtime tool enables users to view and mark an Oracle Book document created by someone else. Oracle Book Designer is the primary tool for the creation of Oracle Book documents. Oracle Sound allows developers to create or add sound effects to Oracle Book documents. This chapter first discusses the creation of a document using Oracle Book Designer and Oracle Sound and then the reading of a document using Oracle Book Runtime.

OVERVIEW OF DOCUMENT CREATION

Creating documents with Oracle Book requires the use of a text editor or word processor (to create build files), the Oracle Book Tag Language, and the Oracle Book executables. (See Figure 7.1 for an overview.)

The Document Source File

At the foundation level, Oracle Book requires a source text file created with almost any text editor or word processor. Developers can use any word processor to create the starting document, as long as it can create ASCII or EBCDIC documents. The basic ASCII document is then given mark-up enhancements using the word processor and the Oracle Book Tag Language. The word processor may even take advantage of "hidden text" features, as long as the ASCII file contains the hidden text.

Oracle Book Tag Language

The Oracle Book Tag Language allows the application developer to program the standard and special features that make up an Oracle Book document.

Figure 7.1 Overview of Document Creation

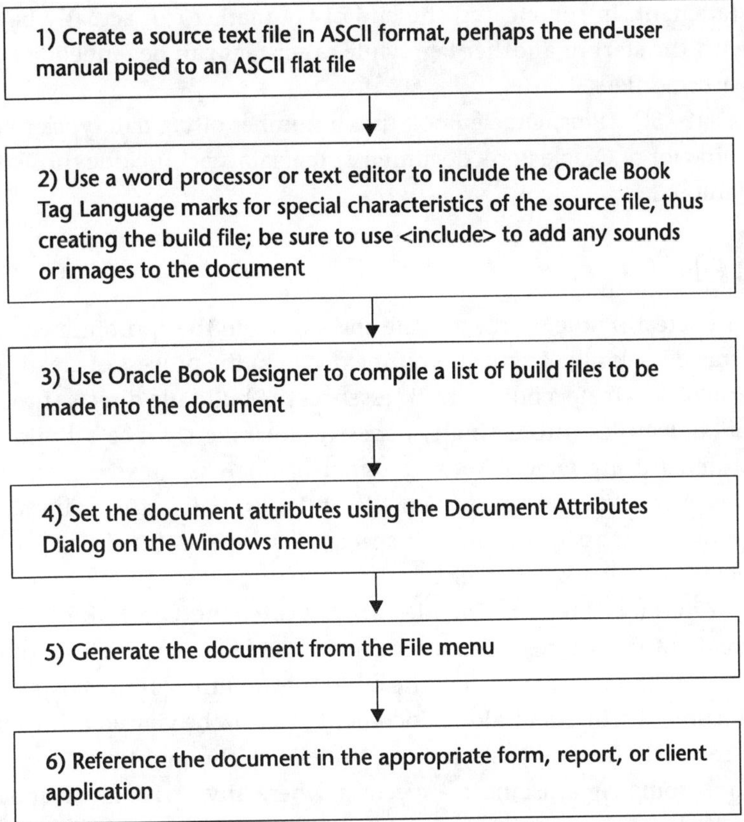

Special features, like boldface or even graphics or audio, are included in Oracle Book documents through the use of *tags*, special markers that tell Oracle how to display the components of the document, such as header styles, indexes, or even video and sound.

Adding an Oracle Book tag to a source file is quite simple, since most tags are structured as follows:

```
<tag_name>TEXT</tag_name>
```

The angle brackets (< >) are required around the tag names. They indicate where the tag begins and ends, while the text between the tags behaves according to the tag characteristics. Some tags, such as <char>, <tabs>, and

<include file>, do not require an end tag, but most end-of-tags must contain the forward slash (/) and the name of the tag shown at the beginning of the statement. In some cases, the end-of-tag marker can actually be substituted with the start of another tag; while other tags can be embedded or "nested" within others.

Like SQL*Plus, Oracle Book uses a number of tag datatypes to control the behavior of Oracle Book documents. Tag datatypes include those described in Table 7.1.

The Build File

After creating the source text file and adding in the appropriate tags using the Oracle Book Tag Language, your next step in the process of creating an Oracle Book is to create a build file. In essence, the build file directs the compilation of source files into a single, cohesive document. Once a build file is constructed using Oracle Book Designer or an ASCII text editor, Oracle Book Designer takes the source text file and tags, builds the pointers to any included files, assigns values for special developer-defined flags, and creates a new Oracle Book document.

Typically, three or four files are left after the Oracle Book Designer has created the document (excluding any included files): the text source file, the marked and tagged text file, the build file, and the completely self-contained document. The stand-alone document can now be viewed using Oracle Book. The source file and build file can be deleted, though it may be unwise to do so in some circumstances, especially where any revisions or updates are expected.

CREATING A BUILD FILE USING ORACLE BOOK DESIGNER

Create a build file by launching Oracle Book Designer from the operating system. Then, list all files used by the document in the build file list. Figure 7.2 shows the Oracle Book Designer interface.

After invoking Oracle Book Designer, include all marked-up files to be processed by first clicking the Add File button at the bottom of the Oracle Book Designer window. When the File dialog box appears, select the file to add from the File dialog box. The file will then appear in the list for the build file. Repeat these steps to add all the necessary files. By default, files are added to the end of the list but can be reordered by highlighting the desired position on the list and then clicking the Add button. When appropriate, use the SAVE BUILD FILE command on the File menu to save the build file and its

Table 7.1 Oracle Book Tags Quick Reference

Tag Name   *Description*

<\character>   Used to enter reserved characters, since it causes Oracle Book to ignore the next character. For example, angle brackets (< >) typically invoke one of the tags. Placing a backslash in front of the angle brackets causes Oracle Book Designer to process them as characters, not a tag entity. To display a backslash, use two backslashes. No end-of-tag is needed.

<char>   Used to insert a special character, like a trademark or copyright symbol, unless the symbol is unavailable on the reader's system, in which case a substitute is used. <char> types include:

<char-box>	check box
<char-bullet>	bullet
<char-c>	copyright
<char-dagger>	dagger
<char-ellipsis>	ellipsis
<char-line>	long line
<char-r>	registered trademark
<char-tm>	trademark

End-of-tags are not required, causing <char> to display the special character at its designated position. However, an end-of-entity tag can be used to reserve text between the start tag and end tag as a hidden comment.

<headingN>   Used to create an automated, navigable table of contents. The heading numbering scheme places the items in an outline form in the table of contents, with level 0 headings at the top (chapter headings) down to level 9 subheadings. Every document must have at least one level 0 heading, though Oracle Book will provide a default <heading0> tag using the document filename if one is not specified. The <heading0> tag divides the document into chapters, allowing users to navigate using the NEXT CHAPTER and PREVIOUS CHAPTER commands in the Navigate menu. For example:

```
<heading0>Oracle Book Designer's Reference</heading0>
<heading1>Preface</heading1>
```

<host>   Invokes a platform-dependent command line, such as a user exit, within an Oracle Book document. The <host> tag appears as an icon in the document; selecting the icon invokes the HOST command. The <host> tag must indicate the platform type and command line, as shown in the following example, and no end-of-tag is required. Common platforms include "mac" for Apple Macintosh, "dos" for Microsoft Windows or DOS, and "unix" for all UNIX platforms. For example:

```
<host platform = "dos" command = "C:\UTILS\SYSINFO">
```

<if>   <if> tags, which cannot be nested, allow conditional performance of an action in the document. Text and commands between the <if> tag and the end-of-tag are processed only if the "flag" has the specified value. By default, the flag is

(continued)

Table 7.1   Oracle Book Tags Quick Reference *(continued)*

Tag Name   *Description*

"TRUE" if no value is specified. Flag values can be assigned in the Build file and in the Document Attributes dialog. For example:

```
<if MACHINE = "dos">
<include file = "table_schema" type = "TIFF">
</if>
```

The TIFF image file will be included in the document only if the flag "MACHINE" has been set to "dos."

<if-not>   Similar to <if> tags, except processing occurs only if the "flag" does not have the specified value or is "FALSE." A flag with no value is considered "FALSE." Except for the tag syntax <if-not VALUE = "some value"> </if-not>, <if-not> tags are otherwise the same as <if> tags.

<include file>   Inserts the contents of an external file into a document. Included files can be just about anything—text, image, sound, or video—though the type clause should specify the format of the included file. The optional caption clause provides a title for video and images. No end-of-tag is needed. The syntax for the <include> tag follows:

```
<include  file = "file name" type = "type name" caption = "label">
```

File types supported by the <include> statement are as follows:

Type	*Format*	*Description*
Text:	TEXT	(ASCII text)
Image:	BMP	(Windows 3.1 bitmap format)
	PCX	(DOS bitmap format)
	PICT	(Macintosh graphics format—image data only)
	PNTG	(MacPaint format—scaled)
	TIFF	(Tagged Image File Format—scaled)
	UBMP	(Windows 3.1 format—unscaled)
	UPCX	(DOS bitmap format—unscaled)
	UPIC	(Macintosh graphics format—unscaled)
	UPNT	(MacPaint format—unscaled)
	UTIF	(Tagged Image File Format—unscaled)
Sound:	AIFC	(sound format)
Video:	AVI	(Audio Video Interleaved—Windows 3.1)
	MOOV	(QuickTime Movie Format—Apple Macintosh)
	SGI	(Silicon Graphics Movie Format)

Scaled images appear at their true size, while unscaled images vary in size depending on the screen resolution; however, unscaled images are generally of better display quality than scaled images. Text and image files can appear within the document text or as icons. Video and sound files can appear as icons only and are activated when clicked. Nonvideo files are inserted into the document at the location of the tag, adding to the physical bulk of the document. Video files

Table 7.1 Oracle Book Tags Quick Reference *(continued)*

Tag Name   *Description*

are not stored in the document. Changes in an included text, image, or sound file do not appear in a document unless the document is regenerated, but changes in video files are reflected immediately. Use the <host> tag to display file types not available under <include>. For example:

```
<include file = "c:\cad\sys_diag type" = "tiff">
<host    platform = "dos" command = "c:\images\vgif.exe 0135PIC.GIF">
```

<index>   Used to create an automated, navigable index for the document in the Index dialog. An <index> tag must be placed with each item to appear in the index. The text of the item itself acts as the default, though a specific primary and secondary index label can be specified using the TERM clause, with a semicolon to separate the two items. For example:

```
<index term = "Dialog Box;Pop-Up Window">
```

<info>   Creates Get Info text for a document. Only one info tag is allowed per document, and it may not contain other tags. For example:

```
<info>
Teacher Grading System User Reference
Version 2.2
Copyright 1995, Smith Corporation.  All rights reserved.
</info>
```

<link>   Creates a source for a hypertext link. Targets for hypertext links are defined by the <target> tag. The <link> tags and <target> tags must be paired with names that match exactly. A separate link is required for each region of hypertext and must have an end-of-tag marker. Targets in other documents must have specified document ID. The link navigates to the first available target with the same target name. The <heading> tags can also serve as targets. The target name is optional and defaults to the text of the tag when no target name is supplied. For example:

```
<link>Tardiness</link> , or
<link>linkname="Tardiness" id="Intro"</link>
```

<style>   Applies a display attribute, or typeface, to a portion of text. Text held between the start tag and end-of-tag is displayed with the specified typeface. Oracle Book supports the following default styles:

_bold	a boldface font
_italic	an italicized font
_emphasis	an emphasized font
_plain	a plain text font
_mono	a monotype font

Style attributes cannot be combined, since <style> tags act as an end-of-tag for any previous <style> tags. Multiple <style> tags must be manually created using Oracle*Terminal (discussed in chapter 8).

(continued)

Table 7.1   Oracle Book Tags Quick Reference *(continued)*

Tag Name   *Description*

<tabs>   Establish tab settings for a region of text. Tab stops can be of two types: *lt* (left tab) or *li* (left indent tab). Text following a tab character and a left tab is indented the specified amount, word-wrapping to the specified column until the next end-of-line character. As many as eight tab stops are allowable per line and continue to be in effect until an end-of-tag marker or another <tab> tag is encountered. Tabs display as blank spaces, though tabs greater than ten characters in length are ignored in the document. For example, where a backslash (\) appears as a source-file tag symbol, the following code:

```
<tabs lt=20, lt=30, lt=40>
\tBike\tCar\tBoat
Wheels\tYES\tYES\tNO
Propeller\tNO\tNO\tYES
Vehicle\tYES\tYES\tYES
Doors\tNO\tYES\tNO
</tabs>
```

appears as:

```
              Bike      Car       Boat
Wheels        YES       YES       NO
Propeller     NO        NO        YES
Vehicle       YES       YES       YES
Doors         NO        YES       NO
```

<target>   Creates a target for a hypertext link, defined by the <link> tag. By default, the text of the tag is used as the target name, or a target name can be applied. A target name must be unique, though the <link> need not be.

<verbatim>   Indicates that a specific region of text should appear exactly as it is typed into the document. The <verbatim> tag prevents word wrapping or proportional spacing when printed or displayed and displays the text <verbatim> tag item in the "_mono" style. For example:

```
<verbatim>
a question mark
  * * * * * *
 * * * * * * * *
* * *     * * *
      * * *
    * * *
  * * *
  * * *

  * * *
  * * *
</verbatim>
```

Figure 7.2 Oracle Book Designer Interface

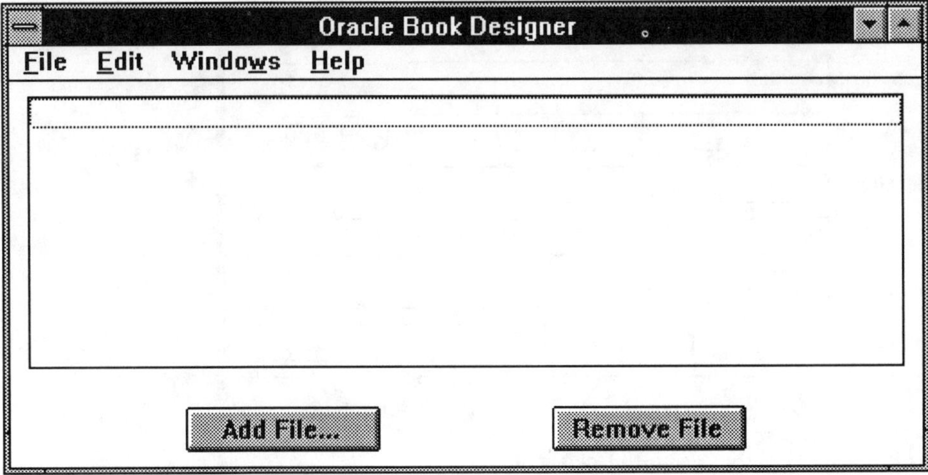

document attributes. Files at or below that position on the list will be pushed down. A file can be removed from the list by highlighting the file and then selecting the Remove File button.

DOCUMENT ATTRIBUTES IN ORACLE BOOK DESIGNER

Only one step remains before the build file can be generated into an Oracle Book document: setting the document attributes. Document attributes can be set by using the Document Attributes dialog box or by embedding document attribute markers in the build file with a text editor. In the Document Attributes dialog box, describe the document title and location, ID number, and any attribute flags. Document attributes can be edited by selecting the DOC ATTRIBUTES command from the Windows menu. The Document Attributes dialog box appears, as shown in Figure 7.3.

The Document Attributes dialog box is fully described in Table 7.2.

USER-DEFINED FLAGS

You can enter user-defined flags, used as values in determining the processing of <if> and <if-not> tags, in the Document Attributes dialog. To create and set these flags in the Document Attributes dialog, follow these steps:

Figure 7.3 Document Attributes Dialog

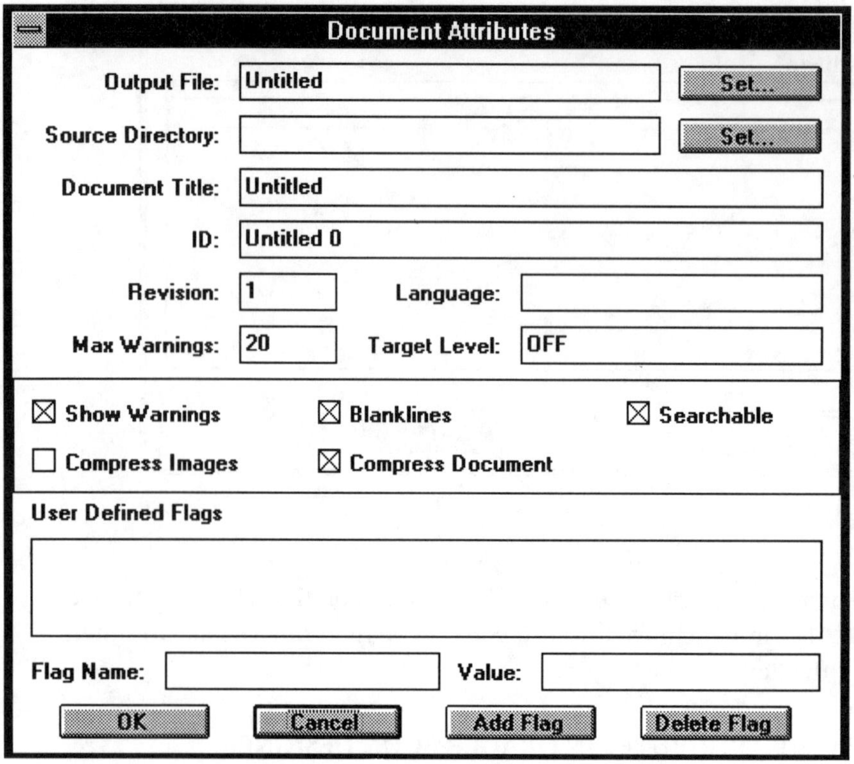

Document Attributes

Output File: Untitled [Set...]

Source Directory: [Set...]

Document Title: Untitled

ID: Untitled 0

Revision: 1   Language:

Max Warnings: 20   Target Level: OFF

☒ Show Warnings   ☒ Blanklines   ☒ Searchable
☐ Compress Images   ☒ Compress Document

User Defined Flags

Flag Name: Value:

[OK]   [Cancel]   [Add Flag]   [Delete Flag]

1. Put the name of the flag in the Flag Name field.

2. Give the flag an initial value in the Value field. Flags can be any alphanumeric value and any length.

3. Use the Add Flag button to add the flag and its corresponding value to the list of flags.

You can edit a preexisting flag and/or its value by selecting it from the list and editing the values in the appropriate field. To remove the flag from the list, select the flag from the list and use the Delete Flag button. All flags that are undefined are set to "FALSE," while all flags with a name but no value are set to "TRUE."

Table 7.2 Document Attributes

Attribute	Description
Document Title	The title for the generated document, which can be up to forty characters long. The title, which defaults to "Untitled," appears in dialog boxes and windows but does not affect the operating system filename.
Output File	The operating system path and filename for the document; "untitled.obd" by default. This field is ignored when saving to the database.
Source Directory	The path and directory where all marked-up and included files are housed. The default is the same directory in which Oracle Book is located. The <include> files and build files must explicitly describe their path, unless the files are in the same directory as Oracle Book.
Document ID	A unique identifier for the document; can be any combination of alphanumeric characters; "UNTITLED0" is the default.
Revision	Keeps track of document version numbers, but defaults to "1".
Language	The National Language Support identifier for the document; "american_america.us7ascii" is the default. This setting allows you to use different language defaults and character sets.
Max Warnings	The maximum number of warning messages stored in the Messages window; can be up to 999. Document generation aborts when reaching the maximum number of warnings. The default is "20."
Target Level	Controls the level of headings processed as a target for the link tag. Heading levels with a number greater than the specified target level are not processed. The default is "OFF," which does not process any headings as targets.
Searchable	Defines the document as searchable through the Oracle Book Find dialog box. Oracle Book appends a search list to searchable documents, increasing the size of the file by one to two times. Documents are searchable by default.
Blanklines	Defines paragraph markers as one or two carriage returns. If checked, two returns start a new paragraph (the default); otherwise, one return starts a new paragraph.
Warnings	Enables or disables warnings while the document is being generated. The default is unchecked, causing no warnings to be displayed.
Compress Images	Compresses all images included with the <include> file tag. Compressed images consume less disk space but are slower to display and build. The default is unchecked.
Compress Document	Compresses the final Oracle Book document. Compressed documents consume less disk space but are slower to build. Viewing time is the same for compressed and uncompressed documents. As a rule of thumb, uncompress only working documents. The default is compressed.

CREATING A BUILD FILE WITH A TEXT EDITOR

Simple build files can contain only a list of files to be processed as chapters, but more complex build files can contain comments and flag settings that affect the usability of the file. Three special types of lines can be added to a build file: comment lines, flag lines, and tag lines. Each line must be terminated by a carriage return or newline character. Table 7.3 describes the document attribute text markers that can be manually added to the build file through a word processor or text editor.

GENERATING THE DOCUMENT

The final step in creating an Oracle Book document is the generation process. By now, the build file should include all the tagged and marked-up text files assembled either by using the Add File button and all the document settings configured through the Document Attributes dialog box or by using a text editor. Now perform these steps to generate an Oracle Book document:

1. Select the GENERATE DOCUMENT command from the File menu.

2. Select the build file to be processed. A status dialog box will appear describing the generation procedure and any errors that arise.

Barring any errors, the document will be created after all files have been processed. You can then view the document using the Oracle Book executable to open and navigate it (refer to "User Capabilities" later in this chapter for more information on viewing documents).

Oracle Book documents can be stored and retrieved from an ORACLE database. However, the SQL scripts provided with the Oracle Book must be processed against the database first. Plus, the database may need expansion to accommodate the size of documents it will maintain. It is assumed that your Database Administrator will be responsible for these procedures.

ORACLE BOOK SOUND

Oracle Book Sound is a sound creation utility that allows the easy and direct creation of sound files that can be included with Oracle Book documents using the <include> tag. Oracle Sound allows you to record sounds and store them in files using the AIFFC format. The development platform must support sound input and output, including accessibility to sound input and output devices. If the hardware and software are set up properly, a few simple

Table 7.3 Document Attribute Text Markers

Text Marker Syntax	Description
#	Comment marker used for inserting "invisible" notes into the text of the build file.
-	Flag marker used to establish the values of <if> and <if-not> tags. Flag lines can indicate a value, but those without a value default to "TRUE." The flag can have any name you wish it to have, as in -GUI = "Macintosh".
_blanklines = TRUE/FALSE	Same as the BLANKLINES document attribute (see Table 7.2).
_directory = path	Corresponds to the Source Directory document attributes.
_imagecompression = value	Enter a value of "LZW" to compresses images; the default value "NONE" prevents compression; otherwise, the same as the Compress Images document attributes (see Table 7.2).
_language = value	Essentially the same as the Language document attributes (see Table 7.2).
_maxwarn = value	Same as the Max Warnings Document Attributes (see Table 7.2).
_nowarn = TRUE/FALSE	Same as the Warnings Document Attributes (see Table 7.2).
_pack = TRUE/FALSE	"FALSE" disallows compression of the final document file; same as the Compress Document document attributes (see Table 7.2).
_searchable = TRUE/FALSE	Same as the Searchable document attributes (see Table 7.2). "TRUE" makes the document searchable.
_targetlevel = value	Same as the Target Level document attributes (see Table 7.2). "Value" is the level of heading that will be recorded as a target for hypertext links. "OFF", the default, suppresses the linking of all headings.
<doc title,...>	Uniquely identifies a document, combining the Document Title, Output File, Document ID, and Revision settings found in the Document Attributes box. Its four main parts are:

filename:	the file system name and extension for the document.
title:	the title identifier for the document used in all windows and dialogs.
id:	a unique thirty-two–character identifier.
rev:	an integer revision number used internally to prevent mismatches between links of differing versions.

Only one <doc> tag is allowed per document, which must appear at the start of the first chapter of the document. A <doc> tag is required; its absence will result in an error. For example:

```
<doc filename="TEGIS.OBD" title="Teacher Grading System" id="A10351 rev=1>
```

<process file = "filename">	Orders the processing of the source text files, saving you the task of ordering them manually. Each <process> file tag lists the file path and name and file extension. <Process> file tags must point to an ASCII file that includes all appropriate Oracle Book Tag Language markers.

Figure 7.4 The Oracle Book Sound Dialog

steps will create a fully usable sound file. First, launch the Oracle Sound application, which allows the recording of sounds through the Sound Recorder box. After recording the sound, save the sound file by selecting the SAVE command in the File menu. Alter the settings of the file by using the OPTIONS command in the File menu. The file is now ready to be incorporated into an Oracle Book document using the <include> tag.

Here is a step-by-step example of how to record and save a sound file:

1. Invoke the Oracle Sound application. Your screen should look something like Figure 7.4.

2. Select the NEW command in the File menu. The Sound Recorder box appears and should look like Figure 7.5.

3. Record the sound and then close the dialog box by selecting the OK button.

4. Use the OPTIONS command to alter the sample rate and/or compression scheme. The Oracle Sound Options box, also called the AIFFC File Format Options, should look like Figure 7.6.

5. Select the OK button when done altering the options.

6. Save the sound to a file using the SAVE command in the File menu.

Oracle Sound commands are shown in Table 7.4.

Figure 7.5 The Oracle Book Sound Recorder

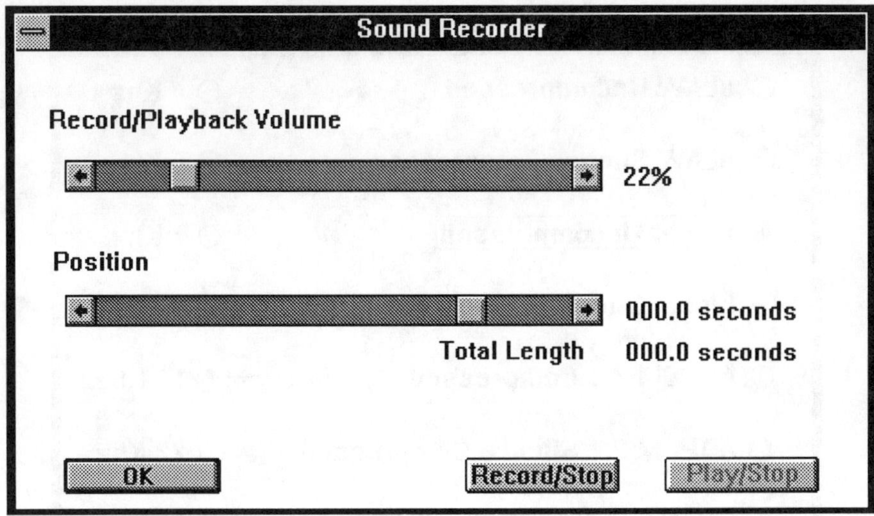

COMMAND-LINE OPTIONS

Oracle Book command-line options can be used to launch the product from the operating system or from other CDE products, such as Oracle Forms. However, this section applies only to platforms that support command-line executables. Use the following syntax to launch Oracle Book from the command line or from another application:

```
Oracle_Book_executable_name
   [document|module=]<filename:suffix>
   target=<targetname>
   userid=<name/password@[network protocol]:database_name
```

"Oracle_Book_executable_name" is the name of the Oracle Book executable file, either Designer or Runtime. The executable name varies from platform to platform, so check with the database administrator for the actual executable name. All parameters are optional.

The document (or module) parameter requires a valid name and path for the document. When no path is specified, Oracle Book looks in the current

Figure 7.6   The Oracle Sound Options Dialog

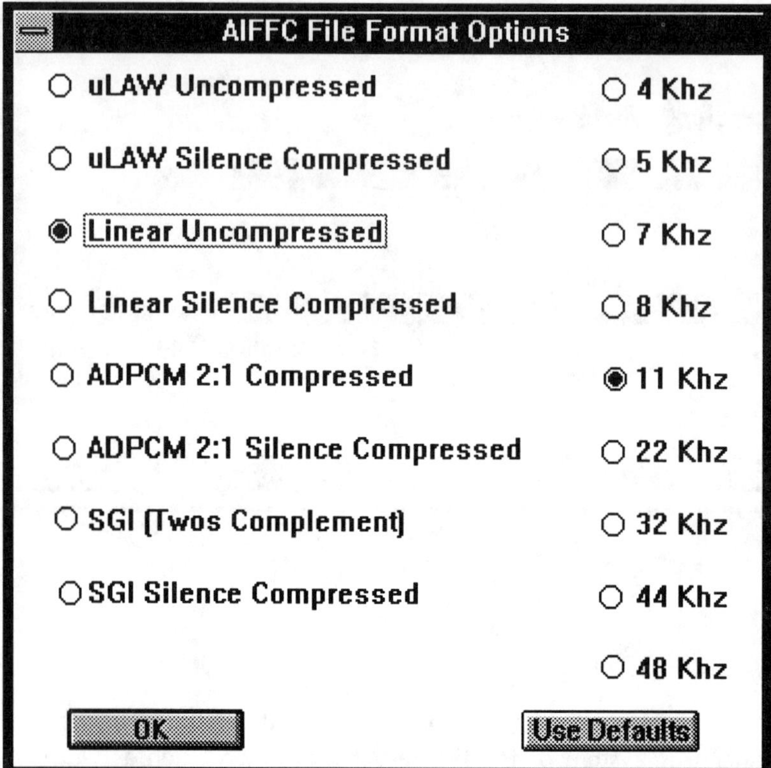

directory. The word "document=" or "module=" is not needed before the name of the document.

The suffix field indicates where the document is located, either in the file system or in the database. When the document is stored in the file system, the suffix is ":FS," and when it is stored in the database, the suffix is ":DB." File system is the default.

The target parameter opens the document to a specified target location. The target parameter works only in tangent with the document parameter.

The userid parameter allows the specification of a remote database and network protocol. This option is not needed when connecting to a local database. Do not include path information for documents opened from the database. By default, documents are opened from the file system. For example:

Table 7.4 Oracle Sound Commands

Command	Description
EXIT	The EXIT command in the File menu, or "Quit" option, aborts the current application session. Oracle Sound will ask to save the sound file if outstanding changes have not already been saved.
NEW	The NEW command in the File menu clears the application settings and allows you to record a new sound in the Sound Recorder box. Oracle Sound will ask to save outstanding changes to a sound file if they have not already been saved.
OPEN	The OPEN command in the File menu recalls a previously recorded sound file through a dialog box that allows you to select the specific sound file to be opened. Oracle Sound will ask to save outstanding changes to a sound file if they have not already been saved.
OPTIONS	The OPTIONS command in the File menu allows alteration of the sample rate and compression scheme used when saving the sound to a file. Sample rate and compression scheme affect the file size, playback quality, and the playback response time of sounds.
RECORD	The RECORD command in the Sound menu invokes the Sound Recorder box, where recording and playback are controlled.
SAVE	The SAVE command in the File menu stores the current sound in a file. The sound is saved either back to the file it originated from or, when the file is being saved for the first time, to a file named by you in the File dialog box.
SAVE AS	Use the SAVE AS command in the File menu to save an existing file to a new filename. Once selected, the File dialog box appears, asking for the name of the new sound file.

```
B10DES document = C:\document\students.obd:FS target = info
B10DES module = students:DB userid = kevin/triangle@t:mydata
```

The first example invokes Oracle Book and opens the file document "students" in the directory "C:\document." It will also open the document at the location of the target, "info." The second example invokes Oracle Book and opens the database document "students," using the username "kevin" and the password "triangle" to open the database "mydata" using the protocol "t" for TCP/IP.

"B10" is the name of the Oracle Book executable file, either Designer or Runtime. The code "-batch" invokes Oracle Book Designer in batch mode. Without this flag, Oracle Book Designer runs in graphical interactive mode. This flag is required in batch mode but is otherwise optional. For example:

```
B1ODES -batch build1
B1ODES build1
```

The first example opens Oracle Book Designer in batch mode with the build file "build1" as the startup build file. The build-file parameter opens a build file when opening Oracle Book Designer. The second example opens Oracle Book Designer in interactive mode with the build file "build1" as the startup build file opened.

USER CAPABILITIES

Oracle Book Runtime automatically includes a number of features that enable end-users to navigate, format, and customize Oracle Book documents. You, as a developer, can encourage the user to take advantage of the customization features of Oracle Book Runtime, or you can even produce a single document that is customizable to meet the needs of many subsets of end-users. From the end-users' point of view, Oracle Book allows the viewing of documents on a computer screen just as if they were paperbound books or manuals with the added features of sound and video. The user can navigate through a document using traditional means, such as a table of contents and an index. Oracle Book provides users with the added power of annotating and customizing the on-line documents they use.

End-users have a great deal of control over the documents they use by constructing a Notes file. The look and feel of an Oracle Book document can be customized to the tastes of each user by allowing individually configured fonts, window size, sound output, and image quality. Users can quickly navigate through a document using standard search methods such as the table of contents and index, as well as performing searches on words, partial words, and phrases through a single document or a set of documents called a *bookshelf*. Users can also enhance navigational control by building their own user-defined links to other files, regions within the same file, and multiple documents. Users can add personal commentary to a document with the annotation feature. Annotations are not limited to text; they can also include sounds and images. And, as with a paperbound book, users can toss in an occasional bookmark to keep their place while reading a document.

Users have access to several distinct components in a typical Oracle Book document: the body of text, headings, the table of contents, and the index. The body of text is all of the text in a document contained under a heading or subheading. Headings and subheadings introduce a new chapter, complete with its own body of text, and are usable for navigation. The table of contents contains a list of all the headings and subheadings in the document as you would expect to find in a regular book. The index is an optional component containing an alphanumeric listing of all words and phrases tagged as index items.

Users can see images in color, gray scale, and black-and-white, depending on the design. Images are often embedded directly into the body of the text. In many cases, users will encounter icons of images, sounds, and video, which can be launched at the users' convenience on platforms that support sound and video.

The Oracle Book Interface is made of many components: the document title, menu bar, document display area, target margin, annotation area, and scroll bars. Figure 7.7 displays and diagrams these features.

The document title contains the name of the document, which identifies the document in all pop-up lists, scroll lists, and dialog boxes. The menu bar displays the menu options available to Oracle Book users. The document display area contains the body of text for the document. The target margin indicates the target of a link or navigational command and appears in the left margin. The annotation area indicates the presence of an annotation and appears in the right margin by default. Each annotation has its own icon, though annotation icons can be suppressed to free up space to display the body of the text.

Navigating in an Oracle Book Document

Users have many options when navigating and searching a document. The next two sections provide information about opening Oracle Book documents, navigating the documents, and searching through documents and bookshelves.

Opening an Oracle Book document is quite easy, as the following steps show:

1. Launch Oracle Book.

2. Select the OPEN DOCUMENT command from the File menu to open a document from the file system or database. The file system indicates the specific path and drive on which the Oracle Book document is saved as a file. The database option opens a document stored in a local or remote Oracle RDBMS. The user must be connected to the local or remote Oracle database.

Figure 7.7   Oracle Book Interface Components

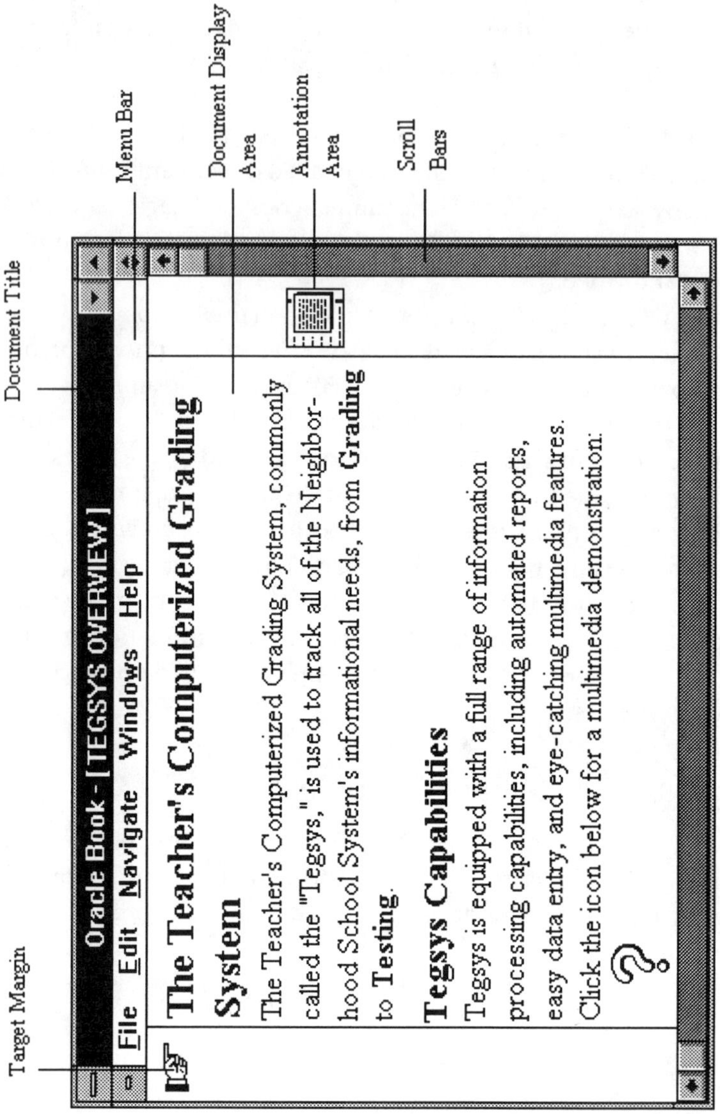

3. Select the FILE SYSTEM or DATABASE subcommand. The File dialog box or the Document dialog box appears with a listing of available Oracle Book documents.

4. Select the specific document. The document, similar to the one displayed in Figure 7.8, will appear.

Even if you are not a heavy user of Oracle Book documents, you will need to navigate your document to test its functionality and judge the aesthetics of its appearance. Once the document has been retrieved, there are seven ways to navigate through the document:

- the scroll bars
- the Navigate menu
- the TABLE OF CONTENTS command
- the INDEX command
- hypertext links
- the NAVIGATOR command
- the HISTORY command

SCROLL BARS

Horizontal and vertical scroll bars allow the user to scroll to regions of the document not shown on the computer screen but included in the open document. By clicking the scroll arrows at the ends of the scroll bar, the user can scroll the viewed region one line at a time. The scroll box on the scroll bar indicates the user's relative position within the body of the text. Users can scroll one complete screen at a time by clicking the region of the scroll bar between the scroll arrow and the scroll box. Users can move to an exact position within the body of the text by selecting and moving the scroll box.

NAVIGATE MENU

The Navigate menu allows a user to travel through a document or user notes. The Navigate menu contains five useful navigation commands: NEXT CHAPTER, PREVIOUS CHAPTER, NEXT PAGE, PREVIOUS PAGE, and GO BACK. Each command is self-explanatory, except perhaps GO BACK, which enables the user to step back one navigational operation at a time.

Figure 7.8 Sample Oracle Book Document

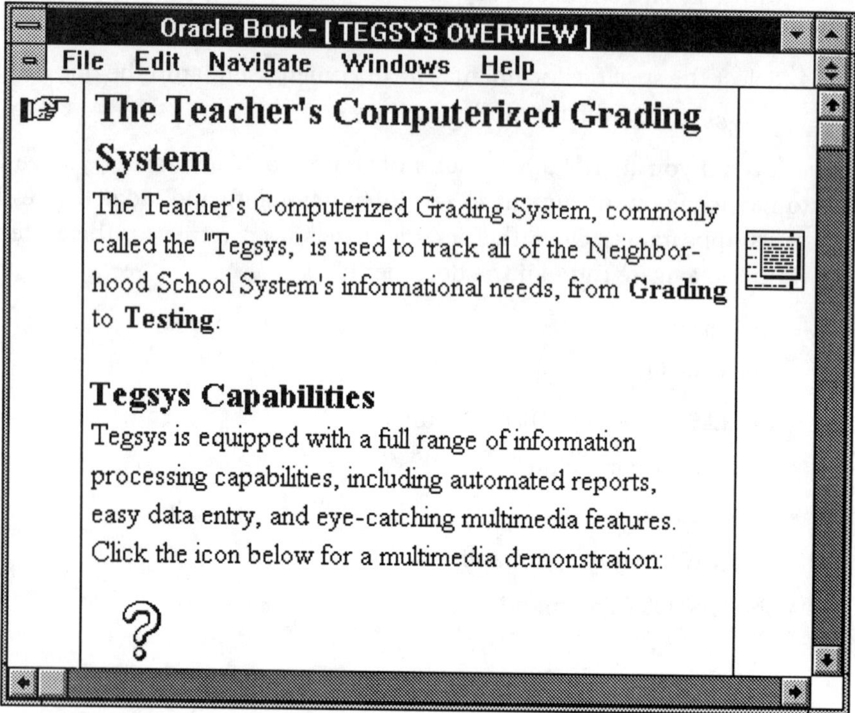

TABLE OF CONTENTS

The Table of Contents dialog lists all chapter headings and subheadings in the order they appear in the document. To travel to a heading or subheading, click on an entry from the list and select the Go To button. Individual chapters with subtopics can be expanded or collapsed to show display levels of detail with the Expand, Expand All, Collapse, and Collapse All buttons. Note: the subtopic indicator (>) indicates that the heading possesses subheadings that are not shown. Figure 7.9 illustrates the Table of Contents dialog box. A Document pop-up list is available just above the topic list to enable you to switch between various documents.

INDEX

Users can search through a listing of all developer-indexed items in a document by selecting the Index dialog box in the Windows menu. The user can

Figure 7.9 Table of Contents Dialog

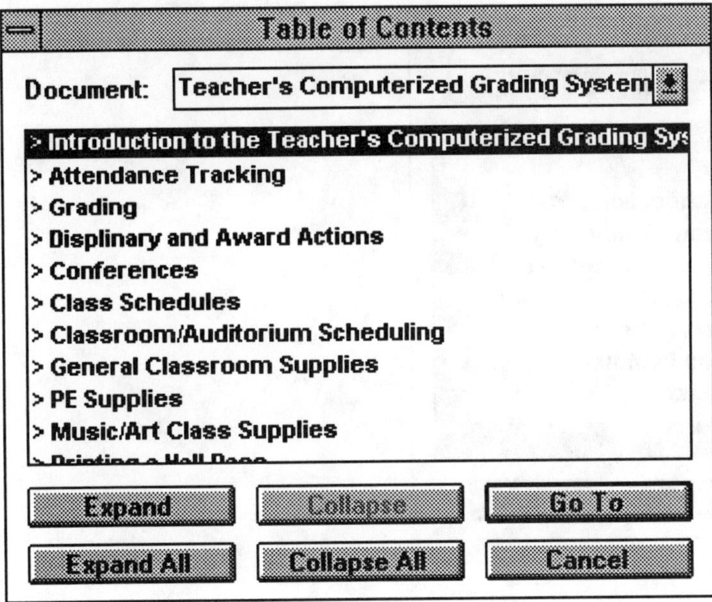

navigate to an item by selecting it from the list, then clicking the Go To button. Occasionally, the index, as shown in Figure 7.10, will appear empty, in which case no items have been marked as index items in the document. A Document pop-up list is available just above the index list to enable switching between various documents.

While Oracle Book navigates to the selected index item, the Index dialog box will remain visible on the screen in case the user wishes to navigate elsewhere using the index. Users can close and exit by selecting the Cancel button.

HYPERTEXT LINKS

Hypertext links allow the user to quickly invoke regions of text from another part of the document or from another document entirely, serving the purpose of a "For More Information Refer to" clause in a traditional book or manual. When displayed, hypertext links appear in a different font than the regular body of text. Hypertext links can be created by both the developer and the user. Navigate using hypertext by selecting the hypertext region, then using the FOLLOW LINK command in the Navigate menu.

Figure 7.10 Index Dialog

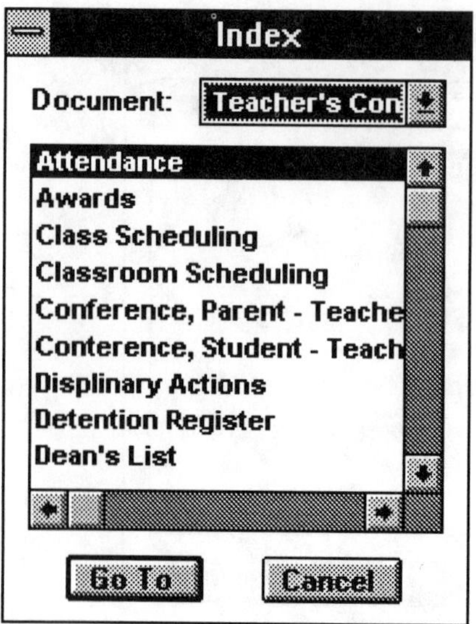

THE NAVIGATOR DIALOG BOX

Located in the Windows menu, the NAVIGATOR command allows the user to directly access any document, chapter, hypertext link (both author and user links), annotation, or bookmark. Figure 7.11 depicts the Navigator Dialog box.

To use the Navigator dialog box:

1. Open the Navigator dialog box by selecting the command from the Windows menu.

2. Select a chapter (or other object) from the list.

3. Go to the selected chapter by pressing the Go To button.

4. Return to your starting point by selecting the Go Back button or use the Cancel button to quit.

HISTORY

All navigation is tracked by the HISTORY command on the Windows menu (except for scroll bar usage and page navigation). The History dialog, shown in Figure 7.12, does have a limit to the number of navigations it will track.

Figure 7.11   The Navigator Dialog

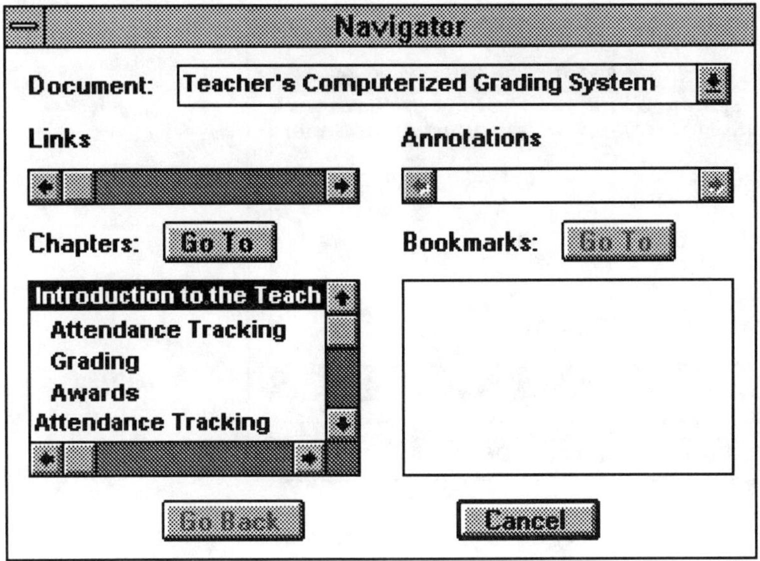

The limit is defined in the PREFERENCES command of the Edit menu. Users can travel to any item in the History list by selecting the item and pressing the Go To button.

Searching

Oracle Book allows users to perform dynamic word and phrase searches in any document that has been set up as searchable through the FIND command on the Windows menu, as shown in Figure 7.13. Oracle Book will notify the user if the document is not searchable.

Users describe the exact text to be located in the Find What field at the top of the dialog box. Users can include the wildcard symbol (%) to find words or phrases that are like the word or phrase in the Find What field. Users can search a single document, multiple documents, or even multiple bookshelves by pressing the Multiple Documents button, then selecting the appropriate documents from the Find in Documents pop-up list, shown in Figure 7.14. The documents do not need to be opened to be searched.

After executing the search by pressing the Find button, Oracle Book displays a list of the documents that contain the selected text in the Resulting

Figure 7.12   The History Dialog

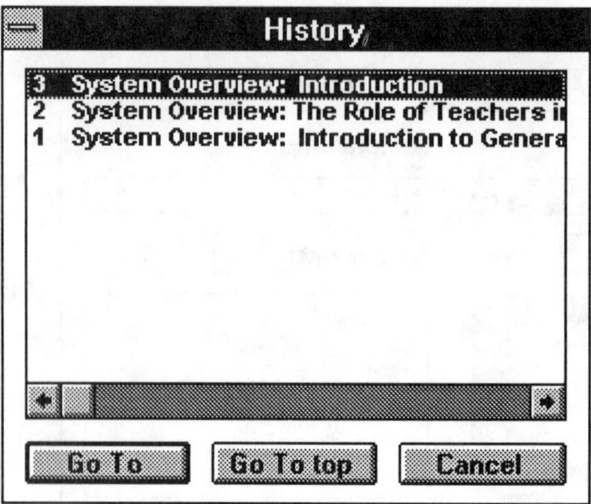

Documents list and text in which the match was found in the Matches list. The user can then navigate to the document and matched text by pressing the Go To button.

1. Select the FIND command from the Windows menu.

2. Enter the search phrase or word, using the wildcard symbol (%) where appropriate.

3. Select the document(s) to be searched from the Document pop-up list; the default document is the current document. Select the Multiple Documents option from the Document pop-up list and then press the Multiple Documents button, when searching multiple documents. Select all desired documents shown on the Open Document list and accept them by pressing the OK button. Search a bookshelf by selecting from the Bookshelves list and pressing OK. After you press OK (or cancel), Oracle Book then returns to the Find dialog box.

4. Click the Find button. Documents that contain a match appear in the Resulting Documents list, while actual matching text appears in the Matches list. Navigate to a match by selecting it and pressing the Go To button.

Figure 7.13 The Find Dialog

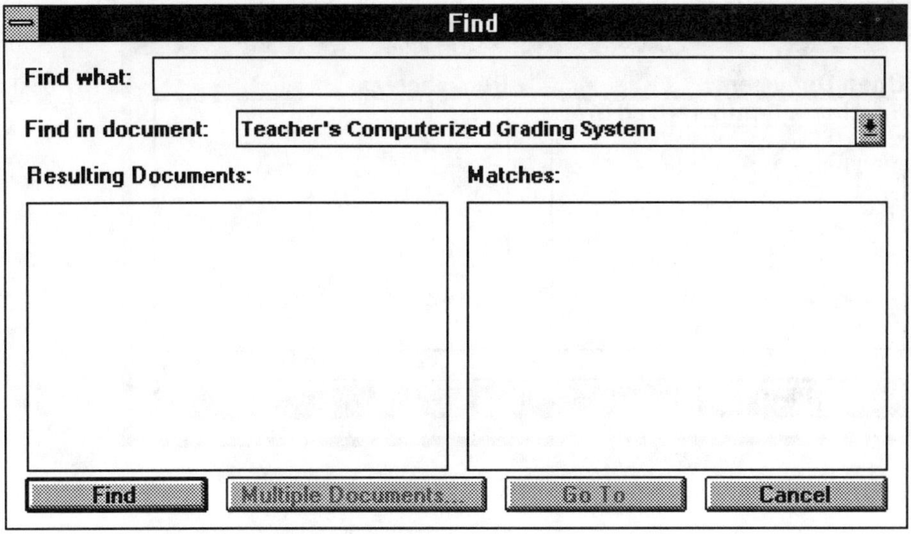

Find

Find what:

Find in document: Teacher's Computerized Grading System

Resulting Documents: Matches:

Find   Multiple Documents...   Go To   Cancel

Creating and Using Bookshelves

A bookshelf is a grouping of Oracle Book documents that have been teamed together using the BOOKSHELVES command on the Windows menu, shown in Figure 7.15. Developers can use bookshelves to group documents on related topics, such as user guides for separate modules of a single application.

The Bookshelves dialog shows all of the previously defined bookshelves and their corresponding documents. A bookshelf is created by pressing the New Shelf button and invoking the Add Bookshelf dialog box. The user then types in the name of the new bookshelf in the Bookshelf Name field and presses the OK button to confirm the new name. Now the user can add documents to the bookshelf by using the Add From File button. The Add From File button invokes the File dialog, where the user can select documents from the list and accept them as part of the working document by pressing the OK button.

User Notes

Users can keep all sorts of notes about a document in an optional Notes file. A Notes file is an assortment of annotations (text, sound, and image), book-

Figure 7.14   The Multiple Documents Dialog

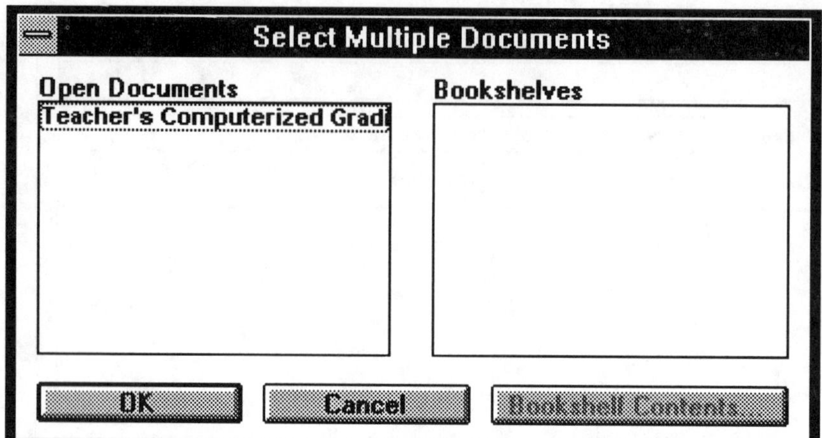

marks, and user links associated with a document or documents. Users and developers can make notes available to each other and even include context-sensitive information. Although users and developers can create, edit, and merge Notes files, doing so does not affect the document files in any way. Users can open one Notes file at a time and can track information for multiple documents in the Notes file. Oracle Book automatically opens all the notes in the current Notes file for a specific document when that document is opened.

Notes can be one of three types: annotations, bookmarks, and user links.

ANNOTATIONS

Annotations are marked by an icon in the right margin of a document. The annotation area can be concealed by setting the preferences in the Windows menu. Each annotation has a specific identifier, as shown in Figure 7.16.

When creating annotations, first select the text that will receive the annotation. Then select the ADD ANNOTATION command from the Edit menu and determine the type of annotation: text, sound, or image. After selecting the type, a dialog box asks for the name of the annotation. The annotation name can be up to forty characters and defaults to the first forty characters of

Figure 7.15 The Bookshelf Dialog

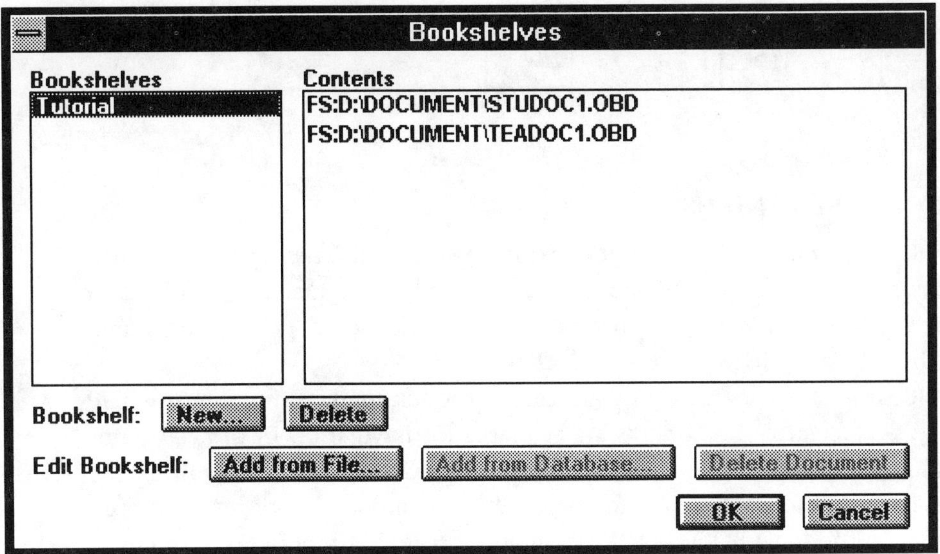

the selected region of text. After you name the annotation, a new dialog box appears depending on the type of annotation:

Text: Text can be manually edited or formatted using the Cut, Copy, Clear, and Paste key equivalents, including copying and pasting text from the document itself.

Image: Images are pasted from the clipboard into the Image Annotation dialog by using CUT, COPY, and PASTE commands from the Edit menu.

Sound: Sound is available only if the user's system possesses the supporting hardware and software to output it. After the user selects the type of sound annotation, the Oracle Sound Annotation box appears, allowing the user to record and play sounds. Creating a sound annotation is otherwise the same as using Oracle Sound.

Annotations can be edited by selecting the annotation icon and selecting the EDIT ANNOTATION command from the Edit menu. Open the annotation and make the necessary changes, then press the OK button. The changes will be saved. To exit without saving the changes, use the Cancel button.

Figure 7.16   The Annotation Identifier

BOOKMARKS AND USER LINKS

Bookmarks and user-created hypertext links are useful for end-users reading a document. You, as a developer, can also use them to assist in testing and readibility. Imagine having to proofread a two-hundred–page user manual without being able to put a bookmark in it!

Bookmarks are identified by an icon in the left margin and appear where they were created. Bookmarks are available for navigation in the Navigator dialog under the Windows menu or from the BOOKMARK command in the Navigate menu. Bookmarks are created by selecting a body of text and then selecting the ADD BOOKMARK command in the Edit menu. You can create an unlimited number of bookmarks in a document, though only twenty are available through the BOOKMARKS command in the Navigate menu. A bookmark will then be attached to the body of text.

User-created hypertext links allow the user to quickly navigate from one body of text to another, possibly outside of the current document. Like bookmarks, user links are created by selecting a body of text to serve as the source of the link, then selecting the ADD LINK command from the Edit menu. You can assign up to forty characters to the link name. Once the source and target text are selected, use the Make Link button to create the link.

Saving and Deleting Notes

All annotations, bookmarks, and user links must be saved to a Notes file to be reused. The Notes file is distinct from any other database or document file and can contain information about more than one document. Thus, a user can store all his or her notes on a multitude of documents in a single Notes file. When a user opens a document, all of the user's notes in the current Notes file become activated. Save user notes to a Notes file by issuing the SAVE NOTES command on the File Menu and entering an appropriate filename and path. Finally, push the Save button to create the Notes file.

Figure 7.17 The Preferences Menu

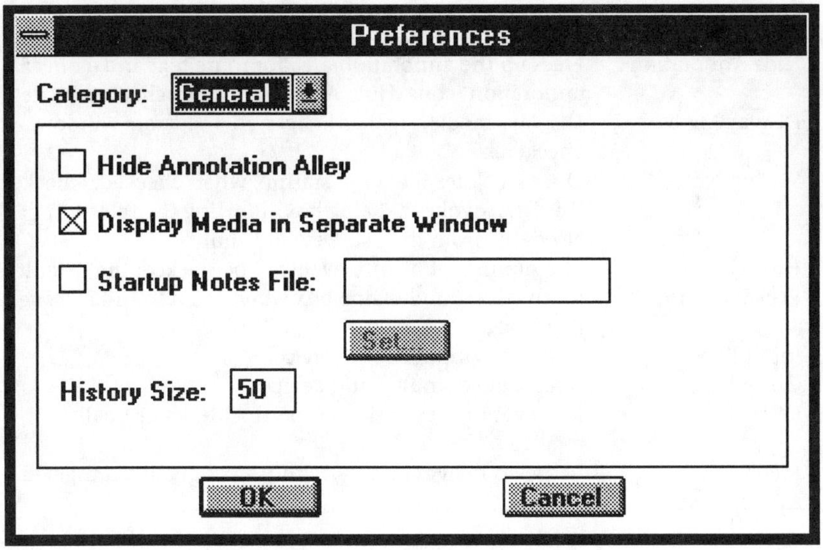

Preference

Developers and users can control important Oracle Book environment settings by using the PREFERENCES command in the Windows menu. To set a session's preferences, select the PREFERENCES command in the Edit menu, as shown in Figure 7.17. Specific preferences are described in Table 7.5.

CONCLUSION

Oracle Book provides developers with a powerful, multimedia on-line help utility. Developers can take help information in the form of an ASCII file and add tags to the file to build in hypertext links and assemble multimedia sound and graphic displays. Developers can create build files by using either the Oracle Book Designer or their favorite text editor. Once the build file is created, the document can be generated and distributed. It can be launched from within other CDE products or directly from the operating system.

After reading this chapter, you should know the uses of and differences between the source file, build file, and the Oracle Book document file. You

Table 7.5 Oracle Book Preferences

Type	Setting	Description
General	Hide Annotation	Frees up the annotation area for more text and conceals annotation icons. Hide Annotation is unchecked by defaults.
	Display Media	Displays media, such as images, in a separate window, when checked.
	Startup Notes	Opens a Notes file upon startup, when checked. Checking this box invokes a dialog box, allowing the selection of the Notes file from the list. Default is null.
	History Size	The number of history events to be tracked; the default is 20.
Sound	Play Sounds	Opens the sound dialog box whenever a sound is played, if checked.
	Input Pop-up	Selects the input sound device.
	Output Pop-up	Selects the output sound device.
Image	Best/Slow	Retrieves images at slower speed with better quality, if toggled.
	Medium/Fast	Retrieves images rapidly, with poorer quality, if toggled.

should know how to create an ASCII source file and how to add Oracle Book Tag markers to create a formatted Oracle Book document, as well as how to assemble several tagged and marked source files into a build file. You should also know how to generate the build file from your collection of source files and, finally, how to include sound and video in the Oracle Book document and how to write effective command-line executables to call Oracle Book documents from other CDE tools, such as Oracle Forms.

Once the document is developed and implemented, users and developers have a wide range of tools to navigate and search the document. Users can even add annotations of all sorts (text, graphics, and sound) to a document, plus bookmarks and hypertext links. From this chapter, you should have a good idea how to navigate a document through several different means. You should also be able to customize a document using annotations, bookmarks, and hypertext links.

8   ORACLE CDE UTILITIES

INTRODUCTION

The CDE presents a number of tools that provide the developer with an integrated life-cycle application development environment. The majority of application development requirements are met using the CDE core products like SQL, Oracle Forms, Oracle Reports, Oracle Graphics, and Oracle Book. However, a variety of additional Oracle tools are available to meet special application development niches or to ease the application development process. It is not the intention of this book to provide complete instructions for application development in each of these additional tools; however, an overview is provided here to acquaint the developer with the basic use and capability of these tools, specifically SQL*Net, Oracle Browser, Oracle Glue, Oracle*Terminal, and SQL*Loader.

SQL*NET

SQL*Net is Oracle's primary tool for enabling a client-server architecture and distributed databases. Client-server architecture is an applications model that separates computers (and their users) into two distinct groups: clients and servers. Client computers execute the application (such as the forms, reports, and graphics described earlier in the book) and provide the main user interface via keyboard, mouse, and screen. The client then accesses data, either across the network or locally, that is stored on the server. Server computers maintain the Oracle RDBMS and handle all processing for data requests and alterations from the client computers. By utilizing client-server architecture, developers are able to lower hardware acquisition and maintenance costs because of the low price of client and server computer platforms, while taking advantage of the high-level graphic capabilities of the client computers.

In addition to offering client-server architecture, SQL*Net enables developers to create distributed databases. A distributed database acts like a single database but is physically located on many geographically dispersed servers. By utilizing sophisticated networking equipment and communication software in addition to SQL*Net, developers can design databases spread across many servers that provide seamlessly integrated data to users, wherever they are located. For example, the Neighborhood Elementary School might maintain its own database concerning the enrollment and grades of its student body, but using a distributed database technique, the downtown office could query all schools in the school system to get an immediate picture of the status of the entire system. Thus, with distributed databases each site can maintain autonomous data but still be treated as a single logical database by higher authorities in the organization.

SQL*Net is designed to be layered on top of the network operating system used by the application. As a result, there are a multitude of version variations within SQL*Net, and when properly installed, they are virtually invisible to the user or developer. For example, SQL*Net for TCP/IP (just one of many different networking protocols) supports networking cards and driver software from 3Com, Excelan, FTP PC/TCP, HP ARPA, Interlan TCP Gateway, Novel, Ungermann-Bass, and more. In order to work properly, the same version of SQL*Net must be installed and set up on both the client and server platforms.

To connect to a server, you must first identify it within the SQL*Net setup. In general, servers are identified by describing information about them in a host file, an ASCII text file that contains mapping for each server the client might wish to connect to. Host files in SQL*Net for TCP/IP should contain the Internet address of the server, the server's name, and an abbreviated alias for the server. For example, the following is a short list of hosts:

```
192.31.126.7    MaximuLibrary        Lib
136.205.62.1    DataCollectors       Datac
192.18.244.8    Newsnet              NN
```

Once the hosts have been set up, clients can use SQL*Net to connect to remote databases just as if they resided on the local machine. The client will need to connect to the database using a valid username and password. Users can add a host connect string that is automatically used by SQL*Net to connect to the remote host. For example, to run a report from a remote server, you might enter the following:

```
r20run kevin/triangle@t:newsnet report=weather_rpt
```

In this example, R20RUN can be any Oracle application that requires a user to connect to the database. KEVIN/TRIANGLE can be any userid and password valid on the remote database. @T:NEWSNET is the entire remote connect string needed to locate the remote server. Note that the parameter RE-PORT=WEATHER_RPT, and any other parameter used by the application, must appear after the network connect string.

The actual network connect string can vary among network operating systems. For example, the entire network connect string for clients using SQL*Net TCP/IP can involve the following articles:

```
@network_prefix:host:((SID),(buffer))
```

The elements of this string are as follows:

@	the required connect string symbol
network_prefix	the network protocol indicator; always a T for TCP/IP
:	the terminating character between strings
host	the name or alias of the server, as described in the host file
SID	an optional system identifier (SID) to differentiate between databases on the host
buffer	the size, in bytes, of data blocks passed between the server database and TCP/IP; on TCP/IP systems the value can be between 6 and 4096, with higher numbers yielding higher performance but greater memory requirements

Many of the parameters used by SQL*Net can be set up as defaults through various means. For example, setting the most commonly called server's alias to SQLNET will allow the user to omit the host name when attempting an operation that requires a database connection, because SQL*Net automatically points to the SQLNET alias. On Windows clients, the user can add the LOCAL and REMOTE strings to the CONFIG.ORA file to ease database connections. The commands might look like the following:

```
local=t:newsnet
remote=t:datacollectors:07
```

Then, whenever the user issues a command that requires a connection to the local database, the setting is substituted. For example, the command

SQLPLUS KEVIN/TRIANGLE would automatically connect the user to the NEWSNET database. Alternatively, to make a connection to the remote database easier, the user need only specify the T: string to connect the default remote database, as in SQLPLUS KEVIN/TRIANGLE@T:. For more information on utilizing distributed databases, such as how to create synonyms for networked databases or how to build database links, refer to specific SQL commands in chapter 3.

ORACLE BROWSER

Oracle Browser is a CDE tool designed to allow end-users to quickly retrieve and format information without using any SQL statements. Instead, Browser uses a graphical data-access technique to give end-users direct and immediate access to data. Browser is especially useful in organizations where the application development staff is heavily burdened in that it allows the end-user to retrieve data in a timely fashion and relieves the developer of the need to code ad hoc queries.

The Oracle Browser interface, shown in Figure 8.1, enables the end-user to graphically define select conditions and to relate data in distinct tables by drawing lines, representing relationships, between the tables. Browser's graphical query tool, called the Worksheet, is very similar to the Data Model Painter in Oracle Reports. Once a query is executed, the results can be printed or stored in many popular file formats, such as WKS, SYLK, DIF, or delimited ASCII, by using the SAVE or SAVE AS commands on the File menu. The query itself can also be saved as text, a SQL statement, or in graphic format.

The Browser interface features many common elements found in other CDE tools, such as the standard pull-down menus, scroll bars and boxes, multiple viewport support, and resizable views. Unique to the Browser is its helpful icon bar that allows easy construction of OR, AND, and NOT SQL clauses, as well as common comparison operators.

Building Queries in Browser

Users begin a query by selecting the NEW command from the File menu, then choosing the Database option and clicking OK. Then, they select the data sources, which can be any valid table, view, or synonym the users have access to, both locally and remotely. After the data source is chosen, it is graphically displayed in the worksheet. Users choose the specific items they want to appear in the query by double-clicking the item in the data source.

Figure 8.1 The Oracle Browser Interface

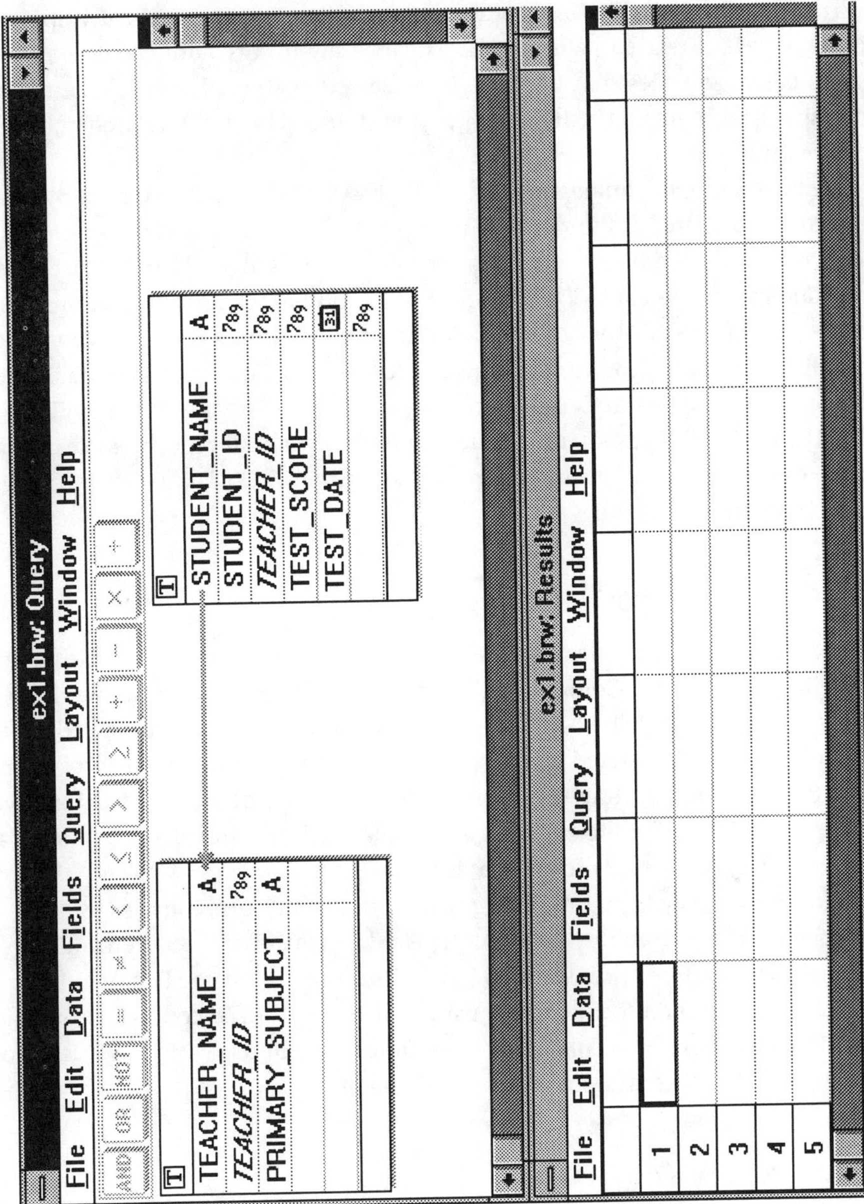

When data is selected from multiple sources, Browser automatically applies joins based on related columns. Users can draw in any additional relationships between tables that they desire by selecting the column in one table, pressing and holding the [Control] key, and dragging to the related column of the other table.

Selection criteria, analogous to a SELECT's WHERE clause, are built by first clicking the desired columns, then the operator to apply to the column (such as =, <, >, etc.), and finally the operator value. AND, OR, and NOT clauses can be added with the click of a button on the icon bar. Conditions can also be nested within each other or even disabled temporarily. Users can also have conditions use functions or columns not found in the query by pasting in the object (that is, the function or nonquery column) using the PASTE FIELD or PASTE FUNCTION command on the Edit menu. Once all aspects of the query have been completed, it can be run by issuing the EXECUTE command from the Query menu.

Formatting Output in Browser

Browser output is very flexible. The user has full control over the sizing and ordering of columns. Column width can be altered by clicking the right border of a column's title box and dragging to the desired size. Column ordering in the query can be altered by moving the point to the column title box, then using [Shift]-click to drag the column to the desired position. Additionally, columns can be added to the query (or removed from the query) by double-clicking the column title in the Datasource window.

Columns can be formatted using custom or default format masks by selecting the appropriate command from the Fields menu. Users can even add page headers and footers using the PAGE SETUP command on the File menu. Formulas and computations, created using the SUMMARIZE command on the Fields menu, can be displayed at specific break points, which are defined using the BREAK command on the Fields menu.

Special Features

Browser is a client application and, as such, links to data sources wherever they may reside, even on physically remote computers. Conversely, data retrieved by Browser is stored on the client computer. Because Browser is a client application, the database server performs relatively light duty (just executing the query), while the client computer performs the heavier processing of testing the query, sorting the data, and formatting it locally.

Queries can be saved to ASCII files (using the SAVE command from the File menu) and can be used by other users (by invoking the OPEN command on the File menu). In fact, if the MS-Windows Dynamic Data Exchange is used, queries can be linked to other Windows applications such as Excel™.

ORACLE GLUE

Oracle Glue takes data from third-party software and "glues" it to the Oracle database or application. Using Oracle Glue, developers can link e-mail, popular desktop spreadsheets and databases, and palmtop computers to the Oracle RDBMS, making the differences in hardware, software, and operating systems invisible to the user. In this sense, Oracle Glue serves as a universal application programming interface (API), uniting data on a diverse set of computers running a wide variety of applications.

With Oracle Glue, developers can link to Oracle databases, non-Oracle databases (using the Oracle Open Gateway), Oracle*Mail, and Microsoft products such as Excel and Visual Basic™. Oracle Glue transfers data between these products and the database using data *containers*. Containers can include local variables, internal variables within Oracle Glue, spreadsheet cells, and even Visual Basic controls. For example, to select data into an MS-Excel cell range, Oracle Glue would use a command such as the following:

```
=execsql ("select teacher_name into [a1:a30] from students")
```

To perform the same action using Visual Basic, you would enter the following:

```
result=execsql ("select teacher_name into :names.list:from students");
```

Again, to do the same thing in an Oracle Glue internal command, you would enter the following:

```
result=execsql ("select teacher_name into :names: from teachers")
```

Note that each command is essentially the same, differing only in the destination of the data. Oracle Glue uses routines like execsql, execmail, dosql, dolink, and domail to execute many processes, including piping data from one source into another. For example, a query can be constructed that would fetch the results of a database query into an e-mail message. In this case, all honor students are brought to the attention of the principal:

```
execsql ("for all select student_name into :honor_roll: from
student_grades where average_grade >= 90 and grade_date between
:begin_date: and :end_date:")
```

```
execmail ("send message 'Outstanding Students This Quarter',
:honor_roll: from 'Admin' to 'Principal Stallings'")
```

Used in this fashion, Oracle Glue serves to unite data across diverse software, hardware, and network systems. In fact, Oracle Glue's connectivity extends to a variety of palmtop computers, such as the Sharp Wizard™.

ORACLE*TERMINAL

Oracle*Terminal is a CDE tool that allows developers to modify the default device and key mapping for other CDE products. Using Oracle*Terminal, developers can alter keystroke or mouse operations to provide greater uniformity between differing client computers for the implementation of their application. Oracle*Terminal also allows the developer to modify the appearance of an application, such as the fonts and colors used, or to accommodate differences in hardware and firmware via terminal definitions. Once a definition is created, the developer can apply it to a single application or to a specific type of terminal. This capability provides some potent advantages in designing an application for a heterogeneous computer environment. Primarily, a developer can use Oracle*Terminal to ensure uniformity of keystrokes, even when one group of users might be working with old block-mode terminals, while another group uses high-resolution graphic workstations.

Terminal definitions built with the Oracle*Terminal resource editor are called *resource files*, or simply *resources*. Resources contain all the information needed to describe the appearance and behavior of an application or terminal type. Resources containing information about the physical configuration of a terminal device are stored in the terminal definitions file (or termdef), while resources containing information about applications are stored in an application-specific resource file. By changing these resources, developers can alter important key functions. For example, the developer might remap the print screen function from [Shift]-F8 to [Alt]-P for anyone using the specific Oracle application. This process is called *key binding*.

In addition to binding various functions to specific terminal keystrokes, developers can alter the visual attributes, such as fonts and the background color of text fields, using the Oracle*Terminal resource editor. These visual attributes are also called *logical attributes* and exist for almost every aspect of an application's visual interface. In a mixed-platform environment, where some users have terminals that support bit-mapping and others have terminals that support only character mode, developers can use the CMDEVAT (character-mode device attribute) to accommodate the character-mode machines. These resource definitions can be applied to entire classes of terminals, so that all VT-100 emulators and terminals use one specific termdef and all PC terminals use another. (Note that termdefs are used only on character-mode platforms; regular resource files are used on all other platforms.)

Termdefs can be used to alter the height or width of the screen, the description of screen coordinates, whether the terminal has graphics capabilities, attribute names and coding (like ReverseBold or UnderlineBold), command key names and encoding (like [Control], [Alt], and [Tab]), and the way attributes are displayed after they are edited. Termdef also controls how the terminal redisplays the screen, on-screen navigation between and in fields, and scrolling. Once defined, a termdef can be assigned as the default terminal style for an application, causing the application to utilize that terminal definition unless explicitly told not to.

To alter a resource file, open (or create) a resource file, then specify the hardware device and software product. Select the FUNCTION/EDIT KEYS command to alter or create the specific key bindings in the Key Binding Table. Attributes can be edited by selecting the Attributes pop-up list. Key names can be entered in the Key Binding Table as complete words, such as "Backspace," or by entering macro mode and typing the desired key. Once the process is completed, the developer can preview the binding alterations before testing the new settings. Additionally, the developer should save all the changes made to the key binding, then generate a new compiled version of the key binding.

A new termdef (as opposed to a resource) can be created by first opening the resource file and specifying the device, then issuing the FUNCTIONS/EDIT DEVICE command. Next, enter the name of the device to be created. The Add and Duplicate command buttons will be initialized. Create a new device by selecting its parent object, then clicking Add, or click an existing object and the Duplicate button to copy the existing object type. Duplicated objects can then be customized to the developer's needs. When creation of the new termdef is completed, click OK to accept the changes and dismiss the dialog. Finally, save the changes.

To select a device as the default for a given application, first open the resource file and specify the device to be edited. Issue the FUNCTIONS/EDIT DEVICE command to call the device editor window. Using the Select Default Device pop-up near the bottom of the dialog, select the desired default device. Finally, save the modifications to the resource file.

Because of the hardware-dependent nature of programming in Oracle*Terminal, developers must have access to information about the key binding and visual attributes of the target platform. This usually means the developer must have a fairly good understanding of the way the platform's operating system works, as well as access to technical documents describing information about the platform's key bindings and visual attributes.

SQL*LOADER

SQL*Loader is Oracle's tool for loading data into Oracle databases from non-Oracle external files. SQL*Loader provides a great deal of control over the way in which records are loaded into the table and accepts a wide variety of data formats. It is not uncommon for applications to require data from external sources. SQL*Loader has a wide variety of data-handling capabilities, including the ability to do the following:

- accept delimited, fixed-position, and variable-length records;

- accept data from multiple files and multiple file types;

- support all Oracle datatypes;

- handle and load multiple records as if they were one logical record, or a single record as if it were many logical records;

- load multiple tables concurrently;

- load specific records based on specific search criteria;

- provide and load a sequential identifier in specified columns;

- load from anywhere on the file system path, including tape and CD-ROM;

- provide a direct loading facility that quickly loads data at the speed of the disk subsystem; and

- provide detailed log, discard, and error reports.

To run SQL*loader, developers must provide a control file that specifies how the data is to be loaded and a data set. The data set is usually stored in a separate, external file but can be included in the control file itself. The control file, called a CTL file, manages all aspects of the data load, including the creation of the various output files. Output files include a detailed log file showing the results of the load process, a bad file that contains any records that were not loaded because of errors, and a discard file that contains any records excluded by the load procedure's WHERE clause.

Data loaded by SQL*Loader can come in a number of formats, including both binary data, which is not human-readable, and character data, which is human-readable. In fact, SQL*Loader can load files such as image or sound files into the Oracle database.

The data records can be stored in fixed positions or in variably sized records. Fixed-position records require that every column of the record falls within designated columns. For example, the first column of a record might start on column 1 and end on column 12; the next column would then start on column 13 and end on column 20, and so on, with the columns of each record falling within the same bounds in every instance. Variable-length records possess columns that fall within fluctuating boundaries. If the first column value of a record is six characters, but the same column value in the next record in twelve characters, then the first record will be shorter.

Consequently, variable-length records require somewhat more management, usually in the form of a *delimiter*. One type of delimiter, called an *enclosing mark*, is used to mark the beginning and end of each field. Another type, called a *terminal mark*, merely marks the end of the field. For example, the following two records show a record with enclosing marks and termination marks, respectively:

```
"1","2","3","4"
1, 2, 3, 4
```

Records that use delimiters must also use an end-of-line mark of some kind, such as a newline character or semicolon (;), to designate the end of the variable record. Data can also be distinguished in terms of its physical and logical representation. The physical record is the actual record from the beginning of the record to the end of the record. Physical records are stored in file-system records. The logical record is analogous to a row in a database table. Logical records can correspond directly to physical records or can be composed of several physical records using continuation fields.

SQL*Loader Examples

What follows are several SQL*Loader examples. Example 1 is a simple load procedure using enclosing marks and data contained in the CTL file. Example 2 loads positional data in a fixed-length file. Finally, Example 3 loads data into multiple tables simultaneously, while accessing multiple physical records.

EXAMPLE 1

Here data is loaded from within the CTL file into the database. Note that the double-dash comment mark (--) can appear anywhere in the CTL file, except in the data itself. The remarks also describe how to build a similar program that reads the data from a flat file. The command used to invoke this routine would look like the following:

```
sqlload userid=kevin/triangle control=loader1.ctl
```

The LOADER1.CTL control file would look something like this:

```
load data
-- The LOAD DATA statement must appear at the beginning of the file.

infile *
-- Data appears in the CTL file. If data were to be read from a file,
-- the statement would read INFILE PATH/FILENAME.

into table teachers
-- The default INTO statement requires the table to be empty in order
-- to insert records.

fields terminated by ',' optionally enclosed by '"'
-- The fields are terminated by commas and may be enclosed by
-- semicolons. Developers may specify their personal preferences for
-- the terminating character or the enclosing character.
```

```
(teacher_name, teacher_id, primary_subject)
-- When loading data into every database column, the developer does
-- not actually need to list every field. The developer may load data
-- into as few columns as the table's NOT NULL constraints allow.

begindata
"CHEU, KAREN", "CK12", "HISTORY"
"JUAREZ, MIKE", "MJ09", MATH
"SCHAEFFER, HELEN", HS72, SCIENCE
-- BEGINDATA indicates the beginning of the data block. If data were
-- to read from a file, the BEGINDATA statement and data block would
-- be excluded.
```

EXAMPLE 2

Example 2 loads fixed-length, positional data from a flat ASCII file; otherwise, the data load is quite straightforward. The command used to invoke this procedure would look like the following:

```
sqlload userid=kevin/triangle control=loader2.ctl data=flat.list
```

The LOADER2.CTL might look like this:

```
load data
infile flat.lst
-- The name of the data file.

discardfile junk.lst
-- Indicates that any discarded records should be placed in a file
-- called JUNK.LST.

discardmax 45
-- Indicates that the procedure should terminate after 45 records have
-- been discarded.

replace
-- This command tells SQL*Loader to delete all records from the table
-- before attempting to load.

into table teachers
(teacher_name    position(01:20) char,
teacher_id           position(22:26) char,
primary_subject    position(28:48) char)
-- Loads data based on position within the data file.
```

Here are few sample lines from the FLAT.LST:

```
CHEU, KAREN           CK12 HISTORY
JUAREZ, MIKE          MJ09 MATH
SCHAEFFER, HELEN      SCIENCE
```

As the program executes, it will create both a log file and a bad file, whether or not any data was bad. Since the TEACHER table constrains the TEACHER_ID field as NOT NULL, the SCHAEFFER record would appear in the bad file, allowing the developer to examine the rejected record and track down the reason the record was rejected.

EXAMPLE 3

Example 3 compiles multiple physical records into multiple database tables. The commands to run this load are stored in a file called LOADER3.CTL, shown below:

```
load data
infile flat3.lst
badfile bad.lst
-- Stores information concerning any errors or anomalies while
-- loading takes place.

discardfile junk1.lst
discardmax 45
replace
continueif this (1) = '@'
-- This command tells SQL*Loader that if an at symbol (@) appears in
-- column 1, then the next physical record should be considered an
-- extension of the data on the first line. Note that column 1 must
-- now be null or contain an @.

into table teachers
(teacher_name        position(01:30) char,
teacher_id           position(32:36) char,
primary_subject      position(38:58) char,
ssn                  position(60:68) number,
yrs_of_service       position(70:80) decimal external)
-- Will load the data into a second table based on the WHEN condition.

into table class_schedule
when homeroom_class != ' '
(teacher_id          position(32:36 char,
```

```
primary_subject        position(38:58) char,
homeroom_class         position(82:85) char)
-- Loads data based on position in the data file.
```

SQL*Load Command Keywords

There are a number of command keywords that can be associated with the SQL*Load executable. Many of the keywords are assumed—that is, if a value appears in the logical order (shown in Table 8.1), then the keyword is assumed to be associated with the value on the command line, even though the keyword does not appear.

Table 8.1 SQL*Load Keywords

Keyword	Default Value	Usage
userid	prompts/automatic	The Oracle userid and password. If none is given, the operator is prompted. If the slash (/) is given, the automatic logon is used.
control	prompts	The path and name of the control file.
log	control file	The path and name of the log file. Defaults to the name of the control file with a LOG extension.
bad	control file	The path and name of the bad file. Defaults to the name of the control file with a BAD extension.
data	control file	The path and name of the data file. Defaults to the name of the control file with a DAT extension.
discard	control file	The path and name of the discard file. Defaults to the name of the control file with a DSC extension.
discardmax	all	Indicates the number of discard records before the process aborts.
skip	0	Indicates the number of logical records from the beginning of the file to be skipped (i.e., not loaded).
load	all	Indicates the maximum number of records to load. The DIRECT option can be specified to load data directly into the table. This option provides extremely fast data loads, especially on long or cumbersome data files.
errors	50	Indicates the maximum number of insert errors to allow before the process aborts.
rows	64	Indicates the number of rows to buffer before inserting and committing data.
bindsize		Indicates the maximum byte size of the bind array. Default size is system-dependent.
silent		Suppresses the specified messages (header, feedback, errors, discards, or all).

CONCLUSION

In addition to the core development tools of SQL, Oracle Forms, Oracle Reports, Oracle Graphics, and Oracle Book, a variety of additional Oracle tools are available to perform special functions or aid in applications development. After reading this chapter, you should understand the role SQL*Net plays in facilitating client/server architectures and distributed databases. You should know how to use Oracle Browser to extract basic queries and how to format basic ad hoc queries. You should understand the role of Oracle Glue in linking data from e-mail, desktop spreadsheets and databases, and personal laptop and palmtop computers to the Oracle RDBMS, while making the differences in hardware, software, and operating systems invisible to the user. You should know how Oracle*Terminal enables developers to modify the behavior of default devices and key mapping for other CDE products and hardware devices. Finally, you should have a good grasp of how to load non-Oracle data using SQL*Loader.

APPENDIX 1

RESERVED WORDS

Reserved words have special meanings in SQL and/or PL/SQL; therefore, never use a reserved word to name an application object (such as a block, field, or image item) or a programming variable.

ABORT	CONNECT	EXIT	LOOP
ACCEPT	CONSTANT	FALSE	MAX
ACCESS	COUNT	FETCH	MAXEXTENTS
ADD	CRASH	FILE	MIN
ALL	CREATE	FLOAT	MINUS
ALTER	CURRENT	FOR	MOD
AND	CURSOR	FORM	MODE
ANY	DATA_BASE	FROM	MODIFY
ARRAY	DATABASE	FUNCTION	NEW
AS	DATE	GENERIC	NOAUDIT
ASC	DBA	GOTO	NOCOMPRESS
ASSERT	DEBUGOFF	GRANT	NOT
ASSIGN	DEBUGON	GRAPHIC	NOWAIT
AT	DECIMAL	GROUP	NULL
AUDIT	DECLARE	HAVING	NUMBER
AUTHORIZATION	DEFAULT	IDENTIFIED	NUMBER_BASE
AVG	DEFINITION	IF	OF
BEGIN	DELAY	IMMEDIATE	OFFLINE
BETWEEN	DELETE	IN	ON
BODY	DELTA	INCREMENT	ONLINE
BOOLEAN	DESC	INDEX	OPEN
BY	DIGITS	INDEXES	OPTION
CASE	DISPOSE	INDICATOR	OR
CHAR	DISTINCT	INITIAL	ORDER
CHAR_BASE	DO	INSERT	OTHERS
CHECK	DROP	INTEGER	OUT
CLOSE	ELSE	INTERSECT	PACKAGE
CLUSTER	ELSIF	INTO	PARTITION
CLUSTERS	END	IS	PCTFREE
COLAUTH	ENTRY	LEVEL	PRAGMA
COLUMN	EXCEPTION	LIKE	PRIOR
COMMENT	EXCEPTION_INIT	LIMITED	PRIVATE
COMMIT	EXCLUSIVE	LOCK	PRIVILEGES
COMPRESS	EXISTS	LONG	PROCEDURE

PUBLIC	ROWTYPE	SUBTYPE	UPDATE
RAISE	RUN	SUCCESSFUL	USE
RANGE	SAVEPOINT	SUM	USER
RAW	SCHEMA	SYNONYM	VALIDATE
RECORD	SELECT	SYSDATE	VALUES
RELEASE	SEPARATE	TABAUTH	VARCHAR
REM	SESSION	TABLE	VARGRAPH
REMARK	SET	TABLES	VARIANCE
RENAME	SHARE	TASK	VIEW
RESOURCE	SIZE	TERMINATE	VIEWS
RETURN	SMALLINT	THEN	WHEN
REVERSE	SPACE	TO	WHENEVER
REVOKE	SQL	TRIGGER	WHERE
ROLLBACK	SQLCODE	TRUE	WHILE
ROW	SQLERRM	TYPE	WITH
ROWID	START	UID	WORK
ROWNUM	STATEMENT	UNION	XOR
ROWS	STDDEV	UNIQUE	

APPENDIX 2

THE ORACLE DATA DICTIONARY

Oracle uses its data dictionary to store information about Oracle objects and events. Developers may find these views and tables particularly useful to validate certain users' access, to control application development, and to maintain security. A description of all user- and developer-accessible views and tables follows:

View	*Description*
ACCESSIBLE_COLUMNS	columns of all tables, views, and clusters
ACCESSIBLE_TABLES	tables and views accessible to the user
ALL_CATALOG	accessible tables, views, synonyms, and sequences
ALL_COL_COMMENTS	comments on columns of accessible tables and views
ALL_COL_GRANTS	grants on columns for which the user is the grantor, grantee, or owner, or PUBLIC is the grantee
ALL_COL_PRIVS_MADE	grants on columns where the user is grantor or owner
ALL_COL_PRIVS_RECD	grants on columns where user or PUBLIC is grantee
ALL_CONSTRAINTS	table constraints accessible to the user
ALL_CONS_COLUMNS	columns used in constraints accessible to the user
ALL_DB_LINKS	database links accessible to the user
ALL_DEF_AUDIT_OPTS	table- and system-level default auditing options
ALL_DEPENDENCIES	dependencies between PL/SQL objects stored in the database
ALL_ERRORS	current errors for stored objects
ALL_INDEXES	descriptions of indexes on accessible tables
ALL_IND_COLUMNS	columns comprising indexes on accessible tables
ALL_OBJECTS	objects accessible to the user
ALL_SEQUENCES	descriptions of the user's own sequences
ALL_SOURCE	text sources for all stored objects
ALL_SNAPSHOTS	snapshots accessible to the user
ALL_SYNONYMS	synonyms accessible to the user
ALL_TABLES	description of tables accessible to the user
ALL_TAB_AUDIT_OPTS	auditing options for accessible tables and views
ALL_TAB_COLUMNS	columns of all tables, views, and clusters
ALL_TAB_COMMENTS	comments on tables and views accessible to user
ALL_TAB_PRIVS	grants on objects where the user is the grantor, grantee, or owner, or PUBLIC is the grantee
ALL_TAB_PRIVS_MADE	user's grants and grants on user's objects
ALL_TAB_PRIVS_RECD	grants on objects where user or PUBLIC is grantee
ALL_USERS	information about all users of the database

ALL_VIEWS	text of views available to the user
AUDIT_ACTIONS	each action code and its description
COLUMN_PRIVILEGES	same as ALL_COL_PRIVS_MADE and ALL_COL_PRIVS_RECD
CONSTRAINT_COLUMNS	accessible columns in constraint definitions
CONSTRAINT_DEFS	constraint definitions on accessible tables
DICTIONARY	description of data dictionary tables and views
DICT_COLUMNS	columns in data dictionary tables and views
INDEX_STATS	results from the ANALYZE INDEX UPDATE STATISTICS command
RESOURCE_COST	costs of each resource
ROLE_ROLE_PRIVS	roles granted on other roles
ROLE_SYS_PRIVS	system privileges on roles
ROLE_TAB_PRIVS	table privileges on roles
SESSION_PRIVS	privileges for the current user and session
SESSION_ROLES	roles available for the current user and session
TABLE_PRIVILEGES	same as ALL_TAB_PRIVS
USER_AUDIT_CONNECT	audit trails for user logons and logoffs
USER_AUDIT_OBJECT	audit trail for statements affecting objects
USER_AUDIT_SESSION	audit trail for user connections/disconnections
USER_AUDIT_STATEMENT	audit trail for GRANT, REVOKE, AUDIT, NOAUDIT, and ALTER SYSTEM commands issued by users
USER_AUDIT_TRAIL	audit trail entries relevant to the user
USER_CATALOG	accessible tables, views, synonyms, and sequences
USER_CLUSTERS	descriptions of user's own clusters
USER_CLU_COLUMNS	mapping of table columns to cluster columns
USER_COL_COMMENTS	comments on columns of user's tables and views
USER_COL_PRIVS	grants on columns where the user is the owner, grantor, or grantee
USER_COL_PRIVS_MADE	grants on columns of objects owned by the user
USER_COL_PRIVS_RECD	grants on columns where the user is the grantee
USER_CONS_COLUMNS	columns used in constraints created by the user
USER_CROSS_REF	cross ref for the user's views, synonyms, and constraints
USER_DB_LINKS	database links owned by the user
USER_DEPENDENCIES	dependencies involving objects owned by the user
USER_ERRORS	errors involving objects owned by the user
USER_EXTENTS	storage space comprising segments owned by the user
USER_FREE_SPACE	free extents in tablespaces owned by the user
USER_INDEXES	descriptions of the user's own indexes
USER_IND_COLUMNS	columns comprising indexes on the user's tables
USER_OBJECTS	objects owned by the user
USER_OBJ_AUDIT_OPTIONS	audit options on tables and views owned by the user
USER_RESOURCE_LIMITS	resource limits for the current user and session
USER_ROLE_PRIVS	the user's roles
USER_SEGMENTS	storage allocated for all database segments
USER_SEQUENCES	descriptions of the user's own sequences

USER_SOURCE	text sources for the user's stored objects
USER_SNAPSHOT	snapshots accessible to the user
USER_SYNONYMS	the user's private synonyms
USER_SYS_PRIVS	the user's system privileges
USER_TABLES	descriptions of the user's own tables
USER_TABLESPACES	description of accessible tablespaces
USER_TAB_AUDIT_OPTS	auditing options for the user's tables and views
USER_TAB_COLUMNS	columns of the user's tables, views, and clusters
USER_TAB_COMMENTS	comments on tables and views owned by the user
USER_TAB_PRIVS	grants on objects where the user is the owner, grantor, or grantee
USER_TAB_PRIVS_MADE	grants on objects owned by the user
USER_TAB_PRIVS_RECD	grants on objects where the user is the grantee
USER_TS_QUOTAS	tablespace quotas for the user
USER_TRIGGERS	the user's database triggers
USER_USERS	information about the current user
USER_VIEWS	text of views owned by the user

APPENDIX 3

SQL COMMAND REFERENCE

The SQL command reference is included in this book to give developers a general understanding of the scope and application of the wide variety of SQL commands. Because many of the important SQL commands are already detailed in the book and the sheer volume of information needed to discuss all the SQL commands would require a great deal of space, this section lists a brief description of all SQL commands and their particular uses. If a developer needs detailed information for a specific command, use the HELP command_name function available in SQL*Plus or refer to the Oracle *SQL Language Reference Manual* (Oracle Corp., (415) 506-7000, publication # 5142-31-1192). In fact, there are many useful commercial books that treat SQL commands as their sole topic.

Command	*Usage*
ALTER CLUSTER	Redefines storage allocations for a cluster.
ALTER DATABASE	Alters an existing database by: 1) mounting the database; 2) converting an Oracle, Version 6 data dictionary to Oracle7; 3) opening the database; 4) choosing archivelog/noarchivelog mode for redo log file groups; 5) performing media recovery; 6) adding/dropping a redo log file or group; 7) renaming a redo log file or group; 8) backing up the current control file; 9) replacing an old data file with a new one; 10) taking a data file online or offline; 11) enabling/disabling a related group of redo log file groups; 12) changing the database's global name; 13) changing the MAC mode; and 14) setting DBHIGH or DBLOW to an operating system label.
ALTER FUNCTION	Recompiles stand-alone, stored database functions.
ALTER INDEX	Changes future storage allocation for data blocks in an index.
ALTER PACKAGE	Recompiles a stored package.
ALTER PROCEDURE	Recompiles a stand-alone, stored procedure.
ALTER PROFILE	Adds, modifies, or removes a resource limit in a profile.

ALTER RESOURCE COST	Specifies a formula to calculate the total resource cost used in a session. For any session, this cost is limited by the value of the COMPOSITE_LIMIT parameter in the user's profile.
ALTER ROLE	Changes the authorization needed to enable a role.
ALTER ROLLBACK SEGMENT	Alters a rollback segment by: 1) bringing it online; 2) taking it offline; and 3) changing its storage characteristics.
ALTER SEQUENCE	Changes the sequence by: 1) changing the increment between future sequence values; 2) setting or eliminating the minimum or maximum value; 3) changing the number of cached sequence numbers; and 4) specifying whether or not sequence numbers must be ordered.
ALTER SESSION	Alters the current session by: 1) enabling or disabling the SQL trace facility; 2) changing the values of NLS parameters; 3) changing the DBMS session label in Trusted Oracle (a version of Oracle used by the federal government on secrect projects); 4) changing the default label format for the session; 5) closing a database link; 6) sending advice to remote databases for forcing an in-doubt distributed transaction; 7) permitting or prohibiting procedures and stored functions from issuing COMMIT and ROLLBACK statements; and 8) changing the goal of the cost-based optimization approach.
ALTER SNAPSHOT	Alters a snapshot by: 1) changing its storage characteristics; and 2) changing its automatic refresh mode and times.
ALTER SNAPSHOT LOG	Changes the storage characteristics of a snapshot log.
ALTER SYSTEM	Dynamically alters the Oracle database by: 1) enabling or disabling resource limits; 2) managing shared server processes or dispatcher processes for the multithreaded server architecture; 3) explicitly switching redo log file groups; 4) explicitly performing a checkpoint; 5) verifying access to data files; 6) restricting logons to Oracle to only those users with RESTRICTED SESSION system privilege; 7) enabling distributed recovery in a single process environment; 8) disabling distributed recovery; 9) manually archiving redo log file groups or enabling or disabling automatic archiving; 10) clearing all data from the shared pool in the System Global Area (SGA); and 11) terminating a session.
ALTER TABLE	Alters the definition of a table by: 1) adding a column; 2) adding an integrity constraint;

	3) redefining a column (datatype, size, default value); 4) modifying storage characteristics or other parameters; 5) enabling, disabling, or dropping an integrity constraint or trigger; and 6) explicitly allocating an extent.
ALTER TABLESPACE	Alters an existing tablespace (an area of storage space on a hard disk used to hold the Oracle database) by: 1) adding or renaming data file(s); 2) changing default storage parameters; 3) taking the tablespace online or offline; and 4) beginning or ending a backup.
ALTER TRIGGER	Enables or disables a database trigger.
ALTER USER	Changes any of the following characteristics of a database user: 1) password; 2) default tablespace for object creation; 3) tablespace for temporary segments created for the user; 4) tablespace access and tablespace quotas; 5) limits on database resources; and 6) default roles.
ALTER VIEW	Recompiles a view.
ANALYZE	Performs one of the following functions on an index, table, or cluster: 1) collection of statistics about the object used by the optimizer and storing of them in the data dictionary; 2) deletion of statistics about the object from the data dictionary; 3) validation of the structure of the object; and 4) identification of migrated and chained rows of the table or cluster.
ARCHIVE LOG	Manually archives redo log file groups or enables or disables automatic archiving.
AUDIT (SQL Statements)	Chooses specific SQL statements for auditing in subsequent user sessions.
AUDIT (Schema Objects)	Chooses a specific schema object for auditing.
COMMENT	Adds a comment about a table, view, snapshot, or column into the data dictionary.
COMMIT	Ends the current transaction and makes permanent all changes performed in the transaction. This command also erases all savepoints in the transaction and releases the transaction's locks.
CONSTRAINT	Defines an integrity constraint. An integrity constraint is a rule that restricts the values for one or more columns in a table.
CREATE CLUSTER	Creates a cluster. A cluster is a schema object that contains one or more tables that all have one or more columns in common.
CREATE CONTROLFILE	(Always perform a full backup before using this command.) Recreates a control file if: 1) All copies of the existing control files have been lost through media failure; 2) The name of the database must be

	changed; or 3) One of the following attributes must be changed: the maximum number of redo log file groups, redo log file members, archived redo log files, data files, or instances that can concurrently have the database mounted and open.
CREATE DATABASE	Creates a database, making it available for general use, with these options: 1) establishment of a maximum number of instances, data files, redo log file groups, or redo log file members; 2) specification of names and sizes of data files and redo log files; and 3) choice of a mode of use for the redo log. This command erases any data currently in use.
CREATE DATABASE LINK	Creates a database link, which is an object in the local database that allows you to access objects on a remote database or to mount a secondary database in read-only mode. The remote database can be either an Oracle or a non-Oracle database.
CREATE FUNCTION	Creates a stand-alone, stored function. A stored function is a set of PL/SQL statements that can be called by name.
CREATE INDEX	Creates an index on one or more columns of a table or a cluster. An index is a database object that contains an entry for each value that appears in the indexed column(s) of the table or cluster and provides direct, fast access to rows.
CREATE PACKAGE	Creates the specification for a stored package. A package is an encapsulated collection of related procedures, functions, and other program objects stored together in the database.
CREATE PACKAGE BODY	Creates the body of a stored package. A package is an encapsulated collection of related procedures, functions, and other program objects stored together in the database.
CREATE PROCEDURE	Creates a stand-alone, stored procedure. A procedure is a group of PL/SQL statements that can be called by name.
CREATE PROFILE	Creates a profile, which is a set of limits on database resources. Once a profile is assigned to a user, that user cannot exceed those limits.
CREATE ROLE	Creates a role, which is a set of privileges that can be granted to users or to other roles.
CREATE ROLLBACK SEGMENT	Creates a rollback segment, which is an object that is used by Oracle to store data necessary to reverse, or undo, changes made by transactions.
CREATE SCHEMA	Creates multiple tables and views and performs multiple grants in a single transaction.

CREATE SEQUENCE	Creates a sequence, which is a database object from which multiple users can generate unique integers. Sequences can be used to automatically generate primary key values.
CREATE SNAPSHOT	Creates a snapshot, which is a table that contains the results of a query of one or more tables or views, often located on a remote database.
CREATE SNAPSHOT LOG	Creates a snapshot log, which is a table associated with the master table of a snapshot. Oracle stores changes to the master table's data in the snapshot log and then uses the snapshot log to refresh the master table's snapshots.
CREATE SYNONYM	Creates a synonym, which is an alternative name for a table, view, sequence, procedure, stored function, package, snapshot, or another synonym.
CREATE TABLE	Creates a table, the basic structure to hold user data and specifies this information: 1) column definitions; 2) integrity constraints; 3) the table's tablespace; 4) storage characteristics; 5) an optional cluster; and 6) data from an arbitrary query.
CREATE TABLESPACE	Creates a tablespace, which is an allocation of space in the database that can contain objects like tables and views.
CREATE TRIGGER	Creates and enables a database trigger, which is a stored PL/SQL block that is associated with a table. Oracle automatically executes a trigger when a specified SQL statement is issued against the table.
CREATE USER	Creates a database user, an account that allows connection to the database, and establishes the means by which Oracle permits access by the user. Optionally assigned properties include 1) default tablespace; 2) temporary tablespace; 3) quotas for allocating space in tablespaces; and 4) a profile containing resource limits.
CREATE VIEW	Defines a view, a logical table based on one or more tables or views.
DELETE	Removes rows from a table or from a view's base table.
DISABLE	Disables an integrity constraint or all triggers associated with a table. Note the following: 1) Oracle does not enforce its disabled integrity constraints. However, disabled integrity constraints appear in the data dictionary along with enabled integrity constraints; and 2) Oracle does not fire disabled triggers if its triggering condition is satisfied.
DROP	Erases an integrity constraint from the database.
DROP CLUSTER	Erases a cluster from the database.
DROP DATABASE LINK	Erases a database link from the database.

DROP FUNCTION	Erases a stand-alone, stored function from the database.
DROP INDEX	Erases an index from the database.
DROP PACKAGE	Erases a stored package from the database.
DROP PROCEDURE	Erases a stand-alone, stored procedure from the database.
DROP PROFILE	Erases a profile from the database.
DROP ROLE	Erases a role from the database.
DROP ROLLBACK SEGMENT	Erases a rollback segment from the database.
DROP SEQUENCE	Erases a sequence from the database.
DROP SNAPSHOT	Erases a snapshot from the database.
DROP SNAPSHOT LOG	Erases a snapshot log from the database.
DROP SYNONYM	Erases a synonym from the database.
DROP TABLE	Erases a table and all its data from the database.
DROP TABLESPACE	Erases a tablespace from the database.
DROP TRIGGER	Erases a database trigger from the database.
DROP USER	Erases a database user and optionally removes the user's objects.
DROP VIEW	Erases a view from the database.
ENABLE	Enables an integrity constraint or all triggers associated with a table.
EXPLAIN PLAN	Determines the execution plan Oracle follows to execute a specified SQL statement. This command inserts a row describing each step of the execution plan into a specified table. This command also determines the cost of executing the statement, in cost-based optimization environments.
GRANT	Grants system privileges and roles to users and roles. Alternatively, grants privileges for a particular object to users and roles.
INSERT	Adds rows to a table or to a view's base table.
LOCK TABLE	Locks one or more tables in a specified mode. This lock manually overrides automatic locking and permits or denies access to a table or view by other users for the duration of the operation.
NOAUDIT (SQL Statements)	Stops auditing chosen by the AUDIT command (SQL Statements).
NOAUDIT (SchemaObjects)	Stops auditing chosen by the AUDIT command (Schema Objects).
RECOVER	Performs media recovery.
RENAME	Renames a table, view, sequence, or private synonym.
REVOKE	Revokes system privileges and roles from users and roles. Revokes object privileges for a particular object from users and roles.
ROLLBACK	Undoes work done in the current transaction. Also, can be used to manually undo the work done by an in-doubt distributed transaction.

SAVEPOINT

Identifies a point in a transaction to which you can later roll back.

SELECT

Retrieves data from one or more tables, views, or snapshots.

SET ROLE

Enables and disables roles for your current session.

SET TRANSACTION

Performs one of these operations on the current transaction: 1) establishes the current transaction as either a read-only or a read-write transaction; and 2) assigns the current transaction to a specified rollback segment.

STORAGE

Specifies storage characteristics for tables, indexes, clusters, and rollback segments, and the default storage characteristics for tablespaces.

TRUNCATE

Erases all rows from a table or cluster.

UPDATE

Changes existing values in a table or in a view's base table.

APPENDIX 4

GLOSSARY

accelerator key: A shortcut key used to quickly execute a menu operation.

alert: A dialog box that calls attention to some special condition that requires a response.

alias: A secondary, and usually easier, name used in a SQL statement to refer to a table, view, or column.

alignment: In Oracle Reports, the method used to position data within a field.

anchor: In Oracle Reports, a layout object that holds two or more objects to their current relative positions.

anonymous block: An unnamed block of PL/SQL code.

antecedent: An object that appears above another object in a hierarchy. All objects below the antecedent are its decendants.

application: One or more forms, menus, displays, documents, or reports.

argument: An expression displayed in the parentheses of a subprogram, supplying a value for the subprogram to use. For example, in NEW_PROC(xxx), the argument is xxx.

ASCII: Literally, the acronym for American National Standard Code for Information Interchange, but in practice, the de facto standard for text files.

axis chart: In Oracle Graphics, a chart with two or three axes whose data is plotted according to where it lies on the chart's axes.

background element: In Oracle Graphics, the white part of a pattern (which can be altered by the developer).

background menu: A menu of common commands accessible from any part of a menu.

baseline value: In Oracle Graphics, the starting value used for plotting fields on the continuous axis of a chart.

base table: The database table on which a block is based in Oracle Forms.

base table block: An Oracle Forms block that is based on a table in the database.

base table item: An item based on a column in the base table of a base table block.

bind reference: A reference to a variable, always prefaced by a colon (:) and used to replace a literal value appearing in a SQL or PL/SQL construct statement.

block: A group of functionally and hierarchically related objects in an Oracle Forms module.

block menu: A menu displaying all form blocks; used for navigation.

body: In Oracle Reports, the bulk of the report's hard copy (text, graphics, data, and computations), situated between the header and trailer pages.

boilerplate: Text, art, and/or images that cannot be altered and appear in an application every time it is run.

border: In Oracle Reports, an outline surrounding a layout object; used to highlight its contents.

break column: A column within a break group.

break group: In Oracle Reports, a grouping of records used to break data into distinct sets.

break order: In Oracle Reports and SQL*Plus, a column property setting the order, either ascending or descending, in which to display a break column's data.

break report: A report containing at least one break group.

built-in: A predefined PL/SQL procedure, function, or trigger that is provided by the CDE tools. Each built-in performs a specific action.

button: An item that allows the operator to initiate an event and possibly execute a block of PL/SQL code by means of a mouse click.

canvas view: The background object on which the designer lays out interface objects, which operators see at runtime.

category axis: A discrete axis.

CGM: The Computer Graphics Metafile image format.

chart element: A bar, line, pie slice, or other graphical object used to represent a single value for a field.

chart template: The attributes and properties that define the format of a chart.

check box: An object that can be toggled on or off.

clipboard: An area of buffered memory where an object remains until the developer cuts or copies another object or until the developer quits the application.

column: A vertical list of data contained in a database table, with attributes describing its name and datatype.

command line: An operating-system prompt invoking a CDE tool.

commit: The process of saving changes to data (made via INSERT, UPDATE, and DELETE commands) to the database in a permanent fashion.

compile: The process of translating PL/SQL code into binary, executable format.

connect: The process of logging on to a database.

constraint: A database-level rule or restriction limiting the behavior or use of a database object, such as a NOT NULL constraint on a database column.

context: The hierarchical level of operation at which the developer is working (i.e., form-level, block-level, or object-level).

continuous axis: In Oracle Graphics, an axis whose values begin at one point and progress mathematically until they reach another value; also called a value axis.

control block: An Oracle Forms block not based on a database table or view.

control item: An Oracle Forms item not based on a database column in a database table.

control points: The corner points of a visual object that appear when the object is selected in the Layout Painter, allowing the developer to drag the control point out, modifying the shape of the object.

coordinate system: The unit of measure used to designate x,y coordinates in the CDE layout tools (e.g., centimeters, pixels, characters, points, or inches).

coordinates (x,y): The horizontal (x) and verticle (y) location points for objects appearing in the layout.

cross-product: In Oracle Reports, a group that owns two or more other groups and correlates the values between them.

crosstab: A matrix cell similar to those found in a spreadsheet.

cursor: An internal pointer to data retrieved by a query. Cursors point to only one row of data at a time.

database: A collection of related tables and data.

database cursor: The memory assigned to a SQL command.

database field: The value at a specific intersection of a column and a row; synonymous with field.

data dictionary: A set of tables and views owned by the DBA used to control and administrate the operation of the database.

data model: A graphically depicted relational model that defines the composition and nature of data used for an application, for example, a query, group, column, parameter, or link used in a report.

data type: The primary behavior characteristic of data (i.e., numbers, characters, dates, etc.)

date axis: In Oracle Graphics, a continuous axis that plots date values.

DBA (database administrator): An individual responsible for the use and administration of a database. The DBA creates and maintains the database, as well as the user accounts.

Debug mode: A runtime mode that allows the developer to execute an application while monitoring the underlying processing.

default: A value assigned to an object, parameter, or attribute by Oracle when the user or developer does not specify one.

definition level: The context in which a trigger is attached and all levels below that. The definition level determines what events will cause the trigger to fire.

dependent data: Data that depends on other data for its value; also called value data.

descendant: An object that appears below another object in the hierarchy. All objects above the descendant are its antecedants.

deselect: To move an object or tool from an active state to an inactive state.

Designer: The CDE component in each tool that provides the developer with abilities to create and modify the application.

detail block: A block in a master-detail relationship whose records are associated with the records of a master block.

dialog box: A window that requires information to complete an operation.

disabled: The status of an object that disallows keyboard response or mouse input.

discrete axis: In Oracle Graphics, an axis that plots distinct values at fixed intervals where the values have no mathematical relationship; also called the category axis.

display: An Oracle Graphics application.

display item: In Oracle Forms, a display-only item that cannot be entered or modified.

EBCDIC: Literally, the extended binary-coded decimal interchange code, but in practice, a standard for text files made popular by IBM.

edge: The outermost boundary of an object.

Edge/Fill/Text Display: A display box on the Tool palette that controls settings of and displays the current settings for the edge, fill, and text patterns and colors.

Edit mode: An Oracle Forms Runform mode in which all keystrokes are accepted as data entry and no triggers fire.

editor: A work area in which you perform a specific set of tasks, such as designing a display or a chart template.

enabled: The status of an object that allows keyboard response or mouse input.

enclosing object: In Oracle Reports, an object that completely surrounds another object.

Enter Query mode: An Oracle Forms Runform mode that accepts query conditions and establishes the query SELECT statement, but otherwise limits the operations of the user.

event: A point in the execution of the application where the developer or end-user can take action. Developers often associate PL/SQL code with an event in the form of a trigger.

event trigger: A block of PL/SQL code that executes in response to a runtime event.

executable argument: An argument passed to a CDE tool on the command line that alters its behavior when invoked.

export: The process of moving a copy of the selected object to a file.

field template: In Oracle Graphics, the attributes and properties that determine how values are represented as chart fields, such as bars or pie slices.

file column: In Oracle Reports, a column whose value is a filename and whose contents may be populated by the specified file.

fill area: In Oracle Graphics, the area in an object where color and pattern fills can be applied.

foreground element: The black part of a pattern, which can be altered by the developer using the Foreground Color palette.

foreign key: A column in one table that refers to a primary key in another table.

format mask: The customized appearance of an item specified by the developer and enforced by the application (e.g., "10-FEB-95," as opposed to "January 7th, 1996").

format trigger: In Oracle Reports, a block of PL/SQL code that allows the report to dynamically configure the formatting attributes of an object before printing.

form layout: In Oracle Reports, a default layout style where labels appear on the left of fields, with only one record per logical page.

form letter layout: In Oracle Reports, a default layout style where boilerplate and fields are intermixed with lines wrapping at the appropriate word breaks.

formula column: In Oracle Reports, a customized column whose data is derived from PL/SQL code, a user exit, a SQL statement, or any combination.

frame: In Oracle Graphics, the basic definition of a chart, independent of data, stored in the chart template. In Oracle Reports, a layout object that encloses other layout objects and is used to control the formatting, frequency, and positioning of all objects within the frame.

function: A block of PL/SQL code that performs a specified sequence of actions and then returns a value.

function key: A key on the keyboard that performs a specific function, like inserting a new record ([Insert Record]).

generate: To create a binary executable of a module in a file or the database.

global variable: A variable available to all modules in an application, until the session is ended or the variable is erased.

grant: To give a user access privileges to a module, database table, view, or synonym.

group: A collection of objects that behave as one single object in the Layout Painter. In Oracle Reports, an object in the data model that contains all of the columns selected by a query and often serves to create breaks within a report.

group filter: In Oracle Reports, PL/SQL code that restricts the data displayed by a group. The data is still fetched, but it is not displayed.

GUI: The Graphical User Interface, commonly in a bit-mapped mode.

handle: In Oracle Graphics, an internal pointer needed by PL/SQL for some objects.

header: In Oracle Reports, an area of the report that precedes the actual body of the report. Headers are commonly used to display introductory material about the report.

hidden: The property of an object that exists in an application and may actually have a value, but is not displayed or visible to the end-user.

horizontal sizing: In Oracle Reports, the setting that assigns how objects will behave to accommodate various sizes of print objects at runtime (valid settings are Contract, Expand, Fixed, and Variable).

horizontal spacing: The amount of horizontal space printed between instances of a repeating frame.

icon: A button with a meaningful graphic image.

image item: An Oracle Forms item that displays an image from a database, a file, or the clipboard.

import: The process of bringing object or file contents in from externally stored files or databases.

independent data: A piece of data that has informational value by itself and does not depend on other data for its value.

index: A database structure, built on tables, that serves to quickly locate rows of a table.

Insert mode: A text-editing mode in which each character is inserted at the cursor, pushing the following characters to the right, as opposed to Replace mode.

interface objects: The graphic objects like radio buttons, check boxes, records, and boilerplate text that are available only on a bit-mapped terminal.

item: An object owned by a block and used to represent a column value, perform data manipulation, or initiate actions.

join: A query that combines data from two (or more) tables in a single SELECT statement.

key mapping: The functionality assigned to specific keystrokes, such as the [TAB] key serving as the Next Field function

label: Boilerplate text identifying the values or meaning of elements within an application.

layout: The area in the various Layout Painters where developers create, modify, position, or delete objects while viewing their graphical representations.

Layout Editor: The WYSIWYG, graphical design facility available in CDE tools as a component of the Designer.

lexical reference: A reference to a variable, always prefaced by an ampersand (&) and used to replace an entire clause in a SQL statement.

library: A collection of one or more PL/SQL programs stored together in a file or database and available to be referenced by other applications.

link: In Oracle Reports, a data model object that defines the relationship between a group and a query.

link file: In Oracle Reports, the name of a file whose contents are imported into a report at runtime.

list item: An Oracle Forms interface item that displays a predefined list of choices from which users may select a value.

lock: Assignment of a resource to a specific user or object. For example, rows in the database are locked to a specific user until that user releases the rows. Alternatively, design objects can be locked, for example, locking boilerplate in a window.

logical page: In Oracle Reports, one page of the actual report, which may be displayed on one or more physical pages.

look-up item: An Oracle Forms item whose value is based on a value from a table other than its own base table.

LOV: A scrollable pick list where operators can select a single, distinct value.

mailing label layout: In Oracle Reports, a default report layout that displays records in columns across the page with fields appearing beneath each other in a single repeating frame.

margin: In Oracle Reports, an area on a report that surrounds the body of each logical page.

master block: A block in a master-detail relationship whose records control and are associated with the records of a detail block.

master/detail layout: In Oracle Reports, a default report layout where the detail records appear in the tabular layout style below the master records, which appear in form layout style.

master-detail relationship: A defined relationship between blocks that reflects a primary-foreign key relationship between the base tables of the blocks.

matrix layout: In Oracle Reports, the default report layout used for matrix reports, designed to format data in a grid.

matrix report: In Oracle Reports, a cross-tab report using four sets of data: one set as headers across the page; one set as labels down the left side of the page; one set as the cross-product (building the relation between the headers and labels); and one set as the "filler" of the matrix cells.

menu item: In Oracle Forms menus, a choice that users can select at runtime to perform an action.

message line: A line on the screen where information is displayed, such as error messages, prompts, and similar information.

modal window: A window that requires a response from the user before any action outside the window can take place.

mode: The method of an application's operation, which may or may not limit a user's or developer's capabilities.

modeless window: A window that may be opened while the user performs actions outside the window.

modifier key: A key that alters the meaning of a counterpart key when pressed together, such as the [ALT], [CTRL], and [Shift] keys.

module: A definition file of a single form, menu, report, display, or library. Modules can be saved into the database or into a file.

multiline field: A field in a window or dialog that extends for several lines, allowing vertical as well as horizontal scrolling.

multirecord block: A block that displays more than one record, either horizontally or vertically.

navigable: The condition of an Oracle Forms item in which it can be reached via the keyboard or mouse.

nonquery record group: In Oracle Forms, a record group that does not have a query associated with it; used for special programmatic purposes.

NULL: The absence of any value.

object: An item within an application that can be copied, moved, or deleted in a single operation.

object hierarchy: The relationship of objects in which higher-level objects own lower-level objects.

object layer: A memory buffer that stores changes that have been applied but not saved to disk or the database.

overflow: In Oracle Graphics, when an object's contents cannot fit on the current logical page and spill over to the next logical page.

package: A database object of logically related PL/SQL types, objects, and procedures.

page break: In Oracle Reports, the setting that controls when to move an object to the next logical page.

page-dependent reference: In Oracle Reports, a value in the report that relies on the formatting of the report.

palette: An object that displays tools, colors, or patterns available in the Layout Painter.

panel: In Oracle Reports, the number of physical pages required to print one logical page.

parameter: A variable that can be changed at runtime by the end-user.

parameter list: A named list of parameters defining all the parameters and parameter values to be passed to another product at runtime.

pattern: The graphical property of an object that governs the appearance of the object's edge or fill.

physical page: A single sheet of paper printed by the printer.

plot type: In Oracle Graphics, the appearance of a plot for a field on a chart, such as in bar, line, or symbol form.

pop-up list: An Oracle Forms list that pops up from nowhere when programmatically made to do so or when the user performs a particular action.

preference: A setting that affects the behavior of the CDE Designer or Runtime interface.

primary key: A group of one or more columns (in a table) or text items (in an Oracle Forms block) that enforce a record's uniqueness.

procedure: A block of PL/SQL code that performs a specified sequence of actions.

program unit: A block of PL/SQL code.

property: An attribute.

property sheet: A window that allows the developer to define the properties and attributes of objects in an application.

protocol: A user-provided string that connects the user to a remote database.

query record group: An Oracle Forms record group fetched from the database.

radio button: One of a related group of mutually exclusive options depicted as buttons.

radio group: An Oracle Forms item that provides a group of radio buttons.

read consistency: The process of checking all issued queries to ensure that related data is internally consistent.

record: A construct that defines one row of related items and the data the items contain.

record group: A customizable, internal Oracle Forms data structure for storing ordered sets of records.

record locking: A database feature that prevents two users from updating the same row of data at the same time.

reference line: In Oracle Graphics, a line displayed at a specified value on a chart.

relation: A similarity between tables, characterized by the presence of a primary key in one table and foreign keys in other tables.

relation object: An object that defines the relationship between objects in a master-detail relationship.

repeating frame: In Oracle Reports, a layout object used to display repeating rows of data.

Replace mode: A text-editing mode in which each character overwrites the current character at the cursor; as opposed to Insert mode.

resource file: A file containing the definitions for device behavior, product behavior, and application behavior when a specific application or device type is in use.

role: A set of privileges available to users that help control and secure applications.

root window: A window showing the default menu and the title bar.

runtime: The time when an application is in execution.

runtime file: A definition file of all objects, behaviors, and processes in a single module.

scope: The context at which a trigger fires.

screen cursor: The visual marker indicating the current user's or developer's current position on the screen.

script: A file containing SQL and SQL*Plus commands that are run as programs.

search criteria: The actual values to be fetched by a query based on the comparison operators.

session: The period between opening and exiting an Oracle application.

single-record block: A block that displays only one record at a time.

stacked canvas: In Oracle Forms, a programmatically controlled canvas that overlays another canvas in the same window.

status line: A line on the screen, similar to the message line, where the CDE tool displays information about its current status.

subprogram: A PL/SQL procedure or function.

substitution parameter: A variable that represents a value for use in the command line of an application.

system variable: A variable containing information about the current status of the application, such as the current date or the current location of the screen cursor.

table: The basic functional unit of relational databases in which data is stored in a two-dimensional grid composed of rows and columns.

tabular: In Oracle Reports, a default report layout displaying as a table, with labels at the top of the page and records beneath the labels.

text item: In Oracle Forms, an object, commonly called a field, that can display textual data and, optionally, can accept textual data entry.

TIFF: Acronym for tagged image format file.

timer: A mechanism available within the CDE tools to schedule a specific processing event.

title bar: A horizontal area at the top of the application that contains the name of the application or window.

toggle: A setting that can be either on or off.

tool: An icon that appears in the Layout Painter palettes; used to create and manipulate objects.

trailer: In Oracle Reports, an area of the report displaying closing material at the end of a report.

transaction: A set of SQL statements that Oracle treats as a single unit and executes at one time.

trigger: An anonymous PL/SQL block that executes in response to a runtime event.

user area item: An Oracle Forms item whose control is handed over to a user exit.

user exit: A third-generation language program that is linked to the application's executable file.

view: 1. The portion of the application that is displayed in the window at runtime, that is, the portion of the application shown on the screen. 2. A database construct that acts as a virtual table.

visual attribute: The display properties of an object.

window: An Oracle Forms object where canvases are displayed at runtime.

INDEX